COMPUTER
SECURITY

PROTECTING

DIGITAL

RESOURCES

COMPUTER SECURITY

PROTECTING DIGITAL RESOURCES

Robert C. Newman
GEORGIA SOUTHERN UNIVERSITY

JONES AND BARTLETT PUBLISHERS

Sudbury, Massachusetts

BOSTON   TORONTO   LONDON   SINGAPORE

World Headquarters
Jones and Bartlett Publishers
40 Tall Pine Drive
Sudbury, MA 01776
978-443-5000
info@jbpub.com
www.jbpub.com

Jones and Bartlett Publishers
Canada
6339 Ormindale Way
Mississauga, Ontario L5V 1J2
Canada

Jones and Bartlett Publishers
International
Barb House, Barb Mews
London W6 7PA
United Kingdom

Jones and Bartlett's books and products are available through most bookstores and online booksellers. To contact Jones and Bartlett Publishers directly, call 800-832-0034, fax 978-443-8000, or visit our website www.jbpub.com.

Substantial discounts on bulk quantities of Jones and Bartlett's publications are available to corporations, professional associations, and other qualified organizations. For details and specific discount information, contact the special sales department at Jones and Bartlett via the above contact information or send an email to specialsales@jbpub.com.

Production Credits

Acquisitions Editor: Timothy Anderson
Production Director: Amy Rose
Senior Production Editor: Tracey Chapman
Editorial Assistant: Melissa Potter
Senior Marketing Manager: Andrea DeFronzo
V.P., Manufacturing and Inventory Control:
    Therese Connell
Composition: Spoke & Wheel/Jason Miranda

Illustrations: Accurate Artists, Inc.
Cover Design: Kristin E. Parker
Cover Image: © Tyler Olsen, ShutterStock, Inc.;
    © Andrea Danti/ShutterStock, Inc.;
    © John Vernon/Dreamstime.com
Printing and Binding: Malloy, Inc.
Cover Printing: Malloy, Inc.

Library of Congress Cataloging-in-Publication Data

Newman, Robert C.
  Computer security : protecting digital resources / Robert C. Newman.
      p. cm.
  Includes bibliographical references and index.
  ISBN-13: 978-0-7637-5994-0 (pbk.)
  ISBN-10: 0-7637-5994-5 (pbk.)
  1. Database security. 2. Computer security. 3. Computer networks—Security measures. I. Title.
  QA76.9.D314N49 2009
  005.8—dc22

                        2008047272

6048

Printed in the United States of America
13 12 11 10 09   10 9 8 7 6 5 4 3 2 1

Contents

CHAPTER 3 SCAMS, IDENTITY THEFT, AND FRAUD   63

PART TWO COMPUTER SYSTEMS AND NETWORKS   107

CHAPTER 5 THE INTERNET AND WEB NETWORK ENVIRONMENT   109

CHAPTER 8 E-COMMERCE SECURITY MECHANISMS   191

PART THREE SECURITY AND OPERATIONS ADMINISTRATION   223

CHAPTER 9 BUSINESS CONTINUITY AND DISASTER RECOVERY PLANNING   225

PART FOUR SECURITY RESOURCES, EDUCATION, AND STANDARDS   317

CHAPTER 12 SECURITY SOLUTIONS FOR DIGITAL RESOURCES   319

CHAPTER 13 STANDARDS, SPECIFICATIONS, AND PROTOCOLS   335

APPENDICES   385

APPENDIX C ANSWERS TO CHAPTER SECURITY REVIEW QUESTIONS   401

APPENDIX D COMPUTER SECURITY ACRONYMS   411

APPENDIX E INTERNET PROTOCOL ADDRESSES   415

APPENDIX F SECURITY APPLICATIONS AND SOLUTIONS   417

Preface

Computer Security: Protecting Digital Resources was developed because a number of issues have surfaced concerning computer use on the Internet and the Web. The impact on the entire population is understated. Criminals, sexual predators, child predators, con artists, and terrorists are among those using the network for numerous nefarious purposes. An old proverb states "ignorance is bliss". This certainly does not apply to the use of the Internet, commercial networks, and myriad Web sites.

Numerous scam and fraud schemes are being directed toward public Internet users. A serious issue involves identity theft and identity fraud. Internet criminals are using personal information to steal personal assets from savings and checking accounts. Criminals are using phishing techniques to trick Web users into providing Social Security numbers, birth dates, and other information that are then used to commit cybercrimes. Numerous techniques are being used to learn confidential financial information. Even more serious is the possibility of terrorists using the Internet for hostile purposes.

Computer technology has been growing at an unbelievable pace, and security preparedness has not kept pace with this growth. This is due in large part to the expansion of Internet access to almost all sectors of society. Everyone on the planet with network access can access the Internet. Children are introduced to the Web at an early age at school and at home. Handheld electronic devices and portable computers are available to everyone. The opportunity for expansion of services for the entire population is astronomical. Corporate, government, and other information technology/information systems organizations must step up to these security challenges.

Even more urgent and important, the use of the Web to conduct electronic transactions requires an appreciation of the consequences of not being security "savvy". Many wireless network users are initiating e-commerce transactions from hotspots in coffeehouses, bookstores, fast-food stores, and airports. There are many new threats that can have a significant impact on these users. It is possible for rogue users to illegally access portable wireless computers and other wireless devices. This book addresses the multitude of security issues that affect personal and organizational digital resources.

This book is oriented toward the average computer user, business, government, and education community, with the expectation that the user can learn to use the network with some degree of safety and security. This book provides a broad approach to computer-related crime, electronic commerce, corporate networking, and Internet security topics. Emphasis is placed on the numerous vulnerabilities and threats that are inherent in the Internet environment. Efforts are made to present techniques and suggestions to avoid identity theft and fraud. Also included is information that can be used to protect against child molesters and predators. Information presented is applicable for protection of both personal and business resources from unscrupulous individuals.

Additionally, a considerable amount of information is presented concerning wireless electronic commerce, namely e-commerce, which includes business-to-business (B2B), business-to-consumer (B2C), and consumer-to-consumer (C2C). A large number of business transactions are now being transmitted over the Internet. It is imperative that these transactions possess a high degree of integrity. Because e-commerce transactions can occur any time during the day or week, from any location across the planet, those individuals responsible for network security and integrity must be constantly vigilant. There are many hardware and software products and solutions to address these critical issues. Education and awareness are the first steps toward addressing these issues. There are a number of certification programs that can prepare network staff for the tasks at hand. Two familiar certification programs are the Certified Information Systems Security Professional (CISSP) and Security+. Chapter 14 provides information on numerous security courses and training providers.

Corporate, government, and education management must be concerned about the confidentiality, integrity, and availability of computer and database assets and resources. Several chapters are devoted to the topics of computer contingency planning, disaster recovery, intrusion detection, and intrusion prevention. These initiatives require very expensive solutions and a significant amount of understanding and planning.

The orientation of the book is, therefore, toward giving the general public, student, network administrator, and business professional the tools to identify and apply a number of techniques to the Internet, internetwork, and Web environment for the various applications of security solutions. This book is also useful for those engaged in corporate security and network management. Both wireless and wired networks can be the source of financial and personal security compromises. These topics are covered in several of the chapters.

In summary, this book is not highly technical—just enough detail is provided to allow the reader to apply the information provided to be successful in addressing the security issues prevalent in the e-commerce, networking, Web, and Internet environment. This book has been written to provide any reader with an understanding of the issues that must be addressed when using the Internet or a corporate network for personal, business, government, or academic pursuits. This book is especially relevant for curricula offered in business, information systems (IS), information technology (IT), and network studies in two- and four-year institutions of higher learning and technical schools.

Disciplines that would benefit from this book include:

- Computer Science
- Management
- Management Information Systems (MIS)
- Business Information Systems (BIS)
- Computer Information Systems (CIS)

- Networking
- Telecommunication Systems
- Data Communications
- Criminal Justice
- Network Administration

ORGANIZATION OF THIS BOOK

This book is divided into four parts. Part One provides basics and general understanding of security and integrity issues of computer and networking systems that are part of the Internet environment. This part is relevant to all readers and should be read before attempting Part Two. It includes a background and general overview of the security issues. A section is included on cyber-terrorism, which should be on everyone's mind. Also addressed are the vulnerabilities and threats that may well be encountered when accessing the Web. Part One also includes chapters on both personal safety and security, along with a chapter on property and asset security. It includes chapters on security issues; vulnerabilities and threats; personal and property security; and Internet, network, and WWW security.

Part Two provides a look at the various systems and components that comprise the computer networking infrastructure. This part includes more details that will be useful to the student or commercial user. Part Two includes chapters on basic information and issues concerning the Internet and the global network environment. This part includes a chapter devoted to wired and wireless local area networks, which are prevalent in the business and educational environment. The chapter on computer systems security provides a solid understanding of how this infrastructure is part of the security and privacy issues. The last chapter in Part Two is dedicated to a very relevant topic of this book—e-commerce and Internet security.

Part Three provides considerable information concerning business continuity and disaster recovery planning and intrusion detection and prevention. These are "must" chapters for anyone who has any connection with computer and data systems. The last chapter addresses troubleshooting and problem-solving in this computer environment. A section is included on computer forensics relating to computer, e-mail, and wireless devices.

Part Four includes a chapter that identifies security solutions for digital resources and a chapter that presents various computer security standards, specifications, and protocols. The last chapter addresses security training and certifications and the all-important issue of security careers.

More than 300 key terms are provided throughout the book (**bold type**) and the definitions of these can be found in the Glossary.

Several appendices are provided:

A. Computer and Information Systems Security Review
B. Information Security (InfoSec) Acceptable Use Policy
C. Answers to Chapter Security Review Questions
D. Computer Security Acronyms
E. Internet Protocol Addresses
F. Security Applications and Solutions

INSTRUCTOR UTILIZATION OF THIS BOOK

Instructors' materials include copies of PowerPoint slides for classroom and employee presentations. The instructor material includes a test bank of true/false and multiple-choice questions, varying in complexity, that can be used to support the material that has been presented. End-of-chapter exercises test the understanding of the material presented. Answers to these questions are found in Appendix C. Chapter research exercises require external resources, including the Web, where many of the solutions can be developed.

Many Web resources were utilized in developing this book. Several books that were used to prepare for the CISSP and Security+ exam were extremely useful in completing this work. These included *Security+ Certification for Dummies*, and *The CISSP Prep Guide*. Significant input was provided from presentations attended at the 2005–2007 Kennesaw Cybercrime Summits. The amount of information and data available today on the security subject is staggering and will take considerable effort for the reader to keep up-to-date.

SUPPLEMENTS

Supplements for the text can be found on the catalog page at *http://www.jbpub.com/catalog /9780763759940*, including PowerPoint slides and test items.

ACKNOWLEDGMENTS

Thanks to the following reviewers for providing valuable feedback: Dr. Sunil Hazari, State University of West Georgia; Benjamin Halpert, Nova Southeastern University; and Barbara Endicott-Popovsky, University of Washington.

Thanks to the two academic department chairs in the Information Systems department of Georgia Southern University—Dr. Tom Case and Dr. Susan Williams—who provided support and guidance in the development of this book.

Finally, I would like to thank the many individuals responsible for the publication of this book. These include Tim Anderson, Acquisitions Editor; Melissa Potter, Editorial Assistant; and Tracey Chapman, Senior Production Editor.

CHAPTER 1

Cyber Environment and Security Issues

🔒 CHAPTER CONTENTS

- Look at the historical and current status of the cyber environment.
- See how computer and network security issues will affect the user community.
- Understand the difference between trusted and untrusted networks.
- Identify threats that could be encountered when accessing the Internet and Web.
- Look at the various methods of protecting computer and network resources.
- Become familiar with issues relating to cybercrimes and cyber-terrorism.
- Identify intellectual property theft categories.
- Understand the issues relating to Internet and Web access for children.

INTRODUCTION

Chapter 1 sets the stage for a discussion of the various aspects of computer, database, network, and Internet security. Discussions include security issues involving all segments of the populace as they relate to the Internet infrastructure and the Web.

Basic security concepts are established to provide a framework for the rest of the book. Issues relating to the current security atmosphere that permeates the Internet and Web networking environment are presented. Efforts will be directed at presenting the "who, what, where, and how" concerning security issues.

Throughout the text, sections delve into security basics, security technologies, and security goals. The concept of trusted and untrusted networks is presented. An overview of the issues that affect physical and personal security includes various alternatives to counter malicious activities and threats.

Three major grouping descriptors are identified that reflect the current state of the computer and networking environment. The three main goals and objectives of secure computing, which include *confidentiality*, *integrity*, and *availability*, are discussed. Most business, academic, and government offices have access to a common local area network (LAN) that is accessible from the Internet. There are numerous issues that relate to computer security and the electronic commerce environment.

Considerable emphasis is placed on security threats and vulnerabilities to personal, government, and business networks, hardware, and software systems. Introductions are also provided on data and database security and integrity. The concepts and issues introduced in this chapter are explored in detail in subsequent chapters. Data are concentrated on large database systems, allowing for significant opportunities for information theft and fraudulent activities.

An introduction is provided concerning cybercrime and cyber-terrorism and their impact on the network. The reader should be aware of the global issues that are relevant in today's cyber environment. Efforts have been made to provide a "one-stop shopping" for a majority of the issues relating to cybercrimes; however, Internet security is a moving target, and constant vigilance is necessary.

Pornography, violence, predation, and obscenity are available on numerous Web sites. Predators can compromise the Internet safety of minors. What can parents, guardians, and educators do to ensure a safe and secure experience with Internet resources? Suggestions oriented toward child pornography, child molestation, and Web safety are presented.

AN HISTORICAL PERSPECTIVE

In the past, security was not a major issue, because all computer resources were contained in a central location. In today's environment, security lapses can bankrupt a company and destroy a wealth of information. Individuals can lose their life savings and have their credit ratings ruined. What are these new threats, and what can be done to negate their impact? This book explores the computer and network environment and provides a number of possible solutions and suggestions to counter a multitude of pervasive threats.

In the 1960s and 1970s, the computer industry was in its infancy. Hardware and software resources were only available to those users who were located at the central host-computer location. Remote access did not exist for network or computer communications. The next technology evolution provided users with the capability to access the host computer site using a dial-up, slow-speed connection. From very slow transmission speeds to today's megabit speeds, many of the networking developments pervasive in industry today started in the educational environment. With the development of the Internet, connectivity is available to everyone on the planet. This includes cyber criminals, predators, and terrorists!

Because the computer resource was contained in a protected central location, it was fairly easy to build protection into the physical facility, and a guard could be employed to watch this physical asset. As technology progressed, and the capability to access computer resources from distant locations became feasible, different issues and challenges surfaced. Another important aspect of computer security is the protection and integrity of the data and databases located on an individual's personal computing device and those in commercial computer centers.

As more and more members of the general public become computer literate and because computing devices are readily available to most of the population, issues relating to computer security has increased. The *Internetstatstoday.com* Web site for Internet market research indicates the estimated number of Internet users at **1.463 billion** people and the world Internet penetration rate at **21.9 percent** as of June 2008.

A number of horror stories made the computer industry aware that something must be done to quell the threat to computer resources that has taken the form of computer viruses and identity theft on various electronic media. Because these attacks are being perpetuated over the Internet, the physical controls that were used to protect centralized facilities have become obsolete. New approaches are necessary to protect public and private assets and resources.

Security Concerns Today

The Internet is plagued with individuals who enjoy the electronic equivalent of creating graffiti on other people's walls with spray paint or causing some type of vandalism to property. Thousands of virus attacks are a recurring menace. Organizations are plagued by "denial of service" attacks. Many computer and network users are attempting to get real work done over the Internet and have sensitive or proprietary data they must protect. The objective is to keep the undesirables out of the network while accomplishing required activities or tasks.

Two major issues must be addressed when discussing network and computer security: accidental and malicious events. An accidental situation can cause as much grief as a destructive attack. It is, therefore, necessary to protect resources from both of these situations. There are a multitude of methods and procedures available that can address these issues. Various suggestions and alternatives are presented in subsequent chapters.

Industry analysts estimate that in-house security breaches account for a majority of business computer network attacks. Many of these intrusions may go undetected. A disgruntled employee may seek revenge by deleting or altering files or applications. Another may participate in corporate espionage after being given a promise of large rewards. Still another may be looking for insider information for a stock purchase. Others are just inquisitive and try to access forbidden sites and information. Most organizations can successfully discourage insider attacks by assigning specific access rights that provide restrictions to this type of information. Internal attacks often occur because of the knowledge possessed by the personnel who operate on the organization's computer and network systems. Security and computer-use policies that address the proper use of resources must be established in all organizations with information systems departments.

COMPUTER AND INTERNET ENVIRONMENT ISSUES

There are many individuals in today's society whose goal is to "get something for nothing" or who are willing to cause havoc for havoc's sake. The law enforcement establishment could usually handle the task of guarding against these individuals. However, in today's computer and networking environment, these individuals can appear anywhere in the world—at any time—to cause distress to individuals; corporations; and government, education, health care, and public resources. This means that legitimate users must initiate activities and actions that can minimize or eliminate these threats. Security boundaries can be set up around groups, departments, and data centers within an organization. Such boundaries can make it difficult for internal personnel to access restricted systems while also making it more difficult for outside attackers to penetrate into an organization's network. These barriers will probably take the form of firewalls, routers, and gateway devices along with the software that provides for security and integrity functions. Additional safeguard information is presented in subsequent chapters.

Three major grouping descriptors reflect the current state of the computer and networking environment: (1) the value of the resource, (2) the portability and size of the resource, and (3) the personal contact required. Each of these descriptors is described in the following sections.

Value of the Resource

Access to computer resources can improve productivity by making applications, processing power, and data available to employees, students, customers, and business partners. If this access is impeded, productivity can and will be degraded. Networks, however, make organizational data and information stored in databases more vulnerable to abuse, misuse, and external attack.

The computer and network resource might consist of a desktop, palmtop, PDA, cellular phone, smart phone, laptop computer, client/server, or a mainframe computer. The cost of the physical device can be small or can run into millions of dollars. The cost of the hardware, however, is only a small part of the resource. The value of the data and information stored in a computer system can be substantial. (*Note that* data *refers to any material represented in a formalized manner so that it can be stored, manipulated, and transmitted by machine, whereas* information *is the meaning assigned to data by people.*) Computer systems contain confidential information about the population's taxes, investments, medical history, education, criminal history, military records, and so on. Even more sensitive information may be stored concerning business operations, which may include new product lines, marketing strategies, sales figures, and other strategic and tactical information. Governmental computers may store information on military targets, troop movements, weapons, intelligence, and other state secrets. New systems concerning health care are being planned for nationwide access. New products for law enforcement allow the officer on the beat to access the Internet for record checking. The value of these assets is enormous, and the repercussions of losing them can be quite devastating to the country, its organizations, and the general public.

Of particular interest is the protection of the data and assets of the general public. Every day new revelations surface about cybercrime victims who have lost their life's savings to some computer criminal. Even more insidious are the incidents of identity theft and fraud that appear to occur on a daily basis. Life savings or retirement funds of an individual can be stolen overnight because of identify theft. Organizations that store customer data have recently been compromised, which can lead to identify theft and fraud. E-mail address books are susceptible to attack and compromise; and the list of threats and compromises continue to grow daily. Chapter 3 will provide a wealth of information addressing these issues.

Portability and Size

The first computers filled up rooms with hardware and were very expensive. The use of software was cumbersome and difficult and was part of the technical realm. The palmtop, MP3 player, and cell phone that can be carried on the body have more computing power than the original mainframe computers. Device size has significant implications on portability. It is now possible to access the Internet from anywhere in the world using a handheld computer. The other element associated with device size is the cost. An attaché case can hold thousands of dollars' worth of computer and networking equipment. The information stored on these portable devices will probably be a subset of that resident on the corporate client/server and mainframe systems. It is now possible to lose or misplace these portable devices, which could compromise the corporate, educational, or governmental resource.

Implications for security are immense. Laptops can be left in airports and coffee shops where they disappear with ease. Many students use laptops, smart phones, and PDAs in their daily lives. These devices are very susceptible to theft. Data stored on these devices can be used for illegal activities. Often the cost to replace these data are more expensive that the value of the original device. New computer and data storage devices enter the market on a daily basis. The amount of data and information that can be contained on such storage media is immense. Flash storage now contains in excess of 8 gigabytes of data storage and hard drives have a storage capacity in excess of 1.5 terabytes.

Personal Contact

In the near past, most transactions were one-on-one and up-front and personal. Either cash or personal check was the common medium of exchange. The time is probably at hand where hard money, per se, will not be necessary or viable. Stores are now scanning checks at the checkout lane. Most citizens and organizations utilize some form of credit or debit card to conduct financial transactions. They are not only easier to use, but provide an electronic audit trail of the transactions. Electronic funds transfers (EFTs) account for most transfers of money between and among banks and other financial institutions. Many organizations pay employees by direct deposit to the employees' bank account. The government is using direct deposit for Social Security, tax refunds, and payrolls. Mortgage companies, credit unions, utilities, insurance companies, and other institutions can automatically process deductions against their clients' bank accounts. It is now possible to make banking transactions and stock market transactions from portable and remotely deployed computer and networking devices.

Commerce is aided via electronic data interchange (EDI) capabilities, which provide for electronic orders and shipments. There are many opportunities for fraud and loss in this worldwide electronic environment, and the lack of personal contact plays to the dishonest individual whose goal is to defraud as many computer users as possible. A recent report developed by the Federal Bureau of Investigation (FBI) shows that many of the network computer frauds are initiated from outside the United States.

Transactions concerning purchases over the Web have increased dramatically. These Web organizations have incorporated security methods, including electronic signatures to protect against illegal activities; however, the individuals making the buy and sell transactions must be vigilant against a cyber attack. It is essential that transactions across the network possess a high degree of integrity and be "trusted."

TRUSTED SYSTEMS

Trust is the composite of availability, performance, and security, which includes the ability to execute processes with integrity, secrecy, and privacy. Solutions and suggestions that provide support to trusted systems are presented in subsequent chapters, including computer policies, biometric systems, secure protocols, and secure electronic transactions. Each of these systems provides a part of the total solution for protection of the organization's computer and network assets. The task of online systems is to develop and implement security solutions that will protect the organization from the untrusted networks. Likewise, individual users must also initiate processes for protection of personal computer assets and data. Concepts and details concerning confidentiality, integrity, and availability (CIA) are discussed in subsequent sections.

Trusted and Untrusted Networks

In computer networking, *trust* refers to the ability of an application to perform actions with integrity, to keep confidential information private, and to perform its functions on a continuing basis. The components of trust in a network computing system consist of availability, performance, and security. **Trusted networks** are inside the security perimeter, whereas known untrusted networks, such as the Internet, are outside the security perimeter. An unknown network is also considered an untrusted network.

Someone in an organization usually administers the computers that comprise the trusted networks, and the organization controls security measures. The internal trusted network consists of a number of devices, including firewalls, routers, gateways, and secure servers. Subsequent chapters provide information on these computer and network solutions and describe how unscrupulous individuals can compromise them.

An **untrusted network** is outside the organization's control, and there is no control over the administration or security policies for these sites. They consist of private, shared networks with which the trusted network often communicates. Much of the information presented in this book addresses the issue of untrusted network traffic; however, there are also significant internal threats. Technical solutions are available to operate in this untrusted environment. They may take the form of a demilitarized zone (DMZ) or computer devices such as proxy servers. There are also many software products that address these security issues. These solutions are presented in a subsequent chapter.

THE CYBER ENVIRONMENT

A number of components make up the cyber environment, including the Internet infrastructure, the Web, the computer systems, client/server systems, the network, and individual workstations. Major components of the computer and network systems include system and application software. System software includes a set of instructions that provides functionality between the computer hardware and application programs, whereas application software's purpose is to provide functionality to a user. This software can be a major contributor to computer and network incidents. These major components are but a small part of the enormous network infrastructure that makes up this environment. An overview is provided for each of these network subset components.

Cyber is a prefix used to describe new things that are being made possible by the spread of *computers*. Cyberphobia, for example, is an irrational fear of computers. It is easy to see why someone would be afraid to use a computer to access critical systems. **Cyberspace** is defined as the global network of interconnected computers and communication systems. Anything related to the Internet also falls under the cyber category. Additional terms, described later, include cybercrime and cyber-terrorism.

The Internet and the World Wide Web

It is essential for the reader to become familiar with the numerous terms that relate to Internet and Web use and, specifically, to the issue of crime and criminal activities that exist in the network as vehicles to prey on the general public. Each chapter provides an understanding of the various terms and describes situations that might arise from using the Internet. Subsequent chapters provide more detail and guidance on the safe and secure methods of conducting sessions over the Internet. A good place to start is to briefly describe the computer environment, its components, and how they play in the cybercrime arena.

Briefly, the *Internet* (capital *I*) is a self-regulated network of computer networks, and an *internet* (small *i*) is a government, education, or corporate internal network. An *intranet* is an internal network, usually within a department or business. An *extranet* is a secure network that allows business partners to access parts of an organization's resources via some security technique such as logons and passwords. There are different security implications for each type of network. Additional details are provided in Chapter 6.

The terms *Internet* and *World Wide Web* (aka the *Web*) are often used interchangeably; however, the two terms are not synonymous [Ciampa, 2004]. The Internet and the Web are two separate but related entities. The Internet is a massive network of networks, a networking infrastructure. It connects millions of computers together globally, forming a worldwide network in which any computer can communicate with any other computer as long as they are both connected to the Internet. Information that travels over the Internet does so via a variety of computer network languages known as *protocols*. Elements of the infrastructure include Internet Service Providers (ISPs) and Network Service Providers (NSPs) for accessing Web servers. Network access points (NAPs) provide the connectivity between these elements.

FIGURE 1-1 provides a graphical representation of this network environment. Additional details on the Internet are provided in Chapter 5.

The World Wide Web (WWW), or Web, provides a method of accessing information over the medium of the Internet. It is an information-sharing process that is built on top of the Internet. The Web uses the Hypertext Transfer Protocol (HTTP) to transmit data. Web services, which use HTTP to allow applications to communicate in order to exchange business logic, use the Web to share information. The Web also utilizes *browsers*, such as *Internet Explorer* or *Netscape*, to access Web documents called Web pages that are linked to each other via hyperlinks. *Hyperlinks* associate text or graphics with some Web page location. Web documents also contain graphics, sounds, text, and video. Web pages are usually constructed using a programming language called Hypertext Markup Language (HTML). Web sites are addressed by a universal resource locator (URL). An example of a URL is *www.weather.com* or *www.google.com*.

The Web is just one method of information dissemination over the Internet. The Internet, not the Web, is also used for *e-mail*, which relies on Simple Message Transport Protocol (SMTP), *Usenet* news groups, instant messaging, and File Transfer Protocol (FTP). Note that e-mail and messaging systems are often the vehicles for fraudulent and destructive activities, and numerous security solutions are available to provide some level of security. SMTP and FTP details are provided in Chapter 13.

Client/Server Environment

In today's networking and Internet environment, remote access to computer systems and resources can be achieved quickly and easily with very little expense to the user. Advances in usability and accessibility have been countered by losses in security of the resources. It is still necessary to have the physical site security of locked doors and alarms; however, additional controls are necessary to provide security for remote access. The client/server explosion has provided the impetus to develop additional security programs. Why is this environment

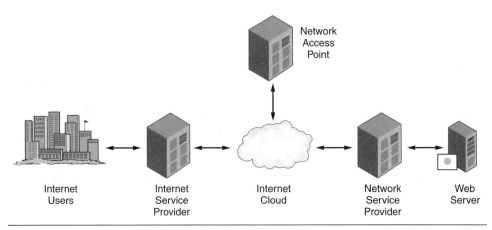

FIGURE 1-1 Internet Infrastructure

a candidate for security initiatives? The client/server model is defined as a desktop computing device or program "served" by another networked computing device. Computers are integrated over the network by an application, which provides a single system view. The server
can consist of a number of computer processor devices with attached storage devices. A client
can be served by a number of servers. Different operating system software can be resident on
a number of different server systems. The user is not usually aware of the location of these
server resources.

FIGURE 1-2 provides a graphical view of the client/server environment.

The distributed computing environment consists of both distributed computing and a
distributed database. A database contains raw information about some subject or entity. Portions of the applications and data are broken up and distributed among the server and client
computers. A distributed database is an application in which there are many clients as well as
many servers. All databases at remote and local sites are treated as if they were one database.
Users are not usually aware of the location of the database assets, nor do they care, because
computer and network resources are transparent to the user. The downside to distributed
networks is the difficulty of management and control. Distributed networks that utilize the
Internet also offer the attacker or intruder additional opportunities to commit harm to assets
and resources. Computer virus attacks can quickly spread across countries because of this
distributed network architecture. Situations have occurred in which a virus has spread so far
and fast that it starts to attack itself around the world.

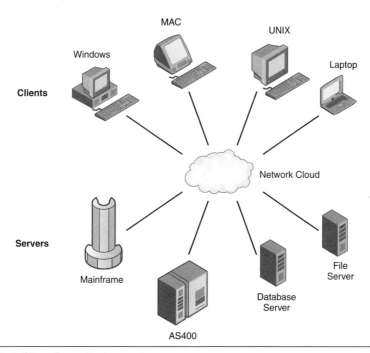

FIGURE 1-2 Client/Server Environment

CYBERCRIMES

Cybercrime encompasses any criminal act dealing with computers and networks (sometimes called *hacking* or *cracking*). Additionally, cybercrime includes traditional crimes that are now being conducted through the Internet and the Web. For example, telemarketing and Internet fraud, identity theft, sex crimes, and credit card account thefts are considered to be cybercrimes when the illegal activities are committed through the use of a computer and the Internet. Criminals are becoming technically literate, and their activities are more difficult to track because of the worldwide nature of the Internet. Criminal activities can be initiated anywhere in the world using the Internet and other networks.

Criminal activity has increased in the area of networking with the advent of worldwide access to the Internet. This in turn has increased the vulnerability of the computer assets that are accessible through the organization's networks. The U.S. Department of Justice (USDOJ) provides guidance to investigators and prosecutors in the areas of cybercrime and intellectual property matters. This support is provided under the Computer Crime and Intellectual Property Section (CCIPS) umbrella. Many computer crime documents containing computer crime guidance and case studies are available at the Web site located at *www.cybercrime.gov/ccips.html*. The Computer Crime Initiative is a comprehensive program designed to combat electronic penetrations, data thefts, and cyber attacks on critical information systems. CCIPS prevents, investigates, and prosecutes computer crimes by working with other government agencies, the private sector, academic institutions, and foreign counterparts.

There are many categories of cybercrime and security policy issues that must be addressed in today's networking environment. The major issues can be summarized as follows:

- Identity theft and fraud.
- Pornography and minors.
- E-commerce legal issues.
- Encryption and computer crime.
- Federal code related to cybercrime.
- Intellectual property crime.
- International aspects of computer crime.
- Privacy issues in the high-tech context.
- Prosecuting crimes facilitated by computers and by the Internet.
- Protecting critical infrastructures.
- Searching and seizing computers, and obtaining evidence in criminal investigations.
- Speech issues in the high-tech context.

There are a number of statutes that are used to prosecute computer and networking crimes. A sample of these statutes includes the following:

- Title 18 USC 1029. Fraud and Related Activity in Connection with Access Devices.
- Title 18 USC 1030. Fraud and Related Activity in Connection with Computers.
- Title 18 USC 1362. Communications Lines, Stations, or Systems.

- Title 18 USC 2511. Interception and Disclosure of Wire, Oral, or Electronic Communications Prohibited.
- Title 18 USC 2701. Unlawful Access to Stored Communications.
- Title 18 USC 2702. Disclosure of Contents.
- Title 18 USC 2703. Requirements for Governmental Access.

These documents are normally associated with domestic computer and networking crimes; however, these crimes are starting to bleed over into the military and international environments and are called *information warfare* and *cyber-terrorism*. After looking at the list of cybercrimes, it should be apparent that employment opportunities are good in the security field. It is essential that security students understand the numerous terms that are part of this environment. Various security dictionaries, such as *alphadictionary.com*, are available on the Web.

CYBER-TERRORISM

While not generally an issue with home and personal computer systems, it is essential that the user be aware of any potential threat. The FBI defines **terrorism** as the unlawful use of force or violence against persons or property to intimidate or coerce a government, the civilian population, or any segment thereof, in furtherance of political or social objectives. Cyber-terrorism could thus be defined as the use of computing resources to intimidate or coerce others. An example of cyber-terrorism could be hacking into the Federal Aviation Administration (FAA) computer system and making modifications that could cause havoc with air transportation. Another example of cyber-terrorism would be an attack on any public resource, such as the power grid, that depends on the computer network to provide services. General computer users and computing professionals all over the world need to be aware of possible areas of weakness to such terrorism in order to better protect their computer systems and possibly help put an end to terrorist activity.

Cyber-terrorism is the convergence of terrorism and cyberspace. A cyber attack would include unlawful attacks and threats against computers, networks, and databases; however, when done to intimidate or coerce a government or its people in furtherance of some political or social objective, such actions become cyber-terrorism. Cyber-terrorism includes attacks that result in violence against infrastructure, persons, and property and often lead to death or bodily injury, explosions, plane crashes, water contamination, or severe economic damage. The terrorists are interested in instilling fear in the general populace. The current complement of terrorists' objectives is to destroy all elements of modern civilization, which includes the computer and network infrastructure, computers, assets, resources, and personnel.

Cyberspace is constantly under assault because cyber spies, thieves, saboteurs, and thrill-seekers break into computer and networking systems. They steal personal data and trade secrets, vandalize Web sites, disrupt service, sabotage data and systems, launch computer viruses and worms, conduct fraudulent transactions, and harass individuals and organizations. These attacks are facilitated with increasingly powerful and easy-to-use software tools, readily available on the Internet. The scary part is that the terrorists can be located anywhere in the world and can create turmoil if access to the Internet is available.

The next generation of terrorists will grow up in a digital world, where more powerful and easy-to-use hacking tools will be available. They might see greater potential for cyber-terrorism than the terrorists of today, and their level of knowledge and skill relating to attacking personal, business, and government resources will be greater. Hackers and insiders might be recruited by terrorists or self-recruiting cyber-terrorists. Some might be moved to action by cyber policy issues, making cyberspace an attractive venue for carrying out an attack. Cyber-terrorism could also become more attractive as the real and virtual worlds become more closely coupled, with a greater number of physical devices attached to the Internet. Web-based resources are available for individuals or organizations bent on terror, fraud, and other illegal acts 24 hours a day, 7 days a week (24/7). These people have a number of tools to ply their trade. One technique used by terrorists is steganography.

Steganography

Steganography or *stego* is the art and science of hiding information by embedding messages within other, seemingly harmless, messages. Steganography works by replacing bits of useless or unused data in regular computer files (such as graphics, sound, text, HTML, or even floppy disks) with bits of different, invisible information. This hidden information can be *plain text*, cipher text, or even images. Stego is used by cyber-terrorists or criminals to hide messages in standard transmissions that are not readily visible to the general network user. However, the intended fellow terrorist would know where to look for any hidden messages.

As an example, a terrorist might send a broadcast message to millions of Internet users. This message could be a meaningless spam e-mail that would probably be deleted by most recipients; however, the designated terrorist would decode and read the message. Pretty slick! Another example is too simple. It is possible to code messages in the comment statements of Web page HTML. These comment statements could be plain text or encrypted. This is another opportunity for individuals interested in counter-hacking.

Steganography is sometimes used when encryption is not permitted. Or, more commonly, steganography is used to supplement *encryption*. An encrypted file may use steganography to hide information, so even if the encrypted file is deciphered, the hidden message is not seen. Special software is needed for steganography, and there are freeware versions available at many download sites.

Steganography (literally meaning covered writing) dates back to ancient Greece, where common practices consisted of etching messages in wooden tablets and covering them with wax, and tattooing a messenger's shaved head, letting his hair grow back, then shaving it again when he arrived at his contact point.

Information Warfare

Information warfare is the offensive and defensive use of information and information systems to deny, exploit, corrupt, or destroy an adversary's information, information-based processes, information systems, and computer-based networks while protecting one's own. Such actions are designed to achieve advantages over military or business adversaries. An allied term is **INFOSEC**, meaning information security, which describes the protection of classi-fied information stored on computers or transmitted by radio, telephone, teletype, or any other means.

Acronyms associated with this new category of crime include a number of unique terms. A sampling of information warfare definitions follows:

- CARNIVORE: an FBI system used to monitor e-mail and other traffic through ISPs.
- Defense Information Structure (DIS): the worldwide shared or interconnected system of computers, communications, data, applications, security, personnel, training, and other support structures serving the military's information needs.
- Defense Information Security Administration (DISA): the military organization charged with responsibility to provide information systems to fighting units.
- van Eck monitoring: monitoring the security of a computer or other electronic equip-ment by detecting low levels of electromagnetic emissions from the device.
- Electromagnetic pulse (EMP): a pulse of electromagnetic energy capable of disrupting computers, computer networks, and other forms of telecommunications equipment.
- High-Energy Radio Frequency (HERF): a device that can disrupt the normal operation of digital equipment such as computers and navigational equipment.
- Information security (INFOSEC): protection of classified information that is stored on computers or transmitted by radio, telephone, or other means.

Note that some of these acronyms relate to advanced forms of security attacks.

RESOURCE AND ASSET PROTECTION

One of the primary concerns of most organizations is protecting its computer and networking assets. Of particular interest is the security and integrity of the data and database resources of the users and the organization. Companies can lose competitive position, and even fail, if information gets into the wrong hands. Securing data against illegal access and alteration is even more of an issue on networks, because there are many opportunities for snooping and interception when transmitting data between computers and between LANs.

It is obvious that security in the computing and networking environment has a high priority with corporate entities. The purpose of this book is to develop a broad and general understanding of the security issues that relate to the computing and communications envi-ronment. Various areas of organizations are visited to identify candidates for security solutions. Vulnerabilities are identified and countermeasures or controls are suggested. In addition, a number of risks and their related costs are identified. Corporate and site computer policy is addressed, followed by topics on basic threats, attacks, and vulnerabilities of the networking asset. Protection of database assets is a priority because this issue applies to everyone that uses networking services.

Many techniques are available for computer and network protection: from user passwords to biometrics and from firewalls to intrusion detection technologies. The challenge is to employ appropriate security measures that will provide sufficient protection of the organization's assets without impeding productivity. Organizations and individual users should not spend more on protection than the asset is worth. One effective technique is to code the transmissions so they are not readily understandable by the casual reader. Concepts introduced include a cryptanalysis study, a cryptography art, and encryption and decryption translations.

Cryptanalysis

Cryptanalysis is the study of a cryptographic system for the purpose of finding weaknesses in the system and breaking the code used to *encrypt* the data without knowing the code's *key*. Cryptanalysis has a number of uses—not all good. It can be used for military and diplomatic surveillance, or by enterprises and other organizations to test the strength of security procedures, or by malicious *hackers* in exploiting weaknesses in Web sites.

Cryptography

Cryptography is the art of protecting information by transforming it (encrypting it) into an unreadable format, called *cipher text*. Only those who possess a secret key can decipher (or decrypt) the message into plain text. Encrypted messages can sometimes be broken by cryptanalysis, also called *code breaking*, although modern cryptography techniques are virtually unbreakable.

As the *Internet* and other forms of electronic communication become more prevalent, electronic *security* is becoming increasingly important. Cryptography is used to protect *e-mail* messages, credit card information, and corporate data. One of the most popular cryptography systems used on the *Internet* is Pretty Good Privacy (PGP) because it is effective and open source. PGP, described in Chapter 13, is used primarily with encrypting e-mail transmissions.

Cryptography systems can be broadly classified into *symmetric-key* systems that use a single key that both the sender and recipient have and *public-key* systems that use two keys—a public key known to everyone and a private key that only the recipient of messages uses.

Encryption/Decryption

The translation of data into a secret code and back is called *encryption* and *decryption*, respectively. Encryption is the most effective way to achieve data security. To read an encrypted file, users must have access to a secret key or password that enables the decryption. Unencrypted data are called plain text; encrypted data are referred to as cipher text. There are two main types of encryption: asymmetric/public-key encryption and symmetric/private-key encryption. The Data Encryption Standard (DES) and Advanced Encryption Standard (AES) are examples of cryptographic algorithms that protect unclassified computer data. There are additional algorithms that can be used to protect data. Details are provided in subsequent chapters.

CONTENT MANAGEMENT

Content management has usually been a concern of business; however, this issue is also becoming important for the general public. Security involves the protection of data and database resources as well as the contents of these assets. Content management is a critical issue because the owner loses control over the data after the data are downloaded, and their ultimate destination and use are unknown. Completing a survey or a warranty card might provide information to undesirable entities. The individual does not know who will end up with this information. Organizations sell mailing lists, so everyone must be aware of the information that is being made available. The process of information sharing becomes valuable only when the "right data" are communicated to the "right people" at the "right time."

For organizations, extranets lend themselves to the aggregation of tactical information, which can have a strategic value over time. This can become a security issue if content control and the time value of information are not considered as part of the security equation. Partners or contractors, who are also competitors, can realize an undue advantage if certain short-term data can be aggregated over the long term, which would provide a strategic advantage. This means that the same information should not be accessible in the same form to all corporate partners.

An extranet is a situation in which an organization exposes its proprietary information to a semi-open audience. Sound content management means that the resource owner must never assume that the partner will be the final user of the information. Ease of information flow is inherent to achieving success; however, it must be recognized that revealing too much information is a recipe for disaster. It is, therefore, incumbent upon content owners to implement information security systems that permit content control and dynamic changes to minimize exposure to risk.

Two terms should be introduced that emphasize the need for controlling the content distribution of private data and information. **Aggregation** means obtaining information of a higher sensitivity by combining information from lower levels of sensitivity. **Inference** allows users to infer or deduce information about data at sensitivity levels for which they do not have access privileges. In English: intruders, attackers, competitors, spies, and any others without a need to know, given enough data and information, can arrive at some conclusion that might be correct and secret.

ELECTRONIC THREATS

There are numerous types of infections that can affect the integrity of the network. Daily news reports highlight many different forms of electronic infections in both the public and private sectors. Specific types of threats might include an integrity threat, a denial of service (DoS) threat, or a disclosure threat. Briefly, an *integrity threat* is any unauthorized change to data stored on a computer or network resource or in transit over the network; a *DoS* is an attack that attempts to deny network resources to legitimate users; a **disclosure** is where dissemination of information has occurred to someone other than the intended individual. Briefly, the most common threats encountered by the general public are as follows:

Virus. A virus is a small piece of software that piggybacks on real programs. For example, a virus might attach itself to a program such as a spreadsheet program. Each time the spreadsheet program runs, the virus runs, too, and it has the chance to reproduce (by attaching to other programs) or wreak havoc.

E-mail virus. An e-mail virus moves around in e-mail messages and usually replicates itself by automatically mailing itself to dozens of people in the victim's e-mail address book.

Worm. A worm is a small piece of software that uses computer networks and security holes to replicate itself. A copy of the worm scans the network for another machine that has a specific security hole. It copies itself to the new machine using the security hole and then starts replicating from there, as well.

Trojan horse. A Trojan horse, or Trojan, is simply a computer program. The program claims to do one thing (it may claim to be a game) but instead does damage when you run it (it may erase your hard disk). Trojans have no way to replicate automatically.

Threats, attacks, and vulnerabilities are described and discussed in Chapter 2. Also described are computer network vulnerabilities that are subject to attacks and threats.

CYBER SECURITY GOALS AND OBJECTIVES

This section is devoted to the goals and objectives of secure computing. The three main goals discussed include availability, integrity, and confidentiality. Information provided in Chapter 9 provides insights into continuity planning of computer and network systems.

Availability

Availability means computer and network resources are accessible to only authorized parties. This also means they are available to illegitimate users. An authorized party should not be prevented from accessing the resource. It is possible to make the resource so secure that it is difficult even for the authorized user to access. Availability is sometimes known by its opposite, which is denial of service. The goals of availability include the following:

- Controlled concurrency—multiple users served.
- Fair allocation—fair and equitable share of resources.
- Fault tolerance—protection from failures.
- Timely response—prompt and adequate.
- Usability—useful and relevant.

Integrity

Integrity is defined as rigid adherence to a code or standard of values; the quality or condition of being unimpaired and sound. An integrity threat is any unauthorized change to data stored on a network resource or in transit between resources. A system is compromised when the integrity of the data has been maliciously or otherwise altered. Note that the integrity of the network resource can be compromised by both authorized and unauthorized modifications. This book is primarily concerned with unauthorized integrity threats.

An integrity threat can cause both minor and major consequences. Advance preparation can reduce the severity of the integrity compromise. If there is a backup copy of the data, then the impact of a breach will be less severe than a situation in which a backup is not available. Loss of stored critical information can be disastrous, particularly when financial, health, or national security issues are involved.

A system fabrication or modification can compromise the integrity of a network resource. Forgeries or counterfeit objects may be fabricated and placed on a system. A modification can occur when an unauthorized party tampers with an asset. Changes can be made to database files, operating systems, and even hardware devices. It is, therefore, essential that controls be in place to ensure that only authorized parties make system modifications.

Confidentiality

Confidentiality means maintaining security and secrecy. This means only authorized people can see protected data or resources. The main issue here is to decide what is confidential and who has the right to access it. Confidentiality is probably the best understood of the security properties. When the statement is made, "This is confidential," most will understand that access is limited to a select few. Confidentiality may affect availability. Confidentiality includes the following issues:

- What resources are confidential?
- Who can access the resource?
- How often can the resource be accessed?
- Who can modify or delete the resource?
- Can the status be changed?

ETHICS

Ethics are the rules or standards governing the conduct of the members of a profession. The computer and networking industry has been associated with a lack of ethical behavior in the past. This can be attributed to the lag of protective legislation with respect to electronic data and privacy issues. As a result, acceptance of ethical behavior throughout the industry has been less than satisfactory.

Ethics is not often addressed in computer and telecommunications classes; however, the implications are too significant to ignore. A number of conflicting issues arise: the user's need for privacy, the public's right to know, and the organization's necessity to protect proprietary information. There are a number of consequences that result from a system's ethical, integrity, and security lapses. Several significant incidents that must be addressed are as follows:

- Plagiarism of copyrighted work.
- Eavesdropping on e-mail and other communications.

- Cracking or hacking a computer system.
- Unauthorized access to private or protected systems.
- Illegally copied software and videos.

There are a number of initiatives that can be undertaken to mitigate these situations, including awareness training sessions and communications to employees and users of a system regarding the issue of ethics. Specific activities that the organization can employ to address this issue include the following:

- Develop and publish policies that outline acceptable behavior and repercussions for failure to abide by them.
- Develop and schedule regular training sessions for users and employees on the subject of ethics in the organization's environment.
- Conduct normal business activities in an ethical way, providing an example to employees and users.

ISSA Code of Ethics

The primary goal of the Information Systems Security Association (ISSA) is to promote practices that will ensure the confidentiality, integrity, and availability of organizational information resources. To achieve this goal, members of the Association must reflect the highest standards of ethical conduct. Therefore, ISSA has established the following Code of Ethics and requires its observance as a prerequisite for continued membership and affiliation with the Association. Membership requirements in this organization include the following:

- Perform all professional activities and duties in accordance with all applicable laws and the highest ethical principles.
- Promote generally accepted information security current best practices and standards.
- Maintain appropriate confidentiality of proprietary or otherwise sensitive information encountered in the course of professional activities.
- Discharge professional responsibilities with diligence and honesty.
- Refrain from any activities that might constitute a conflict of interest or otherwise damage the reputation of employers, the information security profession, or the Association.
- Not intentionally injure or impugn the professional reputation or practice of colleagues, clients, or employers.

INTELLECTUAL PROPERTY PROTECTIONS

Intellectual property offenses include copyright and trademark infringement and theft of trade secrets. Civil intellectual property suits include copyright, trademark, and patent infringement. Most educational institutions advertise intellectual property guidelines. Plagiarism can be an issue on educational campuses. Issues discussed in this section include copyrights, trademarks, and trade secrets.

Copyright

Copyright is a form of protection provided by the laws of the United States (Title 17 of the U.S. Code [USC]) to the authors of "original works of authorship," including literary, dramatic, musical, artistic, and certain other intellectual works. This protection is available to both published and unpublished works. Section 106 of the 1976 Copyright Act generally gives the owner of copyright the exclusive right to do and to authorize others to do the following:

- Reproduce the work in copies or phonorecords.
- Prepare derivative works based upon the work.
- Distribute copies or phonorecords of the work to the public by sale or other transfer of ownership, or by rental, lease, or lending.
- Perform the work publicly, in the case of literary, musical, dramatic, and choreographic works, pantomimes, and motion pictures and other audiovisual works.
- Display the copyrighted work publicly, in the case of literary, musical, dramatic, and choreographic works, pantomimes, and pictorial, graphic, or sculptural works, including the individual images of a motion picture or other audiovisual work.
- Perform the work publicly by means of a digital audio transmission in the case of sound recordings.

Note: A phonorecord is what most people would refer to as a "recording." This can be a vinyl record, a compact disc (CD), a tape, or any other fixed medium containing a song—the exact medium is not important for status as a phonorecord.

Trademark

A **trademark** is a word, name, symbol, or device that is used in trade with goods to indicate the source of the goods and to distinguish them from the goods of others. A *service mark* is the same as a trademark except that it identifies and distinguishes the source of a service rather than a product. The terms "trademark" and "mark" are commonly used to refer to both trademarks and service marks [Consumer Law Page].

Trademark rights may be used to prevent others from using a confusingly similar mark but not to prevent others from making the same goods or from selling the same goods or services under a clearly different mark. The registration procedure for trademarks and general information concerning trademarks is described on a separate page entitled "Basic Facts about Trademarks" [USPTO]. The federal criminal statute that applies is Title 18 USC 21320.

Trade Secrets

In most states, a **trade secret** may consist of any formula, pattern, physical device, idea, process, or compilation of information that provides the owner of the information with a competitive advantage in the marketplace. This process is treated in a way that can reasonably be expected to prevent the public or competitors from learning about it, absent improper acquisition or theft.

Unlike other forms of intellectual property such as patents, copyrights, and trademarks, trade secrecy is basically a do-it-yourself form of protection. Owners don't register with the government to secure a trade secret; owners simply keep the information confidential. Trade secret protection lasts for as long as the secret is kept confidential. Once a trade secret is made available to the public, trade secret protection ends. Federal criminal statutes that apply include Title 18 USC 1831 and 1832.

INTERNET ACCESS FOR CHILDREN

Relevant Internet issues for children are predation, pornography, violence, fraud, identity theft, and obscenity. There are a number of issues relating to the easy access that children have to the Internet. These include the content of the Web sites and the opportunity for exploitation. This section addresses the issues of pornography and violence as they relate to the welfare of minors. Chapter 3 provides information on issues concerning computer fraud and identity theft.

Pornography and Violence

Pornography is generally described as the presentation of sexually explicit behavior, as in a photograph, intended to arouse sexual excitement. It has been said that pornography is in the "eye of the beholder." How are minors protected from viewing material that might be offensive? A search of the Cornell Law Center index shows 35 entries, including Titles 18, 19, 20, 22, 28, 42, and 47 of the U.S. Code. This pornography law index can be viewed at the Web site [Cornell Law Center].

Under Title 18 USC 2256, *child pornography* means any visual depiction, including any photograph, film, video, picture, or computer-generated image or picture, whether made or produced by electronic, mechanical, or other means, of sexually explicit conduct, where:

- The production of such visual depiction involves the use of a minor engaging in sexually explicit conduct.
- Such visual depiction is, or appears to be, of a minor engaging in sexually explicit conduct.
- Such visual depiction has been created, adapted, or modified to appear that an identifiable minor is engaging in sexually explicit conduct.
- Such visual depiction is advertised, promoted, presented, described, or distributed in such a manner that conveys the impression that the material is or contains a visual depiction of a minor engaging in sexually explicit conduct.

Child pornography is illegal in nearly all countries, although enforcement varies across the globe. Most countries agree on the basic definition of child pornography: sexually explicit material made with actual minors, usually less than 16 to 18 years of age, as subjects.

Pornography is not the same thing as obscenity. **Obscenity** is a legal concept that applies to those forms of pornography that society considers the most harmful to sexual morality and that it punishes under criminal law. In the United States, for example, the Supreme Court limits the definition of obscenity to "hard-core" pornographic depictions, meaning extremely explicit portrayals of sex.

Another issue concerns children and their ability to access network sites from computers at school, friends' homes, and at home. Violence and pornography is only a mouse-click away. Children are more Internet "literate" than their parents and usually more inquisitive. What can be done to provide some level of safety and security for minors? Education and controls such as parental locks might prove to be only a stopgap solution. Children are often home alone without parental or guardian supervision. What sites are children accessing when away from parental supervision?

Violence is another issue with Web access. Should parents or guardians be held liable for Internet crimes committed by minors? Who is responsible for the content of the Web? Does anyone really care? An organization called NetSmartz apparently cares.

NetSmartzKids is one of a number of Web sites dedicated to network safety for minors. The NetSmartz Workshop is an interactive, educational safety resource that teaches kids and teens how to stay safer on the Internet. NetSmartz combines the newest technologies available and the most current information to create high-impact educational activities that are well received by even the most tech-savvy kids [NetSmartz]. Parents, guardians, educators, and law enforcement also have access to additional resources for learning and teaching about the dangers children may face online. NetSmartzKids was created by the National Center for Missing and Exploited Children® (NCMEC) and Boys and Girls Clubs of America (BGCA).

A report related to Internet violence that consists of interviews with a nationally representative sample of 1,501 youth ages 10 to 17 who use the Internet regularly, "Online Victimization: A Report on the Nation's Youth" [Finkelhor, Mitchell, & Wolak], found that:

- Approximately 1 in 5 received a sexual solicitation or approach over the Internet in the last year.
- One in 33 received an aggressive sexual solicitation—a solicitor who asked to meet them somewhere; called them on the telephone; or sent them regular mail, money, or gifts.
- One in 4 had an unwanted exposure to pictures of naked people or people having sex in the last year.
- One in 17 was threatened or harassed.
- Approximately 25 percent of young people who reported these incidents were distressed by them.
- Less than 10 percent of sexual solicitations and only 3 percent of unwanted exposure episodes were reported to authorities such as a law enforcement agency, an Internet Service Provider, or a hotline.
- About 25 percent of the youth who encountered a sexual solicitation or approach told a parent. Almost 40 percent of those reporting an unwanted exposure to sexual material told a parent.

- Only 17 percent of youth and approximately 10 percent of parents could name a specific authority, such as the Federal Bureau of Investigation, CyberTipline, or an ISP, to which they could make a report, although more said they had "heard of" such places.
- In households with home Internet access, approximately 33 percent of parents said they had filtering or blocking software on their computer at the time they were interviewed.

Note that a considerable number of these solicitations had some sexual orientations or connotations. This report suggests that the Web is fraught with sexual predators and scam and fraud artists. The Web provides access via blog sites, e-mail, and chat rooms where predators can prey on unsuspecting children. An update to this study, entitled "Online Victimization of Youth: Five Years Later," was published in 2006 [missingkids].

🔒 CHAPTER SUMMARY

Requirements for security have increased in importance because computer assets are now accessible from remote users. Database assets are available from a host of portable and desk-top computing devices. Historically, a centrally located database could only be accessed onsite by local personnel. With the advent of the Internet, Web, and the derivations of intranets and extranets, many people could possibly have a need to communicate with a centrally located data center. Both site security policies and corporate security polices must be developed to ensure that the corporate resource will be protected from external threats. These are especially relevant to e-commerce organizations, which often utilize untrusted networks to conduct business activities and transport electronic transactions.

Threats can come from anywhere in the world. It is essential that vulnerabilities are identified and methods developed to counter the threats identified. Specific attacks can threaten the integrity of the data, database, and the system. Specific attacks can include the denial of service, which limits access to legitimate users, and the disclosure threat, which allows the dissemination of secret information to unauthorized parties.

Security goals and objectives include confidentiality, integrity, and availability. The system must be accessible in a timely manner, usable, and accurate. It must also be secure from unauthorized people and organizations. Software threats include worms, Trojans, and viruses. Both the data and the database must be protected from these threats, as they are the foundation and lifeline of the organization.

Management issues of ethics and content management must be considered. Awareness training sessions and communications to employees and users of a system regarding the issue of ethics are a requirement. Content owners must implement information security systems that permit content control to minimize exposure and risk to the organization.

Cybercrime and cyber-terrorism share common attributes. Orientations are different; however, both use the Internet and can exploit the same assets and resources, worldwide. Cyber-terrorism includes unlawful attacks and threats against computers, networks, and databases, to intimidate or coerce a government. Considerable efforts are under way to thwart these types of crimes.

Intellectual property theft offenses include copyright and trademark infringement and theft of trade secrets. Copyright applies to original works of authorship, including literary, dramatic, musical, artistic, and certain other intellectual works. A trademark is a word, name, symbol, or device, and a trade secret may consist of any formula, pattern, physical device, idea, process, or compilation of information.

Pornography, predation, violence, and obscenity Web sites can compromise Internet safety of minors. There are a number of laws that apply to sexually explicit crimes. Information is available at the Cornell Law Center Web site. There are also additional laws that apply to security and privacy of network resources. The NetSmartz Web site provides tools to educate minors in the safe use of the Internet.

 KEY TERMS

aggregation	cyberspace	pornography
availability	cyber-terrorism	steganography
confidentiality	disclosure	terrorism
content management	ethics	trademark
copyright	inference	trade secret
cryptanalysis	information warfare	trust
cryptography	INFOSEC	trusted network
cyber	integrity	untrusted network
cybercrime	obscenity	

 SECURITY REVIEW QUESTIONS

1. What are the three major grouping descriptors that reflect the state of the computer and networking environment?
2. What are the components of trust in a network computing system?
3. Describe the difference between an *internet* and the *Internet*.
4. Define *cybercrime*, and provide several examples.
5. Provide several examples of cyber-terrorism.
6. Describe steganography.
7. What are some examples of techniques that can be utilized to protect computers and networks?
8. Provide a short list of threats that can compromise computer and network assets.
9. What is CIA?
10. What are relevant issues that apply to children and Internet usage?

RESEARCH ACTIVITIES

1. Review the case studies presented at *www.cybercrime.gov.*
2. Review the statutes and laws pertaining to computer and networking crimes.
3. Research the topic of steganography.
4. Identify the various systems that are engaged in information warfare.
5. Become familiar with the functions of cryptography and cryptology.
6. Identify techniques for encryption and decryption.
7. Identify and explain threats and attacks currently active in the network.
8. Develop a case for Web ethics.
9. Describe why the network user should be concerned with content management.
10. Document any Internet horror stories personally experienced.
11. Produce a report identifying cybercrimes directed at children.
12. Identify and describe the intellectual property theft categories.
13. Search the Web for current virus attacks.

CHAPTER 2

Attacks, Threats, and Vulnerabilities

🔒 CHAPTER CONTENTS

- Describe threats and vulnerabilities to computer networks and systems.
- Understand virus, worm, and Trojan threats.
- Look at techniques to counter digital attacks and threats.
- See how spam and scams affect digital resources and users.
- Determine how to combat social engineering techniques.
- Identify malicious threats that affect the network and information systems.
- Identify a number of security breaches affecting digital resources.
- Become familiar with computer and network security challenges.

INTRODUCTION

A *threat* is an unwanted deliberate or accidental event that may result in harm to an asset. Often, a threat is exploiting a known vulnerability. A threat to the computer network is described as any potential adverse occurrence that can do harm, interrupt the systems using the network, or cause a monetary loss to the organization. Threats are also extended to include the individual user's computer assets and resources. Information is presented on the threat categories of security and privacy threats, integrity threats, delay and denial threats, and intellectual property threats.

To counter these threats, awareness is required to identify those vulnerabilities that are susceptible to some malicious activity. It should be noted that *vulnerability* is the absence or weakness of a safeguard in some asset or resource. This absence or shortcoming makes a threat or attack potentially more harmful or costly and more likely to occur.

As intruders continue to create more ingenious methods for penetrating the network, administrators and individual users must take a comprehensive approach to security. The use of anti-virus programs, anti-spyware, anti-adware, firewalls, and the triple-A techniques are a good start; however, much more is required to ensure network security.

Attackers use a number of methods to gather information about network users and the organizations they represent. Countermeasures include policies, procedures, plus software and hardware that can detect and prevent computer networking security threats. Various countermeasures, when used in a coordinated effort, can help protect against system integrity, security, and blocking attacks.

THREATS

A threat is an unwanted deliberate or accidental explicit or implicit message event that may result in harm to an asset. Often, a threat is exploiting a known vulnerability. This threat can come from an individual, a group of individuals, or an organization. It is regarded as a possible danger or menace and can be very expensive if not countered by some form of protection. A **threat** to a computing device is defined as any potential occurrence, either accidental or malicious, that can have an undesirable effect of the assets and resources of the individual or organization. The asset might be hardware, software, databases, files, or the physical network itself. A threat is significant from a security viewpoint because the computer security goal is to provide insights, methodologies, and techniques that can be employed to mitigate threats. These goals can be achieved by recommendations that provide guidance to computer and network system administrators, designers, developers, and users toward the avoidance of undesirable system characteristics called vulnerabilities.

There are many opportunities for threats to occur in the computer, Internet, and networking environment. This is particularly true in the internet working environment, where attackers, crackers, and hackers abound. A *hacker* is someone who enjoys exploring and learning about computer systems. It is often confused with *cracker,* which refers to a person who has a mischievous attitude and often attempts to break into computer systems. A threat from these individuals can have a potentially adverse effect on the assets and resources of users and organizations. Threats can be listed in generic terms; however, they usually involve fraud, theft of data, destruction of data, blockage of access, and so on.

It is essential to identify the various threats and rank them as to their importance and impact. These assignments can be made on the basis of dollar loss, embarrassment created, monetary liability, or probability of occurrence. The most common threats to an individual or organization include the following:

- Virus/Trojan/worm.
- Predator.
- Device failure.
- Internal hacker.
- Equipment theft.
- External hacker.
- Natural disaster.
- Industrial espionage.
- Terrorist.

Surveys have shown that the most common network security problem today is the virus. This type of threat is often communicated via e-mail. The relative importance of a threat to the user usually depends on the type of transmission. For example, an educational institution or financial organization might be a frequent victim of an attack, whereas a fast-food store might be spared. It should be noted, however, that an attacker might feel more secure in attacking a small network or an individual's laptop. The impact of a threat could have different ramifications between these two types of sites. A survey conducted by CBS News revealed Internet users at home are not nearly as safe online as they believe, according to a nationwide inspection by researchers. They found most consumers have no firewall protection, outdated anti-virus software, and dozens of spyware programs secretly running on their computers.

Not all breaks in security are malicious; however, the results can be just as damaging. Some may stem from a purposeful interruption of a system's operation or may be accidental, such as a hardware failure or a software abnormality caused by a lack of controls. Security breaches must be minimized, whether they are malicious or accidental. The overall goal is to protect the network and computer system from any attack and to prevent theft, destruction, and corruption of the resources of the individual user or organization.

As described in Chapter 1, a new threat has arisen with the advent of cybercrime, information warfare, and cyber-terrorism. The federal government is actively engaged in identifying and defeating these types of threats.

THREAT TARGETS

There is information resident on the Internet that explains how to attack almost any type of computer, protocol, operating system, application, device, or hardware environment. From the previous discussions, it should be obvious that threats require a considerable amount of vigilance. After identifying the various threats, the next step is to identify the various computer and networking components that compose the threat environment. These include any hardware device or software component that might be assessable to the threats previously identified. Potential candidates include the following:

- Computers, servers, PCs, administrative workstations, laptops, and personal digital assistants (PDAs).
- Communication circuits (DSL and cable).
- Cell phones, BlackBerrys, iPhones, and other smart phones.
- Network devices such as routers, gateways, and switches.
- Local area network devices such as hubs, repeaters, and bridges.
- Communication devices such as modems, data service units (DSUs), and splitters.
- Front-end processors, communication controllers, and multiplexers.
- Network and operating system software.
- Application software.
- Power and air-conditioning systems.

From this list, it should be obvious to the reader that opportunities abound for an attacker to wreak havoc on the individual user's computer or an organization's assets and resources. Information concerning these digital assets is presented in Chapter 7. There are a number of resources and tools that the organization and individual user can use to mitigate the effect of the various threats. Three major categories of threats include integrity, denial of service, and disclosure.

Integrity Threat

Integrity of digital resources includes the assurance that information has been created, amended, or deleted only by the intended authorized means. An **integrity threat** is any unauthorized change to data stored on a network resource or in transit between resources. A system is compromised when the integrity of the data has been maliciously or otherwise altered. Note that the integrity of the network resource can be compromised by both authorized and unauthorized modifications. Administrative and operational incidents can, and often do, affect the integrity of the computer and network resources. This chapter, however, is only concerned with unauthorized integrity threats.

Advance preparation can reduce the severity of the integrity compromise. If there is a backup or duplicate copy of the data, then the impact of a breach will be less severe than in a situation where a backup is not available. Loss of stored critical information can be disastrous, particularly when health or national security issues are involved. While not on the scale of national issues, the loss of a personal database might be just as disastrous to the individual. Additional details are provided on contingency and disaster recovery planning in Chapter 9.

A system modification can compromise the integrity of a network resource. A modification can occur when an unauthorized party tampers with an asset. Changes can be made to database files, operating systems, application software, and even hardware devices. It is, therefore, essential that assets be modified by authorized parties or only in authorized ways. Modifications include creating, changing, deleting, and writing information to a network resource. There are techniques available that provide for an audit trail involving these activities on a database. This includes the very important process of "change management" in business operations.

Denial of Service Threat

Denial of service (DoS) is defined as an attack that attempts to deny computer and network resources to legitimate users. This situation arises when there is an intentional blockage as a result of some malicious action by a user. This occurs when a legitimate user requires access to a resource and another user prevents this access by some malicious activity. This situation can be either a temporary or permanent blockage for the legitimate user. An interruption of service can occur when an asset becomes unavailable or unusable.

Common examples of DoS attacks involve users overloading shared resources such as processors or printers so that other users cannot access them. This type of attack may be bothersome or benign, depending on the criticality of the access. An example of such an attack would involve a number of rogue users transmitting numerous messages to a computer port (such as port 80) on a server, thus making this port unavailable for legitimate users. If this network resource was part of a mission critical system, the impact could be severe. Educational institutions are often victims of such attacks as students see an opportunity to harass competitors. Department of Defense and other high-profile systems, such as transportation, utilities, and financial systems, would be candidates for efforts to avoid denial of service attacks.

It may be difficult for the user to identify poor response time with denial of service. In today's networking environment, oversubscription of network facilities can make the situation look like a denial of service, when in fact it is a provider or network issue. *As a note, oversubscription is a technique that can be used by vendors to increase revenue at the user's expense.* The inability to reach some network resource may be caused by the provider or an error in the user's actions. The provider may have put all interfaces in an inactive state to accomplish a system update or modifications are being made to a Web site. A technique termed *throttling* can be used by administrators to reduce network traffic. The user will probably not know the difference, and the network provider might not be forthcoming with status information.

A **distributed denial of service (DDoS)** is a type of DoS attack in which an attacker uses malicious code installed on various computers to attack a single target. An attacker may use this coordinated method to have a greater effect on the target than is possible with a single attacking machine. This threat is so serious that a high priority is assigned to prevent or mitigate such attacks. Hackers might hijack hundreds of thousands of Internet computers and plant software "time bombs" on the victim systems. The hackers then instruct these time bombs to bombard the target site with forged messages, overloading the site and effectively blocking legitimate traffic.

Disclosure Threat

Disclosure occurs when information has been disseminated to someone other than the intended individual. The **disclosure threat** compromise occurs whenever some confidential information stored on a network resource or in transit between network resources is transmitted to someone not cleared to receive such information. This is sometimes called a "leak" when it has been purposely disseminated without proper authorization.

A significant amount of raw data and information stored on computer systems is not for general distribution. This could take the form of personal information on a user's computer or confidential records stored in a massive database. Dissemination of a user's personal information could cause some embarrassment; however, public disclosure of a citizen's private records could cause severe repercussions. This could be even more problematic if government secrets or intelligence files are disclosed. An interception by an unauthorized party, who copies programs or files and may do so without any trace, also adds to the disclosure problem.

Considerable resources have been devoted to the disclosure issue. Research and development in security have focused on the disclosure threat and how to counter it. A reason for the emphasis on disclosure issues is the impetus given it by the federal government. Sabotage and espionage are two techniques that could be employed to obtain or modify data and information illegally and without any obvious trace. *Sabotage* is generally defined as the destruction of property or obstruction of normal operations, whereas *espionage* is the act of spying to obtain secret information. Terrorists and enemy agents might well be involved in activities to obtain sensitive government information that would be used to perpetuate future attacks.

ATTACKS

An **attack** on a computer system or network asset involves the exploitation of vulnerabilities, which can result in a threat against the resource. An attack is often *heuristic,* which means the attacker has some knowledge of the vulnerabilities of the resource. This book is not concerned with general programming and operational errors that can occur at any time in this environment. These types of errors, however, can be just as devastating as a virus attack. The objective, therefore, is to reduce the possibilities that would allow an attacker into the network resource.

Four general categories of attacks include fabrications, interceptions, interruptions, and modifications. An attack might well consist of all or a combination of four categories of attacks:

- *Fabrications* involve the creation of some deception in order to deceive some unsuspecting user.
- An *interception* is the process of intruding into some transmission and redirecting it for some unauthorized use.
- An *interruption* causes a break in a communication channel, which inhibits the transmission of data.
- A *modification* is the alteration of the data contained in the transmissions.

Attacks are classified as either active or passive. An *active* attack involves some modification of the data stream or attempts to gain unauthorized access to computer and networking systems. This is a physical intrusion. A *passive* attack would include monitoring and eavesdropping on a transmission. An example would include the use of a "keylogger" or "sniffer" device that would not be obvious to the user. Both can be detrimental to the organization and individual user.

Identifying and responding to threats, vulnerabilities, and attacks are complicated and nontrivial tasks and may be too expensive and time-consuming to eliminate. Efforts must be made to reduce the occurrences as much as possible; however, the cost of protection may be more than the value of the asset or resource.

Additional discussion is directed toward specific types of threats that include the techniques called "social engineering," "phishing," and "phreaking." These techniques are used to identify information that can be used to compromise a network, computer system, or a user's computer.

Social Engineering

Internet and network attackers often use a deception technique called **social engineering** to gain access to a resource. The easiest way to accomplish this intrusion is by obtaining a password or other identification by lying and impersonating some authorized user. The person who uses this technique is often a fast and smooth talker, is usually aggressive, and possesses "quick thinking" abilities. The objective of this person is to test the computer and network resource security without getting caught.

The main objective of social engineering is to place the human element in the "network breaching" loop and use it as a weapon. A forged or stolen vendor or employee ID could gain entrance to a secure location, where the intruder could then obtain access to sensitive assets. If this intruder possessed the proper dress and equipment, it would be easy for some employee to escort this intruder to an equipment room or network interface, where an attack could occur. By appealing to employees' natural instinct to help a technician or contractor, it becomes easy to breach the perimeter of an organization and gain access to sensitive resources. Social engineering is most effective when directed at new and inexperienced employees.

Receptionists, secretaries, and new employees are often targets of these deceptions. Clueless users and inept employees also contribute to the problems associated with social engineering. There are a number of techniques to reduce these occurrences:

- Ensure that employees are educated on the basics of a secure environment.
- Develop a security policy and computer-use policy.
- Enforce a strict policy for internal and external technical support procedures. Require some sort of user, contractor, or customer ID.
- Limit data leakage by restricting the detail of information published in directories, Yellow Pages, Web sites, and public databases.
- Be especially careful about using remote access. Validate the destination.
- Learn the techniques for sending and receiving secure e-mail.
- Remove the opportunity of "dumpster diving" in corporate and personal trash.

Phishing

Phishing is a type of fraud whereby a criminal attempts to trick his or her victim into accepting a false identity presented by the criminal. The common application of this approach is to send fake e-mails (*e-mail spoofing*) to a victim purporting to come from a legitimate source and requesting information or directing the victim to a fake Internet Web site where this information can be captured (*Web page spoofing*). Fraud is a growing problem on the Internet as people are tricked into providing personal information including credit card numbers, passwords, mother's maiden name, date of birth, bank account numbers, automated teller machine (ATM) pass codes, and Social Security numbers. Virus protectors and firewalls do not catch most phishing scams because they do not contain suspect code, while spam filters let them pass because they appear to come from legitimate sources.

A **phishing scam** is an identity theft scam that arrives via e-mail. The e-mail appears to come from a legitimate source, such as a trusted business or financial institution, and includes an urgent request for personal information usually invoking some critical need to update an account immediately. Clicking on a link provided in the e-mail leads to an official-looking (spoofed) Web site. This Web page would look identical to the official page except a link on the page would forward the user's information to the scammer's Web site. Personal information provided to this Web page goes directly to the scam artist and not to a legitimate organization.

It is difficult for most users to identify a phishing target by looking at the Web page. However, clues in the address can sometimes reveal the deception. Similar looking characters might be substituted in the spelling of the link for the real character so that a "1" (numeral one) is used in place of a lowercase "L." For example, phishers have used *paypa1.com* rather than *paypal.com*. (See the difference?) Phishing scams have become so sophisticated that phishers can also appear to be using legitimate links, including the real site's security certificate. Another variation of the phishing scam is called the verification scam. For several years, individuals have purchased domain names that are similar to those of legitimate companies. It may be in a form such as: *abcname-order.net*. The real company is abcname, but it does not have a "-order" in its domain. Another ploy is to change the Web page address from .org to .com. These con artists then send out millions of e-mails requesting that consumers verify account information, birthdates, and Social Security numbers. Some computer users will respond and compromise their resources.

The best way to protect against phishing scams is to avoid supplying personal information to an e-mail request. If a user believes the request might be legitimate, call the company's customer service department to verify this before providing any information, but do not use phone numbers contained in the e-mail. Even if the request is legitimate, manually enter the required address in the browser rather than clicking on a link, as a phishing scam could conceivably run concurrent with legitimate business. Computer forensic techniques can be employed to identify suspect e-mail transmissions.

A variation of the phishing attack is called spear phishing. **Spear phishing** is an e-mail spoofing fraud attempt that targets a specific organization, seeking unauthorized access to confidential data. As with the e-mail messages used in regular phishing expeditions, spear phishing messages appear to come from a trusted source.

The Anti-Phishing Working Group (APWG) is the global pan-industrial and law enforcement association focused on eliminating the fraud and identity theft that result from phishing, pharming, and e-mail spoofing of all types [Anti-Phishing Working Group]. The Federal Trade Commission (FTC) also has advice for consumers, an e-mail address for reporting phishing, plus a form to report identity theft. The Web site is located at *www.ftc.gov*.

Pharming

Pharming is similar in nature to e-mail phishing as it seeks to obtain personal or private financial-related information through domain spoofing. Rather than being spammed with malicious and mischievous e-mail requests to visit spoofed Web sites that appear legitimate, pharming "poisons" a domain name system (DNS) server by infusing false information into the server, resulting in a user's request being redirected. The browser, however, will show the correct Web site, which makes pharming a bit more serious and more difficult to detect. Phishing attempts to scam people one at a time with an e-mail, while pharming allows scammers to target large groups of people at one time through domain spoofing.

Phreaking

Phreaking is a slang term coined to describe the activity of a subculture of people who study, experiment with, or explore telephone systems, the equipment of telephone companies, and systems connected to public telephone networks. **Phone phreaking** is the art of exploiting bugs and glitches that exist in the telephone system.

VIRUS THREATS

A computer virus passes from computer to computer like a biological virus passes from person to person. A computer virus must piggyback on top of some other program or document in order to get executed. Once it is running, it is then able to infect other programs or documents.

In today's environment, a virus can destroy an individual's credit record, bankrupt a company, and destroy a wealth of information. A **virus** is a computer program that infects other programs via replication. It clones itself from disk to disk or from one system to the next over computer networks. A virus executes and accomplishes its damage when the host program executes. Some new viruses attack macros in programs like Microsoft Word® and do their damage when the macro is executed. (*Note that a* macro *is a set of instructions in a computer source language, such as Assembler.*)

The modifications caused by viruses may be harmless, such as a birthday greeting on a certain day; however, they often cause considerable damage by destroying computer system records, file tables, and user data. To maintain a protective stance against virus threats, the user must keep abreast of the current virus threats and update virus protection daily. There are a number of Web sites that provide information on viruses, such as recent activities and hoaxes.

There are a number of virus classifications set forth by TruSecure and the Computer Security Institute (CSI). A **worm** is similar to a virus except it is designed to self-replicate and can cause damage to systems and large networks. Unlike a virus, a worm does not necessarily require a host file for attachment. Worms are easily spread across the Internet via e-mail and chat programs. Computer viruses and worms are often part of a botnet attack.

A **botnet** (also known as a *zombie army*) is a number of Internet computers that, although their owners are unaware of it, have been set up to forward transmissions (including spam or viruses) to other computers on the Internet. Any such computer is referred to as a zombie—in effect, a computer "robot" or "bot" that serves the wishes of some master spam or virus originator. Most computers compromised in this way are home-based. According to a report from Russian-based Kaspersky Labs, botnets—and not spam, viruses, or worms—currently pose the biggest threat to the Internet. A report from Symantec came to a similar conclusion.

COUNTERING THE VIRUS THREAT

The **Computer Emergency Response Team (CERT)** is an organization with teams around the world that recognizes and responds to computer attacks. The **CERT Coordination Center (CCC)** is responsible for studying Internet security and responding to security incidents reported to it. CERT publishes various security alerts and develops plans for individual computer sites to improve their security. CERT is part of the networked systems survivability program in the Software Engineering Institute, which is a federally funded research and development center at Carnegie Mellon University [Software Engineering Institute]. The program was established to:

- Study Internet security vulnerabilities.
- Provide incident response services to victimized sites.
- Publish a variety of security alerts.
- Research security and survivability in WAN computing.
- Develop information to help improve host security.

A system becomes contaminated with a virus through file system activity. A contaminated file is either copied from a floppy disk or flash drive or is downloaded from an online service. Users can transport viruses from home and work on their portable computers, which have access to the Internet and other network services.

When files are contaminated, they may increase in size, which makes it relatively easy for a virus detection program to report such problems. However, stealth viruses are able to spoof the pre-infected file size of a document so it appears that nothing has changed. Active stealth viruses can fight back against virus detection programs by disabling their detection functions. Advanced steganography techniques can also hide data on computer systems.

It is, therefore, smarter to protect against a virus instead of fixing the damage. It is easy to avoid viruses if the user is careful to never copy files from unknown or untrusted sources. This is easier said than done. The Internet and Web have created a whole new way to spread viruses. It is now possible to execute programs while browsing the Web without actually copying a file to the user's system disk. Users must be vigilant for spyware and adware programs. There are a number of Web security programs that can give the user some tools to avoid this situation.

Trojan programs, backdoors, and worms are usually installed by employees or contractors inside the organization, who have specific intentions to capture data or damage some system. The best protection is to limit system availability, restrict access, and carefully monitor the activity of employees and contractors. These restrictions apply particularly to employees who might be leaving the organization or who are suspected of being malicious for some reason.

Even after detecting and eliminating a virus infection, there is still a chance that the virus is lurking somewhere in the organization, ready to re-infect systems. If the virus is detectable, all systems must be checked for its existence. It might be necessary to run a virus scan on all storage devices.

The network administrator must develop a security program for addressing viruses and other destructive elements. The administrator should keep up with the latest virus information by reading weekly computer journals or joining organizations like the National Cyber Security Alliance (NCSA). Frequently checking the NCSA and CSI Web sites for virus information is also recommended. There are many anti-virus products that prevent the spread of viruses and clean specific ones off the system.

Virus Control Policies

An effective anti-virus strategy must include policy, procedures, and technology. There are six general policies that can be established that will assist in controlling viruses:

- Create an education program oriented toward virus protection.
- Post regular bulletins about virus problems.
- Never transfer files from an unknown or untrusted source unless the computer has an anti-virus scan utility installed.
- Test new programs or open documents on a "quarantine computer" before introducing them to the production environment.
- Secure computers to prevent malicious people from infecting systems or installing Trojan horse programs.
- Use an operating system that uses a secure logon and authentication process.

As collaborative applications such as groupware have become more commonplace in organizations, a new method of virus infection and virus re-infection has emerged. Viruses can be quickly spread throughout the network because groupware messages and data are stored in a shared database. Documents may then be distributed throughout the network for document conferencing or workflow automation applications. Because groupware servers replicate their databases to other servers, a virus will continue to spread. Even if the virus is eliminated from the originating server, responses from still-infected servers will re-infect the original server. This infection/de-infection/re-infection cycle can continue until the virus is purged systemwide.

Software Detection

Computer viruses provide ever-changing means for hacking attacks on personal and business networks, and anti-virus measures are an essential element of defense against these attacks. Most networks employ anti-virus software at numerous points throughout the network. Anti-virus checking is most effective when it is performed automatically, which means it is always working and vigilant. The downside of anti-virus software is that a virus cannot be countered if it is new and unknown. Hackers are constantly inventing new viruses; therefore, it is important to constantly update anti-virus software with the latest versions. An effective approach is to run a virus protection program with every logon.

There are a number of virus protection programs for desktop computers and networks. Virus detectors attempt to detect known viruses that have infected files or memory locations. On workstations, activities can be monitored to detect and stop system functions that might indicate virus activity. Another technique is to look for unique identifiers that indicate a virus. These methods are called **signature scanning**. So that an anti-virus program may detect the latest viruses, it must be periodically updated with the latest identifiers from the software vendor. The downside is that signature scanning is only as good as the most recent signature file.

E-Mail Viruses and Worms

Anti-virus software is only part of the solution. An e-mail worm can spread worldwide in just minutes, but it takes hours for anti-virus vendors to analyze, create, and deploy signature updates. There are five activities that users can take to help close that window of vulnerability and help keep e-mail worms off the computer system: identification, known user, relevant, secure the client, and patch the system.

- *Identification.* Understanding the nature of the attachment is the first step toward e-mail safety. Any executable type attachment has the potential to be infected. Don't open an e-mail attachment from an unknown source.

- *Known user.* An executable type attachment should not be opened unless it was specifically requested or expected. (*Note that an* executable *is a binary file containing a program in machine language that is ready to be executed [run].*) Because e-mail worms are sent to addresses found on infected users' machines, just knowing the sender is no proof of intent—they may well be infected. In fact, odds are an e-mail worm will arrive from some known person and the sender is oblivious to the viral e-mail being sent. Worse, today's worms spoof the "From address," so it is possible the e-mail is not even from a known user. Also, be suspicious of e-mails that have been forwarded or contain no subject.

- *Relevant.* This is the simplest rule to follow, but most often ignored. If an attachment is not needed or requested, don't open it. Delete the e-mail instead.

- *Secure the client.* Many e-mail worms and viruses have taken advantage of security vulnerabilities found in Microsoft Outlook® and Outlook Express®. However, any mail client that supports HTML and scripting should be considered at risk. Mail clients might include Eudora, Netscape Mail, Outlook/Outlook Express, and Pegasus. Check the Internet for known worms and viruses.

- *Patch the system.* Microsoft routinely releases numerous security patches per year. Keeping abreast of these and understanding which are applicable to the system can be a daunting task. Microsoft provides a Windows update site, which will automatically scan the system and provide a list of recommended updates specific to the operating system. Install any updates marked "Critical." And remember: security is never passive. It's an ongoing process and new vulnerabilities are constantly discovered. Visit the Windows update site monthly to ensure all necessary patches are installed.

Virus examples might be found under the headings of network worms, classic viruses, file and boot viruses, and script viruses. Additional categories could include Trojans and other malware. A Web site that provides an exhaustive list of this malware is located at *www.viruslist.com* [Virus List]. The human willingness to double-click on the executable fuels viruses. Attackers can count on Web users to be inquisitive and sometimes gullible.

An Ounce of Prevention

Users can protect against viruses and worms with a few simple steps:

- Purchasing virus protection software is probably the most effective safeguard.
- Avoid programs and downloads from untrusted sources, like the Internet.
- Using commercial software purchased on CDs eliminates almost all of the risk from traditional viruses.
- Disable floppy disk booting—most computers now allow this, and that will eliminate the risk of a boot sector virus coming in from a floppy disk accidentally left in the drive.
- Enable "Macro Virus Protection" in all Microsoft applications, and never run macros in a document unless their functions are known.

Comparing Virus, Worm, and Trojan Software

The most common misconception when the topic of a computer virus arises is that computer users will often refer to a worm or Trojan as a virus. While the words *Trojan*, *worm*, and *virus* are used interchangeably, they are not the same. Viruses, worms, and Trojans are all malicious *programs* that can cause damage to a computer, but there are differences among the three, and knowing those differences can help users better protect computers from their often damaging effects.

A **Trojan horse** or **Trojan** is a type of computer program that performs an ostensibly useful function but contains a hidden function that compromises the host system's security. These programs can be installed on a computer when the user leaves the computer logged in when unattended. One of the most insidious types of Trojan horse is a program that claims to rid computers of viruses but instead introduces them. The Trojan, at first glance, will appear to be useful software but will actually do damage once installed or run on a computer. Those on the receiving end of a Trojan are usually tricked into opening them because they appear to be receiving legitimate software or files from a legitimate source.

The Trojan program is the most widely used class of computer attack methods. An attacker must trick the user into running a Trojan program by making it appear attractive and disguising its true nature. Some Trojan programs are merely designed to destroy data or crash systems, while others allow attackers to steal data or even remotely control computer systems. Another attacker method closely allied with the Trojan is called the backdoor. A **backdoor** is an alternate method of accessing a system. It is an electronic hole in software left open by accident or intention. This type of program may also be called a "backdoor Trojan." Backdoors are used by criminals to get remote control of a person's computer. Once criminals have gained control, they can use the computer to steal data, store illegal files, and launch attacks against other computers.

After installing a Trojan backdoor, attackers often attempt to cover their tracks by manipulating the computer system files. This can be accomplished by deleting or modifying the computer system logs that show all of the processor activity. System log management is important to defend against log-editing attacks. A **logic bomb** is basically a Trojan with a timing device. It initiates some destructive mechanism based upon a clock. As an example, a disgruntled employee may create a bomb to execute after leaving the employ.

A *worm* is often mistaken for a virus. It is a single destructive program on a single system often planted by someone who has direct access to the system. A worm has the ability to copy itself from machine to machine. Worms normally move around and infect other machines through computer networks. Using a network, a worm can expand from a single copy incredibly quickly. For example, the Code Red worm replicated itself more than 250,000 times in approximately nine hours on July 19, 2001. A worm usually exploits some sort of security hole in a piece of software or the operating system. Worms use up computer time and network bandwidth when they are replicating; and they often have some sort of evil intent. Experts predicted that a worm could clog the Internet so effectively that the network would completely grind to a halt.

Another issue that has emerged is called the botnet. A *botnet* consists of a collection of software robots, or bots, that run autonomously. While the term "botnet" can be used to refer to any group of bots, such as Internet relay chat (IRC) bots, the word is generally used to refer to a collection of compromised computers (called zombie computers) running programs, usually referred to as worms, Trojans, or backdoors. (*Note that an* IRC *is a facility that allows computer users, from many different places in the world, to simultaneously chat in real time.*)

Combating Viruses, Worms, and Trojans

The first step to protecting the computer is to ensure the computer operating system (OS) is up-to-date. This is essential when running the ubiquitous Microsoft Windows OS©. Secondly, anti-virus software should be installed on the system, and updates downloaded frequently, to ensure the software has the latest fixes for new viruses, worms, and Trojans. Additionally, anti-virus programs should have the ability to scan e-mail and files as they are downloaded from the Internet. This will help prevent malicious programs from even reaching the computer. If this isn't enough protection, then consider installing a firewall as well. Experience has shown that several different virus protection programs must be installed on a computer system to catch all of the viruses. (*Note that some virus programs are mutually exclusive and will not run with a competitor product.*)

An effective solution for addressing the virus problem is a firewall. A **firewall** is a system that prevents unauthorized use and access to a computer. A firewall can be either hardware or software. Hardware firewalls provide a strong degree of protection from most forms of attack coming from the outside world and can be purchased as a stand-alone product or in broadband routers. Unfortunately, when subduing viruses, worms, and Trojans, a hardware firewall may be less effective than a software firewall because it could possibly ignore embedded worms in outgoing e-mails and see this as regular network traffic. For individual home users, the most popular firewall choice is a software firewall. A good software firewall protects the computer from outside attempts to control or gain access to the computer and usually provides additional protection against the most common Trojan programs or e-mail worms. The downside to software firewalls is that they will only protect the host computer and not a network.

It is important to note a firewall solution in itself will not solve all computer virus problems. When used in conjunction with regular operating system updates and anti-virus scanning software, it will add some extra security and protection for a computer or network. Additional details on the use of firewalls are presented in Chapter 6.

VULNERABILITIES

A characteristic of a computer system or a network that makes it possible for a threat to occur is called **vulnerability**. A vulnerability presence provides an opportunity for problems and disasters to occur. To avoid these undesirable situations, threats to a computer system or network can be mitigated by identifying and eliminating these vulnerabilities. Solutions and suggestions are presented throughout this book.

From remote access, the most vulnerable routes for break-ins are through telephone access facilities and from the Internet. To prevent these break-ins from damaging the computer and network resources, networks can employ firewall and other solutions to block unsafe services and sources. Detection techniques and vulnerability testing can identify and block intrusion attempts. Software products can be used to block virus attacks and are usually available for download from numerous software vendors. It should be noted that, to date, anti-virus software is the best "bang for the buck" to counter the computer virus threat. Anti-spyware and adware software tools are also available from a number of sources. Security solutions are presented in Chapter 12. There are also numerous professional consulting and outsourcing services available for business security planning and deployment.

It should be noted that no security measures or products would completely secure a network. Therefore, users and organizations must strike a balance between user accessibility and the level of protection required for maintaining a safe and secure environment. Higher levels of security might mean inconvenience for users, which could reduce productivity and increase job dissatisfaction. The likely result will be circumvention of security measures by the users. Realistic network protection strategies use measures that meet security needs while causing minimum interference with employee job performance and satisfaction. Chapters 9 and 10 address continuity planning and network intrusion detection and prevention issues. A cost/benefit analysis should be conducted to determine if the cost of the security exceeds the value of the resource.

MALICIOUS ATTACKS

As stated earlier, security threats can be either active or passive; however, both can have negative repercussions for the network. There are a number of malicious attacks in addition to virus infestations that can affect the security of an organization's resources. Active threats include brute force, dictionary masquerading, address spoofing, session hijacking, replay, and man-in-the-middle attacks. Passive threats include eavesdropping and monitoring. This section concentrates on providing descriptions of each and suggests methods to successfully counter them.

A prelude to these attacks might include active port scanning of the network devices. This is the process of connecting to Transmission Control Program (TCP) and User Datagram Protocol (UDP) ports on the target computer systems to determine what services are running or in a listening state. Identifying *listening state* is critical to determining the type of operating system and applications in use. These issues are responsibilities of network administrators and computer and data communication specialists.

Both TCP and UDP use ports and port numbers to identify application protocols. A port is a logical component of the TCP connection. A typical session involves sending packets from a source IP address and port (socket) to a destination address and port. The packet headers contain source and destination port address information and flow between the applications at either end of the connection. Port numbers are published in Request for Comments (RFC) 1700 (assigned numbers) [Request for Comments]. Unused ports would be deactivated to reduce port-scanning attacks. The various technical specifications and protocols are described in Chapter 13. Learning more about ports will help administrators better defend a network by closing off ports and services that are not required. Users can also read more about the well-known ports at the Internet Assigned Numbers Authority (IANA) Web site.

War Dialers

Before an attack can occur, the intruder must identify a target. One method used is called a war dialer, which is a program that tries a set of sequentially changing numbers to determine which ones respond positively. These are usually telephone numbers, but they can also be passwords. There are many computer networks and voice systems that are accessible via some dial-up telephone access. After these identities are established, the attacker can dial back the discovered listening modems and attempt to enter the organization's network. It is essential that the administrator know the criteria being used by the hacker. A general list of factors has been developed that should be considered when employing a security shield against this type of threat:

- System banners do not contain private information.
- The connection has a time-out or attempt-out threshold, and exceeding the threshold drops the connection.
- The connection is only allowed at certain times.
- Authentication levels required include userid, password, or both, and the number of userid and password characters is deterministic.
- The connection has a unique identification method, such as SecurID.

Brute Force Attack

Those who attack computer networks constantly seek out new methods while still hammering away at the old ones. Internal attacks and corporate espionage are real and can take place every day in many different organizations. As many different types of attacks exist as do attackers, and a standard approach is called brute force. A **brute force attack** is a cracker term for trying different passwords until it is successful. The attacker merely applies all possible combinations of a key to an algorithm until the message is deciphered.

Although the government allows the use of 56-bit encryption standards in certain circumstances, this standard has not proven to be hack-proof. Government experts had estimated that 56-bit encryption would take many years to crack, but clever hackers have proven otherwise. With today's large-scale computers, it is possible to try millions of combinations of passwords in a short period of time. Given unlimited time and access to a number of computers over the Internet, it is possible to crack most algorithms. The 128-bit encryption is considered by most as impregnable and would require 4.7 trillion billion times as many calculations as would be required to crack 56-bit encryption.

Server-Gated Cryptography (SGC) enables 128- or 256-bit Secure Socket Layer (SSL) encryption, depending on the browser and host server operating system. When a SSL handshake occurs between a client and server, a level of encryption is determined by the browser, the client computer operating system, and the SSL certificate. High-level encryption, at 128 bits, can calculate 288 times as many combinations as 40-bit encryption. That is more than a trillion times a trillion stronger. A hacker with the time, tools, and motivation to crack 40-bit encryption would require a trillion years to break into a session protected by an SGC-enabled certificate.

The Advanced Encryption Standard (AES) enables 256-bit encryption, much stronger than 128-bit. If the server operating system and the site visitor's browser support 256-bit encryption, then it is possible for SSL certificates to deliver this higher level of protection. Even though an SSL certificate is capable of 128- or 256-bit encryption, millions of people still use older computer systems that are incapable of strong encryption. Internet Explorer browser versions prior to 3.02 and Netscape browser versions prior to 4.02 are not capable of 128-bit encryption with any SSL certificate. Specifics concerning these standards are presented in Chapter 13.

It is important to note that there is more to a key-search attack than simply trying all possible keys. If the message is just plain text in English, then the result is easily observable, although the task of recognizing English would have to be automated. If the text messages were compressed before encryption, then recognition would be more difficult. If the target contained compressed numerical data, it becomes more difficult to automate. To supplement the brute force approach, some degree of knowledge about the plain text is required, and some means of automatically distinguishing plain text from garble is necessary. If the only form of attack that could be made on an encryption algorithm is brute force, the corrective measure is obvious: use longer keys for logins and passwords.

Dictionary Attack

The **dictionary** attack is a simple attack that illustrates the need for carefully chosen passwords. A simple cracker program takes all the words from a dictionary file and attempts to gain entry by entering each one as a password. End-users often select a common dictionary word as a password, which is poor practice. A nonsensical combination of letters and numbers should be selected instead, and they should not reflect any personal information about the user.

Masquerading

A masquerade takes place when an entity pretends to be a different entity. A **masquerade attack** usually includes one of the other forms of active attack, such as address spoofing or replaying. Authentication sequences can be captured and replayed after a valid authentication sequence has taken place, thus enabling an authorized entity with few privileges to obtain extra privileges by impersonating an entity that has those privileges. A sophisticated example of masquerading involves an attacker who social engineers passwords from an Internet Service Provider.

Eavesdropping

Eavesdropping or **snarfing** takes place when a host sets its network interface on promiscuous mode and copies packets that pass by for later analysis. (Promiscuous mode *allows a network device to intercept and read each network packet that arrives in its entirety.*) It is possible to attach hardware and software, unknown to the legitimate users, and monitor and analyze all packets on that segment of the transmission media. Candidates for eavesdropping include satellite, wireless, mobile, and other transmission methods.

A network protocol specifies how packets are identified and labeled, which enables a computer to determine its destination. Because the specifications for network protocols are widely published, a third party can easily interpret the network packets and develop a packet sniffer. A **packet sniffer** is a software application that uses a hardware adapter card in promiscuous mode to capture all network packets sent across a LAN segment. Because some network applications distribute network packets in plain text, a packet sniffer can provide its user with meaningful and sensitive information, such as user account names and passwords. These tools are described in Chapter 11.

An active variation on eavesdropping is called covert channel eavesdropping. Intruders actively probe the network for infrastructure information. A **covert channel** consists of a hidden unauthorized network connection to communicate unauthorized information. Probing is a technique that gives an attacker a road map of the network in preparation for some intrusion or a DoS attack. This type of intrusion along with steganography is a possible tool for cyber-terrorism activities.

Address Spoofing

Spoofing is a type of attack in which one computer disguises itself as another in order to gain access to a system. This is generally done when an outside computer pretends to be a computer that exists on the legitimate network. If the local router is not configured to filter out incoming packets whose source IP address is internal, a spoofing attack can occur. Using IP spoofing, an attacker can easily masquerade as an authorized user. Because of this vulnerability, valuable information should be protected by more than a client's identity. Protection based solely on a client's identity should be limited to situations in which the host computer is completely known and trusted.

IP spoofing is facilitated by using an Internet Protocol (IP) address that is within the range of the network or by using an authorized external IP address that is trusted for specific access to specific resources on the network. An IP spoofing attack is normally limited to the injection of data or commands into an existing stream of data passed between a client and server application or a peer-to-peer network connection. To enable bi-directional communication, the attacker must change all routing tables to point to the spoofed IP address. If the attacker manages to change the routing tables, all network packets addressed to the spoofed IP address can be intercepted. The intruder can then respond to the messages as a trusted user. (See Appendix E for an overview of IP addressing.) It should be obvious to the reader that this is a complex subject.

A CERT advisory on IP spoofing reports that the CERT Coordination Center has received reports of attacks in which intruders create packets with spoofed source IP addresses. This exploitation leads to user and root access on the targets system. This means that the intruder can take over login connections and create havoc.

Hijackers

Hijacking is a type of network security attack in which the attacker takes control of a session between two entities and masquerades as one of them. In one type of hijacking, called a "man in the middle attack" (discussed in more detail a bit later), the perpetrator takes control of an established connection while it is in progress. The attacker intercepts messages in a public key exchange and then retransmits them, substituting their own public key for the requested one, so that the two original parties still appear to be communicating with each other directly. The attacker uses a program that appears to be the server to the client and appears to be the client to the server. This attack may be used simply to gain access to the messages or to enable the attacker to modify them before retransmitting them. Encryption can be implemented to thwart understanding the transmission contents.

Another form of hijacking is *browser hijacking*, in which a user is taken to a different site than the one the user requested. There are two different types of domain name system (DNS) hijacking. In one, the attacker gains access to DNS records stored on a server and modifies them. Requests for the genuine Web page will be redirected elsewhere, usually to a fake page that the attacker has created. This gives the impression to the viewer that the Web site has been compromised; however, only a server has been affected.

In the second type of DNS hijack, the attacker spoofs valid e-mail accounts and floods the inboxes of the technical and administrative contacts. This type of attack can be prevented by using authentication for Internet Corporation for Assigned Names and Numbers (ICANN) records [ICANN]. (*Note that DNS is an Internet service that translates domain names into IP addresses.*)

In another type of Web site hijack, the perpetrator simply registers a domain name similar enough to a legitimate one that users are likely to type it, either by mistaking the actual name or through a typo. This type of hijack is currently being employed to send many unwary users to a pornographic site instead of the site they requested.

Session Hijacking

In **session hijacking**, instead of attempting to initiate a session via spoofing, the attacker attempts to take over an existing connection between two network computers. The first step in this attack is for the attacker to take control of a network device on the LAN, such as a firewall or another computer, so that the connection can be monitored. Monitoring the connection allows the attacker to determine the sequence numbers used by the sender and receiver.

After determining the sequence numbering, the attacker can generate traffic that appears to come from one of the communicating parties, stealing the session from one of the legitimate users. As in IP spoofing, the attacker would overload one of the communicating devices with excess packets so that it drops out of the communications session.

Session hijacking points out the need for reliable means of identifying the other party in a session. It is possible for the legitimate user who initially started a session to suddenly be replaced, maybe unknowingly, by an intruder for the remainder of a communications session. This calls for a scheme that authenticates the data's source throughout the transmission; however, even the strongest authentication methods are not always successful in preventing hijacking attacks, which means that all transmissions might need to be encrypted.

Replay Attack

Replay attacks involve the passive capture of a data unit and its subsequent retransmission to produce an unauthorized effect. The receipt of duplicate, authenticated IP packets may disrupt service or have some other undesired consequence.

Systems can be broken through replay attacks when old messages or parts of old messages are reused to deceive system users. This helps intruders to gain information that allows unauthorized access into a system. This is possible when partial encrypted or decrypted files are left on computer hard drives. It is a good idea to run the computer disk clean-up utility frequently.

Man-in-the-Middle Attack

A **man-in-the-middle attack** is a type of attack that takes advantage of the store-and-forward mechanism used by insecure networks such as the Internet. In this type of attack, an attacker gets between two parties and intercepts messages before transferring them on to their intended destination. Web spoofing is a type of man-in-the-middle attack in which the user believes a secured session exists with a particular Web server. The user then can be duped into supplying the attacker with passwords, credit card information, and other private information.

To use encryption, the user must first exchange encryption keys. Exchanging unprotected keys over the network could easily defeat the whole purpose of the system because those keys could be intercepted. A sophisticated attacker employing spoofing, session hijacking, and eavesdropping (sniffing) could actually intercept a key exchange in an insecure network. The attacker's key could be planted early in the process so that this intruder would appear to the sender as a legitimate recipient, when in fact it was a man-in-the-middle.

The possible uses of such attacks are theft of information and data, denial of service, corruption of transmitted data, gaining access to the organization's internal computer and network resources, and introduction of new information into network sessions.

OTHER SECURITY BREACHES

Some security breaches result from a purposeful disruption of system operations; others are accidental and may be based on hardware and software failures. It matters not whether they are accidental or malicious; a security break damages an organization's credibility. Activities that can cause a security breach are as follows:

- Denial of service.
- Distributed denial of service.
- Browsing.
- Wiretapping.
- Incorrect data encoding.
- Backdoor.
- Accidental data modifications.

Denial of Service

DoS attacks, previously identified, result in the blocking of a resource to legitimate users. They are synchronized attempts to deny service by causing a computer to perform an unproductive task over and over, which makes the system unavailable to perform legitimate operations. When a disk fills up, an account is locked out, a computer crashes, or a CPU slows down, service is denied. The attacks come in many forms and different levels of severity and can cost an organization millions of dollars in lost revenue.

Two basic types of denial of service attacks include logic and flooding. *Logic attacks* exploit software flaws to crash or seriously degrade the performance of remote servers. Many of these attacks can be prevented by fixing the faulty software or by filtering particular packet sequences. *Flooding attacks* overwhelm the victim computer's CPU, memory, or network resources by sending large numbers of spurious requests. Because there is no simple method to distinguish a good request from a bad one, these attacks are especially insidious.

Specific network server applications, such as HTTP or FTP servers, can facilitate attacks that can focus on acquiring and keeping open all the available connections supported by that server. This activity effectively locks out valid users of the server or service. DoS attacks can also be implemented using common Internet protocols, such as TCP and Internet Control Message Protocol (ICMP). Most DoS attacks exploit weaknesses in the overall system architecture being attacked, rather than a software bug or security flaw. A DoS attack can compromise the network by flooding it with undesired and useless packets and by providing false information about the status of network services.

One of the popular techniques for launching a packet flood is called a **SYN flood**. The SYN is a TCP control bit used to synchronize sequence numbers. Another popular technique is called **smurfing**. The smurf attack uses a directed broadcast to create a flood of network traffic for the victim computer.

Insiders can cause DoS attacks as well as outsiders; however, most are perpetuated by anonymous outsiders. Network intrusion detection is usually effective at detecting these attacks because these mechanisms are designed to quickly identify them. RFC 2827 will be a useful source of information for the security administrator; it provides a method for using ingress traffic filtering to prohibit DoS attacks, which use forged IP addresses to be propagated from behind an ISP aggregation point. Details concerning intrusion prevention and detection are provided in Chapter 10.

Web content providers and router companies have placed new rules designed to prevent such an attack in the configuration tables, and the companies and universities whose computers were used to launch the attacks have worked to prevent their systems from being used maliciously. Whether their defenses or the new attacks designed by criminals will prevail remains to be seen.

Distributed Denial of Service

The DDoS attack, previously discussed, involves flooding one or more target computers with false or spurious requests, which overloads the computer denying service to legitimate users. Researchers have estimated that thousands of DDoS attacks are issued against networks each week. This threat is so serious that preventing or mitigating such attacks is a top priority in many organizations.

The term *distributed denial of service* describes the technique by which hackers hijack hundreds of thousands of Internet computers and plant "time bombs" on the victim systems. The hackers then instruct these time bombs to bombard the target site with forged messages, overloading the site and effectively blocking legitimate traffic. Products are currently in the design stage, which will assist the organizations in countering or defending against this type of attack.

Browsing

Browsing is the process of unauthorized users searching through files or storage directories for data and information that they are not privileged to read. The storage could be sections of main computer memory or unallocated space on disk and other magnetic media. Browsing may occur after a legitimate process has completed. This can occur because data still reside on these devices after a legitimate process has terminated and can be accessed by a knowledgeable intruder.

Intellectual property threats are a large problem due to the Internet and relative ease with which a user can access existing material without the owner's permission. Actual monetary damage resulting from a copyright violation is more difficult to measure than damage from secrecy, integrity, or delay and denial threats. Although copyright laws were enacted before the creation of the Internet, the Internet has complicated the enforcement of copyrights by publishers. Many copyright infringements on the Web occur because of ignorance of what cannot be copied. The most misunderstood part of the U.S. copyright law is that a work is protected when it is created and does not require the copyright notice. These topics were explored in Chapter 1.

Wiretapping

Telephone lines and data communication lines can be tapped. **Wiretapping** can be active, where modifications occur, or passive, where an unauthorized user is just listening to the transmission and not changing the contents. Passive intrusion can include the copying of data for a subsequent active attack.

Two methods of active wiretapping are *between the lines* and *piggyback entry*. Between the lines does not alter the messages sent by the legitimate user, but inserts additional messages into the communication line while the legitimate user is pausing. Piggyback intercepts and modifies the original messages by breaking the communications line and routing the message to another computer that acts as a host.

Backdoor

Backdoor software tools allow an intruder to access a computer using an alternate entry method. Whereas legitimate users log in through front doors using a userid and password, attackers use backdoors to bypass these normal access controls. Once attackers have a backdoor installed on a computer, the system can be accessed without using passwords, encryption, or other security controls. This backdoor can be used to bypass controls that the administrator has implemented to protect the computer system. **Netcat** is one of the most popular backdoor tools in use today.

Another form of a backdoor tool is called **rootkits**. The traditional rootkits replace critical operating system executables to let an attacker have backdoor access and hide on the host system. By replacing system software components, rootkits can be more powerful than application-level Trojan horse backdoors. These tools are primarily available on UNIX system platforms.

One of the most frequently discovered vulnerabilities that encourage the use of the backdoor is the default username and password. Almost every network vendor ships devices with a default username and password that must be changed when setting up these devices. This default is usually "administrator."

Finding and removing backdoors from the computer system is next to impossible, because there are many methods of creating one. The recourse for recovery is to restore the operating system from the original media. This would require the task of rebuilding and restoring user and application data from backups, assuming these exist. This becomes more difficult if the system has not been completely documented.

Data Modifications

Problems with data integrity can cause a security breach. These include accidental incomplete modification of data and data values being incorrectly encoded. An incomplete modification occurs when non-synchronized processes access data records and modify part of a record's field. When a record field is not large enough to hold the complete data item, some bits may be truncated and the value distorted. This situation can occur with most programming languages and may be difficult to detect; however, the results can be significant.

ADDITIONAL SECURITY CHALLENGES

Additional challenges to safe and secure communications can originate from spam, hoaxes, spyware, and maybe cookies. A combination of these is also possible.

Spam

Spam is flooding the Internet with many copies of the same message in an attempt to force the message on people who would not otherwise choose to receive it. Most spam is commercial advertising, often get-rich-quick schemes, dubious products, or other services. Spam costs the sender very little to send because most of the costs are paid for by the recipient or the carriers rather than by the sender.

Research by *pcpitstop.com* has estimated that the overall spam volume stabilized in February 2008 for the second month in a row at 78.5 percent of all e-mail. This is up from a 61 percent average for the first half of 2007. Tackling spam not only reduces a company's productivity but also leads to wastage of valuable resources. Software is available that offers effective and holistic e-mail and Web security solutions that provide fail-safe protection against spam, phishing, and other threats. Spam is no longer just a nuisance, and the ability to block it is critical for information technology (IT) security. Spam has become a new way for criminals to solicit individual and company information and a way to plant Trojans and other malware onto user computers. To fight cybercrime, companies must tackle the spam problem.

E-mail spam targets individual users with direct-mail messages. E-mail spam lists can be created by stealing Internet mailing lists or searching the Web for addresses. E-mail is expensive; it costs money for ISPs and online services to transmit spam, and these costs are transmitted directly to subscribers.

One variant of e-mail spam is sending messages to mailing lists of public or private e-mail discussion forums. Because many mailing lists limit activity to their subscribers, spammers will use automated tools to subscribe to as many mailing lists as possible so that they can grab the lists of addresses or use the mailing list as a direct target for their attacks. E-mail spam is unique in that it costs the receiver more than the sender. Spamming forces the receiving user to waste administrative time on cleanup and monitoring of their e-mail.

Spam software invariably comes with a list of names of people falsely claimed to be those who've said they want to receive ads, but actually consisting of unwilling victims culled at random from Usenet or mailing lists. Spammers invariably say they'll remove names on request, but they almost never do. Indeed, users report that when they send a test "remove" request from a newly created account, they usually start to receive spam at that address. Spammers know that people don't want to hear from them, and generally put fake return addresses on their messages so they don't have to bear the cost of receiving responses from users to whom they've sent messages.

Some kinds of spam are illegal in some countries. Especially with pornography, mere possession of such material can be enough to put the recipient in jail. In the United States, child pornography is highly illegal and spammed child porn offers are already on the Web.

One trick the spammers try is to set up fake anti-spam sites or to forge e-mail from anti-spam organizations such as the **Coalition Against Unsolicited Commercial Email (CAUCE)**. Neither CAUCE, as an organization, nor any anti-spammers, as individuals, are soliciting or accepting donations of money or any other valuable consideration [CAUCE]. Another earmark of just such a forgery is use of a throwaway or invalid e-mail address. A supposed anti-spam e-mail or a Web site that is asking for money is probably a fake. Users should report the incident to the nearest anti-spammer and the National Fraud Information Center.

Various state and federal Do Not Call Laws, with some exceptions, prohibit telemarketers who are selling a product, service, or good from contacting those citizens who have chosen to have their phone number placed on the Do Not Call List. Consumer names and phone numbers on the state Do Not Call List were merged into the federal Do Not Call (DNC) registry after it was established in October 2003. The DNC registry, maintained by the FTC, is now the sole registration site for state consumers who wish to ease the burden of unwanted solicitation calls [DNC Registry]. Users should check the Do Not Call sites for requirements to reapply.

Hoax

A **hoax** is some act intended to deceive or trick. These false messages, interspersed among the junk mail and spam, contain dire warnings about devastating new viruses. Added to this are messages about free money, children in trouble, and other items designed for forwarding to others. Most of these messages are hoaxes or chain letters. While hoaxes do not automatically infect systems like a virus or Trojan, they are time-consuming and costly to remove from all the systems where they exist. Much more time can be spent debunking hoaxes than handling real virus and Trojan incidents.

Users are requested to not spread chain letters and hoaxes by sending copies to others. Sending a copy of a cute message to one or two friends is not a problem. However, sending an unconfirmed warning or plea to everyone in an address book, with the request that receivers also send it to everyone known, adds to the clutter already filling mailboxes. Recipients of this kind of mail should not pass it to everyone known. Either delete it or pass it to a computer security manager to validate. Validated warnings from the incident response teams and anti-virus vendors have valid return addresses and are usually Pretty Good Privacy (PGP)–signed with the organization's key. Alternately, get the warnings directly from the Web pages of the organizations that broadcast them to ensure that the information is valid and up-to-date.

Spyware and Adware

Spyware is any software that covertly gathers user information through the user's Internet connection without the user's knowledge, usually for advertising purposes. Spyware applications are typically bundled as a hidden component of freeware or shareware programs that can be downloaded from the Internet. Once installed, the spyware monitors user activity on the Internet and transmits that information in the computer to someone else. Spyware can also gather information about e-mail addresses and even passwords and credit card numbers. Spyware is similar to a Trojan as users unwittingly install the product when they install something else. A common way to become a victim of spyware is to download certain peer-to-peer file swapping products that are available today. It should be noted that the majority of shareware and freeware applications do not come with spyware.

Aside from the questions of ethics and privacy, spyware steals from the user by using the computer's memory resources and also by using bandwidth as it sends information back to the spyware's home base via the user's Internet connection. Because spyware is using memory and system resources, the applications running in the computer background can lead to system crashes or general system instability.

Because spyware exists as independent executable programs, they have the ability to perform a number of operations. They can:

- Monitor keystrokes.
- Scan files on the hard drive.
- Snoop other applications, such as chat programs or word processors.
- Install other spyware programs.
- Read cookies.
- Change the default home page on the Web browser.

Intelligence gathered can be relayed to the spyware author, who will either use it for advertising/marketing purposes or sell the information to another party.

Licensing agreements that accompany software downloads sometimes warn the user that a spyware program will be installed along with the requested software, but the licensing agreements may not always be read completely because the notice of a spyware installation is often couched in obtuse, hard-to-read legal disclaimers.

Anti-spyware software is available from a number of software suppliers. One spyware detector vendor advises that more than 85 percent of computers have spyware installed on them. Spyware is typically not the product computer users install, but small add-ons, that may or may not disable during software installs. In most cases, the End-User License Agreement (EULA) has a few lines telling users about privacy matters, but typically most users don't read the complete EULA and never know they have spyware on their systems.

A less threatening software module is adware. **Adware** is similar to spyware, but it does not transmit personally identifiable information, or at least the collector promises not to sell it. Instead, aggregated usage information is collected. Adware is also often a side-effect of spyware: both monitor users for a sole purpose, which is delivering advertisements tailored to purchasing habits.

Malware

Spyware and adware are also called **malware**. Malware includes files made by publishers that allow them to snoop on browsing activity, see purchases, and send "pop-up" ads. Short for *mal*icious soft*ware,* malware is designed specifically to damage or disrupt a system, such as a virus or a Trojan. It can slow down a PC, cause it to crash, record credit card numbers, and worse. Simply surfing the Internet, reading e-mail, downloading music, or other files can infect a personal computer, without any awareness of the activity. A **pop-up** is a type of window that appears on top of (over) the browser window of a Web site that a user has visited. Pop-ups ads are used extensively in advertising on the Web. Some software products include an option for blocking pop-ups.

Spyware and adware viruses have rapidly become the number-one threat to computers with more than 90 percent of computers already infected. These include Trojans, Web bugs, advertiser software, monitoring software, and more. Fortunately, there are good spyware and adware virus removal tools available. Sorting through them all to find the right one is a challenging task and an important decision to make. Tools and solutions are described in Chapter 12.

Spybots

Spybot is a type of privacy software designed to search and destroy spyware and Trojan programs. The Spybot Search and Destroy® product searches hard drives for so-called spy- or adbots. These are little modules that are responsible for the ads many programs display. Many of these modules also transmit information, including surfing behavior on the Internet. If the product finds such modules, it can remove them. In most cases, the computer operates properly after removing the spyware/adware.

Another feature is the removal of usage tracks, which makes it more complicated for unknown spybots to transmit useful data. The list of last visited Web sites, opened files, started programs, cookies, and more can be cleaned. Supported are the five major browsers, Microsoft Internet Explorer®, Mozilla FireFox®, Apple Safari®, Netscape®, and Opera®.

Cookies

A **cookie** is a message given to a Web browser by a Web server. The browser stores the message in a text file and is entered into the memory of the browser. The message is then transmitted back to the server each time the browser requests a page from the server. To help Web servers track a user's history, browsers allow Web servers to store brief text files on the user's PC hard-disk drive. When the user sends a message to the Web server, the Web server can also get the cookie to see past activity history.

Many Web sites will attempt to place a cookie on a client's system. A client can have hundreds of cookies resident at any time, which can become a nuisance, because they may constantly cause pop-ups, interrupting the current online activity. Web browsers have a feature for controlling cookies, but this feature may cause the user grief. Cookies are somewhat controversial because they allow a Web server to store files on the hard-disk drive. They are text files, however, not programs that could contain viruses.

Cookies personalize the user's experience on the Web site. They can help store personal information so that when users return to the site, they have a more personalized experience. Users returning to a site and seeing personal information mysteriously appear on the screen should not be surprised. This occurs because the user name was stored in a cookie allowing for a personal greeting message. A good example of this is the way some online shopping sites will make recommendations based on previous purchases. The server keeps track of purchases and searches and stores that information in cookies. Cookies also monitor advertisements. Web sites will often use cookies to keep track of the ads it lets users see and how often they see ads.

Cookies do not act maliciously on computer systems. They are merely text files that can be deleted at any time. Cookies cannot be used to spread viruses, and they cannot access the hard drive. This does not mean that cookies are not relevant to a user's privacy and anonymity on the Internet. Cookies cannot read a hard drive to gather personal information; however, any personal information provided to a Web site, including credit card information, will most likely be stored in a cookie unless the cookie feature is turned off in the browser. In only this way are cookies a threat to privacy. The cookie will only contain information freely provided to a Web site.

The user can easily delete the cookies that have been placed on the computing device. In the Windows environment, a right click of the mouse on the browser icon, selecting "Properties," will display a screen that will allow for the deletion of cookies and temporary Internet files.

RESPONDING TO INTERNET AND NETWORK ATTACKS

There are no simple means of protecting the organization against computer attacks. This means the organization must mount a defensive capability that can be used to effectively respond to any vulnerability that might be currently present or may emerge in the future. This is not a small endeavor, but the alternatives are unpleasant.

Although ingenious hackers and intruders continue to invent new methods of attacking computer and network resources, many of these are well known and can be defeated with a variety of tools currently available. Network and security administrators can respond to attacks by providing for rapid restoring of computer and network resources, closing holes in the organization's defenses, and obtaining evidence for prosecution of offenders.

Response to attacks is a combination of planning and policy, detective work, and legal prowess. The lessons learned from a hacker attack should be used to further secure the network against similar attacks on the same vulnerability in the future. Also, there are law enforcement agencies, forensic experts, security consultants, and independent response teams available to assist the organization in responding to a security incident, as well as prosecuting the offender.

Computer and network attacks are a cost of doing business in the information technology field. It is, therefore, essential that responses should be just as aggressively proactive as reactive, looking to prevent attackers as much as responding to them. There are a number of books devoted to the subject of hacking that provide suggestions for countering the intruders. These books provide a step-by-step guide to computer attacks and effective defenses.

Anti-Virus Software Packages

There are a number of anti-virus software solutions available. Two reviews available on the Web are 6starreviews and antivirus-software-reviews [Antivirus-Software-Reviews]. Selected software packages include the following:

- BitDefender.
- PC-cillin.
- Panda Titanium.
- McAfee VirusScan.
- AVG Antivirus Pro.
- Norton Antivirus F-Prot.
- Trend.
- EZ Antivirus.
- Kaspersky Antivirus.

Firewalls

As described earlier, a firewall is a dedicated appliance, or software running on another computer, that inspects network traffic passing through it and denies or permits passage based on a set of rules. A firewall's basic task is to regulate some of the flow of traffic between computer networks of different trust levels. Typical examples are the Internet, which is a zone with no trust, and an internal network, which is a zone of higher trust. A zone with an intermediate trust level, situated between the Internet and a trusted internal network, is often referred to as a *perimeter network*, or demilitarized zone (DMZ). There are numerous firewall solutions available. Prominent firewall vendors include the following:

- Cisco Systems.
- SonicWALL.
- WatchGuard Technologies.
- Check Point.
- ZyXEL.
- Symbol Technologies.
- Nortel.
- Juniper Networks.
- D-Link.
- Multi-Tech Systems.

There are a number of activities that can reduce the impact of computer and network threats. Anti-virus software is a cost-effective method of controlling virus attacks. There are also a number of organizations that are devoted to suppressing Internet intrusions and attacks. Users may decide to use more than one package in the computer to provide a higher level of protection. Experience has shown that different packages provide different levels of support.

NETWORK INTRUDERS

Individuals that are candidates to cause grief on the Web include hackers, crackers, white hats, black hats, script kiddies, and others. Each of these categories will be described in this section.

Hackers

Hacker is a term used to describe different types of computer experts. It is also sometimes extended to mean any kind of expert, especially with the connotation of having particularly detailed knowledge or of cleverly circumventing limits. The meaning of the term, when used in a computer context, has changed somewhat over the decades since it first came into use, because it has been given additional and clashing meanings by new users of the word. Currently, *hacker* is used in two main ways, one disparaging and one complimentary: in popular usage and in the media, it generally describes computer intruders or criminals; in the computing community, it describes a particularly brilliant programmer or technical expert.

As a result of this conflict, the term is the subject of some controversy. This label is disliked by many who identify themselves as hackers and who do not like their label used negatively. Many users of the positive form say the "intruder" meaning should be deprecated, and they advocate terms such as *security cracking, cracker,* or *black hat* to replace it. Others prefer to follow common popular usage, arguing that the positive form is confusing and never likely to become widespread.

A possible middle-ground position observes that "hacking" describes a collection of skills and that these skills are utilized by hackers of both descriptions—although for differing reasons. The companion situation to illustrate this is the skills involved in locksmithing, specifically picking locks, which, aside from its being a skill with a fairly high analogy to classic hacking, is a skill that can be used for good or evil.

The most common usage of *hacker* in the popular press is to describe those who subvert computer security without authorization or anyone who has been accused of using technology (usually a computer or the Internet) for terrorism, vandalism, credit card fraud, identity theft, intellectual property theft, and many other forms of crime. This can mean taking control of a remote computer through a network, or software cracking. This is the disparaging sense of *hacker* (also called *cracker* or *black-hat hacker* or simply *criminal* in order to preserve un-ambiguity).

Web Players

The **cracker** has a hostile intent, possesses sophisticated skills, and may be interested in financial gain. System crackers pose the greatest threat to networks and information resources.

A **black hat** engages in compromising IT security for the mere challenge—to prove vulnerabilities or technical prowess—usually with regard to ethics. A black hat promotes freedom rather than security. Black hats poke holes in systems and do not increase control of information; there are no attempts made to disclose or patch software. A black-hat hacker has private software that exploits security vulnerabilities.

A **wannabe** is capable of becoming a black hat. These people are also called **grey hats** and may ultimately become either criminals or security consultants.

A **script kiddie** is a person with little or no skill. This person simply follows directions or uses a cookbook approach without fully understanding the meaning of the steps they are performing.

A **white hat** or *ethical hacker* is defined as an information security or network professional using various penetration test tools to uncover or fix vulnerabilities. To white hats, the darker the hat, the more the ethics of the activity can be considered dubious. Conversely, black hats may claim the lighter the hat, the more the ethics of the activity are lost.

MALICIOUS TOOLS

There are a number of tools of the trade used by computer criminals and malicious individuals. These software tools included viruses, Trojans, and worms (botnets). Additional tools and techniques could include sniffers, rootkits, cookies, war dialers, hijackers, keyloggers, and scanners. There are software and hardware products that can be used to mediate or counter these malicious tools employed by network intruders and attackers. The network user who wishes to remain safe and secure on the Web must take proactive steps to protect the computer assets.

A brief refresher of viruses, Trojans, and worms is in order. A Trojan consists of a malicious program that is disguised as legitimate software. A Trojan can be used to set up a backdoor in a computer system so that the criminal can return later and gain access. Viruses that fool a user into downloading and/or executing them by pretending to be useful applications are also sometimes called Trojans. A virus is a self-replicating program that spreads by inserting copies of itself into other executable code or documents. Thus, a computer virus behaves in a way similar to a virus, which spreads by inserting itself into living cells. Like a virus, a worm is also a self-replicating program. The difference between a virus and a worm is that a worm does not attach itself to other code. Many people use the terms *virus* and *worm* to describe any self-propagating program.

A **vulnerability scanner** is a tool used to quickly check computers on a network for known weaknesses. Hackers also use port scanners. These check to see which ports on a specified computer are "open" or available to access the computer. (*Note that firewalls defend computers from intruders by limiting access to ports/machines both inbound and outbound.*) The port number identifies the type of port. For example, port 80 is used for HTTP traffic.

A **sniffer** is an application that captures password and other data while it is in transit either within the computer or over the network. Both hardware and software or a combination or both can be deployed as a sniffer. Because a sniffer operates in a promiscuous mode, it is usually invisible to the user. An **exploit** is a prepared application that takes advantage of a known weakness or vulnerability. This is the main reason for the user to identify all vulnerabilities.

As discussed earlier, a rootkit is a toolkit for hiding the fact that a computer's security has been compromised. It contains a set of tools used by an intruder after cracking a computer system. Rootkits exist for a variety of operating systems such as Linux, Solaris, and versions of Microsoft Windows®. These tools can help an attacker maintain access to the system and use it for malicious purposes.

War Dialer

A war dialer is a computer program used to identify the phone numbers that can successfully make a connection with a computer modem. The program automatically dials a defined range of phone numbers and logs and enters in a database those numbers that successfully connect to the modem. Some programs can also identify the particular operating system running in the computer and may also conduct automated penetration testing. In such cases, the war dialer runs through a predetermined list of common user names and passwords in an attempt to gain access to the system.

A network intruder can use a war dialer to identify potential targets. If the program does not provide automated penetration testing, the intruder attempts to hack a modem with unprotected logins or easily cracked passwords. Network system administrators can use a commercial war dialer to identify unauthorized modems on an enterprise network. Such modems can provide easy access to an organization's internal network.

Keyloggers

A **keylogger** is a type of surveillance software or hardware that has the capability to record every keystroke a user makes to a log file. A keylogger recorder can record any information typed at any time using the keyboard. The log file created by the keylogger can then be sent to a specified receiver or retrieved mechanically. Keyloggers could be a technique used by employers to ensure employees use work computers for business purposes only. Unfortunately, keyloggers can also be embedded in spyware, allowing information to be transmitted to an unknown third party.

As a hardware device, a keylogger is a small battery-sized plug that serves as a connector between the user's keyboard and computer. Because the device resembles an ordinary keyboard plug, it is relatively easy for someone who wants to monitor a user's behavior to physically hide such a device in plain sight. Workstation keyboards usually plug into the back of the computer, which makes it hard to detect. As the user types on the keyboard, the keylogger device collects each keystroke and saves it as text in its own miniature hard drive. At a later point in time, the person who installed the keylogger must return and physically remove the device in order to access the information the device has gathered.

A keylogger program does not require physical access to the user's computer. Someone wanting to monitor activity on a particular computer can download the program. It can also be downloaded unwittingly as spyware and executed as part of a rootkit. The keylogger program records each keystroke the user types and uploads the information over the Internet periodically to whoever installed the program.

Although keylogger programs are promoted for benign purposes like allowing parents to monitor their children's whereabouts on the Internet, most privacy advocates agree that the potential for abuse is so great that legislation should be enacted to clearly make the unauthorized use of keyloggers a criminal offense.

🔒 CHAPTER SUMMARY

Threats to business and personal computer and information assets are an everyday menace. It is essential that organizations and individual users identify the vulnerabilities and plan for corrective action to thwart these threats. Threat categories include security and privacy threats, integrity threats, delay, and denial threats. Virus threats are the most common and frequent attack that a user will experience. Anti-virus software is the most effective method of countering a virus attack.

Malicious attacks could emanate from active threats that include brute force, masquerading, address spoofing, session hijacking, replay, man-in-the-middle, and dictionary attacks. Passive threats may include eavesdropping and monitoring. Additional types of programs that are destructive to systems include logic bombs, Trojans, worms, and viruses (botnets).

Specific security breaches might include denial of service, distributed denial of service, browsing, wiretapping, incorrect data encoding, accidental data modifications, and backdoors.

Spam and scams are becoming an issue with Internet usage. Spam is clogging the network with useless and intrusive advertisements. The cost to monitor and clean up spam on computer systems is increasing on a daily basis. Individuals, organizations, and businesses are incurring additional costs because of the increase of spam transmissions.

Threat targets are increasing as more users are added to the Internet. The targets include computer systems, network components, software, electrical systems, and databases. Attacks can be caused by black hats, script kiddies, crackers, and white hats.

Spyware is software that transmits personally identifiable information from a computer to some place on the Internet without the user's knowledge. Adware is similar to spyware, but it does not transmit personally identifiable information. Adware is also often a side-effect of spyware, because both monitor a computer for a sole purpose: delivering advertisements that are especially tailored to user habits.

KEY TERMS

adware	firewall	session hijacking
attack	grey hat	signature scanning
backdoor	hacker	smurfing
black hat	hijacking	snarfing
botnet	hoax	sniffer
browsing	integrity threat	social engineering
brute force attack	keylogger	spam
Coalition Against Unsolicited Commercial Email (CAUCE)	logic bomb	spear phishing
	malware	spoofing
CERT Coordination Center (CCC)	man-in-the-middle attack	spybot
Computer Emergency Response Team (CERT)	masquerade attack	spyware
	netcat	SYN flood
cookie	packet sniffer	threat
covert channel	pharming	Trojan (horse)
cracker	phishing	virus
denial of service (DoS)	phishing scam	vulnerability
dictionary attack	phone phreaking	vulnerability scanner
disclosure	phreaking	wannabe
disclosure threat	pop-up	war dialer
distributed denial of service (DDoS)	replay	white hat
eavesdropping	rootkit	wiretapping
exploit	script kiddie	worm

SECURITY REVIEW QUESTIONS

1. Identify the most common threats to an individual or organization.
2. List a number of potential threat targets.
3. How do you reduce the incidences of social engineering techniques?
4. Describe phishing and spear phishing.
5. What are six general policies that can be established that will assist in controlling viruses?
6. Describe the differences among viruses, worms, and Trojans.
7. Provide a brief description of brute force, dictionary masquerading, address spoofing, session hijacking, replay, and man-in-the-middle attacks.
8. Challenges to safe and secure communications can originate from spam, hoaxes, spyware, and maybe cookies. Provide a brief description of each.
9. Describe the various network attackers that could affect safe and secure network access.
10. Identify those tools of the trade used by computer criminals and malicious individuals.

 RESEARCH ACTIVITIES

1. Review the information presented on the National Computer Security Alliance (NCSA) and the Computer Security Institute (CSI) Web sites. Provide a synopsis of the most serious issues.
2. Identify the current incidents reported on the Computer Emergency Response Team (CERT) Web site.
3. Provide an overview of the information presented on the CERT Coordination Center (CCC) Web site.
4. Identify the current top 10 active viruses.
5. Prepare an overview of the current virus protection software packages.
6. Review the RFC 1700 document, and prepare a list of the most relevant port numbers.
7. Provide an overview of RFC 2827.
8. Present an overview of a computer network attack where you were a victim.
9. Provide an overview of the information presented on the Anti-Phishing Working Group (APWG) Web site.
10. Develop an overview of the Coalition Against Unsolicited Commercial Email (CAUCE) organization.
11. Identify the current phishing activities described on the Anti-Phishing Working Group Web site.
12. Describe the activities and responsibilities of the IANA.

CHAPTER 3

Scams, Identity Theft, and Fraud

🔒 CHAPTER CONTENTS

- Understand scams and how scam artists work.
- Become familiar with the crime of identity theft.
- Look at the issue of Internet fraud.
- Identify the resources for assistance in protecting business digital assets.
- Learn the steps necessary to protect personal computer and data assets.
- Identify methods and techniques to safely use the Internet and Web resources.
- Look at security issues involving children using the Web.
- Become familiar with the laws that apply to the Internet and the Web.

INTRODUCTION

How does the Web or network computer user ensure a safe and secure experience when accessing sites over the network? How can the user protect juveniles from Web sites that might not be educational or safe? Personal safety and security might become an issue if the user is not security savvy. There are many predators, posing both financial and personal risks, waiting for some unsuspecting victim.

One of the most prevalent security issues today is identity theft. Identify theft can occur from a number of sources, with the Internet being the fastest and easiest vehicle for gathering information about an individual. The most likely source of these intrusions is e-mail. This chapter addresses identity theft, fraud, and other threats to network users and provides some guidance to counter these situations.

A pervasive threat to network users is the scam artist. These Internet predators are using techniques to steal the identities of Web users to commit fraud. There is a close relationship among fraud, identity theft, and scams. Techniques and activities are discussed that can be used to counter these threats.

There are numerous activities that Internet users can initiate to counter the crimes of identity theft and fraud. Many Web sites are available that are devoted to crime tips. It is essential that network users become aware of the possibilities of Internet and e-mail scams and fraud. Education and awareness are keys to using the Web in a safe and secure manner.

Another issue concerns children and their ability to access network sites that could affect the family's safety. Children are more Internet "literate" than their parents. What can be done to provide some level of safety and security for minors? Education and controls such as parental locks might prove to be only a stopgap solution. What sites can children access when away from parental supervision? Should parents or guardians be held liable for Internet crimes committed by minors?

SCAMS AND SCAM ARTISTS

A **scam** is a confidence trick or confidence game, *con* for short, that is an attempt to intentionally mislead a person or persons, called *marks,* usually with the goal of financial or other gain. Information presented in this section concerns a number of approaches that a scammer or con artist might take to attempt to steal some user's identity with the intent of committing fraud. These attempts usually look legitimate and can fool many network users into responding with compromising information.

Scammers use spamming techniques to send unsolicited messages in bulk, indiscriminately. Scammers lie to their customers. (*Note that* **spam** *is an Internet term for unsolicited commercial e-mail.*) One ploy is to sell someone a mailing list and tell them the people on it want advertising e-mail. Most of the time, the list is one of the same old spam lists previously available. There are very few lists of people who have actually signed up for ads! Any large list purporting to be of people who want any kind of advertising e-mail is a fraud. The scammers have a new trick—they supply an offshore phone number that users can call to be removed from spam lists. The call costs $2 per minute.

Further, as the "global communications" 809 phone fraud shows, con artists and thieves are gravitating toward massive spam as a way to perpetrate their crimes (*spam.abuse.net/scams/*). For more information on fraud and scams, see the **National Fraud Information Center (NFIC)**, Internet ScamBusters, or the Commodity Futures Trading Commission. Chain letter spam may also be illegal. If there is money exchanged, they are illegal in the United States according to the United States Postal Service. For the definitive word on "make money fast" (MMF) chain letters, see the MMF Hall of Humiliation. See also what other users are saying about MMF, and take a look at some information on pyramid schemes on Usenet. Additionally, users can now report apparent tax fraud and schemes that may not report income to the **Internal Revenue Service (IRS)**.

Removing oneself from lists may not work. There are spam cases that involve claims where users can opt out, when in fact clicking on the link to unsubscribe will simply verify a valid e-mail address. The end result is users can then get lots of spam instead of a little. Several sites available include *donotcall.gov* and *ftc.gov/donotcall*. The FTC, the Federal Communications Commission (FCC), and states are enforcing the national **Do Not Call** registry. Placing telephone and cell phone numbers on the registry will stop most, but not all, telemarketing calls [Do Not Call List].

Scam artists use dumpster diving, mail theft, and lost/stolen wallets to commit their crimes. These criminals are also using other techniques to defraud the general public. Information is gathered:

- By overhearing conversations made on cell phones.
- From faxes and e-mails.
- By hacking into computers.
- From telephone and e-mail scams.
- From careless online shopping and banking.

Scam artists are good at putting together legitimate-sounding scripts, Web sites, and e-mails. Some techniques that can be used to defraud Internet users include promises of free credit reports, "get rich quick" techniques, pyramid schemes, and prizes. A number of techniques include direct questions requesting personal information. The following sections provide samples of potential scammer "tools" such as:

- Free prizes.
- Pyramid schemes and chain letters.
- Work-at-home offers.
- Charities.
- Job advertisements.
- Free credit reports.
- Credit information requests.
- Check cashing.
- Questionnaires.

Free Prizes

Users often receive either a phone call or e-mail offering a free gift or prize; just send credit card info to take care of shipping and handling. Watch out! *Free* means *free,* which means there should be no charge. Also, consider this scam might be a group sending out a cheap gift in exchange for finding a "live" phone number or e-mail address. Responding may result in hundreds of spam messages or telemarketing calls.

Pyramid Schemes and Chain Letters

There are many e-mail chain letters/pyramid schemes. One says, "Will Gaits is testing a new e-mail-tracking program and wants your help. Forward the e-mail to friends and Microsoftware will pay $___ for each person that receives it." Others say, "You will get a gift or money from each person who comes after you." Another says to "Follow the simple instructions below and your financial dreams will come true." Do not respond or forward these e-mails. As Scam-Busters says, "Any e-mail that asks a user to forward it to friends is a possible scam."

Work-at-Home Offers

Advertisements on television and the Web show people making millions working at home. An application would be required to start this work-at-home job. As you probably suspect by now, the application will ask for many personal details including Social Security number, bank account number, and date of birth. This is good information to initiate an identity theft and create a fraud. The components of this fraud include freight forwarding and overpayment for services. Products are shipped to the work-at-home location. These products—say, cameras—are then shipped to other locations. The scammer provides a financial incentive—say, $1,000—to the work-at-home person, using a worthless check. The work-at-home person is asked to provide money—say, $500—in the form of a kickback. The problem is that the credit cards or checks used by the scammer to pay for the cameras are worthless and the incentive check is also worthless. The producer of the cameras is demanding payment from the work-at-home victim, who is actually out $500 in cash and the cost of the cameras and the shipping.

Charities

Telephone scams can involve solicitations from various charities. Do not provide credit card information over the telephone! The millions of dollars donated by individuals to relief efforts in Southeast Asia brought criminals and scammers out of the woodwork. Secondly, scammers may take advantage of the new Do Not Call lists being compiled by state governments. No one from the state will be calling consumers asking if they want to be included on the Do Not Call list, nor will these lists require a consumer to provide a Social Security number via telephone. People who do contribute to charities should determine the percentage of the funds that actually go to "legitimate" charities. Sometimes it is a very small amount, with most of the money going to "administration." "Administration" might really consist of a custom car, large boat, and an island estate.

Job Advertisements

Another opportunity to get scammed involves answering job advertisements. Do not place a Social Security number or date of birth on résumés sent out for jobs. Recently there have been scams involving Internet job Web sites and newspaper want ads. Under no circumstances should an applicant provide a Social Security number to an "HR person" found through a newspaper ad or an Internet ad prior to an actual interview or prior to authenticating both the company and the person asking for the information. If there are any doubts, contact the company directly using a phone number found on the company Web site or in the telephone book. Anyone can set up a Web site. Check out the company with the **Better Business Bureau (BBB)** for that area as well as the state attorney general to make sure they are a legitimate company. Typical tip-offs include e-mail addresses that do not include a company name in the domain section and mailing addresses or fax addresses in cities that differ from corporate headquarters.

Free Credit Reports

Many of the "free credit report" e-mails received are scams or questionable practices. Either the scammer is trying to identify Social Security numbers or will be billing later with a service charge. If there is some suspicion, check out the company via the Better Business Bureau, U.S. Attorney, or the Federal Trade Commission.

Credit Information Requests

Do not respond to e-mails allegedly from eBay® or PayPal® that ask for credit information, Social Security number, and other personal data. Many of these are scams, and the country has been blanketed with them. The e-mail may even threaten that an account or service will be discontinued. Prior to responding, users should contact the company directly via phone or e-mail to verify that the e-mail was legitimate. Do not be fooled by logos and even the **TRUSTe®** seal. Users may also get an e-mail stating that a certain amount of money has been credited to their accounts. Clearly, this is a money-laundering scam. They will ask for a "yes" or "no" to indicate if the service was ordered. Do not respond, but rather forward to the **Identity Theft Resource Center (ITRC)** so that it can be sent to the federal authorities for possible investigation.

Check Cashing

There are a number of schemes involving check cashing from "firms" based in foreign countries. These scammers advise that "due to delays in clearing checks and money orders in Europe, they need 'financial agents' to process payments for their U.S. orders." Basically, checks are received from scammers. These checks would be deposited in the accounts of personal work-at-home victims. These victims would then write checks from these accounts. The original checks received from the scammers would be worthless. Additional details can be found at *www.ic3.gov*. The Internet Crime Complaint Center (IC3) is a partnership between the **Federal Bureau of Investigation (FBI)** and the National White Collar Crime Center (NW3C). IC3's mission is to serve as a vehicle to receive, develop, and refer criminal complaints regarding the rapidly expanding arena of cybercrime. The IC3 gives the victims of cybercrime a convenient and easy-to-use reporting mechanism that alerts authorities of suspected criminal or civil violations [Internet Crime Complaint Center].

Questionnaires

Questionnaires seem to arrive daily in the mail. These include questions that help the person sending it learn birthdates and passwords; they may even blatantly may ask for a Social Security number. Do not answer these, even with false information. Answering the questionnaire lets the other party know they have reached a "live" person and may eventually give away compromising information. These people are slick and can easily convince unsuspecting users to divulge unintended information. That is why they are called con artists.

A response to some scams is called scam baiting. **Scam baiting** is the practice of eliciting attention from the perpetrator of a scam by feigning interest in whatever bogus deal is offered. The scam baiter pretends to be duped, with the intention of making the perpetrators waste time and/or money, and exposing them to public ridicule. Scam-baiters may involve the scammers in a long correspondence or encourage them to travel seeking a payoff. This may not be a desirable activity.

PROTECTING PERSONAL INFORMATION

The best way to avoid scams, fraud, theft, and identity theft is to exercise caution and guard personal information that applies to personal financial assets. Awareness and education are the keys. There are a number of specific suggestions and action items that can assist in realizing this objective.

- Only provide credit card or bank account numbers when actually paying for a purchase. Keep Social Security numbers and birthdates confidential. These are the keys that unlock an identity. Don't give them to any unidentified person. Find out why it is necessary to provide them. Ask health insurers and other companies that may use Social Security number as your ID number to provide a substitute number. If the state department of motor vehicles uses it as a driver's license number, ask for an alternate number.
- Beware of imposters. Crooks pretending to be from companies where consumers conduct business may call or send an e-mail, claiming they need to verify personal information. Be especially suspicious when contacted by someone asking for information they should already possess. Before responding, contact the company directly to confirm the call or e-mail is from them.
- Keep personal mail safe. Mail often contains account numbers and other personal information. Collect it promptly from mailboxes, and ask the post office to hold it while away. Send bill payments from the post office or a public mailbox, not from home. Rural mailboxes are susceptible to mail theft. Remove names from credit marketing lists. Credit bureaus compile marketing lists for pre-approved offers of credit. These mailings are a gold mine for identity thieves, who may steal them and apply for credit in a victim's name. Get off these mailing lists by calling 888-567-8688 (Social Security number will be required to verify an identity). Removing entries from these lists does not hurt chances of applying for or getting credit. Unsolicited applications for credit cards should be disposed of properly. A dumpster diver may be looking through personal trash and use the application to commit fraud.
- Memorize computer passwords and personal identification numbers (PINs). Don't leave them in a wallet or on a desk where someone else could find them. Secure personal data. Keep personal information locked up at home, at work, at school, in a vehicle, and in other places where easy access is restricted.
- Practice safe Internet usage. Don't send sensitive information such as credit card numbers by e-mail because it's not secure. Look for clues about security on Web sites. When asked to provide financial or other sensitive information, on a Web page, the letters at the beginning of the address bar at the top of the screen should change from "http" to

"https" or "shttp." The browser may also show that the information is being encrypted, or scrambled, so no one who might intercept it can read it. But while personal information may be safe in transmission, there is no guarantee that the company will store it securely. Determine how Web sites safeguard personal information in data storage.

The ScamBusters Web site (*scambusters.org*) is an excellent resource to get information on the latest Internet scams. Most scams, by phone or e-mail, prompt the user to provide either credit card account information or a Social Security number. The ITRC recommends that users never give out this information unless they initiate the call and know that they are speaking to a legitimate company representative. A list of current scams can be obtained by accessing the ITRC Web site. If a scam is suspected, forward the entire e-mail to the ITRC's ID theft center [Identity Theft Resource Center]. Users can also contact the FBI at *www.fbi.gov/ majcases/fraud/fraudschemes.htm*, the local state attorney general's office, or the Federal Trade Commission at 877-FTC-HELP, or via e-mail at *spam@uce.gov*.

Credit Card Fraud Prevention Tips

Numerous scams originate because of sloppy use and abuse of the credit card. The ScamBusters organization has developed a number of commonsense approaches for the card-wielding public to avoid credit card fraud [ScamBusters]. Card users should avoid letting the card get out of their sight. This, however, is not always possible because most waiters and waitresses take the card to a back area to run it. Individuals should be suspicious if the worker takes a long time to return the card. The employee might be using a skimmer device on the card. Sign credit cards as soon as they are received and shred all credit card applications received that were unsolicited.

Another major area of concern with card usage involves using the telephone or Web to purchase some item. Card users should not give out their account number over the phone unless they initiated the call and know the company is reputable. Also, never give out any credit card info when receiving a phone call. (For example, the caller advises there has been a "computer problem" and the caller needs to verify confidential information.) Legitimate companies don't call to ask for a credit card number over the phone.

A similar situation occurs when receiving e-mails requesting confidential credit card information. Never respond to e-mails that request verification of personal (and credit card) information. These are called *phishing* scams. Never provide any credit card information on a Web site that is not a secure site.

Another area of concern is the care and maintenance of a credit/debit card. Don't write a PIN number on a credit card or have the PIN anywhere near a credit card (in the event that the wallet gets stolen). Never leave credit cards or receipts lying around the office or workspace. Always shield credit card numbers to avoid copying or capturing by a cell phone or other camera. Don't carry around extra credit cards that are rarely used, and only carry around credit cards that are absolutely needed.

Many card users do not keep track of their purchases and don't save their transaction receipts. This is a very bad practice. Open credit card bills promptly and make sure there are no bogus charges. Treat the credit card bill like a checking account and reconcile it monthly;

save all receipts so they can be compared with the monthly bills. If any charges are found that don't have matching receipts, or are not recognized, report these charges promptly (and in writing) to the credit card issuer. Always void and destroy incorrect receipts.

Last but not least, keep a list in a secure place of all account numbers and expiration dates, as well as the phone number and address of each bank that has issued a credit card. Keep this list updated each time a new credit card is received. If moving, notify all credit card issuers in advance of any change of address.

Monitor Credit Reports

For those on military active duty, put an active duty alert on credit files. The alert will stay in these files for at least 12 months. If someone applies for credit using a false name, the creditors will take extra precautions to make sure that the applicant is not a pretender. Contact the three major credit bureaus to place the active duty alert. The contact information is as follows:

- **Equifax:** 800-525-6285, TDD 800-255-0056, *www.equifax.com*.
- **Experian:** 888-397-3742, TDD 800-972-0322, *www.experian.com*.
- **TransUnion:** 800-680-7289, TDD 877-553-7803, *www.transunion.com*.

Check credit reports regularly. If there are accounts that contain incorrect information, follow the instructions for disputing those items. Check to see who has been inquiring and why. Citizens can ask for free copies of credit reports in certain situations. If denied credit because of information in a credit report, a consumer can ask the reporting credit bureau for a free copy of that file. Victims of identity theft who are on public assistance, or unemployed, but expect to apply for work within 60 days, can ask all three of the major credit bureaus for free credit reports. This generally does not include the credit score. Contact the credit bureaus at the numbers or Web sites just listed.

Everyone can request free copies of their credit reports once a year. In addition to the rights described earlier, a new federal law entitles all consumers to ask each of the three major credit bureaus for free copies of their reports once in every 12-month period. This free annual report program started in late 2004 and is being phased in gradually across the country, from West to East. Go to *www.ftc.gov/credit* or call 877-382-4357 for more details and to see when citizens can make requests. It's not necessary to ask all three credit bureaus for your reports at the same time; requests can be staggered if preferred. Do not contact the credit bureaus directly for these free annual reports. They are only available by calling 877-322-8228 or going to *www.annualcreditreport.com*. Requests can be made by phone or online, or a form can be downloaded to mail the requests.

State law may also entitle individuals to free credit reports. Ask local consumer protection or state attorney general's offices. Rights given by state law are in addition to individual rights under federal law.

Be cautious about offers for credit monitoring services. Why pay for them when credit reports can be obtained for free or very cheap? Read the description of the services carefully. Unless you are a victim of serious and ongoing identity theft, buying a service that alerts individuals to certain activities in credit files probably isn't worthwhile, especially if it costs hundreds of dollars a year. Copies of credit reports and credit scores can be purchased any time through the credit reporting bureaus.

IDENTITY THEFT

Identity theft and *identity fraud* are terms used to refer to all types of crime in which someone wrongfully obtains and uses another person's personal data in some way that involves fraud or deception, typically for economic gain. There are numerous reasons everyone needs to take precautions to protect against identity theft.

Identity theft is the fastest-growing crime in the United States today. Besides mail theft, dumpster diving, and lost/stolen wallets, criminals are stealing information:

- By overhearing conversations made on cell phones.
- From faxes and e-mails.
- By hacking into computers.
- From telephone and e-mail scams.
- From careless online shopping and banking.

The FTC has estimated that more than 20 percent of all cases involve telecommunications and the Internet. It is essential that network users understand how thieves steal information via telephone and computer systems. Scammers, previously discussed, use scamming techniques to succeed in stealing someone's identity.

Individual's fingerprints, which are unique, cannot be given to someone else for their use. However, personal data—especially a Social Security number, bank account or credit card number, telephone calling card number, and other valuable identifying data—can be used by unscrupulous individuals for fraudulent activities. Worldwide, for example, many people have reported that unauthorized persons have taken funds out of their bank or financial accounts, taken over their identities altogether, running up vast debts and committing crimes while using the victims' names. In many cases, a victim's losses may include not only out-of-pocket financial losses, but substantial additional financial costs associated with trying to restore the individual's reputation in the community and correcting erroneous information for which the criminal is responsible.

Many individuals do not realize how easily criminals can obtain personal data without having to break into personal space. Criminals may engage in "shoulder surfing" in public places such as telephones and ATMs. Criminals may be watching from a nearby location, as users enter telephone calling card numbers or credit card numbers, or listen in on conversations, as confidential information is provided over the telephone when conducting personal transactions.

Even the areas near home or office settings may not be secure. Some criminals engage in *dumpster diving*: going through garbage cans or a communal dumpster or trash bin. This is a good location to obtain copies of checks, credit card or bank statements, or other records that typically bear personal information such as name, address, and telephone number. These types of records make it easier for criminals to get control over personal accounts and assume an identity. Shredding any documents that might contain sensitive information is recommended.

Everyone receives applications for "pre-approved" credit cards in the mail, and many discard them without tearing up the enclosed materials. Criminals may retrieve them and try to activate the cards for their use. Some credit card companies, when sending credit cards, have adopted security measures that allow a card recipient to activate the card only from a personal home telephone number, but this is not yet a universal practice. Also, if personal mail is delivered to a place where others have ready access, criminals may simply intercept and redirect this mail to another location. There are numerous stories of thieves stealing Social Security checks and other government checks out of mailboxes. Government agencies are encouraging program recipients to use direct deposit for their benefit payments.

In recent years, the Internet has become an appealing place for criminals to obtain identifying data, such as passwords or even banking information. Network users frequently respond to spam. Personal identifying data might be requested from the user. In some cases, criminals have reportedly used computer technology to obtain large amounts of personal data.

With enough identifying information about an individual, a criminal can take over that individual's identity to conduct a wide range of crimes, for example, false applications for loans and credit cards, fraudulent withdrawals from bank accounts, fraudulent use of telephone calling cards, or obtaining other goods or privileges that the criminal might be denied if a real name was used. The criminal might take steps to ensure that bills for the falsely obtained credit cards, or bank statements showing the unauthorized withdrawals, are sent to an address other than the victim's. The victim may not become aware of occurrences until the criminal has already inflicted substantial damage on the victim's assets, credit, and reputation.

Victims of identity theft and fraud may find the task of correcting incorrect information about their financial or personal status and trying to restore their good names and reputations extremely daunting. Unfortunately, the damage that criminals do in stealing another person's identity and using it to commit fraud often takes far longer to undo than it took the criminal to commit the crimes. Victims of a lost or stolen credit card know how much grief this situation can cause.

Avoid Becoming a Victim of Identity Theft

To reduce or minimize the risk of becoming a victim of identity theft or fraud, there are some basic steps to be taken. Be careful about giving out personal information to others unless there is a reason to trust them, regardless of location. Be suspicious, smart, and aware.

Start by adopting a "need to know" approach to personal data. Credit card companies may need to know the user's mother's maiden name so that it can verify an identity when calling to inquire about an account. A person who calls purporting to represent a user's bank, however, does *not* need to know that information if it is already on file with the bank. The only purpose for such a call is to acquire confidential information for that caller's personal benefit. Individuals should restrict the amount of information printed on personal bank checks. Revealing information such as a Social Security number or home telephone number on personal checks is not a good idea. Don't routinely provide personal data to people who may not need that information.

If a stranger calls and offers a chance to receive a prize or other valuable item, be suspicious. Individuals should not respond over the phone to a caller's requests for personal data such as a Social Security number, credit card number and expiration date, birthdate, or mother's maiden name. Request a formal document via mail and then review the application carefully when received and make sure it's going to a company or financial institution that is well known and reputable. The Better Business Bureau can provide information about businesses that have been the subject of complaints.

When traveling, have personal mail held at the local post office, or ask someone known well and trusted (such as another family member, a friend, or a neighbor) to collect and hold mail while away. If telephoning someone while traveling to pass on personal financial information, don't do it at an open telephone booth where a passerby can listen in on conversations. Use a telephone booth where the door can be closed, or use a less public location to call.

Check financial information regularly and look for what should be there and what should not. Holders of bank or credit card accounts should be receiving monthly statements that list transactions for the most recent month or reporting period. If these monthly statements are not being received, call the financial institution or credit card company immediately and ask about it. When told that statements are being mailed to another address not authorized, advise the financial institution or credit card representative immediately that a change of address was not authorized and that someone may be improperly using the accounts. In that situation, ask for copies of all statements and debit or charge transactions that have occurred since the last statement received. Obtaining those copies will help individuals work with the financial institution or credit card companies in determining whether some or all of those debit or charge transactions were fraudulent. (*Note that some companies may cover credit card fraud charges less than $50.00.*)

If someone has gotten personal financial data and made unauthorized debits or charges against financial accounts, checking monthly statements carefully may be the quickest way to become aware of fraudulent activities. Bank and credit card statements should be verified against transaction receipts to avoid unauthorized withdrawals or charges. This means that consumers must keep all receipts. This includes gas pump receipts! Criminals will take advantage of sloppy personal financial administration.

It is possible for a skimmer to be used on an ATM to capture confidential information. Be wary of odd-looking ATM card readers, as they might be skimmer devices. The machines dispense the correct amount of money to unsuspecting victims while their card details are being recorded onto the suspect device. The captured data are downloaded to the criminal's computer to make new cards, which will be used after some months. There are many ways in which the culprits get card data from ATM machines. One way involves installing an unusual-looking device over the card slots of the machine for skimming. Another method (or modus operandi [MO]) involves installing tiny hidden cameras among brochures near the machine that are focused on where ATM users enter their PINs. Thieves also use transparent and unnoticeable overlays on ATM keypads that record PINs or tamper with the other machines in multiple-ATM locations to make a skimming-device-installed ATM machine the only one available for use.

If someone has managed to get access to personal mail or other data, it will be necessary to take immediate action. Credit cards may have been opened in the victim's name or funds taken from a bank account. Customers should contact the financial institution or credit card companies immediately to report those transactions and to request further action. Ask periodically for a copy of personal credit reports. The credit reports should list all bank and financial accounts under the account name and should provide other indications of whether someone has wrongfully opened or used any accounts in a consumer's name.

Maintain careful records of personal banking and financial accounts. Even though financial institutions are required to maintain copies of checks, debit transactions, and similar transactions for five years, individuals should retain monthly statements and checks until satisfied that their records are correct. Note that the IRS requires supporting documentation for seven years. If the need arises to dispute particular transactions, original records will be more immediately accessible and useful to the institutions that have been contacted.

Even if users initiate all of these suggestions, it is still possible to become a victim of identity theft and fraud. Paper copies of transactions containing personal data, such as credit card receipts, ATM transactions, or car rental agreements, may be found by or shared with someone who decides to use these data for fraudulent purposes. Don't toss these receipts into receptacles where they can be retrieved by anyone (dumpster divers) looking for an easy victim.

The latest technique used by cyber thieves is to use the wireless network to steal information from personal computers. Techniques used include *war driving* and *war chalking*. Internet users frequently purchase laptops for wireless access and do not take the necessary precautions to protect against these criminal activities. Wireless users must change the default logon/password and initiate the security protection attributes of the laptop and PDA.

Generally not associated with Internet fraud and identity theft is the transmission of documents over fax machines. There is a possibility that transmissions from fax machines could be intercepted by some technique and copied without the user's knowledge. If fax transmissions are not encrypted or sent over secure communication links, the possibility exists for an interception. If this were to occur, the objective is more likely to be corporate espionage and not identity theft.

Contacts

Victims of identity theft or fraud should act immediately to minimize the damage and impact on personal funds and financial accounts, as well as personal reputation. There are a number of contact addresses and Web sites that are useful resources for victims of identity theft.

Consumers should contact all creditors where name or other identifying data have been fraudulently used. For example, individuals may need to contact a long-distance telephone company if a long-distance calling card has been stolen or fraudulent charges are discovered on a bill. All financial institutions must be contacted when an identity thief has taken over a personal account or accounts that have been created in someone's name, but without their knowledge. Customers may:

- Need to cancel or block those accounts.
- Place stop-payment orders on any outstanding checks that may not have cleared.
- Change ATM card, account, and personal identification numbers.

The **Federal Trade Commission (FTC)**, under the Identity Theft and Assumption Deterrence Act, is responsible for receiving and processing complaints from people who believe they may be victims of identity theft. This agency can provide informational materials and refer complaints to appropriate entities, including the major credit reporting agencies and law enforcement agencies. Contact the FTC to report the situation at *www.ftc.gov/sentinel/*. A complaint can be filed at FTC Web site [FTC]. Additional information is available on the FTC's identity theft Web pages. Complainants can also call the local FBI or **Secret Service** office to report crimes relating to identity theft and fraud.

If someone suspects that an identity thief has submitted a change-of-address form with the Post Office to redirect mail, or has used the mail to commit frauds involving an identity, contact the local office of the **Postal Inspection Service**. If someone suspects a Social Security number is being fraudulently used, contact the **Social Security Administration (SSA)** at *www.ssa.gov*. The Internal Revenue Service can be contacted at *www.irs.gov* for suspected improper use of identification information in connection with tax violations.

Credit Reporting Agencies

Consumers suspecting a crime can call the fraud units of the three principal credit reporting companies. Check the local telephone directory under headings such as "Credit Reporting Agencies" for names of similar companies. The major **credit reporting agencies** are depicted in **TABLE 3-1**.

Federal Deposit Insurance Corporation

The Consumer Response Center of the **Federal Deposit Insurance Corporation (FDIC)** has responsibility for investigating all types of consumer complaints about FDIC-supervised institutions and for responding to consumer inquiries about consumer laws and regulations and banking practices. The FDIC staff can provide an avenue for efficient and effective resolution of consumer complaints or inquiries. The contact address is:

Federal Deposit Insurance Corporation
Consumer Response Center
2345 Grand Avenue, Suite 100
Kansas City, MO 64108–2638

The FDIC has created a Web page to inform consumers about the new **Fair and Accurate Credit Transactions Act's (FACTA)** consumer provisions—which give new rights to free credit reports. FACTA also provides new rights to obtain credit scores. FACTA became law in December 2003. Consumer Alerts from the Fair and Accurate Credit Transactions Act are available at the FTC Web site [Consumer Alerts].

TABLE 3-1 Major Credit Reporting Agencies

Credit Reporting Agency	Telephone Number	Web Address
Equifax P.O. Box 740241 Atlanta, GA 30374-0241	1-800-685-1111	http://www.equifax.com/
Experian	1-888-EXPERIAN	http://www.experian.com/
TransUnion 2 Baldwin Place P.O. Box 2000 Chester, PA 19022	1-800-916-8800	http://www.transunion.com/

Check Verification Companies

Companies should contact the major **check verification** services if clients have checks stolen or bank accounts set up by an identity thief. In particular, where a particular merchant has received a stolen check, contact the merchant's verification company. These contacts are included in a short list depicted in **TABLE 3-2** [Check Verification].

Others can be identified by typing "check verification" in the search field in Yahoo or Google.

INTERNET FRAUD

Fraud is a deception deliberately practiced in order to secure unfair or unlawful gain. How can the Web user discern whether the offer is valid or a fraud? First, if the offer smells fishy and sounds too good to be true, it probably is a fraud. It is usually not possible to get something for nothing. Human nature, however, sometimes overrules common sense. Fraud is covered under a number of current U.S. statutes. Information concerning Internet fraud and tips to avoid Internet fraud can be viewed at *www.fraud.org/internet/intset.htm*.

The Internet offers a global marketplace for consumers and businesses. But the criminal element also recognizes the potentials of cyberspace. The same scams that have been conducted by mail and telephone can now be found on the World Wide Web and in e-mail, and new cyber scams are emerging. It's often difficult to discern the difference between reputable online sellers and criminals who use the Internet to defraud network users. Network users must learn how to protect themselves by learning how to recognize the danger signs of fraud. It is essential that victims or attempted victims of Internet fraud report scams quickly so law enforcement agencies can shut down fraudulent operations.

TABLE 3-2 Check Verification Companies

Check Verification Company	Web Address
CheckRite	www.checkritesystems.com
CrossCheck	www.cross-check.com
Equifax	www.equifax.com
National Processing Co. (NPC)	www.npc.net
TeleCheck	www.telecheck.com

Internet Fraud Tips

Consumers must research the dealer or vendor. If the seller or charity is unfamiliar, check with the state or local consumer protection agency and the Better Business Bureau. Some Web sites have feedback forums, which can provide useful information about other consumers' experiences with particular sellers. Get the physical address and phone number in case there is a problem later. Look for information about how complaints are handled. It can be difficult to resolve complaints, especially if the seller or charity is located in another country. Check the Web site for information about programs the company or organization participates in that require adherence to standards for reliability and help to handle disputes. Be aware that absence of complaints is not a guarantee. Fraudulent operators open and close quickly, so the fact that no one has made a complaint yet doesn't meant that the seller or charity is legitimate.

Computer users must not believe promises of easy money. If someone advertises claims to earn money with little or no work, get a loan or credit card even with bad credit, or make money on an investment with little or no risk, it's probably a scam. Get-rich-quick schemes are not new, so understand the offer. A legitimate seller will provide all the details about the products or services, the total price, the delivery time, the refund and cancellation policies, and the terms of any warranty. For more information about shopping safely online, go to the *nclnet.org* Web site [shoppingonline]. Here are several tips that can be used to avoid Internet fraud:

- Resist pressure for a quick answer. Legitimate companies and charities will be happy to provide time to make a decision. It's probably a scam if they demand an immediate response or won't take "no" for an answer. Think twice before entering contests operated by unfamiliar companies. Fraudulent marketers sometimes use contest entry forms to identify potential victims.
- Be cautious about unsolicited e-mails. They are often fraudulent. When users are familiar with the company or charity that sent the e-mail but don't want to receive further messages, send a reply asking to be removed from the e-mail list. However, responding to unknown senders may simply verify a working e-mail address and result in even more unwanted messages from strangers. The best approach may simply be to delete the e-mail. These e-mails might also contain computer viruses.

- Beware of imposters. Someone might send an e-mail pretending to be connected with a business or charity, or create a Web site that looks just like that of a well-known company or charitable organization. When not sure of the legitimacy of the organization, find another way to contact the legitimate business or charity and inquire.
- Guard personal information. Don't provide a credit card or bank account number unless actually paying for something. A Social Security number should not be necessary unless applying for credit. Be especially suspicious when someone claiming to be from a personally known company asks for information that the business already possesses.
- Beware of *dangerous downloads*. In downloading programs to see pictures or videos, hear music, or play games, users could download a virus that wipes out computer files or connects the computer's modem to a foreign telephone number, resulting in expensive phone charges. Only download programs from known and trusted Web sites, and read all user agreements carefully.

Credit cards are the safest way to pay for online purchases because consumers can dispute the charges if they never get the goods or services or if the offer was misrepresented. Federal law limits consumer liability to $50 if someone makes unauthorized charges to cardholder accounts, and most credit card issuers will remove them completely when the problem is reported promptly. There are new technologies, such as "substitute" credit card numbers and password programs, that can offer extra measures of protection from someone else using another's credit card.

New Solutions

Bank of America's online customers in North Carolina, South Carolina, and Georgia have a new way to help prevent fraud and identity theft with the launch of an industry-leading protection service with the bank's online banking. A new free service, called **SiteKey**™, allows customers to pick one of thousands of images, write a brief phrase, and select three challenge questions. The customer and the bank can pass that information securely back and forth to confirm each other's identity.

Using SiteKey is like getting a safe deposit box that takes two keys to open. Before the customer and the bank agree to open the box together, they confirm each other's identity. Bank of America, which has the most online banking customers in the country, is the first major financial services company to provide this added level of security.

Internet Fraud Statistics

Statistics have been developed that show the percent of frauds for various scams initiated over the Internet. The top 10 frauds identified by the National Fraud Information Center for 2006 are listed in **TABLE 3-3** [National Fraud Information Center].

Note that the top two scams are oriented toward merchandise purchases where goods were never delivered or misrepresented. Forty-two percent of the crooks were based in foreign countries. The average loss to fraud victims totaled $1,512. Additional details can be viewed at *fraud.org* [Fraud].

TABLE 3-3 Top 10 Frauds

Scam Candidates	Fraud Percentage
Online auctions	34
General merchandise	33
Fake check scams	11
Nigerian money offers	7
Lotteries/lottery clubs	4
Advance fee loans	3
Phishing	2
Prizes/sweepstakes	1
Internet access services	1
Investments	1

Exploiting Children on the Web

A survey by the National Center for Missing and Exploited Children and Cox Communications [missingkids] revealed that 42 percent of parents do not review the content that their teenagers read or type in chat rooms or via instant messaging. Parents also did not know the lingo used by teenagers to communicate over the Web, and 28 percent did not know if their teens talked to strangers online. Parents are encouraged to become more involved with their children's online habits and behaviors.

Studies reveal that many parents are not involved in their children's computer and Internet habits and behaviors. Children may affect the security and safety of the entire family due to their inexperience and naiveté. The same scammers and con artists who compromise adults might use children to gain access to personal and confidential information relating to their parents' accounts and assets. Because there are many "latchkey kids," there are many opportunities for individuals to "use" children in their criminal pursuits.

Children can unwittingly assist scammers and thieves in providing confidential information that can result in property crimes against the family unit. Advise children to never provide personal information to strangers. Information available to a minor that could be used by a criminal includes:

- Address.
- Telephone number.
- Parents' first and last names.
- Parents' work phone numbers and schedules.
- Parents' employer names.
- Names of relatives.
- Credit card and debit card numbers.
- Social Security numbers.
- Family member birthdates.

COMBATING IDENTITY THEFT AND FRAUD

A number of government and private organizations have information about various aspects of identity theft and fraud: how it can occur, what can be done about it, and how to guard personal privacy. To help learn more about the problem and its solutions, the list of Web sites in **TABLE 3-4** provides users with sites they might find interesting and informative on identity theft and related topics. Considerable information is also available at *usdoj.gov* website [USDOJ]. **TABLE 3-4** provides a list of both government and non-government organizations.

AWARENESS AND EDUCATION

Identify theft and fraud can be avoided or minimized if the population becomes aware of the enormity of the problem. Education and awareness is a must. It is obvious criminals are just waiting to take advantage of anyone who lets his or her guard down. After an individual has become a victim of identify theft or fraud, it is too late. There are community forums concerning identify theft and fraud offered in many cities. Many of these are free. Check with the local law enforcement offices, the local Better Business Bureau, and the local **Chamber of Commerce** for possible schedules.

TABLE 3-4 Government and Nongovernment Organizations

Government Organizations	Web Address
Consumer.gov	www.consumer.gov
Federal Bureau of Investigation	www.fbi.gov
Federal Deposit Insurance Corporation	www.fdic.gov
Federal Trade Commission	www.ftc.gov
United States Postal Inspection Service	www.usps.com/postalinspectors
United States Secret Service	www.secretservice.gov/index.shtml

Nongovernment Organizations	Web Address
American Association of Retired Persons (AARP)	www.aarp.org
Better Business Bureau	www.bbb.org
Center for Democracy and Technology	www.cdt.org
Chamber of Commerce	www.uschamber.com/default
National Association of Attorneys General (NAAG)	www.naag.org
National Consumers League	www.nclnet.org
National Fraud Information Center	www.fraud.org
Privacy Rights Clearinghouse	www.privacyrights.org

Shop Online Safely

The Internet is an exciting tool that puts vast information at surfers' fingertips. With a click of a computer mouse, it lets users buy an airline ticket, book a hotel, send flowers to a friend, or purchase a favorite stock. Good deals, convenience, and choice abound on the Internet. But before using all the Internet has to offer, become cyber smart to make the most of the online experience. Cyber thieves can use information provided over chat rooms, blogs, and e-mail to compromise the security of naïve network users.

Security on the Internet

Shopping online offers benefits that won't be found when shopping in a store or by mail. The Internet is always open—24/7—and bargains can be numerous online. Shopping on the Internet is no less safe than shopping in a store or by mail. Keep the following tips in mind to help ensure that the online shopping experience is a safe one:

- *Use a secure browser.* This is the software needed to navigate the Internet. Browsers should comply with industry security standards, such as Secure Socket Layer (SSL). These standards scramble the purchase information sent over the Internet, helping to secure any transactions. Most computers come with a browser installed. Some browsers can be downloaded for free over the Internet.
- *Shop with known companies.* Anyone can set up shop online under almost any name. When not familiar with a merchant, ask for a paper catalog or brochure to get a better idea of their merchandise and services. Also, determine the company's refund and return policies before placing an order. These should be posted on the company's Web site.
- *Keep passwords private.* Be creative when establishing a password, and never give it to anyone. Avoid using a telephone number, birthdate, or a portion of a Social Security number. Instead, use a combination of numbers, letters, and symbols.
- *Pay by credit or charge card.* If paying by credit or charge card online, transactions will be protected by the Fair Credit Billing Act. Under this law, consumers have the right to dispute charges under certain circumstances and temporarily withhold payment while the creditor is investigating them. In the event of unauthorized use of a credit or charge card, cardholders generally would be held liable only for the first $50 in charges. Some companies offer an online shopping guarantee that ensures customers will not be held responsible for any unauthorized charges made online, and some cards may provide additional warranty, return, and/or purchase protection benefits.
- *Keep a record.* Be sure to print a copy of purchase receipts and confirmation numbers for your records. Also, be aware that the Mail and Telephone Order Merchandise Rule covers online orders. This means that unless the company states otherwise, merchandise must be delivered within 30 days; if there are delays, the company must provide a notification.
- *Pay bills online.* Some companies allow the payment of bills and provide the ability to check account status online. Before signing up for any service, evaluate how the company secures financial and personal information. Many companies explain their security procedures on their Web site. If a security description is not evident, call or e-mail the company and ask.

Destroy all diskettes, CDs, and flash drives before they are discarded. Most computer users don't consider the risk of throwing diskettes in the trash. This is a bad mistake as dumpster divers will have a field day. Carefully discarding old storage devices is just as critical as securing the data in the first place. Computer hard drives contain a wealth of information. There are viable security techniques that can be used to destroy this information if a computing device is to be sold or trashed.

LAWS

Individuals and organizations must be aware of various **laws** that have been enacted to protect the privacy of electronic data, such as the following:

- **Health Insurance Portability and Accountability Act (HIPAA).**
  HIPAA, which took effect on April 14, 2006, is a set of rules to be followed by doctors, hospitals, and other healthcare providers. HIPAA helps ensure that all medical records, medical billing, and patient accounts meet certain consistent standards with regard to documentation, handling, and privacy. In addition, HIPAA requires that all patients be able access their own medical records, correct errors or omissions, and be informed how personal information is shared used. Other provisions involve notification of privacy procedures to the patient.

- **Sarbanes-Oxley Act of 2002 (Sarbox or SOX).**
  The Sarbanes-Oxley Act became law in July 2002 and introduced major changes to the regulation of corporate governance and financial practice. The Act establishes a new quasi-public agency, the Public Company Accounting Oversight Board, or PCAOB, which is charged with overseeing, regulating, inspecting, and disciplining accounting firms in their roles as auditors of public companies. The Act also covers issues such as auditor independence, corporate governance, internal control assessment, and enhanced financial disclosure.

- **Gramm-Leach-Bliley Act (GLBA).**
  Under the GLBA, financial institutions must provide their clients a privacy notice that explains what information the company gathers about the client, where this information is shared, and how the company safeguards that information. This privacy notice must be given to the client prior to entering into an agreement to do business.

- **USA Patriot Act of 2001.**
  The Act was passed 45 days after the September 11, 2001, attacks on the World Trade Center in New York City and the Pentagon in Washington, D.C. It substantially expanded the authority of U.S. law enforcement agencies for the stated purpose of fighting terrorism in the United States and abroad. The acronym stands for: Uniting and Strengthening America by Providing Appropriate Tools Required to Intercept and Obstruct Terrorism Act of 2001 (Public Law 107-56).

- **Children's Online Privacy Protection Act of 1998 (COPPA).**
  This Act, effective April 21, 2000, applies to the online collection of personal information from children under 13. The new rules spell out what a Web site operator must include in a privacy policy, when and how to seek verifiable consent from a parent, and what responsibilities an operator has to protect children's privacy and safety online.

- **California Database Security Breach Act of 2003.**
  Senate Bill 1386 requires any company that stores customer data electronically to notify its California customers of a security breach to the company's computer system if the company knows or reasonably believes that unencrypted information about the customer has been stolen. Senate Bill 1, commonly known as the California Financial Information Privacy Act, creates new limits on the ability of financial institutions to share nonpublic personal information about their clients with affiliates and third parties [California Financial Information Privacy Act].

It is essential that efforts be made to keep electronic data secure from criminals, hackers, and malcontents. By ensuring compliance with these aforementioned laws, serious legal consequences can be avoided.

🔒 CHAPTER SUMMARY

Identity theft is the fastest-growing crime in the United States today. Scam artists use a number of techniques, including dumpster diving, mail theft, and lost/stolen wallets to commit their crimes. There are a number of proactive items that the individual can do to protect against identify theft and fraud. These include protecting Social Security numbers and birthdates, being Internet smart, securing personal information, and managing personal mail.

The Internet offers a global marketplace for both consumers and businesses. The criminal element also recognizes the potentials of cyberspace. The same fraud and scams that have been conducted by mail and telephone can now be found on the World Wide Web and in e-mail. New cyber scams directed at the unwary are being initiated every day. There are a number of defenses that can be deployed to counter these computer threats.

Credit reports should be reviewed on an annual or semi annual basis. Free copies may be available from the credit reporting agencies. Credit card statements and bank statements should be reviewed on a monthly basis.

Victims of identity theft and fraud have a number of contacts where reports can be filed. These include the FTC, FDIC, FBI, Secret Service, IRS, and the U.S. Post Office. A number of laws been enacted to protect the privacy of electronic data.

Studies reveal that many parents are not involved in their children's computer and Internet habits and behaviors. Children may affect the security and safety of the entire family due to their inexperience and naiveté.

KEY TERMS

Better Business Bureau (BBB)
Chamber of Commerce
check verification
Children's Online Privacy Protection Act of 1998 (COPPA)
credit reporting agencies
Do Not Call
Equifax
Experian
Fair and Accurate Credit Transaction Act (FACTA)
Federal Bureau of Investigation (FBI)
Federal Deposit Insurance Corporation (FDIC)

Federal Trade Commission (FTC)
fraud
Gramm-Leach-Bliley Act (GLBA)
Health Insurance Portability and Accountability Act (HIPAA)
identity theft
Identity Theft Resource Center (ITRC)
Internal Revenue Service (IRS)
laws
National Fraud Information Center (NFIC)
Postal Inspection Service

Sarbanes-Oxley Act of 2002 (Sarbox or SOX)
scam
scam baiting
scammers
Secret Service
SiteKey™
Social Security Administration (SSA)
spam
TransUnion
TRUSTe®
USA Patriot Act of 2001

SECURITY REVIEW QUESTIONS

1. Provide a list of scammer tools.
2. Name the three credit reporting agencies.
3. Provide a list of personal information that can be used to identify theft schemes.
4. How do scam artists defraud the general public?
5. Provide a list of techniques that can be employed to avoid identity theft.
6. Provide a list of Internet fraud tips.
7. Provide a list of personal information available to a minor that could be used by a criminal.
8. How can exploiters use children in fraud schemes?
9. Identify several safe online shopping suggestions.
10. Identify the various laws concerning privacy of electronic data.

RESEARCH ACTIVITIES

1. Produce a synopsis of the contents of the Web page located at *www.ic3.gov.*
2. Produce a summary of the activities identified on the Identity Theft Resource Center (ITRC) Web site.
3. Compile a list of the current scams located on the ITRC Web site.
4. Produce a report of publications and documentation available at the FBI, the local state attorney general's office, or the Federal Trade Commission Web sites.
5. Request your personal credit reports from the credit reporting agencies.
6. Check out the IRS Web site for identity theft and fraud reporting and assistance.
7. Search the governmental Web sites for fraud and identify theft information.
8. Provide an overview of laws directed toward electronic privacy.
9. Provide details of the Fair Credit Billing Act.
10. Identify check verification services, and provide a list of services provided.
11. Contact your local Better Business Bureau or Chamber of Commerce for identity theft and fraud information.
12. Search for Web sites that might be used to exploit children.
13. Compile a list of blogs. Identify their topics.
14. Search the Web for sites that identify predator, fraud, and scam operations.
15. Identify the function of the TRUSTe® seal.
16. Research the Web for current Internet fraud statistics.

CHAPTER 4

Computer and Digital Assets Security

🔒 CHAPTER CONTENTS

- Look at the security issues for digital devices.
- See how portable devices are vulnerable to theft.
- Identify techniques to protect computer and data assets in the academic environment.
- Develop an awareness of the property theft potential.
- Learn how to protect and keep personal information confidential.
- Look at the physical security requirements for personal and commercial computer and network assets.
- Identify the issues relating to digital resources access.

INTRODUCTION

Personal financial security can be compromised if a computing device is stolen. It is likely that computer users have stored personal information on their laptops or PDAs that would allow someone to commit identity theft or fraud. It is essential that everyone treat their computing devices as they would treat a wallet or purse. This chapter addresses the topics of property theft and security issues such as burglary, carelessness, and leaving computing devices unattended in public places. Sections of the chapter address the security of computing devices used by students in the educational environment of dorms and classrooms.

The workplace is also not a safe place to leave a portable computing device unattended. Business travel provides another opportunity to lose a laptop to a thief. Public transportation systems such as airplanes, taxis, and trains provide the criminal with many opportunities to steal electronic devices. Individuals should also be aware that many nonemployees exist in the workplace. These could include contractors, suppliers, maintenance workers, and visitors. Individuals and businesses must develop plans and techniques to counter Internet threats and attacks.

With the advent of numerous wireless electronic products, criminals have another opportunity to steal users' property and identities. Many of these new wireless products are small and easy to conceal, making them easy targets for the criminal element. There are also implications for the business community, as small storage media devices are easily concealed, making the theft of corporate information an issue. Awareness and education can reduce the impact of criminal activity.

Physical security must be addressed by both the individual computer and network user and the corporate or government data center manager. The scope, obviously, is considerably different. Personal physical security is usually just common sense and costs very little to implement; however, physical security for data centers is another matter. Hundreds of thousands of dollars sometimes must be allocated for the defense of the assets and resources of these large centers. This chapter addresses the issues for both situations.

PROPERTY THEFT AWARENESS

Property theft can occur in any setting, including home, work, school, travel, and vacation locations. A theft might be planned by a professional thief or could be a crime of opportunity. The computer user must be vigilant at all times. Personal well-being or worth could be compromised by a lack of attention to security issues. Protecting personal computing devices is not enough; CDs, memory sticks, and flash drives must also be secured. The loss of data storage devices might cause the user more grief than losing the computer device. Normally honest individuals might be tempted at the possibility of a free laptop. The following sections cover burglaries and electronic equipment losses at school, at home, while traveling on business, on vacation, and in the workplace. There are similarities in all settings; however, there are special situations that need to be addressed. Education and awareness can save the computer and network user from many headaches, including financial losses.

Burglaries

Security of personal property is most vulnerable during holidays and vacations when most **burglaries** take place. Homeowners and renters must pay particular attention to security of the residence during Thanksgiving, Christmas, Easter, and other holidays when visiting relatives and friends. There are a number of activities the computer user can perform that will provide some level of security during weekend trips and extended vacations and reduce the probability of burglaries. Professional burglars might only be interested in stealing electronic devices for the purpose of fencing to some other criminal. Somewhere in this chain of crooks there will possibly be a cyber thief. Cyber thieves can steal an identity when they burglarize homes or offices or when they are part of a conspiracy of receiving stolen computer devices. Most computer users keep their financial and other personal records on laptops or desktop computers at their home location. In addition, many computer users also keep personal information on their work computers.

Commercial property thefts can occur during regular weekends and holidays when the office space is unattended. Losses can also occur at off-hours when maintenance personnel are working. Don't overlook thefts at off-hours precipitated by day employees, given the opportunity. Lax security during normal work hours can also provide the opportunity for theft. Students working part-time and low-paid clerical workers might be tempted, given the opportunity. Critical personal financial difficulties can cause honest workers to cross the line. This chapter contains a section devoted to physical protection of computer systems and electronic devices.

Stolen Computer and Networking Components

It has been estimated that 99 percent of laptops stolen are not recovered! Many laptops are stolen from unlocked vehicles, office areas, coffeehouses, or airport work areas. Theft of computer equipment is a serious problem that can be reduced, even eliminated, by being aware of the surroundings. The network user must be constantly aware of the potential for computer and data theft. In addition to the capital loss of equipment, and the related downtime until it is replaced, the loss of sensitive and confidential information will have long-term consequences.

Thieves look for opportunity. Physically locking down electronic equipment to a fixed object in the office or room makes it difficult to steal. It is possible to purchase equipment that can be physically secured or that has the capability to be secured. Portable equipment should have a locking mechanism. Thefts of opportunity happen in less than 30 seconds. Never leave a room or office without locking the door, regardless of the time being absent. In many office spaces, an office with a door might be a perk reserved for supervisors. This means that the other employees, assigned to a cube, must be vigilant when it comes to protecting the computing asset. This almost sounds like the network user must become a little distrustful or paranoid.

Equipment that can be traced is not attractive to thieves. All equipment should be permanently marked with an identification number that can be traced by police. Private property should be marked with a unique number that can be traced to the owner, for example, a driver's license number. There are many methods of marking property. Most professional organizations use property tags for identification and inventory purposes. If a theft of equipment does occur, investigators will need detailed information on make, model, and serial number and any other distinctive markings. This information is stored on a central law enforcement database. Take photographs of all computer devices, and maintain an inventory database. Store the photos and information in a safe and secure location separate from the equipment. Don't forget that your assets can be destroyed by a number of methods, not just by theft. Also, insurance companies might require a photographic and ID record of any stolen or damaged computing device.

Empty cartons and old equipment left in the hallway or on the loading dock advertise new equipment on site. Do not leave packaging or equipment out where it is visible. Discard all waste packaging by breaking it down and taking it to a recycling area.

The data on a personal computer are more valuable than the hardware itself. Personal and confidential information, research, and expensive software are now in the hands of the thieves. Prevent others from accessing the information by password-protecting your computer or PDA. Numerous options are available, including encryption. So that productive work can be resumed as soon as possible, make sure that important data are backed up regularly. Test backups to make sure they can be recovered, and store them in a different secure location, not with the computing device. Business contingency and recovery plans are discussed in Chapter 9.

Many laptops and handheld devices such as personal digital assistants are stolen from vehicles. Equipment left in an unattended vehicle should be stored out of view in the trunk before leaving the vehicle. Stolen computers are often loaded with company proprietary data, possibly even access to company networks and employee information. Studies have shown that a large number of network breaches originate from stolen computers. With a stolen notebook in hand, thieves can use passwords and cookies saved in the computer's memory to get entry to servers, secured Web sites, and restricted intranets and extranets where they can access confidential organization information. This could include employee salaries, new-product plans, or financial details. Such breaches can cost organizations thousands or millions of dollars.

While corporations and governments may invest hundreds of thousands of dollars in information security measures like firewalls, encryption, and virus protection, they often overlook the fact that if their computers are stolen, their investments may become obsolete. The physical security of laptops is critically connected to the data security of the information that's on the network. (*As a personal note, the author carried around a laptop that contained technical information on the entire broadband network of his employer.*) The bottom line is that a stolen notebook costs an organization a great deal more than just the value of the hardware. A device called a **Kensington security lock** is available for securing notebook computers. This device consists of an aircraft-grade steel cable and a Kevlar fiber attachment.

A laptop security policy is important because everyone in the organization must understand the true implications of notebook theft. Without an effective policy, management and employees will not know what steps to take to prevent theft, whether in the office or on the road.

EDUCATIONAL SITE COMPUTER SECURITY

Generally, educational institutions do not cover losses of private property. Students, staff, and faculty should check personal insurance coverage to see if dorm and classroom losses are insured. Laptop computers have become prime targets on educational campuses for both the casual and experienced thief. With laptops valued up to $5,000, the incidence of thefts is increasing. There are a number of strategies that may either prevent the theft of laptops or aid in their recovery if someone should become a victim. Some of these are just plain common sense, while others feature a more physical approach to the issues.

Students must record the make, model, and serial number of computer and electronic devices. This includes printers, external drives, and any other associated devices. The university might keep a record of personal laptops; however, this is the owner's responsibility. A photograph of personal computer and electronic devices is a good idea. This can be used as evidence for an insurance loss or a report to the authorities.

When residing on a ground floor, keep laptops and other electronics away from accessible windows where a thief can quickly break the window, reach in and remove the machine. In a residence hall, be mindful of leaving a laptop unattended in common spaces such as study rooms and kitchens. Because the residence hall is viewed as home, it is easy to become too trusting and complacent. Although students may know and trust roommates, a roommate's friends may not be as trustworthy. A laptop should be locked in a closet or drawer when not in use, or it should be secured to the desktop with an approved security device.

The doors to labs, office spaces, and residence halls should be secured whenever laptops are left unattended. If possible, the laptop should be stored in a locked file cabinet or secured with one of the locking devices discussed later. Never leave a laptop or other computer component unattended. Sounds like a paranoid response to security! As the end of a semester approaches, those students who have not prepared research papers and projects might be tempted to take the easy way out and find an assignment that has already been completed by some other student. Report any theft of computing devices immediately to university security and/or the local police department. Also report the theft to any relevant professors as some assignment may be turned in that looks familiar. (*P.S.: The professors may not believe such a tale! This excuse is similar to "the dog ate my disk."*)

If faculty or administration offices are equipped with locks, use them when away. It sounds simple, but the fact is that many office thefts are crimes of opportunity often committed by students, strangers, or employees who simply walk through the building looking for items of value. Faculty, staff, and students must report suspicious activity to security immediately.

Be careful with laptops in the library. Secure them when going to the stacks, or use a cable lock to secure it temporarily to the top of a study desk. Bookstores frequently require the placement of book bags and books on storage bins outside the store. Ideally, such containment areas should be lockable. If not, it might be possible to check the laptop in with the store staff; otherwise, leave any laptop at home or with a friend who remains outside the store. Check with the store staff, as electronic devices may not be allowed into the store.

Based on comprehensive studies, the following list of recommendations was developed for educational institutions. These suggestions apply to both administrative and academic organizations. Although directed primarily at computer thefts, these recommendations can be used to reduce theft losses to other types of equipment as well.

Device Security

Step one is to provide a level of physical security for electronic devices. Basic techniques for **device security** include the following suggestions:

- Use tie-down devices to secure computer equipment when practical and appropriate to do so. These devices may not be suitable for portable equipment. In addition, university stores should consider connecting individual computers on display to an alarm device.
- Keep portable equipment, such as laptop computers, out of sight in locked desks, cabinets, rooms, or automobiles when not in use.
- Store new computer equipment that has been delivered but not set up out of sight in a secure location.
- Clearly and permanently mark computer equipment with agency identification to deter theft and improve chances of recovery of stolen equipment.

Administration Security

After providing physical security for electronic devices, the next step is to provide an adequate level of administrative security and control:

- Establish a computer user policy that includes theft prevention information for employees.
- Control access to all computer and server areas, preferably with two-factor security. Some agencies may choose to use a card access system and key lock or other method to secure the building or specific rooms.
- Provide room and building keys only to those individuals who really need them, and maintain a record of all individuals who have keys and cards.

- Increase employee awareness of the possibility of theft, and advise them of their need to be alert to the activities of individuals who do not work in their building or area.
- Place receptionist or other work areas near entrance doors. Security guards or surveillance monitors may be used in certain situations.
- Use intrusion alarms for buildings or rooms where justified.
- Provide video surveillance for equipment labs and building entrances.
- Staff computer labs when the labs are being used, and lock them at other times.
- Establish a building liaison whose responsibility is maintaining awareness of theft prevention.
- Make police departments and local pawn shops aware of specific agency markings on equipment.

Housing Security

Housing security precautions are extremely important for students living in a dorm. Student accommodation is targeted usually because of poor security and the fact that there will be more than one television, computer, stereo, checkbook, credit card, and debit card at the property. Security precautions that can be performed for home and dorm protection are as follows:

- If a member of a neighborhood watch area, let your coordinator know of absences.
- If someone trustworthy is remaining in the dorm over the holidays, try to leave any valuable items with them.
- Keep valuable items away from windows and out of view.
- Students may want to take anything valuable (computers, stereos, MP3s) home during any holiday period.

Precautions

There are number of simple actions that students can take to make the educational experience a safe one. Security can be enhanced by these simple crime prevention measures:

- Make a note of the serial number, make, and model of all electronic items.
- Always keep all doors and windows locked when lodging space is unoccupied.
- Keep doors locked day and night, as thefts can occur all hours of the day.
- Develop a plan in case of an emergency.
- Don't make it look obvious that no one is home. Leave a light on when going out at night.
- Ensure that all locks are working and that keys have been changed from the previous inhabitants.
- When looking to rent a place, check for door and window locks and locks on individual rooms.
- When hosting an activity or party, remember you don't necessarily know your "friends' friends."

Carelessness

Students have a lot of distractions in the daily grind. Computer lab assignments are due and everyone is scurrying around. It is easy to become distracted and leave a storage media device in the computer. Flash drives and disks are easily lost or misplaced. Not only does the student lose all of the work stored on the media; the possibility exits that personal information is also resident.

Students must develop an awareness of the potential for identify theft and fraud that can be the result of this carelessness. Aside from this potential, all of the semester's work may be lost, resulting in some severe headaches. Experience has shown that students often fail to make multiple copies of assignments, so there is no backup when the storage device is lost. Educators often do not believe the "dog ate it" story.

Experience has provided some insight into the length that some students will go to avoid preparing assignments and projects. Many students wait until the last minute to start working on projects or assignments that require the aid of a computer to prepare the documentation. Being careless with magnetic media such as CDs and flash drives can cost the student a semester's work. Always make duplicate copies of research. Don't keep all computer work in a backpack or automobile. Magnetic media is cheap: make several copies and store in multiple locations. Remember magnetic media is also susceptible to erasure and damage from excessive heat.

SECURITY AND INTEGRITY FOR INTERNET USERS

Protecting workspace resources is a major consideration and can be a substantial endeavor involving time, money, and manpower. There are a number of actions that both management and the individual user can take to protect computer resources. The primary access protection mechanism is the *password*. Many computer users do not take this simple method seriously. Password authentication is "job one." Passwords are not generally displayed on a video monitor and are replaced by a number of asterisks.

Passwords

The first line of defense in network security is the password. A **password** is defined as a word or string of characters recognized by automatic means, permitting user access to a location, database, or file storage. It is a secret code required to log into a secure computer system. A successful password system depends on passwords being kept secret. Security is often compromised because users tend to violate security procedures by posting the password on the computer monitor or committing other violations of security policies. Guidelines for password management include the following:

- Keep the password secret.
- Choose a password that is different from a user name or an account name.
- Use an invalid word—not one in the dictionary.

- Change the password when required.
- Change the entire password—not one character.
- Use the longest allowable string of characters.
- Do pick a mixture of letters, special characters, and at least one number.
- Do pick a password that is easily remembered.
- Don't pick a password that someone can easily guess if they know your identity (for example, not a Social Security number, birthday, or maiden name).
- Don't pick a word that can be found in the dictionary (brute force programs can rapidly try every word in the dictionary!).
- Don't pick a word that is currently newsworthy.
- Don't pick a password that is similar to previous passwords.

Passwords are the most widely used network security feature, and almost all organizations employ some password scheme. Office applications and databases are routinely secured with login passwords. They provide a minimum level of security and may be used to restrict user access to specific network facilities during designated shifts or working hours.

An area of vulnerability is the database that contains the password file. This database must be protected from those who would attempt to illegally gain access. Many systems are susceptible to unanticipated break-ins. Once the attacker has gained access, it is possible to obtain a collection of passwords in order to use different accounts for different logon sessions, which could decrease the chances of detection. It is also possible that a password file could become readable, which could compromise all accounts.

There are several actions that would be prudent when managing passwords:

- When an employee leaves the organization, this password must be disabled.
- Login attempts must be limited to three before access is denied.
- An audit trail needs to be created that tracks logins and denials.
- An alert needs to be activated when password violations occur.
- The last login date stamp can be displayed when a user logs in. This will flag the user that someone else has been trying the user's password.
- Don't allow multiple users to know the password for a single user ID.

Some users have accounts on multiple computers in other protection domains, and they might use the same password. Thus, if duplicate passwords are used and are compromised, multiple computers may be affected. Some computer installations utilize a single sign-on (SSO) method.

The use of a password is commonly referred to as first-function authentication. A second-function or two-factor authentication is based on something the user possesses. This could include a disk, token, or unique card. A two-factor authentication might be used to control the access to individual offices within a floor, whereas a password might allow access to common areas on a building. Additionally, a three-factor authentication is possible using a technique termed *biometrics*. This technique includes something personal, such as a fingerprint or retina scan. Biometric techniques are described further in a subsequent chapter.

The password process can be compromised by the following activities:

- Sticky notes containing the password on the front of the display.
- Discovery of the password because it is too simple.
- Password sent in plain text across the network and monitored.

The most common security problem comes from having passwords written down and kept in close proximity to a terminal. An off-hours maintenance or cleaning person could easily discover and copy the information or log on to a system and gain access to a database. Do not assume these people are not knowledgeable; they could be computer science students working their way through college. Remember that most computer system compromises are made by internal people.

A method to prevent the unauthorized use of an intercepted password is to prevent it from being reused. One-time password systems require a new password for each session. These systems relieve the user of the difficulty of always choosing a new password for the next session by automatically generating a list of acceptable passwords for the user.

Many networks require that users change passwords on some periodic basis. **TABLE 4-1** shows samples of valid and invalid passwords. Note that the valid passwords are case sensitive, which allows for a larger number of combinations.

The next issue that must be addressed is the receipt of suspect e-mails. As discussed in Chapter 3, e-mails can be major threats to individuals and organizations.

Fraudulent E-Mails and Letters

Network users frequently receive unsolicited correspondence either in hard-copy letters or as e-mails. Such trash mail should not be answered without due diligence. Businesses and individuals need to be on their guard against a surge in fraudulent letters and e-mails promising large cash payouts in exchange for a small up-front investment. Churches and charities have also been targeted.

Recent successes in combating fraud have forced a change of tactics by the organized criminals behind it. This fraud follows a recognizable pattern. A business or individual receives

TABLE 4-1 Valid and Invalid Passwords

Valid Passwords	Invalid Passwords
Q1wT2p3D (random, alphanumeric, upper/lowercase)	administrator
iAm42YoT (I am 42 years old today, upper/lowercase)	Robert
WySiWyG! (what you see is what you get, upper/ lowercase, special character)	12345678

a letter, fax, or e-mail from an "official" allegedly in a foreign government or agency. An offer is made to transfer millions of dollars (for reasons including paper currency conversion, real estate ventures, business investment, a legacy, or simple fraud) into a personal bank account. Targets are encouraged to travel overseas to complete the transaction and are sent documents with official-looking seals and logos testifying to the proposal's authenticity. Throughout the fraud, the targets are asked to provide advance fees for taxes, legal fees, transaction fees, or bribes. There are actually victims of this fraud!

PHYSICAL PROPERTY SECURITY

Physical security is the most time-consuming and expensive effort when protecting network and computer assets. The scope of physical security is vastly different for the individual as opposed to educational, governmental, public service, or business operations. This issue will be addressed in two separate sections. The first section addresses the physical security for individual users; the second section addresses security for the larger data center operations. Security for individual users is straightforward, but protection of data center assets and resources is very involved.

Physical Security for the Individual Computer and Network User

Physical security is generally oriented toward keeping the computer and network user safe and protecting the assets and resources of the individual. The primary assets are the data and information possessed by the computer and network user. Both can be compromised by a theft of the computing device or the storage media. There are a number of proactive steps that can be taken to ameliorate this situation. Protection of personal property and work-related property is often inextricably commingled.

Personal financial security can be compromised if a computing device is stolen. It is likely that computer users have stored personal information on their laptops or PDAs that would allow someone to commit identity theft or fraud. It is essential that everyone treat their computing devices as they would treat a wallet or purse. Property theft, such as burglary, and carelessness, such as leaving computing devices unattended in public places, can compromise the computer owners.

The workplace is also not a safe place to leave a portable computing device unattended. Business travel provides another opportunity to lose a laptop to a thief. Public transportation systems provide the criminal with many opportunities to steal electronic devices. Individuals should also be aware that many nonemployees exist in the workplace. These could include partners, contractors, suppliers, maintenance workers, delivery personnel, and visitors.

With the advent of numerous wireless electronic products, criminals have another opportunity to steal a user's property and identity. Many of these new wireless products are small and easy to conceal, making them easy targets for the casual thief or criminal element. There also implications for the business community, because small storage media devices are easily concealed, making the theft of corporate information an issue. These devices could include PDAs, cell phones, BlackBerrys, and so on.

Personal physical security is usually just common sense and costs very little to implement. In today's environment, it is essential to take care with any computer asset. This is an individual requirement, and users must take personal responsibility. Several primary considerations include the following:

- Keep portable equipment, such as laptop computers, out of sight in locked desks, cabinets, rooms, or automobiles when not in use.
- Clearly and permanently mark computer devices with identification to deter theft and improve chances of recovery if stolen.
- Photographs of any computer device will assist with potential insurance claims.
- Make a concerted effort to keep track of flash drives and other storage media.

Physical Security for the Data Center

Physical security is the term used to describe protection provided outside the computer and networking system. Typical physical security components are guards, locks, fences, sensors, and cameras to deter direct attacks. Many physical security measures are the result of commonsense thinking and planning and are often obvious solutions. Sources that can compromise an organization's ability to function include:

- Natural events.
- Human vandals.
- Power loss.
- Fire and water.
- Heat and humidity levels.

These physical vulnerabilities to security can and often do occur simultaneously. Issues to be considered include the cost of replacing the resource, the speed with which equipment can be replaced, the need for available backup computing power, and the cost or difficulty of replacing operating systems and application software.

The physical element of computer and network security involves the hardware, the facility, cable runs, and the software and database systems that reside in the physical location. An initial step when evaluating physical security is to conduct an audit that looks at all the elements that comprise the organization's computer environment that must be protected. This document takes the form of a baseline. The Enterprise Systems Security Review in Appendix A is a vehicle for accomplishing this task. Analyzing the results of this audit can reveal shortcomings in the organization's physical environment. Chapter 9 addresses contingency planning and disaster recovery processes.

How easy is it for someone to access sensitive hardware components and software and database storage devices? It is essential to note that in today's distributed and e-commerce environment, a number of physical threats can be located at remote branches and locations. Devices that can be an access point for attackers include remote terminals, communications controllers, multiplexers, servers, printers, and PCs. Also included are cable runs and network demarcation points, which can be a source of eavesdropping and monitoring.

Physical Security for the Database and Storage Devices

Data center management must have a plan for a data center disaster that involves the physical storage devices and the resident database system and files. Of particular interest is a formal program that addresses database backup processes and storage. There are a number of procedures required for the integrity and protection of the database system and physical data storage devices. Because large data centers house a significant number of mass-storage devices, it is essential that off-site drives must be available in the event of some local disaster or incident. There are a number of companies that offer this service of off-site computer system physical device components. Details are provided in Chapter 9 concerning continuity and disaster recovery planning.

PREVENTING DAMAGE TO PHYSICAL ASSETS

Physical security issues cover a broad spectrum of possibilities, which include natural disasters, vandals and destructive individuals, fire and water damage, power loss, and heat and humidity. This section provides an overview of each situation and discusses possible ways to mitigate the cost of such an occurrence.

The organization cannot function without the physical assets that include computer systems and networking systems. In many cases, the database asset that resides on the computer system is the company or organization. Several good examples include the records that are located on the databases of the Social Security Administration, the Internal Revenue Service, stock exchanges, Internet service providers, law enforcement, health care, and the airlines. This section suggests precautions that can be taken to prevent or minimize damage from the disasters discussed in the previous section. Appendix A provides a security review checklist template that can be used as a basis for a facility audit.

Fire Hazards

Fire hazards can be internal or external, with the former the most controllable. An external hazard results when the building is vulnerable to combustion from a fire in the surrounding area, or when the organization is a tenant in a larger building complex and a fire starts in some other part of the building. External fires can be started by hazards ranging from a smoker's carelessness to faulty wiring. The computer and telecommunications systems are assets that must be protected with a fire suppression system. If an external hazard exists, the solution is to cure it or move.

The most controllable fire is one that is localized in an equipment room or demarcation closet. Removing the cause of combustion and combustible materials or using fire suppression systems controls hazards. The first line of attack is good housekeeping, which means removing debris or flammable liquids from the area. Ensure that cleaning fluids and flammable liquids are stored in fireproof cabinets outside the asset area.

There should be some form of fire suppression device or system that provides coverage for the computer and networking assets. Fire codes should be observed and monitored. Proper fire extinguishers must be located throughout the area in easily accessible reach. Personnel must be provided with information on how to use the extinguishers.

The local fire department must be made aware of the critical nature of the computer and networking facilities. They must be informed of the location of the major electronic components so they can take precautions to prevent damage in the event there is a fire alarm. Water damage by the fire department can be a disaster. All equipment rooms must be equipped with smoke detectors and fire alarms that can communicate with a central monitoring operation.

A fire alarm system is an active fire protection system that detects fire, or the effects of fire, and as a result does one or more of the following:

- Notifies the occupants.
- Notifies persons in the surrounding area.
- Summons the fire service.
- Controls all the fire alarm components in a building.

Fire alarm systems can include alarm-initiating devices, alarm notification appliances, control units, fire safety control devices, enunciators, power supplies, and wiring.

Water Damage

One of the most common causes of **water damage** is from overhead sprinkler systems within the facility and runoff from other floors. Another common hazard is from ruptured pipes that can flood equipment rooms. Overhead sprinkler systems should not be installed over sensitive electronic equipment. Other alternatives should be pursued that do not cause damage to the circuit cards. If sprinklers are used for equipment room fire suppression, they should consist of high-temperature heads. They should also not be allowed to activate from a fire in another section of the building that poses no hazard to the equipment rooms.

Flooding is the other source of water damage to electronics. If possible, equipment rooms should not be located below ground level, even in areas that are not subject to flooding. Ruptured water mains and stopped-up drains can cause localized flooding. If the building is located in a flood plain, install the equipment above the high-water mark. Even though the building might be closed during flooding, the electronics can remain dry. There is a real-world example of this situation, where a network carrier's central office had equipment located below a high-water mark and the unexpected happened—water backed up through a drain and flooded the electronics, which cost an enormous amount to repair.

Earthquake Damage

It is not possible to prevent an earthquake and difficult to eliminate **earthquake damage**, so management must decide if the risk is minor. If the facility is located in a high-risk earthquake zone, damage can be limited, provided the building survives. If the building is earthquake-proofed, the equipment should be braced to prevent tipping. It should also be bolted to some major support to reduce movement. There is also the danger of secondary damage from fire and water during an earthquake. Water pipes should not be in the vicinity of equipment rooms in earthquake-prone areas. A damper system might be required.

Storm Damage

Hurricanes, tornadoes, snowstorms, and windstorms can cause severe **storm damage**, but usually only to outside facilities. Structures affected usually include antennas, dishes, towers, and overhead wiring. Most companies with outside plant facilities are installing them underground, so this issue should soon be moot. Microwave and other antennas should be braced to withstand maximum expected wind velocities. They should also be equipped with de-icing equipment when appropriate. Pedestals and wiring vaults are candidates for flooding and forest fires, but they must be located close to media aggregation.

Human-Initiated Damage

Humans cause a high percentage of outages and damage, which can be accidental or deliberate. The incidents range from simple work errors or sloppy work to deliberate sabotage, caused by disgruntled employees. Vandals, competitors, or real saboteurs can also cause destruction. All telecommunications areas, computer rooms, and networking facilities must be kept secure from unauthorized access. The most effective access control method is a card-operated or PIN-activated lock that allows access to authorized people and maintains a record of the event. With this method, it is easy to control access and to determine who was in the area at the time of failure. Good records are essential for recovering from damage. Equipment location, inventory, and configuration records should be kept where they are readily available to anyone restoring service. Contingency and disaster recovery planning are major initiatives required in all computer installations. These processes are discussed in Chapter 9.

In today's post–9/11 environment, another issue has emerged: the terrorist threat. Terrorists do not share the values of civilized states. How can educational, commercial, and governmental administrators protect against such a threat? Implementation of access controls for physical and database systems is a good start. Awareness and education are also major keys. Administrators cannot become complacent. Terrorists may select high-profile targets in a large metropolitan area or some small operation in the hinterland.

PHYSICAL SECURITY CONTROLS

Physical security controls pertain to the physical infrastructure, physical device security, and physical access. The physical infrastructure includes the facilities that house the systems and the networks that are used to access these same assets. The physical network infrastructure encompasses both the selection of the appropriate media type and the path of the physical cabling. It is essential that no intruder is able to eavesdrop on the data traversing the network and that all critical systems have a high degree of availability.

Network Access

Telecommunications access adds another dimension to security because data can be accessed from terminals outside the computer room. A number of questions arise concerning **network access**:

- How is the terminal/computer user identified?
- Is this user authorized to access the computer?
- What operations can this user execute?
- Are the communication lines being monitored or sniffed?

Access control techniques include having a unique identification code for each user and a password to protect against these situations. Users must be required to log on to the network, and this information must be automatically recorded in a central database so that a record can be maintained of all network activities. When someone tries to log on unsuccessfully a number of times, the user's ability to log on should be disabled. This log on failure should invoke a log entry and notification of a security administrator. A supervisor, who could authorize a new password, may approve reactivation of this user.

Dial-up lines are especially vulnerable to unauthorized access. The most common security techniques used with dial-up circuits are *callback* and *handshake*. With callback, the user dials the computer and provides identification; then the computer breaks the connection and dials the user back at a predetermined number that is obtained from the database. The disadvantage is it does not work well with traveling employees who would not be at a predetermined location. The handshake technique requires a terminal with special hardware circuitry. The computer sends a special control sequence to the terminal, and the terminal identifies itself to the computer. This technique ensures that only authorized terminals access the computer; however, it does not regulate the user of the terminal.

Media Access

The provisions of network management should be utilized to ensure the highest level of network access. From a security point of view, the type of media chosen for various parts of the network can depend on the sensitivity of the information that traverses it. The most common **media access** types used in networking infrastructures are coaxial cable (coax), twisted-pair copper, and optical fiber. Unlike copper or coax, optical fiber does not radiate any energy, which provides a high degree of security against eavesdropping. Fiber is also much more difficult to tap into than copper or coaxial cables. The heat-fused cladding of multi-mode graded index and single-mode cable makes them practically impossible to tap. Even if a tap occurs, it can be detected, because the match on the fiber-optic cable must be perfect for light transmission without disruptions.

Wiretaps can sometimes be detected by using tools to measure attenuation (reduction of signal strength) on the cable. These devices are normally used to measure signal attenuation and installed cable length; however, an experienced technician can use it to locate wiretaps. It should be noted that an expert intruder can insert a tap so that it not easily detectable by either device. It is a good practice to take an initial baseline signal level of the physical cable infrastructure and periodically verify the integrity of the entire physical cable plant. Creating a baseline is part of enterprise security management.

The physical path of the media, which is part of the network topography, is an issue that must be addressed to ensure availability of the network and its devices. It is imperative to have a structured cabling system that minimizes the risk of downtime. The cable infrastructure must be well secured to prevent unauthorized access. There are International Telecommunications

Union recommendations that provide specifications and recommendations for the construction, installation, and protection of cable plants.

In the case of access to a controlled environment, such as a computer room or network wiring closet, a restrictive set of access rules should apply. Organizational site guidelines must be developed and implemented to restrict access for cabling to these areas by controlling access to cable trays and overhead cable support systems. Approved methods and access points must be established prior to cable routing and installation. The security system to the area can vary from simple lockable cable feeder openings to dedicated individual fiber and cable runs, each with alarm-equipped access covers and video surveillance. The common areas of exposure when addressing cable security include:

- Cable trays in the crawl space under raised floors.
- Wall-mounted wiring access.
- Overhead cable and wire trays.

Wired local area network (LAN) connectivity occurs where cabling terminates in a centrally located wiring closet. There may be a patch panel in the wiring closet that provides for the interconnection between the wide area network (WAN) circuits and the LAN components. There may also be wiring between a terminal server or communications server and the patch panel. The wiring closet is a major point of vulnerability and must be afforded a high level of security.

Data and Information Security

Data and information stored in databases on hardware storage devices is a priority for security administrators. The online environment of e-commerce activities requires that database assets and resources be assigned a very high security priority. Often the data resources are the company, and the loss or corruption of these assets could spell doom for the organization. Large organizations store data and information on assets called "disk farms," whereas personal laptop users and small computer systems usually use internal hard drives for storage. Considerable funds are allocated to protecting these disk farms, and access is restricted to a limited number of computer operations personnel. Additional details on disaster recovery of database resources are presented in Chapter 9.

Device Security

Device security includes identifying the location of devices, limiting physical access, and the installation of environmental safeguards. All network infrastructure equipment should be physically located in restricted access areas. This means creating a secure space for wiring closets that contain switches, firewalls, modems, Data Service Units, and routers. It is essential that this equipment closet be well secured; however do not forget that intruders can enter through a ceiling opening. This network closet is sometimes called a demarcation point, where all the telephone facilities enter the building. This is an excellent place for an intruder to place a monitor for eavesdropping on all of the organization's network traffic.

Any device with a physical connection is a potential candidate for illegal access. This could include LAN connectivity devices such as repeaters, hubs, and switches. The potential increases if shielded twisted pair (STP) or unshielded twisted pair (UTP) cabling is utilized.

Infrastructure equipment includes more than networking equipment, which must be protected. Other sensitive components of the infrastructure include numerous servers, gateways, and administration terminals. Print servers, terminal servers, file servers, and domain name servers must all be afforded a high level of security and should not be available to the general staff. Consoles and administrative terminals must be secured from the general staff and all other unauthorized personnel, because these devices provide access into the secured infrastructure of the organization.

Often overlooked is the output from the office printer or fax machine. These devices are usually centrally located for the convenience of the staff. This is a good place to look for confidential information, so do not overlook its importance as a candidate for protection. It might be necessary to utilize a shredder and not allow any whole pages out of the facility. Do not forget that there are dumpster divers waiting for someone to dispose of confidential material that can be used for some illegal activity.

Physical Access Security

As mentioned earlier, wiring closets and rooms that house infrastructure devices and networking facilities must be secured from unauthorized people. These areas should be in the interior of an organization's operation. It is necessary to ensure that the exterior access is also protected, which usually addresses control of nonemployees and employees alike. A guard station is usually the method employed for controlling exterior access for many organizations. This means that a process has been developed that includes employee identification and authorization, which determines the access level of the individual.

Part of **physical access** security policies and procedures must address contract personnel, maintenance personnel, temporaries, and others who do not possess unrestricted access. These people may be required to be in controlled area, but they must be escorted by an authorized employee or must sign in before entering the controlled area. Identification cards may be required if these are very sensitive areas. The larger the organization, the more important these measures become, because many employees may not even know who works in the organization.

To ensure enforceable physical security, it is essential to make sure that the employees' work areas mesh well with access restrictions. This includes the flow of personnel within an organization's premises. It is easy for an employee to leave a door chocked instead of locking and unlocking it many times a day. Installing an alarm that will sound when a door is left open can eliminate this type of situation. Employee aggravation will be the result if a logical and workable security plan is not developed without considering the daily workflow.

Many organizations host both visitors and personnel from other departments. Access must be afforded these people on a temporary basis but should be located in a controlled area away from sensitive operations. Sign-ins and temporary identification should also be required of these visitors. Biometric access techniques are described in Chapter 6.

Personnel Security

It is essential that personnel in sensitive positions be screened to ensure their integrity. This process should not be an afterthought and must be part of corporate policy. **Personnel security** involves using one or more of the following techniques:

- Security and background screening of prospective employees before hiring.
- An active security awareness program emphasizing security issues and ramifications.
- Training of employees regarding security issues and their responsibilities.
- Identification of employees, contractors, and maintenance workers.
- Error prevention techniques to detect accidental mistakes and malicious activities.

Customer Security

Physical computer and networking assets may be protected inside a building or may be in a public area. These devices can include ATMs and cash-dispensing machines. **Customer security** has become an issue in commercial areas and at ATM locations. There has been a rising crime rate against these devices and against the customers who use them. Robberies occur shortly after customers withdraw money from an ATM or criminals assault ATM customers and force them to withdraw funds. Physical violence is often part of these attacks. A legal question has arisen as to how far a bank must go to protect ATM customers. The location of these devices and the time of day the transactions occur have an enormous impact on the security realized. Many banks are providing video monitoring and lighting systems; however, these initiatives are no solace to the customer being attacked. Banks do not accept responsibility for these crimes and say consumers bear part of the risk when they use these machines late at night. These situations exemplify the type of societal problems that can and will occur as communications systems become more widely used by the general public. Kiosks are a new issue for the security department. These devices are often installed in shopping malls and transportation centers and provide a number of financial and ticketing services.

Visitor Security

Many organizations schedule tours of their facilities. Hopefully, these visitors are not allowed any access to computer and network components. Visitors can accidentally and on purpose cause a considerable amount of damage to an organization's assets and resources. Company secrets can also be compromised by competitors and saboteurs acting as visitors. Minors can be exceptionally destructive. Rules and procedures should be developed for non-business individuals if tours are going to be allowed. Someone in the organization should be designated as the tour guide.

CHAPTER SUMMARY

Property theft can occur in any setting, including at home, work, or school and on vacations. These crimes might be planned by a professional thief or could be crimes of opportunity. The computer user must be vigilant at all times and pay attention to the security of electronic devices. Security of personal property is most vulnerable during holidays and vacations at educational institutions.

Theft of a cell phone, PDA, or laptop could lead to identity theft and fraud. Don't overlook the media where data are stored. A CD or flash drive might be as good a target as stealing the entire electronic device—and much easier to conceal. This situation could compromise an employee's organization and then employment status.

There are many activities that the computer user can initiate to protect electronic computing devices. These include the use of tie-down devices to secure computer equipment when practical and appropriate to do so. Users must keep portable equipment, such as laptop computers, out of sight in locked desks, cabinets, rooms, and automobiles when not in use. Users must also clearly and permanently mark computer equipment with agency identification to deter theft and improve chances of recovery if stolen.

Organizations can initiate administrative policies for protection of computer assets. All employees should be made aware of the policies governing the use of the organization's computer resources. Efforts might include establishing a computer user policy that includes theft prevention information for employees. Access must be controlled to all computer and server areas; room and building keys should be made available only to those individuals who really need them.

Management must increase employee awareness of the possibility of theft and place receptionists, security guards, or surveillance monitors near entrance doors. Intrusion alarms must be deployed for buildings, work areas, or rooms to provide video surveillance for equipment labs and building entrances.

Physical security issues cover a broad spectrum of possibilities, which include natural disasters, vandals and destructive individuals, fire and water damage, power loss, and heat and humidity. These issues can be just as devastating as the loss of the asset or resource to theft.

KEY TERMS

burglaries	housing security	physical access
customer security	Kensington security lock	physical security
device security	media access	property theft
earthquake damage	network access	storm damage
fire hazards	password	water damage
flooding	personnel security	

SECURITY REVIEW QUESTIONS

1. Why is the theft of laptops a large issue?
2. How can students protect their computing assets?
3. Summarize the list of guidelines for password management.
4. List several actions that can be taken for the recovery of stolen items.
5. What are typical security precautions for business data centers?
6. What are the issues of water and physical security?
7. Identify the various categories of problems that can occur with business data centers.
8. Discuss the security issues of media access.
9. Identify four questions that may arise concerning network access.
10. How can management ensure that employees are not part of the security problem?

RESEARCH ACTIVITIES

1. Provide an overview of current computer and network security products.
2. Research the subject of computer theft in educational institutions.
3. Develop a report concerning the theft of computing devices in the industry.
4. Research the issue of the cost of criminal activities relating to the Web.
5. Identify studies that show the costs of doing business over the Internet.
6. Search the Web for policies concerning Internet security.
7. Research and report on computer-use policies for educational facilities.
8. Provide an overview of the Kensington security device.
9. Attempt to find the hacker password file on the Web.
10. Search for the hacker logon database on the Web.
11. Research the Web for articles relating to physical data center security.
12. Identify the major database hardware and software security tools for physical sites.

PART TWO
COMPUTER SYSTEMS
AND NETWORKS

CHAPTER 5

The Internet and
Web Network Environment

🔒 CHAPTER CONTENTS

- Identify components of the global network environment.
- Identify the uses and advantages of a virtual private network.
- Identify the numerous threats that inhabit the Internet and Web.
- Identify the various network security issues.
- Learn the difference among the Internet, extranets, and intranets.

INTRODUCTION

Organizations, academic institutions, government agencies, and individuals have expanded their use of personal computers, laptop computers, personal digital assistants (PDAs), wireless communication devices, and individual computer workstations to support the information needs of users throughout an organization's network. Today's organizations use small computers for word processing, order processing, messaging, sales reporting, financial analysis, engineering, and many other applications in support of the enterprise's mission. As the use of small computers has grown, so has the need for these computing devices to communicate—both with each other and with a centralized enterprise mainframe computer or client/server system.

Historically, small computing devices were often used in a stand-alone manner to support applications that were local in nature. The data were often stored on the device's hard drive or available on a removable storage medium such as a floppy disk or CD. With the advent of the client/server environment, local storage media might consist of hard drives, CDs, USB storage devices, or individual flash drives. Security for these distributed assets is a major concern.

This chapter provides the reader with a basic understanding of the networking topics involved in the access and use of the Internet and its associated Web components. Topics include information concerning the wide area network, local area networks, and virtual private networks. While the author has attempted to present the relevant facts in layman's terms, some technical terms and information are required for an understanding of the topics. Security terms and definitions are presented the first time they are discussed. They are also incorporated into the Glossary. Many terms can be researched on sites such as *pcwebopedia.com*, *whatis.com*, and *wikipedia.org*. Readers should be aware that contributions to these Web sites are received from numerous sources and need to be collaborated for accuracy and completeness.

There are unlimited opportunities for intruders to cause havoc with both personal and business computer assets and resources. Of particular interest are the numerous opportunities for network intruders waiting to access network and data resources. Efforts are made to provide the reader with an insight into the various malicious activities employed on the Web. Readers should be concerned for the integrity and security of their network assets after reading this chapter.

THE INTERNET

The Internet, sometimes called simply "the Net" or "the Web," is a worldwide system of computer networks—a network of networks in which users at any one computer can, if they have permission, get information from any other computer. Today, the Internet is a public, cooperative, and self-sustaining facility accessible to hundreds of millions of people worldwide. Physically, the Internet uses a portion of the total resources of the currently existing public telecommunications networks. Technically, what distinguishes the Internet is its use of a set of protocols called transmission control protocol/internet protocol (TCP/IP). Two recent adaptations of Internet technology—the intranet and the extranet—also make use of the TCP/IP suite. Many private and public computer systems have a requirement to communicate with each other, and this function is accomplished via a wide area global network system.

To understand the issues, it is essential that the reader have a general understanding of the operating environment of the Internet. This section provides an overview of the various hardware, software, and network components that play a part in the security of the Internet environment. Efforts have been made to make this understandable to all levels of expertise.

The use of the Internet for both business and personal activities in our daily life has brought with it an element of risk for its many users. With the Internet's ease of access and its ubiquitous nature, the opportunity for its exploitation is not surprising. Everyday news items advise of theft of database information, theft of personal identity information, and the Internet being used to defraud someone. Computer fraud and cybercrimes are on the rise. What can the individual user do to protect against the possibility of being a victim to cybercrime? The first step is education! This book addresses the major issues and situations and provides the reader with a general working knowledge of the environment along with numerous suggestions of how to become a more knowledgeable Internet user. Threats and solutions that are specific to four major groups are identified: home/personal, business/commercial, student, and traveler. Some of the threats cut across these groups; however, some are specific to one group. Basically, the user needs to practice "safe Internet."

Information is presented so that students and the general public are able to use it in their everyday interactions with the Internet. Sections are specifically oriented toward commercial or business applications; these sections, however, are not highly technical. Security efforts must be directed toward network, hardware, and software issues. Protection of hardware is possibly the easiest to accomplish. Equipment located at a secure central location is fairly easy to protect and maintain. Software is another issue. Software used to be fairly simple; in today's environment, though, it is exceedingly complex. If software is complex, then the network is several orders of magnitude more difficult to manage. Because network users can access computer facilities from anywhere in the world, and even from space, this task is the most complex of all from a security standpoint. Efforts to make the net reachable from all airplanes are moving forward.

Wide Area Networks

A **wide area network (WAN)** is a group of geographically dispersed networks, data devices, or local networks that can communicate with each other from different cities, different roaming zones, different states, different carriers, and different countries. Its primary function is to tie together users who are widely separated geographically. Many of today's networks employ public telecommunications facilities to provide users with access to the resources of centrally located computer complexes and to permit fast interchange of information among users. Intelligent terminals, personal computers, workstations, minicomputers, and other forms of programmable devices are all part of these large networks. Communication among the various entities and organizations are completed over network media paths that consist of copper wires, coaxial cable, fiber optics, waveguide, and radio path. Each of these media offers different opportunities for security violations. An overview of the technologies that utilize these media, and the associated security issues, is presented in subsequent sections.

Many networks, installed in computer centers, use a number of public telecommunications facilities, which allow an organization's computer resources to communicate over long distances. These networks might be used to provide all users at remote locations access to the resources maintained in a centrally located computer complex. Wide area networks use telephone lines to connect businesses that are separated by long distances. For example, a warehouse in Chicago, connected to its regional sales office in Atlanta by a telephone, is a WAN connection. A WAN is not confined to a limited geographical area, and various connection configurations are available. Selection of an appropriate WAN connection depends on factors such as quality of service needed, speed, price, compatibility with the current computer systems at any given location, and the amount of traffic between locations. The types of WAN services and technologies available include:

- Digital subscriber line (DSL) services.
- Wireless and personal computer services (PCS).
- T-1 (1.544 Mbps).
- Cable modem.
- Dial-up, 56 kbps.
- Broadband.
- Private/leased lines.

WAN Access

Communication circuits are connected between telephone company network buildings and the users' or customers' physical locations. A wiring closet or other areas in which network components are installed in a user location is a potential source of network vulnerability. Because WAN circuits terminate in these locations where local area network (LAN) cabling may also terminate, there is ample opportunity for an intruder to gain access to both the LAN and WAN resources at this single point. The wiring closet often houses a patch panel and/or a punch-down block where physical cabling connections are terminated. If uncontrolled access is allowed, eavesdropping and monitoring can occur without the knowledge of the users.

The WAN **demarcation point** in the wiring closet is often in close proximity to the network communication equipment room. This area may house the various data communication devices that provide connectivity between the LAN and the WAN. Both the wiring closet and the equipment room must be secured against all unauthorized access. This security could include locks, pass cards, biometrics, and cameras.

The telephone company also has a demarcation point at the customer's physical site. It is usually on the outside of the facility and is connected to another demarcation point near the street right-of-way via some type of cable. This demarcation point is usually called a *pedestal*. Graphically, these components are usually part of the network cloud.

NETWORK ACCESS COMMUNICATION DEVICES

There are a number of communication devices that are deployed in network topologies. These include modems, data service units (DSUs), splitters, wireless interface cards, and network terminations. Readers should understand the functions of these devices as they provide the interfaces to the various communication networks. The most likely device to compromise a network is the modem. The modem is the device of choice for **Internet service provider (ISP)** access. The ISP provides the vital link between the user and the Internet. Wireless devices use a wireless access point for connectivity. **FIGURE 5-1** provides a logical view of this access. Individual users can access the ISP from wireless and wired devices via network facilities.

Modem

The four basic elements of a data communications system are a transmitter, a receiver, a transmission medium, and communications equipment. **FIGURE 5-2** provides a logical view of these basic elements. A **modem** (which means modulator/demodulator) is a data communication

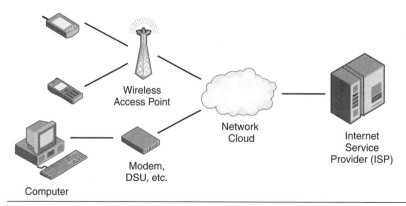

FIGURE 5-1 Wireless Access Point to an ISP

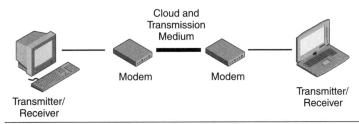

FIGURE 5-2 Communication System Elements

equipment device that modulates and demodulates signals (performs analog to digital conversion). The modem provides an interface between digital devices and network analog circuits and equipment. Modems are designed for different applications and are available in a number of configurations and speeds. Many PCs are currently being shipped with a 56 kbps (56,000 bits per second) modem card for Internet access. The use of modems in business operations should be regulated and monitored for potential security violations.

The standard interface for connecting external modems to computers is called RS-232. Consequently, any external modem can be attached to any computer that has an RS-232 port, which almost all personal computers possess. There are also modems that come as an expansion board you can insert into a vacant computer expansion slot. These are sometimes called *onboard* or *internal* modems. The individual user often only sees the telephone wire jack in the back of the computing device. A cable with RJ11 (four wires) plugs is attached between the computing device and the telephone wall jack.

Most modems have built-in support for the more common protocols, and most modems can communicate with each other. A *communication protocol* is generally defined as a set of rules that govern transmissions between hardware and software components. At high transmission speeds, however, the protocols are less standardized. Aside from the transmission protocols that they support, the characteristics that distinguish one modem from another include speed in bits per second, whether it can operate using voice or data, if it can auto-answer a call, if it can transmit and receive faxes, and if it uses data compression or encryption. Some modems possess a secondary communications channel that allows for network management capabilities.

Modem and Access Server Considerations

Business users should not be allowed to install a modem, even temporarily, without proper authorization. Dial-up access through a modem is a good way to compromise the organization's network. All modem access should be logged and monitored on a regular basis. It would also be a good idea to require one-time passwords when using a dial-up access. It would also be helpful if there was a single dial-in point into a modem pool so that all users could be authenticated by the same method.

A different complement of modems should be used for any dial-out services, and both dial-in and dial-out services should be authenticated. If modems and access servers support callback, then it should be activated. With **callback**, after a user dials in and is authenticated, the system disconnects the call and calls back on the specified telephone number. This provides a level of security because the system calls back the actual user, not a hacker who might be masquerading as the user. As with a number of security mechanisms, callback can also be compromised.

Nonsecure modems provide one of the easiest ways to illegally enter a network. To locate these modems, attackers can employ war dialing, which is a technique that dials different telephone numbers repeatedly looking for modem carrier tones. For war dialing, attackers use telephone number ranges found on a number of sources, including Web sites and newsgroups. After discovering modems, the attackers look for systems without passwords.

Modems and access servers should be carefully configured and protected from intruders who might reconfigure them. Modems should be programmed to reset to the standard configuration at the beginning and ending of each call, and modems and access servers should terminate calls cleanly. Servers should force a logout if the user hangs up unexpectedly.

DSU

The **data service unit (DSU)** is a device that connects a terminal to a digital line. The DSU is a device that performs protective and diagnostic functions for a telecommunications line. This device is basically a very high-powered and expensive modem. Such a device is required for both ends of a digital connection, and the units at both ends must be set to the same communications standard. Common speeds range from 56 kbps to 44.736 Mbps. This device is usually not a security issue because it is connected to a private communication line.

Splitter/DSLAM

Digital subscriber line (DSL) technologies use sophisticated modulation schemes to pack data onto copper wires. They are sometimes referred to as *last-mile technologies* because they are used only for connections from a telephone switching station to a home or office, not between switching stations. When the telephone company receives a DSL signal, the modem with a frequency **splitter** detects voice calls and data. Voice calls are sent to the telephone devices, and data are sent to the computer devices and vice versa. The physical splitter device is often located where the telephone cable enters the home or premise. This is called the demarcation point. The cabling on the user's side of the demarcation point is normally the responsibility of the computer user. There is a distance limitation (usually three miles) between the user and the local central office for the splitter to operate properly. The device located at the central office is called a digital subscriber line access multiplexer (DSLAM).

Wireless Network Interface Card

A **wireless network interface controller (WNIC)** is a network card that connects to a radio-based computer network, unlike a regular network interface controller (NIC), which connects to a wire-based network such as Ethernet LAN. This card uses an antenna to communicate through microwaves. A WNIC in a desktop computer may be located in the peripheral component interconnect (PCI) slot; however, newer models incorporate the WNIC into the computing device. In an infrastructure mode network, the WNIC needs an access point.

All data are transferred using the service access point (SAP). All wireless nodes in an infrastructure mode network connect to an access point. The SAP controls wireless devices and is a bridge between the main wired LAN and the wireless LAN.

All nodes connecting to the access point must have the same service set identifier (SSID) as the access point.

WORLD WIDE WEB (WWW), AKA THE WEB

Today, the **World Wide Web (WWW)**, or the Web, is the premier application for most Internet users. The Web is a collection of servers accessed via the Internet that offer graphical or multimedia presentations about an organization's ideas, products, personnel, or services. Web browsers integrate e-mail and newsreaders and support an increasingly interactive, visual, and even animated interface to the Internet. Companies wishing to use the Web as a marketing tool establish a Web site on the Internet to publicize the address of that location. The Web site and Web server presentation design, implementation, and management can be done in-house or be contracted out to a professional Web site development and management service. Most access for personal use is via an Internet service provider.

Almost any of the current data processing and data communications applications are candidates to ride the Internet. Some major application areas are as follows:

- Customer service.
- Distance learning.
- Electronic commerce.
- Internet access.
- Telemarketing.
- Web design.
- Web hosting.

Reasons people use the Web include the following:

- Browsing.
- Business.
- Chatting socially with other Web users.
- Entertainment.

Virtually all classes of businesses can use the Internet in the following ways.

- Advertising via Web pages and e-mail.
- Communicating via e-mail.
- Providing travel services.
- Providing reference materials.
- Selling goods and services.
- Selling stocks or other financial instruments.
- Transferring documents via electronic data interchange (EDI).

Web Threats

Web threats can be categorized as either active or passive. *Active* attacks include impersonating another user, altering messages in transit between client and server, and altering information on a Web site. *Passive* attacks include eavesdropping on network traffic between browser and server and gaining information on a Web site that is normally restricted.

Web threats can also be grouped according to threat location, whether it involves a Web server, Web browser, or network traffic between the browser and server. Issues of server and browser security are the purview of computer system security, whereas issues of traffic security are part of network security. **TABLE 5-1** provides a summary of security threats pervasive in the Web environment.

TABLE 5-1 Summary of Web Threats

	Threats	**Consequences**	**Countermeasures**
Authentication	User impersonation Data forgery	Misrepresentation of user Belief that false information is valid	Cryptographic techniques
Confidentiality	Eavesdropping Server info theft Client data theft Client/server connection information Network configuration information	Information loss Privacy loss	Encryption Web proxies
Denial of service	Killing user threads Flooding with bogus requests Filling up disk or memory DSN attacks	Annoying Disruptive Prevent user productivity	Difficult to prevent
Integrity	User data modification Trojan horse browser Memory modification Message modification in transit	Loss of information Compromise of machine Vulnerability to all other threats	Cryptographic checksums

INTRANET AND EXTRANET NETWORKS

Historically, computer systems were self-contained entities located at a central location. A network did not exist, which meant security from remote access was not a major issue. Protection of the system was straightforward—controls were added on the centrally located hardware and software. With the proliferation of distributed computer systems, which are accessible by various types of communications networks, the security task has become much more complex.

Networks are now being implemented to support remote access, which was historically outside the corporation or organization. Access to the Internet has gained wide acceptability. An **extranet** provides an access path for contractors and suppliers to components of the local computer system resources. Corporate users are communicating over an **intranet**. The differences between intranets and extranets are subtle, but they are significant from a security standpoint. An intranet is an internal network that implements Internet and Web technologies. Contrast this with an extranet, which is an intranet extended outside the organization to a business partner, with transmissions moving over the Internet or across private facilities. **TABLE 5-2** compares attributes of the Internet with those of an intranet and extranet. The interconnection of networks may be one of the most important factors for future business successes, but it has the potential for the greatest security risks. Intranets and extranets are being utilized as vehicles to complete electronic commerce transactions. There are serious ramifications for financial applications utilizing networks that interface with the Internet.

VIRTUAL PRIVATE NETWORKS

A **virtual private network (VPN)** is a private data network that makes use of the public telecommunications infrastructure, which maintains privacy through the use of tunneling and security procedures. The VPN is so named because an individual user shares communications channels with other users. A **tunnel** is simply a logical connection through which packets of data travel. Switches are placed on these channels to allow an end-user access to multiple

TABLE 5-2 Attribute Comparisons of the Internet, Intranet, and Extranet

Attribute	Internet	Intranet	Extranet
Geographics	Worldwide	Within an organization	Between an organization and a supplier
Accessibility	The entire population	Corporate users	Corporate users and suppliers
Security level	Many risks from everywhere	Internal risks	Risks from suppliers

end-sites. A VPN can be contrasted with a system of owned or leased lines, which can only be used by one company. The connection between sender and receiver acts as if it were completely private, even though it uses a link across a public network to carry information.

The idea of the VPN is to give the user and organization the same capabilities at much lower cost by using the shared public infrastructure rather than a private one. Telephone companies have provided secure shared resources for voice messages. A VPN makes it possible to have the same secure sharing of public resources for data. **FIGURE 5-3** depicts a VPN using a logical tunnel between Charlotte, North Carolina, and New Orleans, Louisiana, that utilizes the Internet for transport. Access to the Internet cloud occurs at Charlotte and then again at New Orleans, which saves on transport costs. The transmissions in the tunnel are secure, except in the case of a massive network failure.

Using a VPN involves encrypting data before sending the data through the public network, and decrypting the data at the receiving end. An additional level of security involves encrypting not only the data but also the originating and receiving network addresses. Often these data have also been compressed before encryption. Attackers and intruders continue to require the attention of the network administrator. Security must be at the forefront of virtual network design and implementation.

Equally important to a VPN's use is the issue of privacy or security. At its most basic, the *private* in VPN means that a tunnel between two users on a VPN appears as a private link, even when running over shared media. For business use, especially for LAN–LAN links, *private* has to mean security that is free from prying eyes and tampering. VPNs need to provide four critical functions to ensure the security of data:

- *Authentication*—ensuring that the data are coming from the claimed source.
- *Access control*—restricting unauthorized users from gaining admission to the network.
- *Confidentiality*—preventing anyone from reading or copying as the data travel across the network.
- *Security*—ensuring that no one tampers with the data as the data travel the network.

Although tunnels ease the transmission of the data across the network, authenticating users and maintaining the integrity of the data depend on cryptographic procedures such as digital signatures and encryption.

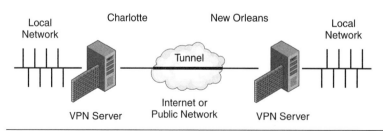

FIGURE 5-3 VPN Network with Tunneling across the Internet

SECURITY ISSUES IN VIRTUAL NETWORKS

Security has been a concern for virtual network users; however, years of research have resulted in solutions that allow transmission of sensitive data over these networks. It is now possible for employees to access data remotely from almost anywhere there is Internet connectivity. It is also possible for customers to access Web sites and transfer credit card information without being concerned about security.

Ensuring security, however, is a major issue when implementing virtual networks and should not be treated lightly. Security problems can be solved with various techniques such as tunneling. Securing tunnels for private communications between corporate sites will do little if employee passwords are openly available or if other holes in the security of the network exist. VPN-related security management of keys and user rights must be integrated into the rest of the organization's security policies.

Tunneling

A key component of VPN is **tunneling**, which is a vehicle for encapsulating packets inside a protocol that is understood at the entry and exit points of a given network. These entry and exit points are defined as tunnel interfaces. The tunnel itself is similar to a hardware interface, but is configured in software. **FIGURE 5-4** depicts a VPN between two remote locations. The transmission is secure between the endpoints but can be compromised at the router location if security is not provided on the LAN devices.

Several areas of security that are implemented in VPNs include authentication, encryption, integrity, nonrepudiation, and content filtering. Additionally, a compression process is also implemented in the VPN data transmission.

Authentication

Authentication is a vital part of a VPN's security structure. Before users can connect to a site, they must first authenticate themselves; that is, they must be able to prove they are who they say they are. Passwords offer only weak forms of authentication; VPNs must use stronger forms. Strong authentication implements at least two forms of authentication, which could include a key or token card, a password, or some biometric method.

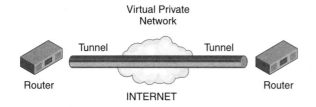

FIGURE 5-4 VPN Tunnel Access across the Internet

The most secure VPN communications use authentication methods to identify the recipient before the message is sent. The purpose of authentication is to ensure that messages are sent to legitimate recipients. The simple authentication of passwords and PINs is vulnerable to attackers. Certificates can be utilized to enhance the protection of the VPN.

Digital certificates based on public/private key pairs are used in message encryption. Each certificate contains a private key that identifies the recipient. A trusted **certificate authority (CA)**, such as an enterprise network or a commercial certificate organization, produces the private key. The sender can verify the recipient certificate by using a matching public key to decrypt it.

Encryption

In normal packet network use, packets containing information are sent over the network and collected at the receiving address. The message content is removed from each packet and reassembled to form the original message. One method of protecting VPN messages from interception is to use *packet encryption*. The contents of the packets sent over the network are encrypted and, when received at the far end, are decrypted to the original message. This prevents anyone who intercepts the message along the transmission path from understanding the content.

A more secure method is to encrypt an entire VPN message at the source and send the encrypted message in the form of packets. These packets are collected at the receiving end and the encrypted message is reassembled and then decrypted. Message encryption allows the use of powerful encryption methods without slowing VPN communications. It is also possible for a VPN to use both packet and message encryption, because they need not interfere with each other. There are a number of encryption techniques that can be employed to protect the security of VPN transmissions.

Integrity

The danger exits that someone will change IP packets in transit. Integrity checks ensure that packets have not been destroyed, changed, or reordered in their passage from the sender to the receiver. Powerful encryption methods must be used, because simple encryption is subject to penetration by attackers. The Data Encryption Standard (DES), described in Chapter 13, is the most popular encryption method used in VPNs; however, other encryption methods are also acceptable. VPN standards use public-key encryption. All messages sent to a given user are encrypted using a public key designed specifically for that recipient. Public keys can be made widely available, and there is no need to take special measures to protect them, because they cannot be used to decrypt messages. Message recipients have a unique and secret private key that matches their public key, and only that key can be used to decrypt received messages. The public-key method avoids the security exposure caused by exchanging encryption keys between sending and receiving parties.

Nonrepudiation

What is nonrepudiation, and why is this concept important to the success of virtual networks? **Nonrepudiation** is a mechanism that prevents a user from denying a legitimate, billable financial transaction. This mechanism provides for monitoring all network endpoints during the course of the exchange, so any applicable charges might be supported in the event they are challenged. It provides a means of proving that a given message came from the party who sent it. Someone who ordered an item and alleges that the item was not ordered and refuses to pay or return the item can be refuted by a system that contains a nonrepudiation function. This is a necessary function for e-commerce transactions.

Content Filtering

A danger exists where a user is authenticated who may send unauthorized requests to the network resource. To prevent inappropriate behavior after authentication, it is necessary to pass each subsequent message from the user through a content filter. **Content filtering** is the technique whereby content is blocked or allowed based on analysis of its content, rather than its source or other criteria. It is most widely used on the Internet to filter e-mail and Web access.

Content management was described in Chapter 1. Some companies check transmission for improper content such as viruses. If the computers used at the sending and receiving ends of a VPN are vulnerable to outside attacks, the security offered by the VPN can be undermined. One widely used method of securing these computers is to employ firewalls. Many products now bundle firewall and VPN protection into one solution.

Compression

Data **compression** is the process of encoding information using fewer bits by implementing specific encoding schemes. As with any communication, compressed data communication only works when both the sender and receiver of the information understand the encoding scheme. Compression is useful because it helps reduce the consumption of expensive resources, such as hard disk space or transmission bandwidth. Compression should be used before the encryption process.

NETWORK, HARDWARE, AND SOFTWARE COMPONENTS

There are various threats that can affect network, hardware, and software components. Each have different identities and repercussions. Everyone should be aware of the various threat levels advertised by the Department of Homeland Security (usually yellow). Some have suggested that the threat level of the Internet is always red.

Threats to Network Components

What exactly is a network? It may be a computer network, a telecommunications network, a wide area network, a local area network, or a metropolitan area network. A computer network is a data communications system that interconnects computer systems at various sites. A network may include any combination of LANs, WANs, and MANs: a **local area network (LAN)** is typically a communications network within a building or a campus, which is used to link together computers, servers, and printers; a **metropolitan area network (MAN)** is a high-speed data network that links multiple locations, usually LANs, within a city, large campus, or metropolitan area; the **wide area network (WAN)** uses network carrier facilities to link dispersed network locations, typically LANs. **FIGURE 5-5** provides a graphic of a hypothetical network. The WAN can be a MAN if the locations of the various networks are located in a metropolitan environment. Each of the three LANs depicted are associated with a limited geographic distance, such as a building or a campus.

The networking environment has two new candidates that will require sophisticated security protection systems: wireless and virtual networks. Wireless networks are being integrated into all aspects of the enterprise environment, including LANs and WANs. Virtual private networks and other tunneling networks are being implemented at a fast pace in all sectors of the economy and provide a secure alternative for communications over the network.

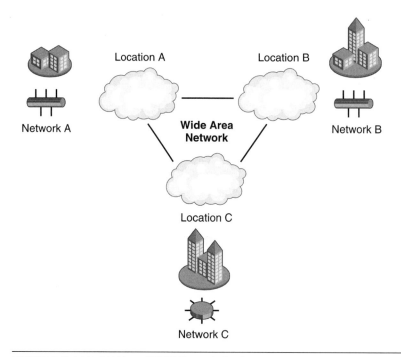

FIGURE 5-5 LAN, MAN, and WAN Network Configuration

Threats to Hardware Components

Because hardware devices such as computers and routers are physical, they are supposedly easy targets. They are also the most visible components, so it would seem that security efforts should be increased for computer systems; however, reasonable safeguards are usually already in place. Security programs for computer systems have been in place since the early 1970s, during the Vietnam War era. Motion detectors, cameras, locks on doors, pass codes, access restrictions, physical location, and a number of other security precautions are commonplace.

There are a number of other situations that can cause havoc with computer and network hardware devices. Hardware devices have been subjected to water, fire, gas, and electrical surges, which can be as devastating as sabotage. Humidity, or even a lack of humidity, can affect the electrical components of these devices. Dust and dirt and cleaning materials are equally harmful. Abuses by employees and visitors from spilled food and drink have caused considerable damage. Smoking used to be a problem before it was restricted. Rough handling by employees and delivery personnel can cause damage to these components. Circuit cards can become dislodged and connector pins damaged through handling abuses.

Because there are so many opportunities for hardware components to become damaged, how can one determine if a specific situation is a vicious act? Both employees and nonemployees can be candidates for security violations. Physical security programs are usually directed at the nonemployee; however, internal attacks may be more insidious and harder to detect. It is fairly easy to sabotage a computer system by dislodging circuit cards or disconnecting power sources, but these are easy to detect. Management must be aware of any situations in which a disgruntled employee or service personnel might cause damage to the system.

Most of the comments so far have been directed at centrally located computer and network control systems. What can be done to ensure the integrity of office and desktop computing devices? Often personal computers, calculators, palmtops, scanners, and printers are left unattended on office desktops. These assets account for thousands of dollars. Service personnel, maintenance personnel, and even employees can damage or pilfer these devices at will. Management must be vigilant in enforcing procedures for the protection of computer and network assets.

A computer system includes many components. Computer systems may be classified as mainframe or client/server. A mainframe configuration includes a central processor, often called a mainframe; a communications processor, called a front-end processor (FEP); and database and file storage devices. A client/server configuration includes a server device with storage media and workstations. These collective devices are called hardware. In addition to these hardware devices, there are operating systems and application programs, collectively called software. The combination of network, hardware, and software comprises the computer system. The next section identifies the various hardware, software, and network components that make up the threat universe.

Threats to Software Components

Software components include operating systems, utility programs, network software, and application programs. Additions, modifications, and deletions to software are possible by both authorized and unauthorized people. How can one limit these activities to authorized personnel?

If hardware failures are fairly easy to detect and correct, the same cannot be said for a software attack. If a personal computer has been left logged on and unattended, the opportunity to create software attacks increase. It makes sense that someone wishing to cause damage through a software attack would not use a personal login. This situation could be especially disastrous if this were an administrator's workstation, which had root (highest) directory privileges.

A hardware device might show evidence if it has been altered; however, software may not display any outward evidences of tampering. Subtle modifications to software might not be evident if the primary function is retained. A number of software threats contain code components that are set to execute at some future date and time. A particularly difficult software threat to counter is called a *logic bomb*. A software modification can be made that will cause some unintended action based on a particular incident or activity. A program could work correctly for years and fail based on some trivial piece of data, such as the temperature on a certain date.

Where modifications and additions to software may be difficult to spot, deletions are usually obvious very quickly. Almost everyone has accidentally deleted software and data files. Some have even deleted the backup files. It is imperative that users keep backup copies of development software and databases for their own protection. If software and databases are deleted due to some illicit activity, it is incumbent that the deleted elements be quickly restored. A good change management system for production software that backs up and restores systems will alleviate this problem. Computer and database backups and restores are addressed in Chapter 9.

Intelligent software can be used to monitor access across internal security boundaries and also to monitor the use of applications and protocols throughout the network. Such monitoring allows network administrators to identify users who are accessing or trying to access unauthorized software and applications.

Special categories of software modifications include information leaks, trap doors, Trojan horses, and viruses. An information leak makes information from a program accessible to unauthorized people. A trap door is a hidden process that allows system-protection mechanisms to be circumvented. A Trojan horse is a computer program that appears to function normally, but actually performs unauthorized actions. A virus is a type of Trojan horse program that infects a computer, causing the operating system to lose integrity.

Another issue of importance is the unauthorized copying of software. Software developers and distributors do not receive compensation for their products when this activity is allowed. Legal action has been pursued in a number of instances. It is essential that administrators have a plan in place to ensure only legal copies of software are in the library and installed on the organization's computer platforms.

NETWORK RESOURCE ACCESS

Access into computer and network facilities, and buildings, has become an issue with most organizations, especially those with large asset bases. It is essential that only authorized personnel be allowed, unattended, into a facility. Not only is ingress an issue, egress can be just as important, because hardware, software, documentation, and other items can "walk" if not protected. The chapter concludes with a discussion of access control for personnel, contractors, and visitors.

A basic requirement of a security system is to identify the user trying to gain access to the network. The owner of the network must determine whether this user is a friend or foe. It is essential that networks, computers, and information be protected from unauthorized disclosure. This concept is called *confidentiality*. In a computer system or network there must be a method of identifying everyone who is allowed into the environment. This takes the form of identification, authentication, authorization, and accounting—collectively called AAA, or triple-A.

Identification

This section examines techniques for identifying entities responsible for initiating specific actions on a computer system or network. This class of techniques is called identification. **Identification** is defined as procedures and mechanisms that allow an external entity to notify a system of its identity. The requirement to perform an identification technique occurs when it is necessary to associate an action with a user or entity that causes each action. Computer systems and network devices can determine who invoked an operation by examining the reported identity of the entity that initiated the session in which the operation was invoked. This identity is usually established via a login sequence.

A system administrator may have assigned this login. The login is the simplest type of mechanism that comprises identification. Once users are logged in, they are allowed to access various resources based on the rights and privileges assigned to their user accounts or the objects they possess. Identification is usually combined with another procedure, authentication, which allows a system to determine if the identification sequence was correct.

Authentication

Authentication is the process whereby a user proves they are who they claim to be. Additionally, *to authenticate* is to establish that a transmission attempt is authorized and valid. There are several techniques for authenticating a user. The first is to enable network logon, which ensures that only valid users are allowed to access the network. The next step is to provide user authentication on servers. Authentication at the server level operates independently of the network logon. Authentication is also required for message exchange, to verify that a particular message has not been fabricated or altered in transit. A username/password is the most common form of identification for network security. This authentication method can be used as either a manual or dynamic entry.

- A manual username/password allows users to choose their own passwords. The password remains the same until the user changes it.
- When using the dynamic username/password, the password continually changes. A device such as a security card can be used to implement the dynamic technique.

Accounting

Accounting services are provided by some network operating systems to track the users who access the resources. Network resources that are commonly tracked are as follows:

- Disk space utilized.
- User logons and logoffs.
- Applications started.
- Files accessed.
- Traffic volume.
- Resources engaged.

In many cases, it is possible for the administrator to set limits and boundaries on the user and the amount and types of resources used. If this information is captured, it can be useful in security forensics.

Authorization

Authorization refers to securing the network by specifying which area of the network—whether it is an application, a device, or a system—a user is allowed to access. The authorization level varies from user to user. For example, payroll personnel have access to the payroll systems and engineers have access to design systems, which means that access is based on the need to know. This also means that access to system resources and services to users or processes, previously authenticated, is selectively granted. It is possible to explicitly grant or deny authorizations. By explicitly denying access, only access to confidential information is restricted. This compares with explicitly granting access, which does not allow access to any information without specifically granting an access. Authorization can be defined as systemwide or limited to specific data elements. Authorization can be based on the type of access, which includes read, write, delete, or execute. There are different authorization processes for routers, gateways, servers, and switches. **FIGURE 5-6** shows the authentication and authorization flow of a computer login session. The user is first authenticated as a legitimate user and then authorized as a user for a specific application or database access.

Network devices such as routers, gateways, and switches require authorization so that unauthorized personnel do not change configurations. Access is limited to a server because directory integrity must be preserved. Often a user is allowed a maximum of three attempts to enter the correct authorization before the access attempt is terminated. Additional authentication and authorization concepts are presented in Chapter 8.

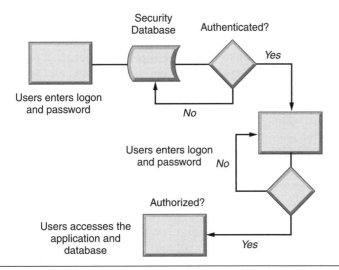

FIGURE 5-6 Authentication and Authorization Flow

A concept closely related to authentication and authorization is trust. Trust is the composite of security, availability, and performance. It includes the ability to execute processes with integrity, keep confidential information private, and perform the required functions without interference or interruption. It follows that a trusted system is one in which a computer, network, or software can be verified to implement a given security policy. A framework for an organizational secure systems policy that addresses resource authorization is called a *trust model*.

Trust is essential among organizations that engage in business transactions. Internet users are often required to trust someone they have never met. Likewise, commercial transactions between diverse enterprise computer systems often contain sensitive and proprietary information. Trust must be established in both cases before secure transactions can occur.

A trust relationship is the link between two entities on a network (e.g., two servers) that enables a user with an account in one domain to have access to resources in another domain. Trust relationships are established between systems so those systems can exchange information without the need for an administrator to actively monitor and authorize these exchanges. Security and system administrators establish relationships for trust in a cooperative way. Access control techniques that support trust systems are presented in subsequent sections. Also presented are technical solutions that can provide support to organizational trust systems.

One-Time Passwords

A method to prevent the unauthorized use of an intercepted password is to prevent it from being reused. **One-time password** systems require a new password for each session. These systems relieve the user of the difficulty of always choosing a new password for the next session by automatically generating a list of acceptable passwords for the user. **S/Key** was developed by Bellcore to provide one-time passwords.

S/Key uses a secret pass-phrase, generated by the user, to generate a sequence of one-time passwords. The user's secret pass-phrase never travels beyond this local computer and does not travel on the network, which precludes it from replay attacks. Because a different one-time password is generated for each session, an intercepted password cannot be used again, and there is no information provided relating to the next password.

One-time password systems require that the server software be modified to perform the required calculations to generate the password, and each remote computer must have a copy of the client software. These systems may not be highly scalable, because it is difficult to administer the password lists for a large number of users.

Password Maintenance

The cost of maintaining passwords includes the many calls to the help desk wanting to know a forgotten password. It has been estimated that this activity costs organizations approximately $30 for each occurrence. This includes the technician's time and the downtime of the user. In addition, it is necessary to maintain a database of legitimate users and their associated passwords. This password database must be afforded a high level of security, or an intruder could compromise the organization's network resources through this single database.

To summarize, any integrity check would be meaningless if the identity of the sending or receiving party is not properly established. Authentication accomplishes this task. Choosing the proper authentication technology largely depends on the location of the entities being authenticated and the degree of trust placed in the particular facets of the network or computer system. Authentication is tightly coupled to authorization in most resource access requirements.

Security Cards

Security cards keep the network secure by preventing access to users who don't possess one. This card requires a permanent username and a temporary password. The password changes after a specific amount of time, often 60 seconds. The passwords belonging to a specific security card are synchronized with a security card server. The steps involved with using this dynamic username/password pairing are as follows:

- The user turns on the card and types in the username.
- The card displays a password for the user to enter for network access.
- The user types in this dynamic password.
- This password is validated through a central security card server.
- If the password is correct, access is allowed to the resource; if not, the user must restart the process.

Smart card systems allow users to access data by inserting a card into a card reader. The card system provides access for authorized users to any reader-equipped workstation or computer. Automatic teller machines (ATMs) use this type of security combined with a personal identification number (PIN). Smart cards containing microprocessor chips can perform such tasks as online encryption and user activity logging as well as perform user identification. Some smart card setups require two individuals to perform an entry procedure before admittance is granted. Smart cards are more difficult to administer than passwords and more inconvenient for end-users.

INTERNET SEARCH TOOLS

A variety of tools have been developed to help one navigate the Internet. Although many of these tools have rendered themselves obsolete due to the advent of WWW browsers, they are still extensively used as reference tools by the WWW. These tools include FTP, anonymous FTP, Telnet, Gopher, Veronica, Archie, and wide area information servers (WAISs).

Browsers

Navigating the Web requires the use of a program called a *client*. Client software provides the communications protocol to interface with host computers on the network. The more common name for client software is a *Web browser*. A Web browser is a program that handles most of the details of document access and display and permits the user to navigate the Web by accessing Web documents that have been coded in a language called HTML.

In addition to text, an HTML document contains tags that specify document layout and formatting. Some tags cause an immediate change; others are used in pairs to apply an action to multiple items. To make document retrieval efficient, a browser uses a cache. The browser places a copy of each document or image on the local disk where the user can then view it. When a document is needed, the browser checks the cache before requesting the document from a server on the network. The latest Web browser products display all reachable resources, from the local PC to the worldwide Internet, on a single hierarchical file tree display.

Documents written in HTML are plain-text ASCII files that can be generated with a text editor. They reside on the Web server and can be identified with an ".html" or ".htm" file extension. Several Web browsers are used to navigate the Web (e.g., Internet Explorer, Mozilla Firefox, Safari, Opera, and Netscape). Each browser must contain an HTML interpreter to display documents. One of the most important functions in an HTML interpreter involves selectable items. The interpreter must store information about the relationship between positions on the display and anchored items in the HTML document. When the user selects an item with the mouse, the browser uses the current cursor position and the stored position information to determine which item the user has selected.

File Transfer Protocol

To download or transfer information back to their client PCs, users would access another TCP/IP protocol called file transfer protocol (FTP) or anonymous FTP servers. Users can access FTP servers directly or through Telnet sessions (explained shortly). The difficulty with searching for information in this manner is that users must know the Internet address of the specific information server they wish to access.

FTP makes it possible to move files across the Internet and handles some of the details involved in moving text and other forms of data between different types of computers. Although FTP is not a highly graphical application, it remains an important tool for individuals and organizations that must exchange files containing data or documents. The FTP function is available from the disk operating system (DOS) command line and takes the form of FTP "IP address."

Trivial File Transfer Protocol

Trivial file transfer protocol (TFTP), described in Chapter 13, is a simplified version of FTP that transfers files but does not provide password protection or user-directory capability. It depends on the connectionless user datagram protocol (UDP) datagram delivery service and is associated with the TCP/IP family of protocols. Precautions must be taken to prevent hackers from accessing files; therefore, it is a good idea to limit access of TFTP to non-critical files. A remote intruder could easily use TFTP to obtain copies of password, system, or user files.

Another way to add security to TFTP is to first access *Telnet*, which checks whether the user has the right to access the system and the corresponding file. It then calls the TFTP client and passes the file name to the client. The client then makes the TFTP connection to the TFTP server.

Gopher

Gopher is a menu-based client/server that features search engines, which comb through all of the information in all of the servers looking for a user's specific request. Gopher provides a way to index and organize all types of textual data collections. Before the introduction of the WWW, Gopher was the premier tool for browsing the Internet to look for information. Gopher was named after the mascot of the University of Minnesota, where the system was developed.

Gopher client software is most often installed on a client PC and interacts with software running on a particular Gopher server, which transparently searches multiple FTP sites for requested information and delivers that information to the Gopher client. Gopher users do not need to know the exact Internet address of the information servers they wish to access.

Newsgroups

Based on a TCP/IP service known as USENET, **newsgroups** provide a way for individuals to exchange information on specific, identifiable topics or areas of interest. This technology lets users read information on a variety of subtopics that are pertinent to a newsgroup's focus. More than 10,000 newsgroups covering selected topics are available. USENET servers update each other on a regular basis with news items that are pertinent to the newsgroups housed on a particular server. For technical matters, this is an especially useful way to exchange opinions and information on a broad range of topics.

Telnet

Text-based information stored in Internet-connected servers can be accessed by remote users logging into these servers via a TCP/IP known as Telnet. **Telnet** permits a user on one computer to establish a session on another computer elsewhere on the Internet, as if the local computer was directly attached to the remote computer. Given the proper access to remote machines, this program lets users achieve many tasks remotely that they might ordinarily only be able to accomplish locally. Telnet is an application of choice for configuring all kinds of networking equipment, especially routers and hubs. The TELNET function is available from the DOS command line and takes the form of TELNET "IP address."

The administrator must ensure that only legitimate users can access the various devices via a Telnet session. The main defense is in the use of passwords. A Telnet password checklist is as follows:

- Cannot be shared.
- Should be encrypted.
- Restricted by device location.
- Contain at least eight characters.
- Changed every six months.
- Callback required for remote access.
- Access logged.
- Profiles of legitimate users.
- Audit the use.

Browser Security

A browser can expose private information, allow harm to a workstation, or just display bogus information.

To access and display information from remote servers, a browser makes connections over the Internet. The requests and responses are in plain text and can be read or altered by anyone with access to some part of the Internet path between the browser and the server. Additionally, some responses contain active content such as scripts and programs that may send information back to the server, install Trojans, or cause harm to a workstation.

Privacy, integrity, and authenticity are security goals that can be accomplished by using the built-in capabilities and features of a browser. *Privacy* ensures that information is seen only by authorized persons and services. *Integrity* ensures that the information is intact and that the workstation is not harmed. *Authenticity* ensures that the browser and the server have been correctly identified and that all requests and responses are between those two parties and none other.

These goals are accomplished by use of cryptography, *authentication*, and *browser restrictions*. Cryptography is used to ensure the privacy and integrity of the requests and responses. Cryptography scrambles messages so that they can be read only by others who know the key. Cryptography is used to ensure message integrity, continuity of authentication, and even authentication itself. *Authentication* ensures the identity of the parties to a communication. *Restriction* blocks use of risky or undesirable methods.

The primary cryptographic technology used by browsers is Secure Socket Layer (SSL). SSL, described in Chapter 13, provides authentication of the remote server and privacy and integrity of the connection to that server. Once such a secure connection is established, the Web site can use forms of HTTP basic authentication to identify the user.

SOFTWARE

Software Issues

Two types of software are of interest in the security arena: system software and application software. Both can be compromised to the detriment of computer and network systems. *System software* refers to the operating system and all utility programs that manage computer resources at a low level. *Application software* comprises programs designed for an end-user, such as word processors, database systems, and spreadsheet programs. An example includes Microsoft Excel®. Systems software includes compilers, loaders, linkers, and debuggers. Electronic mail systems are classified as systems software.

Electronic Mail

Although e-mail remains primarily character oriented, its ability to permit individuals to easily exchange information and files makes it the most popular networked application of any kind.

Millions of users are connected worldwide to the Internet via the global e-mail subsystem. From a business perspective, Internet e-mail offers one method of sending intercompany e-mail. Most companies have private networks that support e-mail transport to fellow employees, but not necessarily to employees of other companies. By adding Internet e-mail gateways to its private network, a company can send e-mail to users almost anywhere.

Internet electronic mail hosts exchange messages through the simple mail transport protocol (SMTP), which is in the TCP/IP architecture. E-mail hosts hold the mail until the subscriber is ready to read it. This allows the receiver to work on a client PC, which will often be turned off. E-mail hosts also transmit outgoing messages to other mail hosts. Together, mail hosts function as a network of electronic post offices.

E-Mail Security

Millions of users rely on e-mail for a variety of purposes, including business correspondence and personal information. Many of these messages are sensitive, and users want to ensure their privacy is protected. The challenges of e-mail security include message confidentiality and encryption.

The contents of a message can be encrypted using a conventional encryption scheme such as the Data Encryption Standard (DES). The most difficult technical challenge for such schemes is the secure exchange of encryption keys between pairs of correspondents. The goal is to prevent anyone but the intended recipient from reading the message.

Message authentication is often referred to as digital signature security. A digital signature, implemented using public-key encryption, makes use of two keys: a public key and a private key. If a block of data is encrypted with the sender's private key, any recipient may decrypt that block with the sender's public key. The recipient is assured the block must have originated from the alleged sender, because only the sender knows the private key.

Another development that might help in message security is the adoption by e-mail vendors of the Privacy Enhanced Mail (PEM) standard, which describes a common method of encapsulating encrypted messages. This standard, described in Chapter 13, should help bring standard, secure e-mail to all users more quickly.

SECURITY IN THE NETWORK

Obviously, the WAN is massive and there are numerous opportunities for an intruder or attacker to cause disruption and damage to the assets. The responsibility of the security administrator is to block or mitigate these efforts. This task is enormous and ongoing. There are many facets of security, and there are many techniques and methods that can be deployed to assist the administrator in providing security in the WAN.

As with LAN security, attention must be directed toward protecting physical components, facilities, and buildings that house the various hardware and software components of the wide area network. This includes the massive databases and terminal inventories that support the WAN infrastructure.

Of particular interest are the processes necessary to restore network functions during an outage or disaster. Disaster recovery and contingency planning are major parts of network security and network integrity assurance activities. Without the WAN infrastructure, the corporate network will not function.

Security Issues

WAN security means employing security operations to achieve three major goals, authentication, integrity, and confidentiality. The types of Internet security services available can be summarized as follows:

- *Access control*—prevention of unauthorized use of a resource.
- *Authentication*—assurance that traffic is sent by legitimate users.
- *Confidentiality*—assurance that a user's traffic is not examined by unauthorized users.
- *Integrity*—assurance that received traffic has not been modified after the initial transmission.
- *Nonrepudiation*—inability to disavow a transaction.

Two primary methods for encrypting network traffic on the Web are SHTTP and SSL. Secure HTTP is a secure version of hypertext transfer protocol that requires both client and server SHTTP versions to be installed for secure end-to-end encrypted transmission. It is based on public-key encryption and provides security at the document or application level. It uses digital signature encryption to ensure the documents possess both authenticity and message integrity. SSL is described as wrapping an encrypted envelope around HTTP transmissions. Whereas SHTTP only encrypts Web documents, SSL can be wrapped around other Internet service transmissions, such as FTP, Telnet, and Gopher, including HTTP. SSL is a connection-level encryption method providing security to the network link.

An Internet e-mail specific encryption standard that also uses digital signature encryption to guarantee authenticity, security, and message integrity of received e-mail is called Pretty Good Privacy (PGP). PGP overcomes inherent security loopholes with public-/private-key security schemes by implementing a web of trust, in which e-mail users electronically sign one another's public keys to create and interconnect groups of public-key users. Specific details for PGP are described in Chapter 13.

Internet Security

Computer and network managers develop documentation called a *baseline* that inventories everything concerning the enterprise resources and assets. This baseline development is especially important in the event of an attack from the Internet. Such data and information can be used to reconstruct the systems from a disaster caused by some intruder or attacker. While the organization's personnel are developing this information, the potential attackers are attempting to develop a profile of the organization. It is the responsibility of the enterprise staff to ensure that they do not contribute to this diabolical endeavor.

These attackers are looking for specific information that can aid their cause. Items of relevance to these people can be related to the Internet, intranets, extranets, and remote-access elements. Details that can assist the attacker include the following:

- IP addresses reachable by the Internet.
- TCP and UDP services running on which systems.
- System architecture.
- Access control mechanisms.
- Intrusion detection systems.
- Routing tables and access control lists.
- Network management information.
- Demographics.

- Organization structure.
- Personnel lists.
- Contact lists with telephone numbers.
- Network equipment type, model, and configurations.

This looks like a formidable list; however, an attacker has the capability of gathering this information. Maybe the organization should hire this person! Don't help the attacker by providing any of this information on the organization's Web page.

Many security incidents have occurred recently, affecting numerous network sites. The most serious types of attacks included IP spoofing, in which intruders create packets with false IP addresses and exploit applications that use authentication based on IP addresses. Incidents also included various forms of eavesdropping and packet sniffing, in which attackers read transmitted information, including logon information and database contents. In response to these security issues, authentication and encryption are included as necessary security features in the next-generation IP address, issued as IPv6.

A security mechanism employed by the U.S. government includes security labels. An optional IP header field that contains a security classification and handling label is used. This field allows computers and routers to label IP traffic based on its security level. Other computers and routers can then check these labels for arriving datagrams. Traffic can be accepted, rejected, or forwarded based on the labels. This labeling allows the implementation of government access control policies based on security clearances and information classifications.

Privacy on the Internet

Technology now provides companies with the ability to collect personal information and potentially give or sell that information to others. While the Internet can serve as a tremendous resource for information, products, and services, users can safeguard their privacy online by following these tips.

- *Keep personal information private.* Don't disclose personal information, such as address, telephone number, Social Security number, or e-mail address. If information is provided, users should know who is collecting the information, why they are collecting it, and how they will use it. Parents should teach children to check with them before giving out personal or family information online.
- *Look for an online privacy policy.* Many companies post their privacy policies on their Web sites. This policy should disclose what information is being collected on the Web site and how that information is being used. Before providing a company with personal information, check its privacy policy. If a policy is not evident, send an e-mail or written message to the Web site to ask about its policy and request that it be posted on the site.
- *Make choices.* Many companies give users a choice on their Web site as to whether and how personal information is used. These companies allow users to decline or "opt-out" of information dissemination. E-mail addresses may be used for marketing purposes or shared with other companies. Look for this choice as part of the company's privacy policy.

Security Services

Security is implemented at the lower levels of the open system interconnection (OSI) model, the data link, and network layers. Deploying security services at these OSI layers makes much of the security services transparent to the user. Implementation of security at these levels can take two forms, which affect the user's responsibility for securing personal data. Security can be implemented for end-to-end communications, such as between two computers, or between network components, such as firewalls and routers. The latter case refers to node-to-node security.

Using security on a node-to-node basis can make it more transparent to the end users and relieve them of some of the heavy-duty computational requirements such as encryption. Node-to-node security, however, requires that networks behind the node be trusted networks. This means that they are secured against attacks from unauthorized users. End-to-end security, because it involves each host, is inherently sounder than node-to-node security. End-to-end security increases the complexity for the end user and can be more challenging to manage.

The traditional security policy for a centrally located computer system identified all the assets in the organization's information infrastructure that required protection. With the advent of distributed information systems, security policies had to embrace departmental LANs as well. This meant adding policies for accessing resources belonging to departments with diverse requirements. Because security must be woven into any distributed system design, a number of questions need to be asked before proceeding:

- Which Internet services does the organization plan to use?
- Which departments within the organization will be part of this network?
- Will access to network services be accessible remotely or locally?
- What security methods will be required and supported?
- What are the risks for providing distributed access?
- What is the cost to provide secure distributed access?
- How will security affect usability?
- What will be the availability of the network resources?
- What are the backup capabilities of the network?
- Will users and employees require any training to use the system?

CHAPTER SUMMARY

The network infrastructure consists of the Internet, intranets, and extranets. In addition, a multitude of commercial and governmental internetworks permeates the communication industry. There are many threats that can affect the network, hardware, and software components. Each has different causes, identities, and repercussions.

The World Wide Web (WWW), or the Web, is the premier application for most Internet users. The Web is a collection of servers accessed via the Internet that offers information concerning products, personnel, or services. Web browsers integrate e-mail and support an increasingly interactive and visual interface to the Internet. Companies wishing to use the Web as a marketing tool establish a Web site on the Internet to publicize the address of that location.

A VPN is a private data network that makes use of the public telecommunications infrastructure, which maintains privacy through the use of tunneling and security procedures. The VPN is so named because an individual user shares communications channels with other users, often over the untrusted Internet.

There are numerous hardware, software, and protocols that support security functions within network configurations. Internet security services address access control, authentication, integrity, and nonrepudiation issues.

 KEY TERMS

accounting	Gopher	smart card
authentication	identification	splitter
authorization	Internet service provider (ISP)	Telnet
callback	intranet	tunnel
certificate authority (CA)	local area network (LAN)	tunneling
compression	metropolitan area network (MAN)	virtual private network (VPN)
content filtering	modem	wide area network (WAN)
data service unit (DSU)	newsgroups	wireless network interface
demarcation point	non-repudiation	controller (WNIC)
digital certificate	one-time password	World Wide Web (WWW)
digital subscriber line (DSL)	security cards	
extranet	S/Key	

SECURITY REVIEW QUESTIONS

1. Identify the various communication devices that can be used to access the network.
2. What are some of the major application areas that can be accessed through an ISP?
3. What is the purpose of a VPN?
4. How are security issues resolved in virtual networks?
5. Compare and contrast intranets, extranets, and the Internet.
6. Provide an overview of the threats that can affect an organization's hardware components.
7. Identify and describe Internet search tools.
8. Identify information that can assist a network attacker.
9. Describe the requirements for network access security.
10. What security issues must be addressed when implementing a computer network?

 RESEARCH ACTIVITIES

1. Identify the security provisions inherent in the OSI model.
2. Identify five ISPs, and describe the security features available to network users.
3. Describe the security features available in IPv4 and IPv6.
4. Provide an overview of the SHTTP and SSL encryption methods.
5. Provide an overview of the protocols used for secure communication over the network.
6. Explain the security issues and vulnerabilities for intranets, extranets, and the Internet.
7. Develop an overview of the various encryption methods that can be used by network security.
8. Arrange for a tour of a wiring closet and network demarcation point in the local school. Produce a graphic of the contents and configurations.

CHAPTER 6

Wired and Wireless
Local Area Networks

🔒 CHAPTER CONTENTS

- Identify the components and topologies of local area networks.
- Look at the differences between wired and wireless LANs.
- Analyze the various security and integrity issues pertinent to wired and wireless networks.
- Learn how firewalls, routers, and gateways can provide a level of security for the network.
- Become familiar with the function of a proxy server, DMZ, and bastion host.
- Look at the security options and capabilities available with biometric technology.

INTRODUCTION

This chapter provides an overview of the infrastructure of wired and wireless communication networks. It is essential that the reader have some basic knowledge of the environment so that realistic and effective security precautions can be developed and implemented. A local area network (LAN) is contained in a small area, such as a campus, office space, or building. A WAN, presented in Chapter 5, is geographically dispersed, such as in different cities or countries. Two additional networks discussed include wireless local area networks (WLAN) and virtual local area networks (VLAN). There are also hybrid configurations of these networks. Information is provided for both WLAN and VLAN implementations.

There are numerous safety, security, and integrity issues that are relevant to wired and wireless networks. There are a number of hardware devices, software systems and tools that can be deployed to provide for a safe and secure network. Management must determine the amount of protection that is necessary and sufficient to secure the organization's resources and assets.

A number of protocols and configurations are required to make the network function properly. A considerable amount of semi-technical details are introduced in this chapter; however, further research is required on the reader's part for a thorough understanding. Additional details concerning network protocols are presented in Chapter 13.

LOCAL AREA NETWORK

A **local area network (LAN)** consists of a group of data devices, such as computers, servers, printers, and scanners, that are linked with each other within a limited area such as on the same floor or building. The most common LAN technologies are:

- *Ethernet*—the most widely used LAN access method, which is defined by the Institute of Electrical and Electronics Engineers (IEEE) standard 802.3. Ethernet is normally a shared media LAN, meaning that all devices on the network segment share total bandwidth. Ethernet networks operate from 10 to 100 Mbps.
- *Token ring*—a local area network that is an implementation of IEEE standard 802.5, the standard for the token-ring access method. The access method, more than the ring shape, distinguishes token-ring networks from other LANs. Token-ring LANs operate at speeds of 4, 16, and 100 Mbps.
- *Fiber distributed data interface (FDDI)*—a LAN technology based on a 100-Mbps token-passing network running over fiber-optic cable. Usually reserved for network backbones in larger organizations.

(*Note: The Institute of Electrical and Electronics Engineers is a professional organization whose activities include the development of communications and network standards. IEEE LAN standards are the predominant LAN standards today.*)

A typical network user views a LAN as a collection of computing systems that are capable of communicating with one another. **FIGURE 6-1** depicts a simple LAN consisting of a server, router, switch, two hubs, a print server, and a configuration of workstations. A user primarily interacts with high-level networking software that allows the use of the networked computers. Computer scientists and network technicians must have a working knowledge of this software, also called operating systems. Examples of the most commonly used networking software systems include:

- Windows NT/XP.
- NetWare.
- Appletalk.
- SNA.
- DECnet.

Organizations may want to share data and information among themselves and with other outside entities. This can be accomplished via an internetwork or a collection of interconnected networks. The internetwork provides functionality needed to share information among multiple networks. Security and integrity issues must be addressed when establishing this type of configuration. Router, switch, and gateway devices might be employed in these situations. Wired LAN configurations rely on some media type for device connectivity.

WIRED LAN CONNECTIVITY

To communicate with one another, each device must be connected to a LAN configuration. Connections between devices may be any combination of twisted-pair copper wire, coaxial cable, fiber-optic line, or wireless media. Twisted-pair category 4/5/6 cabling and coaxial cable are the common media for connecting devices to a LAN. Copper cabling is available in shielded (STP) or unshielded (UTP). The category of cabling selected impacts the speed, range, and quality of the transmission. **TABLE 6-1** depicts the various categories of LAN media. Each of the workstations shown in Figure 6-1 can communicate with each other and also with the

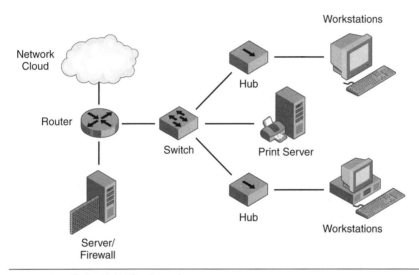

FIGURE 6-1 Typical LAN Configuration

TABLE 6-1 Category 1–6 LAN Media

CAT	Type	Rate (in Mbps)	Distance (in meters)	Normal Use
1	UTP	1	90	Modem
2	UTP	4	90	Token ring—4
3	UTP	10	100	10BaseT
4	STP	16	100	Token ring—16
5	UTP	100	200	100BaseT
5	STP	100	200	100BaseT
6	UTP	1000	200	Gigabit Ethernet

print server. Both users can also access the network cloud and the server through the router. The wiring method depicted in the sample LAN is UTP cable.

There are a number of opportunities for signals to be intercepted, modified, and deleted in the physical cabling environment. Each LAN topology presents a different set of security issues that must be addressed. These topologies include bus, ring, and star configurations.

Bus Topology

A bus is an electrical connection that allows two or more wires or lines to be connected together. All network interface cards (NICs), resident in each computing device, receive all the same information put on the bus, but only the card that is "addressed" will accept the information. With the bus topology, each system is directly attached to a common communication channel, where signals that are transmitted over the channel comprise the messages. As each message passes along the channel, each system receives it and examines the destination address that is contained in the message. If the destination (IP) address is for that system, the message is accepted and processed; otherwise it is ignored. **FIGURE 6-2** illustrates a logical bus LAN topology. All four of the computing devices are physically connected to the bus, usually to a device called a wiring hub or a switch.

Ring Topology

A ring consists of a LAN in which all the PCs are connected through a wiring loop from workstation to workstation, forming a circle or ring. Data are sent around the ring to each workstation in the same direction. Each system acts as a repeater for all signals it receives and then retransmits them to the next system in the ring at their original signal strength. All messages transmitted by any system are received by all other systems, but not simultaneously. The system that originates a message is usually responsible for determining that a message

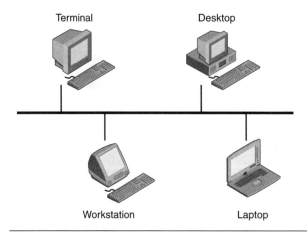

FIGURE 6-2 Logical Bus LAN

has made its way all the way around the ring and then removing it from the ring. **FIGURE 6-3** shows a logical ring topology. Cabling is provided between each of the workstations, forming a ring. This has been the typical topology for IBM LANs. Physically, the computing devices would be connected to a hubbing device, called a multiple station access unit, and possess the connectivity attributes of a physical star.

Star Topology

A star configuration consists of a topology in which all telephones or workstations are wired directly to a central service unit. The central service unit establishes, maintains, and breaks connections between workstations. The star topology requires that all transmissions from one system to another pass through the central point. This device may also play a role in managing and controlling communication and act as a switching device. When one system wishes to communicate with another system, the central switch may establish a path between the two systems that wish to communicate.

The star topology has been utilized for many years in dial-up telephone systems, in which individual telephone sets are the communicating systems and a private branch exchange (PBX) acts as the central controller. **FIGURE 6-4** shows a logical star topology. This is similar to the connectivity of a telephone company central office switch or an organization's private telephone system.

VLAN Described

A **virtual local area network (VLAN)** is a grouping of network devices not restricted to a physical segment or switch. VLANs can be used to restructure broadcast domains similarly to the way that bridges, switches, and routers divide collision domains. (*Note that a broadcast*

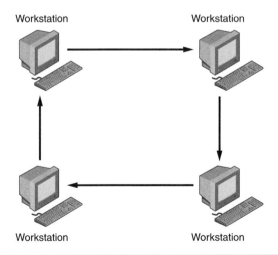

Workstation   Workstation

Workstation   Workstation

FIGURE 6-3 LAN Logical Ring Topology

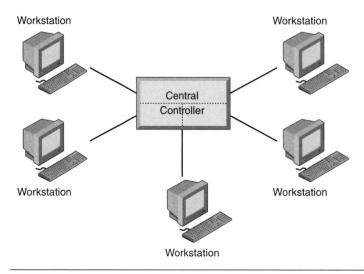

FIGURE 6-4 Logical Star Topology

domain is a group of network devices that receives LAN broadcast traffic from each other.) A VLAN can prevent hosts on virtual segments from reaching one another and can provide isolation from errant broadcasts as well as introducing additional security behind these virtual segments. **FIGURE 6-5** depicts domains A and B connected to a single VLAN switch.

The network administrator can logically divide the LAN without changing the actual physical configuration. These benefits include better traffic control and increased security. Dividing the broadcast domains into logical groups increases security because it is more difficult for an intruder to tap a network port and determine the configuration of the LAN. Additionally, a VLAN allows the administrator to make servers behave as if they were distributed throughout the LAN, when in fact they can be physically locked up in a central location.

As VLANs are defined in the network, there are times when restrictions are needed on certain switch ports. For some organizations, the need to filter certain end nodes is required, which will allow special monitoring for configured ports. There may be instances in which VLAN security is justified by the integrity of the data that travel across the network. VLAN security allows administrators to filter certain confidential transmissions, even at the station level.

There are special methods in which ports can be secured when configuring VLANs. Secure port filtering can be used to block input to an Ethernet port when the media access control (MAC) address of the station attempting to access the port is different from the MAC address specified for that port. (*Note the MAC address in the physical hardware address of the device.*) Common port numbers are:

- HTTP   80
- Telnet   23
- FTP   21
- TFTP   69

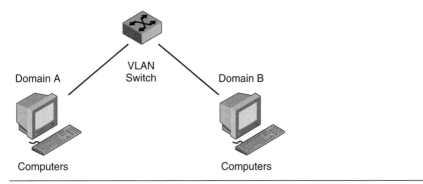

FIGURE 6-5 Different VLAN Domains from a Switch

Frame switches have VLAN capabilities that allow establishment of VLAN groups that correspond to an organization's security policy and also correspond to network management uses. VLANs can be established for diverse departments such as finance, personnel, engineering, and marketing. Controlled communication among these VLANs can make use of any additional appropriate access mechanisms presented in subsequent chapters.

WIRELESS LAN

Using radio-frequency (RF) technology, **wireless local area networks (WLANs)** transmit and receive data over the air, minimizing the need for wired connections; thus, wireless LANs combine data connectivity with user mobility. WLANs are essentially networks that allow the transmission of data and the ability to share resources, such as printers, without the need to physically connect each node, or computing device, with wires. Wireless LANs offer productivity, convenience, and cost advantages over traditional wired networks.

Wireless LAN Connectivity

In local area networks, wireless components act as part of an ordinary LAN, usually to provide connectivity for roving users or changing environments. They may provide connectivity across areas that may not otherwise be networkable, such as in older buildings where wiring would be impractical or across right-of-ways or highways, where wire runs might not be permitted.

The wireless components of most LANs behave like their wired counterparts, except for the media and related hardware involved in the physical connectivity. The operational principles are almost the same. It is still necessary to attach a network interface of some type to a computer device, but the interface attaches to an antenna and an emitter, rather than a wire or cable. Users still access the network just as if they were wired into it.

Access Points

An additional item of equipment is required to link wireless users with wired users or resources. It is necessary to install a transceiver or an access point that translates between the wired and wireless networks. This **access point** broadcasts messages in wireless format, which must be directed to wireless users, and relays messages sent by wireless users directed to resources or users on the wired side of its connection. An access point device includes an antenna and transmitter to send and receive wireless traffic, but is also connected to the wired side of the network. This permits the device to shuttle back and forth between the wired and wireless sides of the network. **FIGURE 6-6** shows an access point device that is connected to a wireless portable personal computer. The access point, workstation, and server depicted are physically attached to a wired (bus) LAN.

Some wireless LANs use small individual transceivers, wall mounted or freestanding, to attach individual computers or devices to a wired network. This permits some limited mobility, with an unobstructed view of the transceiver for such devices.

Roaming

When moving from one wireless network access to another, users roam. When moving out of range of an access point, the client will attempt to find another access point. If there are not any access points in the same network, the client will attempt to find an access point in another network. This means that the wireless user can roam across access points and across networks.

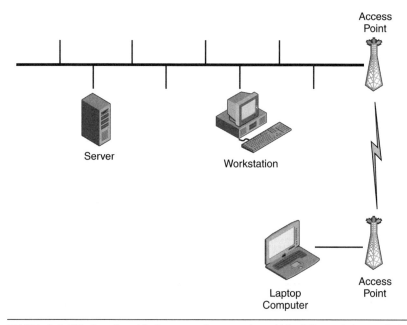

FIGURE 6-6 Wireless Portable Computer Connected to a Wired Network Access Point

LAN NETWORK COMPONENTS

A LAN in the organization is used to connect a number of devices, including PCs and printers. The operating systems on the PCs are user-friendly; however, they are not designed for security functions. An organization's network components, which are security candidates, consist of firewalls, routers, servers, gateways, and workstations. These devices are connected via some media to form the physical network.

Firewalls, Routers, and Gateways

Network security can be augmented with the addition of access control. This additional protection can take the form of a filter, access list, or firewall.

Filters, also called **access lists**, can be configured on routers. Filters enable the router to either accept or reject access based on the contents of the access list. A filter is also called a firewall. It blocks users who are not authorized from accessing segments of the network and allows access only to authorized users. Implementing filters on routers creates a barrier against unauthorized users, thereby preventing access to parts of the network that are off-limits to that user.

Another access control technique is called *route authentication*. The routers verify among themselves that they are valid routers and provide valid paths to other segments of the network. Route authentication is used to verify that the routing paths available on the network are real, not paths to unauthorized devices.

Firewalls

A common method of securing network infrastructure is with a firewall. It is intimately linked with Internet security. The objective of a firewall is to protect trusted networks from untrusted entities. A **firewall** is a combination of hardware and software that limits the exposure of a computer or group of computers to an attack from an outside source. In its most simplistic sense, it controls the flow of incoming and outgoing network traffic. It also ensures that information about the trusted network, such as an address list, is not disclosed to an untrusted network. A firewall can be a single device or a number of different components, such as routers and computers. Typical tasks of a firewall are:

- Authentication based on the source of network traffic.
- Access control based on the service requested.
- Access control based on sender or receiver addresses.
- Logging of Internet activities.
- Virus checking on incoming files.
- Hiding of internal network topology and addresses.

A firewall scans each packet of data to determine if it is to be rejected or forwarded to the corporate resource. (*Note that a* packet *is group of fixed-length binary digits, including the data and call control signals.*) It is basically a hardware or software barrier that provides protection against unauthorized entry. There are three types of firewalls: screened host, screened subnet, and dual-homed gateway. System designers and network administrators would need to research and understand these firewall options.

One technique to enable security on a firewall/router is to create rules, called access lists, that permit or deny various types of network traffic. Permission or denial of traffic can include specific network services. Three functions provided by access lists include the following:

- Control the amount of traffic on the networks to improve performance.
- Control whether network traffic is forwarded or blocked at a router's interface.
- Provide a basic level of security.

Typically, firewalls are deployed at critical ingress and egress points of the network infrastructure. The only access to the server in **FIGURE 6-7** is through the router, switch, and firewall. Separating the packet filtering from other tasks performed by a firewall results in a less complex router and provides better performance. This allows hardware optimization for the routing task and a higher degree of assurance for its security. A proxy server may offer more relevant features.

A primary function of a firewall is to filter traffic, which is the process of selecting the traffic that will be allowed into a certain portion of a network, such as a LAN, MAN, or WAN. Filters can be set to block all packets originating from a specific location (address) or can be set to exclude traffic from specific protocols. **Packet filtering** limits communications based on the type of traffic, source and destination IP addresses, ports, and other information.

Many traditional-style corporations and data centers have computing security policies and practices that must be adhered to. In the case where a company's policies dictate how data must be protected, a firewall is very important, because it is the embodiment of the corporate policy. Frequently, the hardest part of providing access to the Internet is not justifying the expense or effort, but convincing management that it's safe to do so. A firewall provides not only real security, but also plays an important role as a security blanket for management.

Some firewalls permit only e-mail traffic through them, thereby protecting the network against any attacks other than attacks against the e-mail service. Other firewalls provide less strict protections and block services that are known to be problems.

Generally, firewalls are configured to protect against unauthenticated interactive logins from the "outside," untrusted world. This function helps prevent attackers from logging into computers on the network. More elaborate firewalls block traffic from the outside to the inside but permit users on the inside to communicate freely with the outside. Three classifications of firewalls encompass different filtering characteristics. These include circuit filtering, application gateways, and packet filtering.

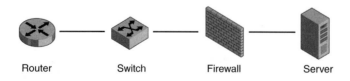

Router   Switch   Firewall   Server

FIGURE 6-7 Firewall Ingress and Egress Points

Firewalls can't protect against attacks that don't go through the firewall. Many corporations that connect to the Internet are very concerned about proprietary data leaking out of the company through that route. For a firewall to work, it must be a part of a consistent overall organizational security architecture. Firewall policies must be realistic and reflect the level of security in the entire network. A firewall can't protect against internal theft and vandalism. Firewalls also can't protect against incompetence. A strong firewall is never a substitute for sensible software that recognizes the nature of what it is handling and behaves appropriately. Remember that the Internet is an untrusted source!

Firewalls can't protect very well against things like viruses. In other words, a firewall cannot replace security consciousness on the part of users. In general, a firewall cannot protect against a *data-driven attack*, which are attacks in which something is mailed or copied to an internal host where it is then executed. Organizations that are deeply concerned about viruses should implement organization-wide virus control measures. Rather than trying to screen out viruses at the firewall, administrators must ensure that every vulnerable desktop has virus-scanning software that runs automatically. Blanketing the network with virus-scanning software will protect against viruses that come in via floppy disks, flash drives, modems, and Internet. Trying to block viruses at the firewall will only protect against viruses from the Internet. The vast majority of viruses transmitted via floppy disks. Newer models of computers are eliminating the floppy disk and replacing it with a DVD drive.

Routers

Two devices deployed in today's enterprise networks include routers and gateways. **Routers** are intelligent devices that connect "like" and "unlike" LANs, MANs, and WANs. They support such broadband technologies as X.25, Frame Relay, and Asynchronous Transfer Mode (ATM). Routers are protocol-sensitive, typically supporting multiple protocols. They commonly operate at the bottom three layers of the OSI model and move network traffic based on a high level of internal intelligence. They can route traffic based on destination address, minimum route delay and distance, packet-priority level, route-congestion level, and community of interest. Because routers have the ability to view an organization's network as multiple physical subnetworks, they are able to confine data traffic within a particular subnet. This process is based on a policy-based routing table, which includes user privileges. Network technicians must have formal training and often are required to possess a certification, such as a certified network administrator (CNA) or Cisco CNA. Chapter 14 describes a number of network certifications and training programs.

A router-based firewall is really a packet-filtering router. Because a router is a computer through which only authorized incoming and outgoing packets may pass, it is often considered a firewall. The router supports network logon as its base level of security for the network. For an additional level of security, it supports access lists to protect servers from unauthorized users and route authentication to prevent other devices from acting as default gateways. A default route is the address of a router on the local network segment that a workstation uses to reach remotes services, sometimes called a default gateway.

Because the router uses login on the network infrastructure, only designated individuals can log into them to change a configuration. Encryption is available on the router to provide data integrity on the network. Encryption can take place at the router and between the workstation and server. To provide the highest data integrity, encryption should be resident on all routers in the network.

The router is the only device that sees every message sent by any computer on either organization's networks. Depending on the time of day and day of the week, some parts of the huge public network may be busier than other parts. When this happens, the routers that make up this system will communicate with one another so that traffic not bound for the crowded area can be sent over less-congested network routes. This lets the network function at full capacity without excessively burdening already busy areas.

Gateway

A gateway is an entrance into and exit from a communications network. In data networks, a **gateway** is typically a node on a network that communicates with an otherwise incompatible network. Gateways often perform code and protocol conversion processes. They connect compatible networks owned by different entities, such as X.25 networks linked by X.75 gateways. Note X.75 defines the connection between public networks such as larger computers and mainframes. Gateways can eliminate duplicate wiring by giving all users on the network access to the mainframe without each having a direct, hard-wired connection. Gateways are commonly used to connect users on one type of network, like Ethernet or token ring, with those on a WAN. See Chapter 13 for additional protocol and standards details.

A gateway is a device that provides mapping at all seven layers of the OSI model. A gateway may be used to interface two incompatible e-mail systems or for transferring data files from one system to another. E-mail systems that sit on LANs often have gateways into larger e-mail systems, like the Internet.

Proxy Servers

A *proxy* is the authority to act for another. Proxy service providers are transparent to the users, who are usually unaware that an intermediary is acting on their behalf, when accessing network services. A **proxy server**, like a firewall, is designed to protect internal network resources that are connected to other networks, such as the Internet. The difference between proxy servers and firewalls is often confusing. Proxies may be services that run on a firewall, where the firewall is a physical device that sits between the internal network and the Internet. Proxy services run on the firewall at the application level to provide a sophisticated traffic control system. A firewall runs proxy services for each different type of Internet application, such as HTTP and FTP, that needs to be controlled. The physical server device running the proxy service has two network interface cards (NICs): one connected to the internal network and the other connected to the Internet. This configuration is called a *dual-homed* or *multi-homed* system. A dual-homed host can act as a simple firewall on a small network as long as there is no direct IP traffic between the Internet and the internal network. In such a case, all Internet applications are run only on the dual-homed host. **FIGURE 6-8** depicts a dual-homed configuration.

If a proxy service does not exist for a particular application, no packets related to the application are allowed to pass through the proxy server. A system on the internal network must communicate with an external Internet system, and vice versa, through the dual-homed host. No direct communication can occur, and all communication may be monitored. When properly implemented, this prevents external hackers from accessing internal systems. While there are advantages, a downside exists to using a dual-homed host because it is difficult to set up and administer.

Proxy services are usually one-way services that block Internet users from any access to the internal network. The services are designed for internal users only, and only packets that are in response to an internal user's requests are allowed back through the firewall. A proxy differs from a standard packet filter function, because a packet filter only determines whether a packet can be forwarded based on its IP address or TCP port number.

For security reasons, incoming response packets may be inspected for viruses or possible alteration by an external hacker. The proxy server may also set up a secure encrypted session with the Web server to ensure that eavesdroppers cannot look at the packets and glean useful information.

Proxy servers also provide caching (local store) functions, where information is stored in memory in anticipation of the next request for information. Because they provide a centralized location where internal users access the Internet, the proxy server can cache frequently accessed documents from sites on the Internet and make them quickly available for other internal users. This can also save overall disk space and provide more efficient distribution of frequently requested documents.

Because a proxy server handles all packets for internal users, it is relatively easy to perform such activities as access control, content filtering, and virus scanning. Packets that contain undesirable content or words can be discarded. Most proxy servers provide proxies for applications like FTP, HTTP, Telnet, and other Internet protocols. Some proxy servers use SOCKS, an authentication protocol, and require clients to have software that can negotiate with

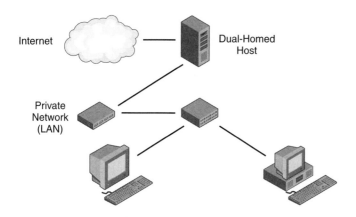

FIGURE 6-8 Dual-Homed Configuration

SOCKS. SOCKS Version 4 provides for unsecured firewall traversal for TCP-based client-server applications, including Telnet; FTP; and the popular information-discovery protocols such as HTTP, WAIS, and Gopher.

There are both advantages and disadvantages to using proxy servers for security. Advantages are:

- Users do not need to log in or have accounts on a bastion host, which allows the bastion host to remain simple and lean.
- The use of a proxy server allows audit trails of user activity. Detection of inappropriate access by internal users is possible.
- Proxies can hide internal IP addresses.
- Logging can include client IP address, date and time, URL, byte count, and HTTP transactions.

Disadvantages include:

- Most Internet services have proxy services; however, a particular service desired may not be available.
- Support for a particular protocol such as simple network management protocol (SNMP) may not be available.

Demilitarized Zone and Bastion Hosts

Users can gain access to semi-trusted networks that provide generally public databases, e-mail, and various servers via a **demilitarized zone (DMZ)**. Confidential and proprietary elements do not reside on this network. The DMZ sits between the Internet and the internal network's security shield and contains a combination of firewalls and bastion hosts. A **bastion host** is designed to defend against attacks aimed at the inside network. On the Internet, a bastion host is the only host computer that a company allows to be addressed directly from the public network and is designed to screen the rest of its network from security exposure. **FIGURE 6-9** provides a graphical representation of a DMZ configuration.

The firewall controls access to the attached network clouds. Internet users cannot directly access internal systems; however, internal users can directly access the Internet through the firewall. Internal users can exchange data with the systems in the DMZ, and the DMZ also allows some external access to a few special systems.

In computer networks, a DMZ is a computer host or small network inserted as a "neutral zone" between a company's private network and the outside public network. It prevents outside users from getting direct access to a server that has company data. A DMZ is an optional and more secure approach to a firewall and effectively acts as a proxy server as well. In a typical DMZ configuration for a small company, a separate computer (or host in network terms) receives requests from users within the private network for access to Web sites or other companies accessible on the public network. The DMZ host then initiates sessions for these requests on the public network. However, the DMZ host is not able to initiate a session back into the private network. It can only forward packets that have already been requested.

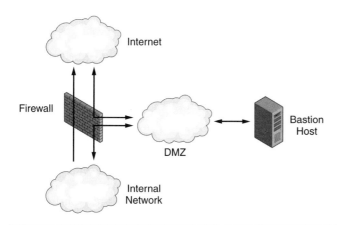

FIGURE 6-9 Demilitarized Zone (DMZ)

Users of the public network outside the company can access only the DMZ host. The DMZ may typically also contain the company's Web pages, so these could be served to the outside world. However, the DMZ provides access to no other company data. In the event that an outside user penetrated the DMZ host's security, the Web pages might be corrupted, but no other company information would be exposed. Cisco, a major router supplier, is one company that sells products designed for setting up a DMZ.

Servers and Workstations

Encryption on a router provides only partial data integrity on a campus network. When data are sent from a workstation to a server, or vice versa, the traffic often crosses two routers. With encryption at the router, the traffic is only encrypted when traversing the backbone. The *backbone* is the network domain responsible for transferring cross-campus traffic as quickly as possible without any processor-intensive operations.

If the data are accessed by another user in the LAN before they reach the router, the data are readable. (*Note the LAN is the network domain that consists of the switching and routing device required to connect users to the network.*) Even more critical, unauthorized users in the server farm can read the data after they pass through the router. Because most network traffic goes to the servers, the server farm is a likely spot for a security breach and information theft. This situation is unacceptable for highly sensitive data. The server farm is the network domain that consists of the enterprise servers, and switching and routing devices required for connection to the rest of the network.

If the network carries extremely sensitive data, workstation and server encryption should be implemented along with router encryption. The level of encryption used at the workstation should be based on the level of confidentiality required for the message to be sent across the network. If the message requires complete confidentiality, then hash functions and asymmetric and symmetric encryption can all be used for data integrity. (*Note that encryption slows down the performance of workstations and some network devices.*)

EXTRANET AND INTRANET LAN ISSUES

These LAN utilization types were introduced in Chapter 5. As a review, an *intranet* provides Internet-type services for in-house, authorized employees. Security issues are not as formidable as for extranets. An **extranet** allows business partners, suppliers, and contractors access to portions of each other's intranets. There are special security arrangements required in this environment.

Extranet Security

Extranets are extensions of corporate intranets and usually allow access via the Internet; however, sensitive data can be kept private via the use of a firewall. Private information and other resources can be kept off-limits by implementing a number of strategies, including packet filtering and intrusion detection. Intrusion detection is described in Chapter 10. When implemented properly, extranets provide access to appropriate resources, while securing others on a selective basis.

The real security challenge involving extranets relates to partners whose business relationships are dynamically changing and complex. Today's partners may become tomorrow's competitors. An extranet must permit dynamic changes in access control to guard against the loss of sensitive and private information. Two key security requirements for extranet access include user authentication and authorization. It should be noted authentication and authorization are commonalities in network security.

The identity of a user wishing to access the extranet must be authenticated. This process is complicated when employees or business partners access information from multiple computers and from remote locations over the Internet. This means remote sites require additional security protocols in order to limit server access. This gives rise to a number of issues:

- There are often many Web servers in large organizations, and users need access privileges for each server.
- Users must remember passwords for many servers.
- Administrators must manage the access controls for each individual server.
- Many separate entries must be added or removed when a user's access privileges change or when there is user turnover.

A security process that lets the organization manage access controls for all centrally located server elements and present users with a **single sign-on (SSO)** to the Web space would simplify security management. After the user has been identified, the access privileges must be determined. Security policies must explicitly grant access rights to Web resources. This access control can be complicated if it is different for each Web server accessed. A centralized authorization framework would simplify this server administration.

A security management system must be easy to implement and administer and must integrate easily into the organization's infrastructure. Complexities in security management increase the possibility of human errors, make the extranet difficult to navigate, and expose it to attack or misuse.

The SSO concept addresses a common problem for users requiring access to multiple systems or applications. With SSO, a user presents a single set of logon credentials to an authentication server. This server transparently logs the user onto all authorized systems and applications. The downside is that this SSO process is difficult to implement and the user has unrestricted access to authorized resources.

Intranet Security

A firewall is implemented in an intranet security system, which is designed to limit Internet access to a company's intranet. The firewall permits the flow of e-mail traffic, product and service information, job postings, and so forth, while restricting unauthorized access to private information residing on the intranet. Security system designers have noted that firewalls used alone may not be sufficient to provide complete protection for the network. They suggest that a layered defense using routers with a proactive intrusion detection system will ensure a higher level of security.

Firewalls are implemented with routers and proxy servers. (*Remember: a proxy server is a firewall component that controls how internal users access the outside world and how Internet users access the internal network.*) In some cases, the proxy blocks all outside connections and only allows internal users to access the Internet, which means the only packets allowed back through the proxy are those returning responses to requests from inside the firewall. Each organization must decide the level of Internet access that is acceptable, which can ensure their resources remain fully protected.

SECURE PROTOCOLS

A **protocol** is a convention or standard that controls or enables the connection, communication, and data transfer between two computing endpoints. In its simplest form, a protocol can be defined as the rules governing the syntax, semantics, and synchronization of communication.

Once keys have been exchanged, clients and servers can engage in secure sessions and transactions. A number of protocols have been developed to handle these secure sessions and transactions. Various protocols address this subject, and the technician would need to research and understand these:

- Private Communication Technology (PCT).
- Secure Sockets Layer (SSL).
- Pretty Good Privacy (PGP).
- Secure Hypertext Transfer Protocol (SHTTP).

Details concerning these protocols are provided in Chapter 13.

Wireless Technologies

In addition to the previously discussed protocol standards, there exist numerous protocols (described further in Chapter 13) and systems for transporting wireless communications. Technical network personnel would need to research and understand these technologies:

- Bluetooth.
- GPRS.
- 3G.
- EDGE.
- UMTS.
- CDMA2000.
- WCDMA.

BIOMETRIC SYSTEMS

Biometrics is the study of biological data and biometric-based authentication, which is an application that uses specific personal traits for access control. Biometrics offers a secure means of limiting access to computer and networking assets. Some of these personal verification methods include iris and retinal scanning, hand and finger geometry, and palm and finger scanning. This "new" technology may increase the accuracy with which security systems can readily identify individuals. The technology relies on measurements of physical characteristics that are unique to an individual. These include behavioral characteristics, handwritten characteristics, and voice recognition. **TABLE 6-2** provides a matrix of techniques along with their comparative accuracy. There are practical biometric techniques currently available that may be acceptable to users. This technology is not in wide use today, mainly due to the lack of standards and the implementation expense. There is also a lack of trust and recognition from users, who are generally not educated on the technology. These concerns include possible invasion of privacy and the association of finger scanning with criminals. This section looks into the various biometric methods that can be deployed to provide for security access.

Biometric methods discussed include finger scanning; finger and hand geometry; palm, retina, and iris imaging; face and voice recognition; and signature verification.

TABLE 6-2 Techniques and Comparative Accuracy

Technique	Comparative Accuracy
Finger scanning	1:500
Hand geometry	1:500
Iris imaging	1:131,000
Retina recognition	1:10,000,000
Signature verification	1:50
Speaker recognition	1:50

Finger Scanning

In the process of **finger scanning**, the user's finger is placed on a reader, where a picture is taken of the fingerprint. The system then converts this picture into a map of minutiae points, which is then put into an algorithm for creating a binary template. This binary template is stored and compared during the authentication and verification process. Common fingerprint patterns are divided into three main groups: arches, loops, and whorls. Approximately 5 percent of the patterns in the population are arches, 30 percent are whorls, and 65 percent are loops.

Finger-scanning imaging techniques include thermal, tactile, capacitance, optical, and ultrasound. Optical images can be captured from images made by a finger on a glass platen. Tactile and thermal images can be captured from a pressure or temperature sensor. Capacitance images are generated from capacitance silicon sensors. Sound waves can generate ultrasound images from finger patterns. There are a number of automated fingerprint identification systems currently being utilized. Finger scanning is highly accurate, and fraudulent deception of the system is difficult. The equipment is easy to use and is readily accepted by users.

Finger Geometry

Some biometric vendors use **finger geometry** or finger shape to determine identity. Unique finger characteristics—such as finger length, thickness, width, and knuckle size—are measured on one or two fingers. Two techniques are utilized for capturing the images. The user can insert the index and middle finger into a reader and a camera takes a three-dimensional image, or the user can insert a finger into a tunnel where sensors take three-dimensional measurements.

Finger geometry systems are simple to use, very accurate, and impervious to deception. Public acceptance, however, is somewhat lower than for finger scanning, because users must insert their fingers into a reader.

Hand Geometry

Some commercial biometric applications are using the two-dimensional shape of the hand for access control, known as **hand geometry**. Users place their hand on a reader, aligning their fingers with specially positioned guides, and a camera captures an image. Measurements center on finger length and the shape of the fingers and knuckles. Commercial systems that perform three-dimensional shape analysis of the hand are under development.

Hand geometry systems are simple to use, accurate, impervious to deception, and readily accepted by users. Hand geometry, however, is less distinctive than finger-scanning techniques, because people can have similar hand geometry.

Palm Imaging

Measurement of palms, or **palm imaging**, is performed by techniques similar to those for finger scanning. A scanner shaped to accommodate the palm scans the ridges, valleys, and minutiae data found on the palm. Alternatively, latent or ink images of the palm can be scanned, and the minutiae data are extracted, processed, and stored in the system. Palm images are useful in crime detection, and some vendors are developing commercial applications. Like finger scanning, palm imaging is simple to use, very accurate, and impervious to deception. User acceptance, however, is not very high.

Retina Recognition

The retina forms a unique pattern for each individual. The user views a green dot for a few seconds until the eye is sufficiently focused for a scanner to capture the blood vessel pattern. The retina pattern is captured by the scanner and then compared with previously stored patterns for identification.

Retina scanning provides very high accuracy, provided the user's eye is properly focused. Reflection from glasses can create interference. Users are resistant to this technique due to the infrared light scanner. Deception of the system is very unlikely.

Iris Imaging

The human iris is a complex structure well suited for unique identification. Each iris contains a complex pattern of specific characteristics such as corona, crypts, filaments, freckles, pits, and striations. A black-and-white video camera can be used to capture an image of the iris. Unique features of the iris are extracted from the captured image by the recognition system. These features are converted into a unique iris code, which are compared to previously stored iris codes for user recognition.

Artificial duplication of the pattern of an individual iris is virtually impossible, and **iris imaging** provides high accuracy. The technique is relatively easy to use, and there appears to be little resistance from users. Fraudulent deception of the system is very unlikely.

Face Recognition

No direct physical contact is required with **face recognition**. The camera captures a facial image, and a number of points on the face are mapped by the system. From these measurements, a unique representation of the individual's face is created. A complete map of the entire face can be created. There is a downside to this system, because people change over time. Some systems compensate for this by combining recently stored information with previously stored images.

Face recognition offers reasonable accuracy but can be affected by poor lighting, aging, glasses, and facial hair. The system can be retrained and updated to recognize changes in users. The equipment is easy to use and readily accepted by users. Current systems can recognize and identify users from distances of 2 to 32 meters.

Signature Verification

Signature-scanning techniques examine the way users sign their names. The system examines the dynamics of the signing process, rather than the signature. Extracted characteristics may include the angle at which the pen is held, the time taken to sign, velocity and acceleration of the signing process, and the number of times the pen is lifted from the document during the signing process.

Ordinary forgery techniques do not work because behavioral characteristics are used rather than a signature. Signature data can be captured with a special pen that contains sensors or with a tablet that senses the motion of a stylus. Acoustic emission measurements of the pen can be captured. A number of signatures can be recorded to build a user's profile.

Signatures are one of the most common methods of establishing identity and are therefore readily acceptable by financial institutions and others that require conventional signatures. Recognition accuracy is high, and the method is considered impervious to deception.

Biometric Security

Biometric technology can be used successfully to identify users; however, it is necessary for the application to be specifically designed, taking into consideration the ease of use, accuracy, cost, and deployment. Finger scanning appears to be the technology of choice. These systems are moderately accurate and easy to use. Acceptance by users is good, and the technique is relatively inexpensive. A biometric technique would be useful as part of a two-factor or three-factor identification scheme.

WIRED LAN SECURITY

Providing appropriate security for the LAN, its data, and users is the combined responsibility of management, the LAN administrator, and the LAN software. Management must establish the environment by providing security polices and by communicating the importance of security to all employees. They must also conduct regular audits of the LAN, which can be performed by both internal personnel and external auditors.

LAN hardware, such as servers and communications controllers, must not be accessible to unauthorized people. Someone, such as the LAN administrator, must assume responsibility for ensuring the security of the LAN components. An orderly process must be in place for establishing and maintaining access control tables in the various LAN devices. Changes must be approved by management and should not be made without proper approval.

There are a number of policies and procedures that must be enacted to ensure the proper level of security on the LAN. These items include but are not limited to the following:

- Use and frequent changing of passwords for logging on to the LAN.
- Sign-off when leaving a workstation.
- Regular backups of disk systems.
- Downloading data to the LAN from foreign systems.
- Scanning disks for viruses.
- Dial-up access to the LAN.
- Utilization of legal, authorized software.
- Encryption of data sent on the LAN or stored on the servers.

Managing and providing a secure LAN requires careful attention at both the management and technical levels of an organization.

A passive attack such as eavesdropping or monitoring can be focused toward e-mail, file transfer, and client/server exchanges in the wired LAN environment. As described in the previous sections, workstations are attached to some type of local wired topology. The user can reach other workstations, hosts, and servers directly on the LAN or other devices that interconnect over other LAN segments. This is an area of vulnerability and must be addressed with a combination of security procedures, including triple-A, firewalls, and routers.

It is possible that the eavesdropper may not be an employee, because it is possible to access the wired LAN through a dial-in capability. The security administrator must look at the possibility of internal and external attackers using a dial-in access line. Access to the outside, untrusted world is almost always available in the form of a bank of dial-out and/or dial-in modems, terminal server, or router.

LAN NETWORK MANAGEMENT

Most network management architectures use the same basic structure and set of relationships. Managed devices such as routers and other network devices run software that enables them to send alerts when they recognize problems or predefined situations that might warrant attention. Upon receiving these alerts, management entities are programmed to react by executing some action including operator notification, event logging, system shutdown, or automatic attempts at system repair.

Management entities can also poll end-network devices to check the values of certain variables. Polling can be automatic or user initiated, but agents in the managed devices respond to all polls. Agents are software modules that first compile information about the managed devices where they reside, then store this information in a management database, and then provide it to management entities within the network management system (NMS).

An important requirement for networking is the ability to manage large networks that consist of hardware and software from a number of providers and manufacturers. Well-known network management protocols include the simple network management protocol (SNMP) and common management information protocol (CMIP). Additional details concerning network management protocols and systems are provided in Chapter 10.

CHAPTER SUMMARY

A LAN consists of a group of data devices, such as computers, printers, and scanners, that are linked with each other within a limited area such as on the same floor or building. The most commonly used LAN technologies are Ethernet, token ring, and FDDI. Wired connections between devices may be any combination of twisted-pair copper wire, coaxial cable, fiber-optic line, or wireless media. Security issues vary depending on the media type and network type.

Using RF technology, wireless LANs transmit and receive data over the air, minimizing the need for wired connections. Thus, wireless LANs combine data connectivity with user mobility. There are a number of security issues associated with wireless devices.

A VLAN is a grouping of network devices not restricted to a physical segment or switch. VLANs can be used to restructure broadcast domains similarly to the way that bridges, switches, and routers divide collision domains. Security and management of a LAN is enhanced with a VLAN configuration.

Network security within the infrastructure can be augmented with the addition of access control. This additional protection can take the form of a filter, access list, or a firewall. The objective of a firewall is to protect trusted networks from untrusted entities. A firewall may consist of a combination of hardware and software.

Two devices deployed in today's enterprise networks include routers and gateways. Routers are intelligent devices, which connect like and unlike LANs, MANs, and WANs. A gateway is an entrance and exit into a communications network. In data networks, a gateway is typically a node on a network that communicates with an otherwise incompatible network. Security features include access control lists and routing tables.

Biometrics offers a secure means of limiting access to computer and networking resources and assets. Some of these personal verification methods include iris and retinal scanning, hand and finger geometry, palm and finger scanning.

An important requirement for networking is the ability to manage large networks that consist of hardware and software from a number of providers and manufacturers. Managed devices such as routers and other network devices run software that enables them to send alerts when they recognize problems or predefined situations that might warrant attention.

KEY TERMS

access list	finger scanning	protocol
access point	firewall	proxy server
bastion host	gateway	retina scanning
biometrics	hand geometry	router
demilitarized zone (DMZ)	intranet	signature scanning
extranet	iris imaging	single sign-on (SSO)
face recognition	local area network (LAN)	virtual local area network (VLAN)
filters	packet filtering	wireless local area network (WLAN)
finger geometry	palm imaging	

SECURITY REVIEW QUESTIONS

1. A _____ consists of a group of data devices—such as computers, servers, printers, and scanners—that are linked with each other within a limited area such as on the same floor or building.

2. What topology is usually found on a commercial telephone system?

3. What is the purpose and function of a VLAN?

4. A _____ transmits and receives data over the air, combining data connectivity with user mobility.

5. A _____ broadcasts messages in wireless format, which must be directed to wireless users, and relays messages sent by wireless users directed to resources or users on the wired side of its connection.

6. _____, also called _____, blocks users who are not authorized to access segments of the network and allows access only to authorized users.

7. A _____ is a combination of hardware and software, which limits the exposure of a computer or group of computers to an attack from an outside source by controlling the flow of incoming and outgoing network traffic.

8. _____ limits communications based on the type of traffic, source and destination IP addresses, ports, and other information.

9. The _____ sits between the Internet and the internal network's security shield and contains a combination of firewalls and bastion hosts.

10. Describe the various biometric techniques.

RESEARCH ACTIVITIES

1. Develop a comparison of LANs, VLANs, and VPNs.

2. Compare the different security issues of wired LANs and wireless LANs.

3. Provide a comparison of the various LAN topologies.

4. Identify the different functions of firewalls, routers, and gateways.

5. Research and identify the most common port numbers.

6. Identify the differences between a bastion host, a dual-homed host, and a screened-subnet host.

7. Explain the differences between an intranet and an extranet.

8. Look up the SNMP RFC on the RFC INDEX. Provide an overview of the trap protocol data unit (PDU).

9. Describe the policies and procedures that can be implemented to protect a network.

10. Construct a feature and function overview of biometric security methods.

CHAPTER 7

Computer, Server, and Database Security Issues

🔒 CHAPTER CONTENTS

- Identify the components and usage of a computer system.
- Look at the current use of client/server systems in the network.
- Learn how to protect computer and client/server systems.
- Understand the security issues inherent in a database management system.
- Become familiar with the various database backup techniques.
- Identify vulnerabilities in the computer systems and infrastructure.
- Understand how voice communication systems work.
- Become familiar with the various options to provide a safe and secure computing environment.

INTRODUCTION

This chapter provides an overview of computer systems, client/server configurations, and telecommunication systems used in a network. Security issues relating to hardware and software components used in these systems are discussed.

Computer system and networking components comprise a major portion of the organization's physical assets. These devices along with their respective operating systems present an enormous opportunity for security breaches. This chapter describes the major hardware components that are part of an organization's computer and networking operations and offers suggestions to protect these assets from both internal and external threats.

The aim of computer networking security measures and countermeasures is to limit damage to the organization's assets. Enhancement to security includes the deployment of hardware devices such as firewalls, gateways, and routers. Sophisticated software products control these hardware devices.

The advent of the client/server environment increases the need for security. These devices provide the processing and storage capabilities for network systems such as e-commerce and distributed computing. Securing mechanized financial transactions has become a priority.

Voice communications systems play a major role in the network. These systems provide access to a number of sensitive resources that must be protected from both internal and external attacks and intrusions. Various approaches to telecommunications security are presented.

COMPUTER SYSTEMS

A computer system consists of a processor, main memory, input/output devices, and devices that interconnect these major components. In addition to the hardware components, there is the software component that includes an operating system, utility programs, and numerous application programs. The material presented in this chapter are oriented toward two categories of computers: mainframes and client/servers. The issues relating to security and integrity are relevant for small client/server and very large mainframe systems.

Historical Overview

Mainframes (often colloquially referred to as "Big Iron") are computers used by large organizations for critical applications, typically bulk data processing such as census, industry and consumer statistics, **enterprise resource planning (ERP)**, and financial transaction processing. The term probably originated from the early mainframes because they were housed in enormous, room-sized metal boxes or frames. Later the term was used to distinguish high-end commercial machines from less powerful units. Many defining characteristics of "mainframes" were established in the 1960s, but those characteristics continue to expand and evolve to the present day.

The advent of communication networks and the Internet ushered in the client/server model. The client/server software architecture model distinguishes client systems from server systems, which communicate over a network. A client/server application is a distributed system comprised of both client and server software. A client software process may initiate a communication session, while the server waits for requests from any client. *Client/server* describes the relationship between two computer programs in which one program, the *client*, makes a service request from another program, the *server*, which fulfills the request. Although the client/server idea can be used by programs within a single computer, it is a more important idea in a network. In a network, the client/server model provides a convenient way to efficiently interconnect programs that are distributed across different locations. Computer transactions using the client/server model are very common. Most Internet applications, such as e-mail, Web access, and database access, are based on the client/server model.

Mainframe Computer System

A **mainframe** is a large, powerful computer, almost always linked to a configuration of peripheral devices such as disk controllers, communication controllers, and high-speed printers. It is used in a multipurpose environment at the corporate, campus, or headquarters level. It contains megabytes and gigabytes of memory and gigabytes and terabytes of disk storage and processes data in the millions of instructions per second (MIPS). The databases that reside on mass-storage devices are attached to the mainframe via high-speed controllers.

FIGURE 7-1 depicts the hardware environment of a mainframe computer. The mainframe is connected to a front-end processor (FEP) and an operator console. Various controllers are connected to the FEP. These controllers are used to connect to various devices such as printers, workstations, and servers. The mainframe also supports massive storage devices on disk farms.

Mainframe Components

Data processing equipment includes communication controllers, disk drives, tape drives, plotters, printers, and front-end processors. These devices are normally part of a mainframe computer system. The component that concerns most users is the disk system, which is where the database resides. Usually the database is transparent to the average user, but if the database belongs to the user, there are numerous challenges, both in terms of integrity and security, that must be addressed. In addition to hardware, an operating system is required that controls the operation of the computer. Very large computer systems often consist of many smaller computers that operate in parallel and process many computer instructions simultaneously.

Front-End Processor

The **front-end processor (FEP)** acts as the traffic cop of the mainframe data communications world. It typically resides in front of the mainframe computer and is designed to handle the telecommunications burden so the mainframe computer can efficiently process its programmed functions. Smaller systems use input/output processor (IOP) modules to accomplish this same task. The FEP must be located close to the processor or connected via some high-speed communication facility. The FEP can be a single point of failure when all communication links for processor access are terminated in one device; therefore, FEPs are often duplicated.

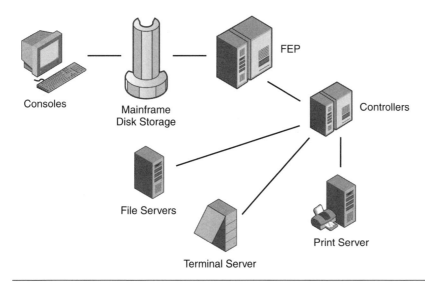

FIGURE 7-1 Mainframe Configuration

Controllers

A **controller** is a device that controls the operation of another piece of equipment. Specifically, in data communications, a controller resides between a host and terminals and relays information between them. Controllers can be housed in the host, can be stand-alone, or can reside on a file server. These devices possess an extremely fast transfer rate. Interfaces and interface cards that provide physical connectivity reside in these devices. Controllers usually do not cause a security problem; however, they can fail and cause an integrity issue. Dual and redundant controllers are a solution that provides sufficient backup in most cases, but there is an expense issue. An integrity issue usually requires a mirroring configuration, where all activities occur to different computer or storage devices simultaneously.

Operating System

The **operating system (OS)** is the software that controls the execution of programs on a processor and manages the processor's resources. Examples are OS/2, MS-DOS, and UNIX. Functions performed by the OS include process and task scheduling and memory management. The OS determines which process should run at a given time. This is accomplished by an interrupt process, which allows the sharing of processor time among numerous processes and users. The process of memory management allows multiple users and processes to share a limited amount of computer main storage. These processes are transparent to the casual user.

The following resources are usually managed and allocated among competing applications:

- CPU processing time.
- Memory access disk storage.
- Input/output devices.
- Retrieval and file system.
- Security.

It should be noted that a computer system is a set of resources for the storage, processing, and movement of data and the control of these functions. The operating system, therefore, is responsible for managing these resources. It is a sophisticated computer program. There are two types of operating systems: batch and interactive. In an *interactive* system, the user communicates with the computer through a terminal device to request the execution of a program. The results often are immediate. In a *batch* system, the user's program is "batched" together with programs from other users and submitted by a computer operator for subsequent execution. The results from batch processing can be delayed for some time. Batch systems are often used by organizations to update databases during the off-hours of business operation. This is similar to banking transactions that close at 4 PM for any given day. Controls must be in place for both interactive and batch-processing OSs to ensure integrity and security of the resources and the data involved.

Directories

A **directory** is a structure containing one or more files and a description of these files. Most network operating systems will create a directory called Users, under which a personal directory is created for each user account. Users typically have full rights to their own directories, which mean they can create new branching subdirectories and share files or directories with other users.

A directory service is the facility within networking software that provides information on resources available on the network, including files, printers, data sources, applications, and users. It also provides users with access to resources and information on extended networks. A directory service is to the network what white pages are to the telephone system. Large organizations have a need for these services to identify distributed and dispersed operations. A universal directory is also a requirement for the Internet and other public service networks.

Common distributed networks have resources and users at many locations. If a user needs to send a message to someone or access a service at a remote location, directory services can help the user locate the intended recipient or service. Because directory services are essential to locating services on the network, they must be continuously available. Directory service information is typically stored in a directory database that can be partitioned and replicated to other locations. This benefits users at remote locations who can access the database locally rather than over wide area network links.

As organizations open up their internal applications to customers and suppliers, they must ensure that only authorized users can access corporate data. Directories have emerged as the primary traffic cop connecting users to needed information. These directories often support digital certificates and electronic signatures that identify users to a network. To simplify this process, suppliers have been developing standards, which would allow robust, end-to-end security for enterprise applications.

X.500 is the designation for a directory standard that permits applications such as electronic mail to access information that is located either at a central location or distributed remotely. The X.500 goal is to make all users on the global networks accessible using directory services. The Internet is an example of an international system through which millions of users can exchange e-mail and search for services that might be available on Internet-connected networks.

Many organizations are not ready to expose their internal employee and resource lists to outsiders. Intercompany directory services and the X.500 standard have limited acceptance due to possible security problems. Another aspect of directory service security is the ability of the service to authenticate users and grant them access to the directory. Many vendors are implementing X.509 public-key encryption standards, which can provide single logon to a variety of network services after users have checked in with the directory. A unique session ID is created to track users during their online sessions. In addition, an encrypted channel can also be implemented to prevent hackers from making sense out of information that crosses the line. Details concerning X.509 are described in Chapter 13.

Disk Technology

Servers require enormous amounts of disk storage. Web servers store thousands of Web pages and associated image, sound, and video files. Storage devices can include small computer system interface (SCSI) disk drives, Fiber Channel, and redundant array of inexpensive disk (RAID) drives. High-end PC servers use SCSI drives, which are somewhat faster, but more expensive than the standard enhanced integrated drive electronic (EIDE) disk drive. For extremely high-speed disk access, high-end servers are moving toward Fiber Channel disk access. Whereas SCSI hosts must be within about 12 meters of their disk drives, Fiber Channel allows disk drives to be hundreds of meters and even kilometers away from their hosts. RAID uses multiple disk drives controlled by a single controller board. System and application software resides on the computer system's disk drives. Technical specifications are included in Chapter 13.

RAID Storage Devices

Redundant array of inexpensive disk (RAID) devices are used to improve performance and automatically recover from a system failure. They can maintain backup files and protect data by continuously writing two copies of the data to a different hard drive. Its primary purpose is to provide fault tolerance and protection against disk failures. RAID separates data into multiple units and stores it on multiple disks by using a process called "striping." There are several levels of RAID available, including RAID 0, RAID 1, and RAID 5, that provide for disk striping, disk mirroring, and duplexing:

- RAID 0 is one method of disk striping in which more than one hard drive is treated as a single volume. Some data are written to multiple drives but are treated as one logical drive.
- RAID 1 is designed to protect data from a hard drive failure by writing data twice—once to each of two drives. This type of disk mirroring allows two hard drives to use the same adapter card. Also supported with RAID 1 is duplexing in which each hard drive has its own adapter card.
- RAID 5, which is disk striping with parity, is a combination of RAID 0 and RAID 1. It improves fault tolerance and drive capacity. Disk striping is a technique for spreading data over multiple disk drives.

Storage Management

Storage is a service that users want available at all times as an unlimited resource. It is more than a collection of disks and tapes. It is an interconnected system of storage devices, software, and servers that receive and deliver data. The role of storage management is to maximize performance, availability, and security at a reasonable cost. A security breach or a failure to the data storage devices can result in a catastrophe to an organization. Disaster recovery is discussed in Chapter 9.

A **storage area network (SAN)** is a high-speed subnetwork of shared storage devices. The storage device is a machine that contains nothing but disks for storing data. A SAN architecture works in a way that makes all storage devices available to all servers on a LAN or WAN. As more storage devices are added to a SAN, they, too, will be accessible from any server in the larger network. The server acts as a pathway between the end user and the stored data. Because stored data does not reside directly on any of a network's servers, server power is utilized for business applications, and network capacity is available to the end user.

CLIENT/SERVER SYSTEMS

A **client/server** is a computer located on a local area network that splits the workload between itself and desktop computers. In most cases, the "client" is a desktop computing device or program "served" by another networked computing device. Computers are integrated over the network by a software application, that provides a single system image. The server can be a minicomputer, workstation, or a larger computer system, and multiple servers can serve a single client. **FIGURE 7-2** depicts four different clients that could access three different servers over some network. These servers have access to common data storage on a storage (disk) farm.

Organizations may institute security policies that constrain how clients and servers communicate, such as partitioning computers into secure and nonsecure components or subnets.

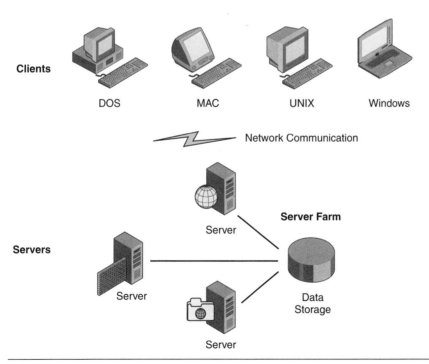

FIGURE 7-2 Client/Server Configuration

To prevent client/server programs from compromising security, the administrator places policy constraints on connectivity, which allows computer-to-computer communication while restricting access to the nonsecure portion of the network. Although such policies might increase security, they can make it more difficult to design and program in the client/server environment. Many of today's network users access a server system somewhere in the world, and there are significant security issues relating to accessing these client/server systems. Efforts will be made in this chapter to provide users with some guidance in the protection of their computer assets.

Client/Server Components

A **server** has a hardware and software component. It is a shared computer on the LAN and a program that provides some service to the other client programs. The server is a component of the client/server environment and connects to a network device. Servers are gatekeepers to systems and information files. The following server systems make the client/server environment possible:

- File server.
- Print server.
- Database server.
- Communications server.

Server Issues

To effectively secure servers, planning and coordination are required. It is necessary to determine possible vulnerabilities in terms of operating systems, communication software, and applications before implementing a security program. It is also necessary to determine different security levels, which assigns specific access levels on a "need to know" basis. This means that one level of security might be "read only," with other levels ascribed to mission-critical and proprietary data. Management must determine who can read what information, who has authorization to modify data, and how the levels relate.

There are several areas for concern when developing a security scheme, most of which revolve around software designed to make more efficient use of the computing environment but that can simultaneously compromise security. These include automatic directory listings and user-maintained directories.

The more a remote hacker can learn about a system, the easier it is to compromise. Automatic directory listings provided on a number of vendors' servers are convenient and allow potential access to sensitive information. Information could include common gateway interface (CGI) scripts, symbolic links, and source-code control logs. As a precaution, users should remove unwanted files from the document root directory.

Some servers allow the extension of the document tree with symbolic links. This is a beneficial feature; it can, however, lead to security breaches when a user accidentally creates a link to a sensitive area of the system. An explicit entry in the server's configuration file would be a more appropriate method to accomplish the same thing. Some servers allow turning off the symbolic link-following feature. It is also possible to enable symbolic link following only if the owner of the link matches the link's target.

Additions (server-side includes) by users are a major security hole. Their use should be restricted to trusted users or turned off completely. Allowing any user on the host system to add documents to a Web site is considered dangerous. Publishing files that contain sensitive system information, CGI scripts, server-side includes, or symbolic links that can compromise security must not be allowed. When creating a home page, it is best to restrict usage to only a portion of the document root. Whether home pages are located in user's home directories or in a piece of the document root, it is prudent to disallow server-side includes and CGI scripts in this area.

Processing the public-key operations required by the Secure Sockets Layer (SSL) can slow down the performance of a server under heavy traffic conditions. Hardware to speed security processing allows servers to perform such processing very rapidly so that commercial transactions are not delayed. There are a number of devices on the market that improve the overall throughput of the enterprise servers and also enhance their security features.

Server Security

Maintaining secure servers is an absolute necessity because they are the gatekeepers to systems and databases. Computer security involves more than setting up a program of firewalls and passwords. It is an ongoing, organization-wide awareness that someone could break into the network and steal information and other resources. Failing to implement protocols and procedures mitigates the effectiveness of the best-designed security program.

Remember that servers consist of hardware and software components. The hardware selected will determine the level of performance provided, whereas the software can determine the level of security of a site. Two approaches to server security include purchasing secure server software packages or in-house development using a variety of packages. Whichever solution is selected, certain elements should be included in this security system. These elements include password protection, encryption, firewalls, and SSL technology. All of these elements offer some degree of security that, when combined, can produce a formidable security scheme.

Server Security Methods

There are a number of ways to secure a server, given the objectives and requirements. The most common security method is access control, which includes user passwords, card or key systems, biometrics, and data encryption. Complex security mechanisms usually increase the inconvenience level for authorized users, which could result in employee resistance. The objective is to develop a protection strategy that does not cause employee complacency or circumvention.

A wide range of access control mechanisms has evolved over time, and many are related to the organization's internal policies. Many of these techniques use authentication mechanisms to establish the identity of a user. An alternative mechanism employs security labels to provide input to rules-based access control policy decisions. Rules-based policies could rely on other inputs, such as time and date, when making access control decisions. In addition to controlling access to databases through a secure server, administrators must evaluate all shared resources that are accessible through the network so that their respective access restrictions can be implemented.

Password protection is the most common means of securing server access. Passwords provide a minimal level of security without requiring special devices such as keys or cards. The downside in implementing only password protection is user ambivalence. If the password method is implemented, several precautions should be mandated:

- Passwords should not contain easily obtainable information.
- They should be dynamic, with mandatory periodic changes.
- A multilevel password protection scheme should be implemented if hierarchical security is an issue.
- A master password file should be maintained and surveyed periodically.

Additional access restriction and control mechanisms include magnetic card systems, biometric systems, and data encryption. These techniques can be used in concert with each other or implemented singularly. A magnetic card and a fingerprint can be used to provide two-factor identification—at the same time the data are being encrypted.

Magnetic card systems allow users to access data from any available workstation with an attached card reader. The card key system allows selective access for each user as opposed to each workstation. Smart cards offer a wide range of security considerations, including eliminating manual passwords. They are viable for both local and remote access control.

Biometrics, discussed in Chapter 6, is a type of identification based on the uniqueness of an individual's physical attributes and traits. These include fingerprints, handprints, voice quality, and retina patterns. The biometric method requires a considerable amount of computer processing, which makes it slower than some other mechanisms. Governments are currently utilizing it to protect national security servers.

Data encryption is a mathematical method of scrambling data to disguise its original content. This is the most popular security mechanism for protecting sensitive information during transmission between computers. Data confidentiality is achieved by encrypting the message at the sender and decrypting at the receiver. Because attackers, including those using network monitors (sniffers), cannot read encrypted data, it has a high probability of remaining secure.

An additional security technique, called *inactivity time-out*, can be utilized for servers that perform remote access. Servers can be configured to automatically terminate calls when there has been no activity for a specified time interval. All of these different approaches in combination provide a high level of security at the server level.

PORTABLE COMPUTER AND ELECTRONIC DEVICES

A portable computer, electronic device, or storage device is a component that is designed to be moved from one place to another. These devices could contain a number of different operating and application systems. The primary categories of portable computing devices include:

- Laptop computer.
- Personal digital assistant (PDA).
- Portable data terminal (PDT).
- Tablet personal computer.
- Smart phone.

Additional devices that have a computing or communication capability include:

- Handheld computers.
- Cell phones.
- iPods.
- Tablets.
- BlackBerrys.
- iPhones.
- Portable monitors.

Of particular concern are the portable storage devices that permeate the public and private computer and network environment. These devices are often lost, stolen, or damaged and could contain an enormous amount of sensitive, personal, or confidential information. Security issues for these storage devices are significant. These issues were explored in Chapter 4. Security policies and computer-use policies need to be developed that address the use and misuse of these storage devices.

DATABASE MANAGEMENT SYSTEM

A **database management system (DBMS)** is a software program that operates on a mainframe system or database server to manage data, accept queries from users, and respond to those queries. Security and integrity are fast becoming issues because databases are being organized so they can be accessed remotely. Most databases are operating "real time," which means that transactions to the database occur instantly when an action is made against the data. In the near past, transactions were collected throughout the business day and batch-processed at night. There were opportunities to correct problems using the batch processing method; however, this is not true with online real-time processing. A DBMS may possess the following features:

- A data dictionary that describes the structure of the database, related files, and record information.
- Input and storage method for the data.

- A query language for data manipulation.
- Multi-user access and user access restrictions.
- Data integrity of the data from multiple modifications.
- Security of the data to authorized users.

Data and Database Security

Data have been defined as any materials, which are represented in a formalized manner, so that they can be stored, manipulated, and transmitted by machine. It follows that a **database** is a collection of data stored electronically in a predefined format and according to an established set of rules. There are many potential threats to data that are located in databases. The data threat is probably more widespread than either a hardware or software attack. Data items appear to have a greater value than hardware or software, because more people know how to use and interpret data. Data become information when people assign them meaning. This means, essentially, that data have no intrinsic value unless they can be converted to information. The cost of data and, by extension, the database can be measured by the cost of creation and the cost incurred if it is lost. It may be expensive or impossible to recreate the data. Confidential data, which come into the possession of a competitor, may cause a business to fail. There might be a liability if certain data are released to the public. Data often lose their importance over time. To summarize, data attributes include the following:

- Data, per se, have little intrinsic value.
- The cost of data is difficult to measure.
- Reconstruction of data may be expensive or impossible.
- Data must remain confidential.
- The useful time period of data is short.
- A data attack is more widespread than a hardware or software attack.

Data and database security can be described by three qualities.

- *Availability*—preventing denial of authorized access.
- *Confidentiality*—preventing unauthorized disclosure.
- *Integrity*—preventing unauthorized modification.

Availability of data and the database requires that a number of expectations be met. Security and accessibility will involve a balancing act. Authorized users will demand fast and easy access; sufficient controls must be in place to ensure both confidentiality and integrity of the data. It is essential that data are available in a usable form, and the system must also provide sufficient capacity to meet the user's requirements. Access to the database must be timely, and response time must be within a reasonable range. An overlay of security procedures can slow down database access and response time. Software audits that might be applied to the database and the data can also create a negative impact on performance. As is often the case with controls, security techniques may cause negative performance issues. Because availability applies to both data access and service, it is essential that both be given a thorough consideration before initiating security controls.

DATA AND DATABASE ATTACKS

There are a number of malicious attacks that might occur on a computer database system. These situations correspond to the threat categories of disclosure, integrity, and denial of service. The results of three database attacks that can affect stored information are as follows:

- Sensitive information is disclosed to an unauthorized individual.
- Information is altered in an unacceptable manner.
- Information is made inaccessible to an authorized individual.

A technique for mitigating database attacks is to consider the architecture of the target database system. Most databases are configured as applications running on some underlying operating system. As a result, database attackers can either attack the database directly or attack the underlying operating system. Several different means exist for unauthorized individuals to obtain information from a database. Several problems discussed include the inference problem and the aggregation problem.

Inference Problem

There are subtle methods for an intruder to obtain information from a database. One method, called the **inference problem**, involves a malicious attacker combining information that is available from the database with a suitable analysis to infer information that is presumably hidden. This means that individual data elements, viewed separately, reveal confidential information when viewed collectively. It is, therefore, possible to have public elements in a database reveal private information by inference from this backdoor approach.

Aggregation Problem

The database disclosure problem called **aggregation** occurs when pieces of information that are not sensitive in isolation become sensitive when viewed as a whole. This is a common problem in military applications, where several related secret documents might be viewed collectively as top secret. Databases could deal with this situation by allowing pieces of data to be labeled as nonsensitive, but when a collection or aggregate is created via some query, the database could upgrade the mode of this aggregate to sensitive.

Security Approaches

Several security approaches have been proposed to deal with the previous two problems. These include polyinstantiation and database porting.

Polyinstantiation means there are several views of a database object existing so that a user's view of the database is determined by that user's security attributes. It addresses the aggregation problem by providing a means for labeling different aggregations of data separately. It also addresses the inference problem by providing a means of hiding certain information that might be used to make inferences.

The other approach is to port a database application—**database porting**—to a secure operating system that counters these malicious attacks. Because most database applications rely on the underlying services of an operating system, it can be used to increase the security of the database. In a scheme in which the underlying operating system provides security services to the database application, a common protection that is utilized is the file system protection afforded within the operating system.

Access Rights

Access rights are the "keys" that define a user's ability to access resources on a network. A network administrator or a departmental supervisor usually assigns them. Access rights affect the ability to access directories and files located on the computer system. Typical access rights or permissions include the following:

- No permission.
- Write-only.
- Write/execute.
- Read-only.
- Read/execute.
- Read/write.
- Read/write/execute.

Access rights also control the resources accessible by the user, which include communications services, printers, and fax machines. They can also dictate the time a user can log in or the specific computers available to the user. Users who have rights to access files and directories are usually called *trustees* of those files and directories. MS Windows provides definitions for both rights and permissions. *Rights* control the actions a user can perform on the system, such as logging on from the network, backing up files, and managing printers. *Permissions* give users access to directories, files, and resources such as printers. Permissions include the ability to read, write, execute, and delete files, among others. There are also shared permissions, which give users the ability to access shared files over the network.

PROTECTING THE DATA AND DATABASE ASSET

Can the organization survive if the database asset is destroyed? How much would it cost to recreate the asset? What are the repercussions if it cannot be recreated? These and other questions are pertinent if the organization utilizes a database to conduct its day-to-day activities. The issue is not *if* the database will be corrupted, but *when?* The organization must take proactive steps to ensure that a complete recovery can be affected in a reasonable time period. Additional details concerning contingency planning and disaster recovery planning are provided in Chapter 9.

It is essential for the administrator to identify the possible causes of a database disaster and the steps that will be required to recover it completely. Enterprise network security is not the same for each file, data item, or database. This means that potential incidents are identified, the ramifications are explored, and corrective measures to be taken are identified for each occurrence.

Integrity of Data and Database Elements

What are data, and what can be done to ensure their integrity and security? *Data* are basically any material, represented in a formalized manner, that can be stored, manipulated, and transmitted by a computer. Data are stored in a database according to a predefined format and an established set of rules, called a *schema*. A database that consolidates an organization's data is called a *data warehouse*. Data warehousing is a software strategy in which data are extracted from large transactional databases and other sources and stored in smaller databases, which makes analysis of the data easier.

The possibility of errors in data transmission exists in all telecommunication networks. Correcting and preventing these errors is called maintaining data integrity. Even though accurate transmission of data is essential, data security may be even more important. Data integrity is addressed by utilizing a number of error-control techniques:

- Parity checking.
- Cyclical parity checking.
- Hamming codes.
- Checksums.
- Cyclical redundancy checks.

Data security can be ensured by implementing the five basic goals of the National Institute of Standards and Technology (NIST). These goals state that secure data messages should be sealed, sequenced, secret, signed, and stamped. NIST is described in Chapter 13.

The NIST 800 Series is a set of documents that describe U.S. federal government computer security policies, procedures, and guidelines. NIST is a unit of the Commerce Department and is accessible at *www.nist.gov*. The documents are available free of charge and can be useful to businesses and educational institutions, as well as to government agencies.

NIST 800 Series publications evolved as a result of exhaustive research into workable and cost-effective methods for optimizing the security of information technology (IT) systems and networks in a proactive manner. The publications cover all NIST-recommended procedures and criteria for assessing and documenting threats and vulnerabilities and for implementing security measures to minimize the risk of adverse events. The publications can be useful as guidelines for enforcement of security rules and as legal references in case of litigation involving security issues.

NIST Security Goals

The NIST goals that should be considered when safeguarding data includes the following:

- An unauthorized party cannot modify a sealed message.
- A sequenced message is protected against undetected loss or repetition.
- An unauthorized party cannot understand a secret message.
- A signed message includes proof of the sender's identity.
- A stamped message guarantees receipt by the correct party.

Backup and Data Archiving

There are immense amounts of data collected and information generated continuously on computer and client/server systems. A **backup** is described as a copy of online storage that provides fault protection, and an *archive* is a historical backup. Hopefully, administrators are aware that some type of backup or data archiving is required in the event of some catastrophic event. There are a number of techniques to accomplish this task, including copying data to magnetic media or copying or replicating data to other systems. **Replication** is the process by which a file, a database, or some other form of computer data in one location is created exactly on another computing device in another location. This process should provide for user data access in both locations.

There are three basic types of backup: normal, incremental, and differential. The backup method depends on issues such as the volume of data, the frequency, and whether off-site storage is utilized.

The **normal backup** process copies all elements selected to a backup device (e.g. magnetic tape, CD, video disk, or flash drive) and "marks" the original elements with a flag to indicate the activity. This method is the easiest to use and understand, because the most recent backup media contains the most current backup. This can become prohibitive due to the volume of media required for the backup process. These backups must be stored somewhere, and a log must be maintained showing location and content.

The **incremental backup** process only copies elements that have been created or changed since the last backup. The elements are marked with an archive flag so that only those changed or added are copied to the backup device. This process requires that a normal backup be conducted on some scheduled time frame, because it will be used with the incremental backup to recreate the original database if there is a problem. These incremental updates do not occupy as many backup media; however, they must be logged and stored somewhere.

With the **differential backup** method, the elements that were created or changed since the last normal or incremental process are backed up. This method does not mark the elements with an archive flag, which means they are included in a normal backup process. A normal backup must be created on a regular basis. If there is a need to restore the database, first restore the normal backup and then restore the last differential backup. It is essential that these backup media are properly labeled and stored.

These three backup procedures assume data and files are being backed up one at a time, which is called a file-by-file backup. An alternative method is the *image backup*, which streams all the elements onto a disk without regard to the file structure. The advantage of this method is speed; however, the entire disk volume must be backed up at the same time, and the restore must be done on a disk that is physically the same as the original. For proper security, a copy of this disk must be part of the off-site storage process.

Data and Database Restoration

With any backup system, a restoration test must be performed to ensure that the data and database can be restored successfully. These tests must be performed on a regularly scheduled basis. It is useful and prudent to have duplicate hardware to test the backup and restoration processes.

In many installations, data items change frequently, while others seldom change. When reconstructing a file, variations in the number and frequency of changes become an important issue. In professional computing and networking systems, periodic backups are performed, in which everything on the system is copied, including system files, user files, scratch files, and directories, so that the system can be regenerated after an incident. This type of backup is called a *complete backup* and is usually conducted during off-hours, like 3 AM Sunday morning.

Many organizations keep three generations of backups. Associated with performing a backup is saving the means to move from the backup forward to the point of failure. In critical transaction systems, keeping a complete record of changes since the last backup solves this problem.

Personal computer users often do not appreciate the need for regular backups. Minor events, such as a failed hardware component, can seriously affect personal computer users. With a backup, users can simply change to a similar machine and continue work. A backup copy is useless if it is destroyed in the disaster. Many major computing and networking organizations rent space some distance from the primary location. As backups are completed, they are transported to the backup location, and the oldest copies are returned to the primary location. It is essential that these backups are labeled both internally and externally and that an inventory is utilized to manage the system.

Personal computer users concerned with integrity and safety can take copies of files home for protection. If both secrecy and integrity are important, a bank vault or another secure place in another location can be used. The worst place to store a backup copy is next to the computing device.

Application Programming Interface

Application programming interfaces (APIs) are the language and messaging formats that define how programs interact with an operating system, with functions in other programs, and with communications systems. APIs are available that interface network services for delivering data across communications systems. In database systems, APIs bind the user applications with the DBMS.

APIs are often called *hooks*. Programmers see APIs as software routines or modules that can be used to quickly build programs for specific systems. A cross-platform API provides an interface for building applications or products that work across multiple operating systems or computer platforms. There are three types of APIs for communications in a network or the Internet: conversational, remote procedure call (RPC), and message. These APIs can be used to provide efficient routing, guaranteed message delivery, priority-based messaging, and security.

Software Threats

Software developed internally for day-to-day operations can be a threat source. Development of Web pages using HTML and common gateway interface (CGI) scripts can unknowingly provide valuable information to hackers and even provide an access point into the enterprise network.

Many Web pages display documents and hyperlink them to other Web pages or sites. Some have search engines that allow for site searches for particular information, which is accomplished through CGI scripts. Hackers can modify these CGI scripts for illegitimate uses. CGI scripts are normally used within the Web-server boundary; however, they can be modified to search outside this server area. Applying a low privilege level to the scripts can reduce this problem. Any CGI script installed on the local server may contain bugs, and every bug has the potential for a security hole.

VOICE COMMUNICATION SYSTEMS

Voice systems include private branch exchange (PBX), automated call distributor (ACD), key, and hybrid systems. These systems are computer based and are controlled by an operating system and a collection of voice system applications. They have similar vulnerabilities as client/ server and mainframe installations. The computer telephony integration (CTI) application provides an interface between the PBX and a computer system. This provides an additional concern for the network because it provides another avenue into the enterprise resource that must be protected.

Private Branch Exchange

In the typical **private branch exchange (PBX)** environment, a T-1 digital trunk interface, which acts like a central office channel bank, resides in a shelf in the PBX system cabinet. As an integral part of the PBX, this T-1 interface is designed primarily around voice circuits; however, newer PBX generations use this interface to provide video and data services. As background information, a voice circuit has a bandwidth of 64 kbps and a T-1 circuit transports 1.544 Mbps. There are 24 voice communication paths in a T-1. The PBX offers some features that are not accessible to a multiplexer or network, including the following:

- Queuing a channel on a T-1.
- Station message detail recording (SMDR).
- Call forwarding.

- Call transfer.
- Conferencing.
- Hunting.
- Least-cost routing.
- Redialing.

The PBX is centrally located and provides direct connections to telephone and other devices. **FIGURE 7-3** depicts a PBX switch with five telephones attached via telephone wire. Digital PBXs can switch data as easily as voice, but office automation does not function well in a circuit-switched environment, and the bandwidth required is often greater than a PBX supports. (*Note the communication path only exists during the call duration with circuit switching.*)

Thieves and hackers use telephone and computer networks to commit fraud by stealing telephone services. Employees, historically, committed this theft by making long-distance calls during business hours. With the increased sophistication of PBXs and the external access afforded to users, intruding into a PBX system is easier and has also become a security and integrity issue. Phone hackers use computers with auto-dialing modems to break security passwords and gain access into PBX systems, where they can use or sell long-distance services at the expense of the PBX owner. Organizations must take preventive measures such as blocking outgoing international telephone calls after hours. Other efforts could include blocking remote access features of PBXs such as direct inward dial access (DISA) and changing access codes and passwords frequently.

Automatic Call Distributors

An **automatic call distributor (ACD)** is a specialized telephone system designed originally for processing many incoming calls, now increasingly used for outgoing calls. An ACD can be integrated into a PBX for multifunctionality support. ACDs are historically used for processing many calls in industries such as airlines, rental car agencies, lodging, computer support, and mail-order houses.

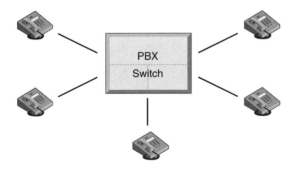

FIGURE 7-3 PBX Centrally Located Switch (Controller)

Computer telephony integration (CTI) is utilized with the PBX, ACD, and computer systems to provide a link for passing information to a database system. The primary CTI service is screen synchronization or "screen pop." In this application, the host computer identifies the caller by calling identification digits passed from the ACD or by prompting the caller for an account number. The computer directs the ACD as to which call center agent should receive the call and simultaneously transmits the customer's record to the agent's workstation display. This situation occurs when ordering a pizza and the order person knows a name based on a telephone number.

E-commerce transactions can be completed over the Internet or over the ubiquitous telephone system. Agents working in an ACD call center process many of these voice-oriented transactions. The database records are accessed and modified from both sources; therefore, security issues relating to computer systems must also apply to voice systems. The following overview provides the reader with an understanding of the relationship of CTI to e-commerce.

The components that are part of a CTI system include:

- PBX.
- ACD.
- Call center.
- Computer system.
- Database.

Access to the CTI system is via a LAN, MAN, or WAN topology. Novell created Telephony Services API (TSAPI) and Microsoft created Telephony API (TAPI) for CTI applications. In some cases, telephony devices might be connected over a network, but the signals that cross the network are for control.

Interactive voice response (IVR) is a CTI application. It is the front-end computerized operator that guides the caller through keypad options. It is possible to have prompts and messages changed based on programmed times and dates. An enhancement to IVR is automatic voice recognition (AVR).

Universal in-boxes are another aspect of CTI. They can provide services such as voice mail, faxing, and e-mail on a companywide basis. Information is stored on disk and is accessible to users who dial into the server by telephone or workstation access.

Screen synchronization (screen pops) is a major function of the CTI system. It relieves the call center agent of asking for a customer identifier such as account number or Social Security number and then entering it via the keyboard. Additionally, if automatic number identifier (ANI) is utilized to identify the caller device, cost savings are realized by a reduction in time required to acquire the customer's database record.

An important part of CTI is the ability to collect information from a telephone call and store it in a database for future use. When a call requires more than one session, the agent can pick up the call where the previous conversation stopped. CTI makes it possible to provide personalized customer services based on knowledge, stored in the computer's database, of callers' preferences. This database is an important asset to the organization and must be protected from malicious activities. This information, in the wrong hands, could prove costly to the organization.

Key Systems

Many key systems are designated by the capacity in central office lines and stations. For example, an 824 system could accommodate a maximum of eight lines and 24 stations. In a key system, each line is terminated via a button on a telephone instrument. The number of buttons that can be physically terminated on the telephone tends to put an upper limit on the feasible size of a key system. At some point, it is awkward to select lines manually for outgoing calls and to use the intercom for announcing incoming calls. A hybrid, in which the attendant transfers calls and the user dials an outgoing call access code, is usually required. Many key systems require proprietary telephone sets and may not use the standard 2500 telephone set. Because key system attendants must announce each call to the called party, most modern systems have an internal paging feature that allows the attendant to hold a two-way conversation over a speaker/microphone that is built into the telephone set.

Hybrid Systems

Private branch exchanges are rarely economical in small line sizes, and large organizations require features and capacity that key systems lack. For companies in between, the market offers a combination PBX and key system that is called a hybrid. A hybrid system has characteristics of both the PBX and key system and can usually be configured as either. Security concerns are the same as a PBX because a database may be accessible from the system.

Voice Over IP Systems

Voice over Internet protocol (VoIP) is a telephony term describing the facilities for managing the delivery of voice using the Internet protocol. It involves sending voice information in some digital form in discrete packets rather than in the traditional circuit-oriented format of the public switched telephone network. One advantage of VoIP is to bypass the tolls charged for ordinary telephone service. Many organizations use VoIP internally over WAN links to reduce telephony service costs.

VoIP security is increasingly important for both enterprises and telephone companies. As VoIP network deployments grow, so too does the threat of VoIP attacks and vulnerabilities. Protecting end-users and real-time Internet communications infrastructure against DoS, DDoS, and spoofing attacks is difficult to do with simple security solutions. The same is true for VoIP spam and other malicious abuses prevalent on the Internet. For hosted VoIP providers and wireless service providers, increasingly sophisticated attacks on previously closed networks mean that comprehensive VoIP security demands more than standard authentication and encryption mechanisms. Organizations need security based on thorough and ongoing VoIP vulnerability research.

Voice Security Issues

Dial-up connections to voice systems still exist today. Dial-up with a modem is the normal method for a vendor to access the voice system remotely for upgrades or maintenance. Dial-up connections that are available continuously invite an intruder into the network. Attackers can use the war dialing method to hack the voice system and then proceed through the voice system to any network resources that might be attached.

Hacking voicemail systems provides another opportunity to access the office telephone system. These instances may occur when there is a layoff of employees or there is a company merger. Mailboxes often remain active after employees depart, which provides for voicemail hacking using a brute force attack. Countermeasures include the deactivation of any mailbox not currently assigned to a warm body. Passwords must be utilized and regularly changed. A lockout mechanism limiting attempts can be installed to counter a brute force attack.

There are general security issues that must be addressed to maintain a secure voice system. The telephone system and PBX may be part of the network administrator's responsibility. Console operator training and staff awareness of security issues must be addressed. Personnel must be sensitive to social engineering techniques that were discussed in Chapter 2. Questions that need to be answered are as follows:

- Are passwords to administrative terminals maintained?
- Are telephone records limited to authorized individuals?
- Are equipment rooms and circuit demarcations kept locked?
- Are cable routes and vaults protected from unauthorized entry?
- Are sensitive communications carried over secure circuits?
- Does the network have virus protection software?
- Does the system allow for dial-in access?
- Are telephone facilities shared within a building?
- How are wireless transmissions controlled?
- Who reconciles the telephone bills to actual usage?
- Is there a system for monitoring and logging long-distance calls?
- Do the employees know how to avoid toll fraud situations?

A checklist for auditing a voice communication system is presented in Appendix A.

PHYSICAL ASSET PROTECTION

There are numerous incidents that can affect the physical network and computer components and assets in a data center. These include both natural and man-made occurrences.

Natural Disasters

It is impossible to prevent natural disasters, but through careful planning it is possible to reduce the damage they cause. The enterprise resources are subject to the same **natural disasters** that can occur to buildings, homes, and vehicles. They can be flooded, burned, and destroyed by earthquakes, storms, and tornadoes.

Water from a natural flood comes from ground level, usually rising gradually and bringing with it mud and debris. All bets are off if the site is below a dam break. There is usually enough time for an orderly shutdown of the systems, losing (at worst) some of the processing in progress. The hardware components may be damaged or destroyed, but hopefully, most systems are insured and can be replaced by the vendor. Organizations with unique or irreplaceable equipment should recognize that the added risk might require a duplicate redundant system available in the event of some disruption.

Hardware is replaceable; the real concerns are the data and programs that are stored locally on magnetic media. Tape libraries and disk packs are usually stored on shelves where they are readily accessible. Many of these media are probably not identified as to importance. There could be thousands of volumes of tapes and hundreds of disk drives that need to be rescued. A simple scheme would be to color code the most important volumes that should be removed quickly in the event of some disaster. Various disaster recovery planning initiatives are discussed in Chapter 9.

Vandals and Destructive Individuals

Because computers and their media are rather sensitive, a vandal could inflict a considerable amount of destruction quickly. Human attackers can include:

- Bored operators.
- Disgruntled employees.
- Saboteurs.
- Ignorant employees.
- Intruders.
- Thrill seekers.

An unskilled vandal may use a brute force attack with an ax or brick; these people will probably be noticed and stopped before any serious damage can occur. More skilled vandals can short-circuit a processor or disable or crash a disk drive with small tools, which would be difficult to detect.

As distributed computing increases, protecting the system from outside access becomes more difficult and important. A protection mechanism and policy are needed to prevent unauthorized people from obtaining access to systems and to verify the identity of accepted users. Physical access methods are addressed in a subsequent chapter.

Fire and Water Damage

Fire and water damage can occur from natural events, structural failures, or from human causes. Fire can be set by an arsonist, or internal water supplies can be broken, or attackers can activate sprinkler systems. All of these situations can be devastating to a computer system. Most computer rooms and electronic systems are protected by something other than a sprinkler system. It is not prudent to install a sprinkler system over electronic systems. Most computer systems are installed over a raised floor, which allows for cabling to run under the devices and out of the way. Air conditioning is also supplied to the computing devices from under the raised floor up into the cabinet or chassis.

It should be obvious that water and all of these electrical connectors and cables do not mix very well. Water under a raised floor will quickly cause an electrical short and shut down the computer system. It would be useful to keep a supply of plastic sheets available to cover the electronic components in the event of a water hazard from above.

Fire is a more serious issue because there is the issue of burning and the subsequent water response from the fire department. There may not be time to react to the fire, which would put personnel in danger and not allow any time to protect any of the computing resources. A computing and network center should have a plan for shutting down the systems in an orderly fashion. Such a process can be accomplished quickly and makes recovery much easier and faster. This plan should include individual responsibilities in the event of a disaster, with backup assignments in case some personnel are not on duty. Every computer system installation should have a master power "kill switch" that would shut off all power.

Power Loss

A constant source of predictable power is required to keep a computer system operating properly. For some time-critical applications, loss of service is intolerable, and efforts must be made to provide some alternative power source if this occurs. Because of possible damage to media by sudden loss of power, many disk drives monitor the power level and quickly retract the recording head if power fails.

One protection against power loss is an **uninterruptible power supply (UPS)**. This device stores energy during normal operation so it can provide backup energy if power fails. One form of UPS uses batteries that are continually charged when the normal power is on, which then provide power if the normal source fails. Several problems with batteries include heat, size, flammability, fumes, leakage, and insufficient output. Size and limited duration of energy output are limitations with the standard UPS system. Some UPS systems use outside generators and motor generators to provide support to the primary backup power supply, but this is a very expensive alternative. If backup power is to be provided for an extended period of time, the outside generator will be a requirement. All telephone central offices use both UPS systems and outside generators because this service is expected to operate continuously and seamlessly.

Another issue with power is its quality. Most people are unaware that AC (alternating-current) power fluctuates ±10 percent, which means that the supply could be between 108 and 132 volts. A voltmeter can be utilized to measure this variation. A disk drive or air conditioner power cycling can cause a temporary drain on the system and cause the lights to dim. When a motor stops, a temporary surge can be sent across the system. It is also possible for lightning to send a momentary large surge across the system. Instead of being constant, the power delivered along a power line shows many fluctuations, called *drops*, *spikes*, and *surges*. A drop is a momentary reduction in voltage, whereas a spike or surge is a rise. For computing equipment, a drop is less serious than a surge, but most electrical devices are tolerant of some fluctuations of current.

Voltage fluctuations can be destructive to sensitive electronic equipment. Simple devices such as surge suppressors filter spikes from a power source, clocking fluctuations that could affect the electronic devices. These surge suppressors are rated in joules—the higher the rating, the more protection afforded. These devices range in price from $20 to several hundred dollars. These protection devices should be installed on every computing and networking device in the installation. This includes PCs, printers, servers, routers, and data communication equipment (DCE) devices such as modems and DSUs.

Another surge that can damage electronic equipment is a lightning strike. To increase protection, personal computers can be unplugged when not in use and during electrical storms. Another source of destruction is lightning striking a telephone line and passing through the modem to the computer. Disconnecting a modem during a storm is also a preventive measure that works. A lightning strike on a telephone line can follow a path to the modem card or stand-alone modem and destroy the electronics. Additional lightning suppression devices may be available from the local telephone company.

Heat and Humidity

Excessive heat and high or low humidity can cause an electronic device to fail. Computer systems are sensitive to heat, and loss of cooling is common due to mechanical failure or electrical disruption. The normal response to this situation is to provide an alternative cooling source or shut down the system, because excessive heat can cause extreme damage to the electronic devices. There is usually adequate time to respond to this situation, assuming that someone is aware of the cooling failure.

Computing systems may perform normally even if the temperature exceeds the manufacturer's recommendations. However, as the temperature rises, components may perform unpredictably, sometimes working apparently well, but producing faulty results. The most serious state is sometimes correct/sometimes incorrect, because this uncertainty can corrupt the entire system, while it appears to function properly.

High or low humidity is another issue that can negatively affect electronic components. When the humidity is extremely low, arcing of electronics components can occur, which can be devastating. High humidity causes moisture to form on the electronic components, which can cause shorts. Either of the humidity problems must be corrected quickly, because the results of both can be circuit card failure. A monitor is available that charts humidity on a 24-hour basis.

Environmental Safeguards Recap

Adequate environmental safeguards must be installed and implemented to protect computer, database, and networking assets. The criticality and sensitivity of each asset will determine the level of security required. The more critical the asset is for accomplishing the mission of the organization, the higher the level of security required. The following safeguards are important elements that should be considered:

- Fire prevention, detection, protection, and suppression.
- Internal water hazard prevention, detection, and correction.

- Electrical power supply provisions.
- Temperature control.
- Humidity control.
- Natural disaster protection from floods, lightning, storms, and earthquakes.
- Protection from electromagnetic magnetic interference (EMI) and radio-frequency interference (RFI).
- Maintenance procedures for dust and dirt.

🔒 CHAPTER SUMMARY

A computer system consists of a processor, main memory, input/output devices, and the interconnecting devices among these major components. A mainframe is a large, powerful computer attached to a number of peripheral devices such as disk controllers, communication controllers, and high-speed printers. A client/server is a computer located on a local area network that splits the workload between itself and desktop computers.

Mainframes and client/server computer systems require enormous amounts of disk storage for system processing and database components. Large amounts of data are collected and information is generated continuously on computer and client/server systems. A process for backup is required to maintain the integrity of the organization's data and information. There are three basic types of backup: normal, incremental, and differential.

A DBMS is a software program that operates on a mainframe system or database server to manage data, accept queries from users, and respond to those queries. Security and integrity are major issues because databases are organized so they can be accessed remotely. There are a number of malicious attacks that might occur on a computer database system. These attacks are exacerbated due to inference and aggregation problems.

Voice communication systems include PBXs, ACDs, key systems, and hybrid systems. These systems are computer based and are controlled by an operating system and a collection of voice system applications. They have vulnerabilities similar to those of client/server and mainframe computers.

An ACD is a specialized telephone system designed originally for processing many incoming calls. CTI is utilized with the PBX, ACD, and a computer system to provide a link for passing information to a database system.

Numerous incidents can affect the physical network and computer components and assets in a data center. These include both natural and man-made occurrences. These can include fire, flood, power loss, heat and humidity, and vandals.

KEY TERMS

access rights	database management system (DBMS)	normal backup
aggregation	database porting	operating system (OS)
application programming interface (API)	differential backup	polyinstantiation
automatic call distributor (ACD)	directory	private branch exchange (PBX)
backup	front-end processor (FEP)	redundant array of inexpensive disk (RAID)
client/server	incremental backup	replication
computer telephony integration (CTI)	inference problem	server
controller	interactive voice response (IVR)	storage area network (SAN)
data	mainframe	uninterruptible power supply (UPS)
database	natural disasters	voice over Internet protocol (VoIP)

SECURITY REVIEW QUESTIONS

1. A _____ is a structure containing one or more files and a description of these files.
2. _____ devices are used to improve performance and automatically recover from a system failure. They can maintain backup files and protect data by continuously writing two copies of the data to a different hard drive.
3. A _____ is a computer located on a local area network that splits the workload between itself and desktop computers.
4. A _____ is a software program that operates on a mainframe system or database server to manage data, accept queries from users, and respond to those queries.
5. The _____ involves a malicious attacker combining information that is available from a database, where individual data elements, viewed separately, reveal confidential information when viewed collectively.
6. The database disclosure problem called _____ occurs when pieces of information, which are not sensitive in isolation, become sensitive when viewed as a whole.
7. _____ means there are several views of a database object existing so that a user's view of the database is determined by that user's security attributes.
8. Identify the typical access rights or permissions.
9. _____ is utilized with the PBX, ACD, and computer system to provide a link for passing information to a database system.
10. This device stores energy during normal operation so it can provide backup energy if power fails.

RESEARCH ACTIVITIES

1. Research data storage devices, and provide a comparison analysis. These include RAID, CDs, flash drives, and so forth.
2. Develop a report on the impact of EMI and RFI in the computing environment.
3. Research the product offerings for uninterruptible power supplies.
4. Provide an overview of NIST security goals.
5. Describe an application for CTI, IVR, and AVR.
6. Develop a scenario for social engineering that uses a telecommunications system.
7. Identify products that can measure heat and humidity in a data center.
8. Provide a comparison of the various types of data backup techniques.
9. Describe the differences between aggregation and inference.
10. Develop a report that addresses security issues with a DBMS.

CHAPTER 8

E-Commerce Security Mechanisms

🔒 CHAPTER CONTENTS

- Become familiar with the variants of e-commerce systems.
- Identify the elements of the e-commerce security environment.
- Look at the numerous security implications for wireless transmission and e-commerce.
- See how security protocols are used to protect the network user.
- Understand the various security management techniques that are employed in the e-commerce computer and networking environment.
- Identify the threats and vulnerabilities inherent in the commercial wireless computing environment.

INTRODUCTION

With the advent of the Internet connectivity to local area network topologies such as the intranet and extranet, it should not be a surprise that commercial interests would want to exploit communications by network computers. These activities are manifested in the form of e-commerce. The implications and ramifications to the organization and its resources are far-reaching.

Personal information such as credit card, debit card, and Social Security numbers must be protected. Major issues include protection of data and information storage and the methods utilized to ensure confidentiality and integrity. The organization must apply security principles and methods, which include authentication and authorization techniques. Integrity of the database and the software that processes the transactions must be ensured.

E-commerce involves Internet use for credit card purchases of such items as airline tickets, computer hardware and software, books, and miscellaneous products. It involves methods of securing transactions, authorizing payments, and moving money between accounts. A number of processes are used to accomplish these transactions. There are enormous security implications for the general public that uses these e-commerce systems.

This chapter explores the subject of electronic commerce and its implication on the computer and networking operations that would process those transactions. Considerable emphasis is placed on the methods and procedures that can be utilized to ensure integrity, privacy, and security of the organization's assets and resources. The future of e-commerce rests on the ability of the network to remain secure and provide a very high level of integrity.

E-COMMERCE ENVIRONMENT

The use of wireless systems and devices is permeating all aspects of the e-commerce environment. Wireless transmissions allow communication to and from a mobile communications device, thus exacerbating integrity and security issues for the user. Subsequent sections present an overview of wireless security issues, along with suggestions and proposals that can provide some level of secure transmission in this insecure environment.

Because millions of dollars are at stake with e-commerce transactions, the security of these transactions is a major issue in today's business environment. When considering e-commerce security, an organization must thoroughly evaluate all aspects of its network access, because users expect a secure and private exchange of information.

Many e-commerce merchants leave the design mechanics to their hosting company or IT staff, but it helps to understand the basic principles. *Ecommerce-digest* states that any system has to meet four requirements [Ecommerce-digest]:

- *Privacy*—information must be kept from unauthorized parties.
- *Integrity*—message must not be altered or tampered with.
- *Authentication*—sender and recipient must prove their identities to each other.
- *Nonrepudiation*—proof is needed that the message was indeed received.

Security management becomes more difficult and important when users have multiple accounts on different computer systems. With systems that provide an open connectivity to the Internet, it is essential that security systems be in place that can provide for a central administrative capability. A broad range of authentication and authorization services and management tools are needed for an effective security program. This is especially true when transporting data from one platform in an enterprise network to a different platform in another.

The boom in the e-commerce arena has spawned a plethora of general security and secure-payment programs for credit card users and financial institutions. The main players are secure electronic transaction (SET), Secured Socket Layer (SSL), and TLS protocols. SET is an open specification for handling credit card transactions over a network, with emphasis on the Web and Internet. In addition, a number of proprietary schemes also exist that serve special purposes, such as EDI, or provide security features within a specific product line.

ELECTRONIC COMMERCE AND TRANSACTIONS

Electronic commerce involves the buying and selling of products and services across a telecommunications network. **E-business** comprises a broader spectrum of business activities that includes customer service and support, business partner collaboration, and enhancing internal productivity. **Business-to-business (B2B)** is defined as e-commerce in which both the buyers and sellers are organizations, whereas **business-to-consumer (B2C)** is a business selling online to individual consumers. Another type of transaction is **consumer-to-consumer (C2C)**, with individuals buying and selling over the Internet. These electronic transactions are all susceptible to fraud and security violations. Especially with consumer transactions, it is "buyers beware."

E-commerce involves Internet use for credit card purchases of such items as airline tickets, computer hardware and software, books, and miscellaneous products. It involves methods of securing transactions, authorizing payments, and moving money between accounts. One process used to accomplish these transactions is called **electronic data interchange (EDI)**. EDI is a process whereby standardized forms of e-commerce documents are transferred between diverse and remotely located computer systems. These forms include purchase orders and invoices. The form and format of EDI documents may be defined by vendor specifications or standards organizations, such as the International Telecommunication Union (ITU-T) and the American National Standards Institute (ANSI). Another major player in e-commerce is electronic mail (e-mail).

EDI and other forms of business transactions have been taking place over public and private networks for some time. The financial system, which consists of banks and branches, executes transactions and moves money over the telecommunications network on a regular basis. Credit and debit card transactions are approved over dial-up or dedicated telephone circuits. Millions of stock market transactions take place every day using electronic means. All of these transactions must possess a high degree of integrity.

Because these transactions are occurring over a public network that is prone to abuse, methods and technologies must be in place to ensure the transmissions are secure. Most buyers and sellers using the Internet may have had no previous relationship. So whom can they trust? This element of trust is missing and must be established in some way.

To support Internet- and Web-based commerce, organizations must make use of extranet, intranet, and security technologies to build a networking infrastructure to support the business. **FIGURE 8-1** depicts a logical representation of the computer and networking structure that could be deployed in this environment. Customers, suppliers, and businesses use the Internet infrastructure to conduct e-commerce and e-business transactions. A database is located at the e-commerce organization. This database could contain customer records, inventory, financial information, or schedules.

The Internet is being used as the communication mechanism to support corporate-to-corporate communications for such activities as joint partnership projects or to support industry organizations. Many organizations maintain Web sites for information related to their products and services. A natural extension to the business use of the Internet is to include commercial transactions on this untrusted network. Even though this is an exciting prospect, it is also a serious security concern because commerce on the network refers to the transmission of financial or financial-related transactions. Commercial applications require the parties involved to authenticate each other and transact business confidentially. An important security element of these commercial transactions is nonrepudiation, which prevents a user from denying a legitimate transaction. The security of the client relationship when using Web browsers and other Internet services must be similar to those when using an automated teller machine (ATM).

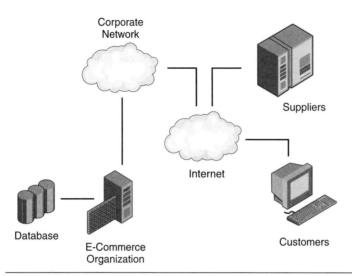

FIGURE 8-1 Logical E-Commerce Structure

When using the Internet to carry transactions using the established payment methods of credit and debit cards, there are usually four entities that are involved. These include:

- The issuer of the credit/debit card.
- The merchant selling the product or service.
- The acquirer of the transaction.
- Security of the transaction by a security authority.

The growing interest in these types of transactions promotes the need for a way of providing proof of identity and confidentiality over a network. Before electronic commerce, there was adequate legal protection against defective goods, fraudulent payments, and failure to deliver. New protection mechanisms are required when engaging in this newer type of commerce. When purchasing from the Web, it is possible to use cryptographic techniques and digital signatures to provide for some protection of the transaction. There are a number of other issues that might arise from such an electronic transaction.

- How does the user return damaged goods for credit?
- How does the user prove nonreceipt of an item?
- What is the recourse if the item arrives damaged or arrives too late?

The availability of a common security authority will help promote commercial transactions on the Internet. Security protocols are being developed and promoted to address the specific problem of transmitting financial transactions on the Internet. Two major credit card companies, along with other partners, have developed the secure electronic transaction protocol to address these security issues.

Secure Electronic Transaction

Secure electronic transaction (SET) is an open specification for handling credit card transactions over a network, with emphasis on the Web and Internet. Secure transactions are critical for electronic commerce (e-commerce) on the Internet. Merchants must automatically and safely collect and process payments from Internet clients; therefore, a secure protocol is required to support the activities of the credit card companies. Also affected by e-commerce requirements are consumers, vendors, and software developers. GTE, IBM, MasterCard, Microsoft, Netscape, and Visa developed SET.

SET is designed to secure credit card transactions by authenticating cardholders, merchants, and banks by preserving the confidentiality of payment data. SET includes the following features:

- Requires digital signatures to verify that the customer, the merchant, and the bank are all legitimate.
- Uses multiparty messages that allow information be encrypted directly to banks.
- Prevents credit card numbers from getting in the wrong hands.
- Requires integration into the credit card processing system.

SET includes a negotiation layer that negotiates the type of payment method, protocols, and transports. This task is the responsibility of the Joint Electronic Payment Initiative (JEPI). Payment methods could include credit cards, debit cards, electronic cash, and checks. Payment protocols, such as SET, define the message format and sequence required for completion of the payment transaction. Transports include such protocols as Secure Socket Layer (SSL) and secure hypertext transfer protocol (SHTTP).

An important part of SET's success will be its overall acceptance by cardholders, credit card issuers, payment processors (acquirers), and certificate authorities (CAs). (*Note that CAs provide digital signatures that are critical for verifying the authenticity of cardholders and others involved in the transactions.*) Microsoft and Netscape have included SET support in their browsers. SET, SSL, and SHTTP protocols are detailed in Chapter 13.

SECURING NETWORK TRANSACTIONS

A number of technology companies have developed protocols for transacting business in a secure environment. This is in addition to securing the operating system (OS) and preventing unauthorized access to the server. Some types of communications require protection between the Web browser and the secure server. The most common mechanisms include the following:

- Secure Socket Layer (SSL) provides for server authentication, data encryption, and data integrity.
- Secure hypertext transfer protocol (SHTTP) allows servers to encrypt responses to browsers, digitally sign replies to browsers, and authenticate the identity of browsers.

- Private Communication Technology (PCT) provides privacy between a client and server, and authenticates the client and server.
- Generic Security Service Application Program Interface (GSSAPI) provides for mutual authentication and data encryption capabilities in Web browsers and servers.

There is an option that allows for the combining of HTTP and SHTTP, which offers the freedom, flexibility, and efficiency of HTTP, while using SHTTP to protect sensitive parts of a transaction. This is possible because SHTTP and HTTP are different protocols that use different ports. This allows merchants to offer catalog information to anyone, while providing protection to the server and client during order entry.

Another issue concerns the use of a firewall component between the Internet and the server. Firewalls, discussed in the next section, are used for creating an internal site or private network that is isolated from the general population of Internet users. Using a server for commercial purposes exposes it to the entire untrusted Internet outside the firewall's perimeter of protection. This means that placing a commercial server within the confines of a protected network is self-defeating unless potential clients are granted accessibility on an individual basis.

Digital Certificates and Signatures

A **certificate** is a unique collection of information, transformed into un-forgeable form, used for authentication of users. A certificate can verify the authenticity of a user who is logging on to a secure server. It follows that a Web server can have a certificate to prove its authenticity to users that access it. Users on these servers must be assured that malicious people are not collecting personal information or distributing infected documents. A **certificate authority (CA)** is responsible for issuing these certificates. This CA is a trusted organization that verifies the credentials of people and puts a stamp of approval on these credentials.

Both certificates and signatures are mechanisms that provide an identity of an individual or user. A **digital certificate** is a password-protected file that contains identification information about its holder. This file includes a public key and a unique private key. The electronic exchange of keys and certificates allows two parties to verify their identities before communicating.

A digital signature is an authentication mechanism that enables the creator of a message to attach a code that acts as a signature. The signature guarantees the source and integrity of the transmitted message. A message can be digitally signed by a system by including a header, a body, and a signature as part of the message. These components are described as follows.

- The header describes the identity of the sender.
- The body contains the message to be sent.
- The signature contains a security feature called a *checksum*.

The receiver can decrypt the checksum using the sender's public key and ensure the checksum matches a computed checksum of the transmitted message. The checksum process provides a sum for a group of items in the message, which is used for error checking.

The risk of message forgery is an important reason to use a digital signature. Forged messages can be used to provide false information about a person or some event. Message forgery can also occur on the Internet if someone wants to smear another or an organization. Another issue related to this subject is called *message repudiation* or denial that a message was transmitted.

Certificates and Certificate Systems

Remember that a digital certificate is a personal digital identifier or digital signature that can be used for authentication, to ensure the sender is validated, and to ensure the message has not been altered in transit. This authenticity verification extends to the server, which can prove its authenticity to users who access it. Server users must be assured that malicious people, who may be trying to collect credit card and personal information or distribute bogus and virus-infected copies of software, are not spoofing (impersonating) a site. Certificates can be used in place of credit card numbers for online buying transactions. The SET scheme, developed by major credit card companies, is designed to hide credit card numbers from merchants by substituting the card number with a digital certificate. A basic certificate contains a public key, an expiration date, serial number, certifying authority, and a name. More importantly, it contains the digital signature of the certificate issuer.

Corporations, government agencies, and universities issue their own certificates, which are signed and issued to clients by a trusted certificate server. A certificate granted to an individual is a signed recognition of the individual's identification and authenticity. Checking the existing certificate against the public key of the certificate server and the public key of the individual can validate it.

Public and Private Keys

A **key** is described as a number of characters within a data record used to identify the data. It may also control the use of that data. Two types of keys are utilized in the security environment: public and private. A **public key** is used in an asymmetric encryption system and is used in conjunction with a corresponding **private key**. For secure communication, only its creator should know this private key. The use of public and private keys, where both types of keys are utilized, is called an *asymmetrical* system.

Historically, secure message transmission relied on single-key encryption, where the sender and receiver used the same key for encryption and decryption. Different methods had to be developed for computer communications to prevent eavesdroppers from listening in on transmissions and intercepting keys to decrypt private messages. These new methods are stored in databases that are trusted by everyone. Messages are encrypted using the public key of the recipient, who decrypts it with a private key known only to the user.

Digital Envelopes

Sometimes it is necessary to protect a single message, in which case secret-key cryptography can be used. The sender and receiver must agree on a session key, and each must have a copy. In accomplishing this task, there is a risk the key will be intercepted during transmission.

Public-key cryptography provides an effective solution to this problem within a framework called a *digital envelope*.

The **digital envelope** consists of a message that is encrypted using private-key cryptography, but that also contains the encrypted **secret key**. While digital envelopes usually use public-key cryptography to encrypt the secret key, this is not necessary. If the sender and receiver have an established secret key, they can use it to encrypt the secret key in the digital envelope.

This method can be used to encrypt just one message or an extended communication. A feature of this technique allows the sender and receiver to frequently switch secret keys. Switching keys often is beneficial because it is more difficult for an eavesdropper to find a key only used for a short time. Note that secret-key cryptosystems are faster than public-key cryptosystems.

DATA SECURITY AND ENCRYPTION

An important issue that must be addressed after a user has successfully gained access to the network and the server is data security. As more and more organizations rely on the network for transport of sensitive information, data security is rapidly becoming an area of significant concern. Networks that require a high level of security can use a method called *encryption*.

Encryption is the conversion of plain text or data into unintelligible form by means of a reversible translation, based on some algorithm or translation table. It is sometimes called *enciphering*. This process of scrambling cannot be read by anyone except the intended receiver. This means that the data must be decoded or decrypted back to their original form before the receiver can understand the data. This encryption process maintains data integrity on the network and ensures the confidentiality of the sender and the receiver from other users on the network.

Encryption is accomplished by the use of an algorithm and a secret key. An algorithm is a well-defined set of rules that solve a problem in a finite number of steps. These algorithms take data and scramble them so as to be unintelligible. The secret key is shared by both participants and must remain secret to protect the communication. The key is the value or data string that allows the sender and receiver to actually encrypt and decrypt the transmission. There are several methods used to encrypt and decrypt data. The three most commonly used methods are symmetric encryption, asymmetric encryption, and hash functions. Each of these methods is now discussed in detail.

Symmetric Encryption

Symmetric encryption is defined as a form of cryptosystem in which encryption and decryption are performed using the same key. It is also known as conventional encryption. It follows that a symmetric algorithm, also called a *secret-key algorithm*, uses the same key for encryption and decryption. Data confidentiality is provided when using symmetric encryption. Two end-stations agree on which algorithm to use and which secret key to share. Symmetric encryption is most widely used for data integrity, partly because it is the least complex method and requires the least amount of processing on the network devices. Several common symmetric key algorithms used are as follows:

- Data Encryption Standard (DES).
- International Data Encryption Algorithm (IDEA).
- Triple DES (3DES).

Asymmetric Encryption

Asymmetric encryption is a form of cryptosystem in which encryption and decryption are performed using two different keys. One key is called the public key and the other is a private key. This system is also known as *public-key encryption*. This method provides for both data security and sender authentication. Asymmetric encryption is more complex than symmetric encryption because each end-station must create a public/private key pair instead of sharing the same secret key.

Symmetric encryption algorithms are not as computationally intensive as those of asymmetric encryption. The additional processing requirements of asymmetric encryption for data security might reduce network throughput to an unacceptable level. Asymmetric encryption is usually reserved for situations in which sender authentication is required. Several common asymmetric encryption algorithms include the following:

- Digital Signature Standard (DSS).
- Rivest, Shamir, and Adleman (RSA).

Asymmetric and symmetric encryption algorithms are discussed further in Chapter 13.

Hash Functions

The third method of encryption is called the **hash function**. A hash function maps a variable-length data block or message into a fixed-length value called a *hash code*. The function is designed in such a way as to provide an authenticator to the data or message. This function is also called a *message digest*. The hash function is used with symmetric or asymmetric encryption to provide for a higher level of data integrity. The flow of this method is as follows:

- A secure hash function accepts input data.
- These data are passed through a complex mathematical computation (hash function) that is used for encryption.
- The output consists of new, encrypted data.

It is almost impossible to reverse this process, which would require the output from the algorithm to be used to regenerate the original input data. This would be similar to the scrambled eggs analogy. Crack three eggs in a bowl, scramble them, cook them, serve them, and then reassemble the original three eggs. With hash functions, keys and the same algorithm are not sufficient to decrypt the data. The same hash function must be produced that was originally used to encrypt the data. The secure hash function is usually not used on the data itself because of its computational complexity. It is usually more useful in proving the sender's identity and ensuring the integrity of the data. Several hashing functions include the following:

- Message Digest Algorithm 5 (MD5).
- Secure Hash Algorithm (SHA).
- Cyclic Redundancy Check (CRC).

Note that the hashing function is used in the computer forensic process of imaging files captured from suspect disk systems. This hash is necessary to preserve the integrity of the data for criminal prosecution. These functions and encryption algorithms are described in Chapter 13.

Encryption can take place between the sending and receiving stations, including servers, and at the router. Full encryption security of the network is provided by encryption on the end-stations and servers; however, only partial encryption security is provided on the network by router encryption methods. Encryption at the end-stations and servers provides the highest level of security because the data are encrypted the entire time they traverse the network. It is possible to steal data before they enter a router and after they exit a router at the destination. Encryption at the router works well over the WAN or Internet, but it does not provide sufficient benefit for a campus LAN because most traffic does not pass through more than two routers.

Network management personnel must decide what level of encryption is required to preserve the security and integrity of the organization's data. If a secure network is required, there must be mechanisms in place to control access to the campus (LAN) resources. These mechanisms can take the form of end-station, server, and router encryption methods.

E-COMMERCE SECURITY AND DISTRIBUTED COMPUTING

There is considerable apprehension concerning lack of security on the Internet. There are a number of initiatives to set security standards for electronic commerce. To transact business, organizations must have a means to conduct secure, confidential, and reliable transactions. To achieve this goal, four cornerstones of secure electronic transactions must be present. These include the following attributes:

- Possess the ability to prevent unauthorized monitoring of traffic.
- Prevent the content of messages from being altered after transmission and provide a method to prove they have or have not been altered.
- Determine whether a transmission is from an authentic source or a masquerade.
- Prevent a sender from denying the receipt or transmission of a message (non-repudiation).

Cryptographic systems provide a method to transmit information across an untrusted communication system without disclosing the content of the information to a snoop. Cryptographic systems provide confidentiality and can also provide proof that a transmission's integrity has not been compromised.

Securing Electronic Transactions

Organizations, industries, and commerce utilize the Internet to transmit e-mail, purchase goods and services, transact banking, and for other unique services that depend on security transmissions. There are methods that can provide secure transmissions for each.

E-mail often contains confidential information such as credit card numbers or Social Security numbers. It is essential that the contents and the sender of a message be authenticated. An e-mail might be considered a legal document when conducting a transaction such as responding to an official competitive bid; therefore, it is essential that the sender and recipient be assured of the integrity of the transmission.

Many network users purchase goods and services over the Internet. Buyers select the items and authorize payment using the Web. These items are then delivered through normal shipping channels. Typical items include books, CDs, and auction items. Software and recordings can be delivered immediately by downloading through the Internet. These transactions must all be validated and tracked.

It is now possible to conduct banking transactions through an electronic bank, which offer users virtually all the services and functions provided by conventional banks. Functions include checking of account balances and statements, transferring funds between accounts, and electronic bill payments. Authentication and authorization are two security functions that must occur with these transactions. This means that the user is identifiable and has authority to access a particular account, with a particular transaction.

There are a number of Internet transactions that fall in the general category. The Internet lends itself to the supply of small quantities of information and other services to many users. The development of the Web as a high-quality publishing medium depends on the extent to which information suppliers can obtain payments from users for that information. The use of the Internet for voice and videoconferencing is another service that is likely to be supplied when it is paid for by end-users.

Transactions such as these can be safely executed only when protected by appropriate security policies and mechanisms. A client must be protected against the disclosure of credit and debit card numbers during transmission and against a fraudulent vendor who obtains payment without delivering the goods or service. Conversely, vendors must obtain payment before releasing the items selected for purchase, whether online or through the normal delivery conduit. In addition, the required protection must be achieved at a cost that is reasonable in comparison with the value of the transaction.

Security Services

Security services provide a range of services and protocols for e-commerce, including private communications, access controls, security in business transactions, and electronic cash management. Users who engage in business transactions over the Internet need secure connections. This level of security is provided by a secure channel service called SSL protocol.

With SSL, the client and server use a handshaking technique to agree on the level of security required during a session. Authentication takes place over a security channel, and all information transmitted during the sessions is encrypted. The protocol authenticates the client, then exchanges a master key, which is used to encrypt subsequent data exchanges.

With the growth of e-commerce, security over the Internet has become increasingly important. SET was designed to replace the SSL standard and provide electronic customers and merchants with the assurance that e-commerce can be conducted in a secure manner. (*Note that SET is an encryption standard for secure credit card authorization over the Internet.*) SET offers the prospect of lower business costs, because nonsecured credit card transactions on the Internet carry high fees and are generally considered high risk by credit card companies. The SET standard addressed the following major business requirements:

- Guarantee confidentiality of payment information.
- Guarantee integrity of all transmitted data.
- Provide cardholder authentication.
- Provide vendor authentication.
- Provide security practices to protect e-commerce transactions.
- Develop an open protocol.
- Provide for interoperability between software and network components.

Many problems have occurred with SSL, which prompted the need for a new standard such as SET. With SSL, online merchants encrypt confidential information during transmission, so there is not a method of preventing fraudulent use of this information. SET provides increased security to prevent such occurrences, because it authenticates both merchants and cardholders. The specification guarantees that transaction content is not altered during the transmission between the originator and recipient. Also unlike SSL, SET allows impromptu shopping expeditions by consumers equipped with digital certificates. To meet the business requirements of e-commerce, SET incorporates the following features:

- Cardholder account authentication.
- Confidentiality of information.
- Integrity of data.
- Merchant authentication.

Private Communication Technology (PCT) is an alternative to SSL. It provides many of the same functions as SSL but uses different keys for authentication and encryption. Secure hypertext transfer protocol (SHTTP) goes a step further by providing a method to attach digital signatures to Web pages. This verifies to users that the pages are indeed from the intended source. SHTTP is useful in workflow and document routing applications where documents must be signed and verified using digital signatures. SHTTP will promote the growth of e-commerce as its transaction security features will promote spontaneous commercial transactions.

New technologies and tools have been developed to make Internet e-commerce secure, but they lack acceptance. The industry has been working to develop the methodologies that will make public acceptance more widespread. Security has increased overall on the Internet. Firewall technology has vastly improved, providing a method of keeping intruders out while letting real customers in.

The Electronic Frontier Foundation (EFF) and CommerceNet are working to overcome some of the issues users have with trust on the Internet. They have implemented **eTRUST**, an initiative meant to establish more consumer trust and confidence in electronic transactions. The purpose of this initiative is to build a log system that consumers will associate with trust and to make the eTRUST brand known worldwide.

CommerceNet brings together a number of organizations to focus on the advancement of e-commerce worldwide. It accelerates the development and implementation of important new technologies and practices on the way companies conduct business. CommerceNet serves as a focal point for the collaborative development of solutions that will affect all businesses in the future.

FINANCIAL TRANSACTIONS

Financial transactions are the lifeblood of e-commerce, which is why it is vitally important to keep these transactions secure. Unfortunately, unsecured and insufficiently secured financial transactions are more commonplace than most consumers realize. While industry statistics indicate improvements in security technologies have been implemented, many organizations are still not using them to their fullest advantage. Studies have indicated financial losses can be attributed to computer-related breaches, stolen credit card numbers, and stolen logon passwords.

To help mitigate these security breaches, many organizations have implemented a security program that is supposed to protect them and their customers from data theft, fraud, and misuse. All is not well, however, because internal policies, monitoring of security measures, and follow-up of security breaches are often disregarded.

Technology alone will not protect an organization or a financial transaction. If there is a vulnerable spot within an enterprise's security framework, an intruder will find a way to access and exploit it. For this reason, multiple security technologies, combined with a well-thought-out and well-monitored security plan, must be implemented to ensure that financial transactions are secured and protected.

It is expensive to maintain a comprehensive security system for financial transactions; however, it is much more expensive to maintain one that is inadequate. If an organization is going to participate in the e-commerce game, it must provide those security systems necessary to provide an adequate level of support. The components most often utilized to provide this support include the following technologies:

- Digital signatures.
- Public key infrastructure (PKI).
- Secure Socket Layer (SSL).
- Authentication certificates.
- Firewalls.
- Border managers.
- Biometrics.
- Passwords.

Outsourcing is an alternative if an organization does not have the available capital to improve or develop the infrastructure for electronic transaction security. It should be noted that outsourcing might be considered as an interim solution, with a plan to provide these functions in-house.

Payment Protocols

The SET protocol was developed so merchants could, automatically and safely, collect and process payments from Internet clients. Basically, SET secures credit card transactions by authenticating cardholders, merchants, and banks. It also preserves the confidentiality of payment data. SET requires digital signatures to verify that the customer, the merchant, and the bank are legitimate. It also uses multiparty messages that prevent credit card numbers from ending up in the wrong hands. Electronic money schemes include electronic cash, wallets, and cybercash.

Electronic cash is a scheme that makes purchasing easier over the Internet. One method is for electronic cash companies to sell "Web dollars" that purchasers can use when visiting Web sites. Web sites would accept these Web dollars as if they were coupons.

A *wallet* is an electronic cash component that resides on the user's computer or another device such as a smart card. It stores personal security information such as private keys, credit card numbers, and certificates. It can be moved around, so users can work at different computers and have its access controlled by policies. The Personal Information Exchange is a protocol that enables users to transfer sensitive information from one environment or platform to another. With this protocol, a user can securely export personal information from one computer system to another.

Cybercash uses the wallet concept: a consumer selects items to purchase and the merchant presents an invoice and a request for payment. The consumer can then have the cybercash wallet pay for the purchase electronically. Encrypted messages are exchanged among the merchant server, the consumer, the cybercash server, and the conventional credit card networks to transfer the appropriate funds.

Smart Card

A **smart card** is about the size of a credit card and contains a microprocessor for performing a number of functions. A phone card is an example of a simple smart card. Unlike stripe cards, which have magnetic stripes on the outside, smart cards hold information internally and are more secure. They are often used as token authentication devices that generate access codes for secure systems. They have gained industry acceptance for a number of applications.

Smart card manufacturers are hopeful that the SET standard will help build a market for the cards in the United States. Visa has led the way, but adoption of the SET standard has been slow. Adoption of the Visa offering within the United States could boost the SET standard, which would benefit e-commerce.

Credit Card Transactions

If e-commerce is to succeed, a method must exist for consumers to use credit cards over the Internet. Credit card usage on the Internet is still low but is likely to grow in the future. SET and SSL are utilized in the credit card transaction to provide security provisions.

SSL encrypts a credit card number and other information using a 40-bit key. Due to its size, this key can be hacked; however, it may be adequate for some needs. Even though SSL keeps the credit card number and information private while being transmitted, it does not address the issue of whether the card is valid, stolen, or being used without permission. SET addresses these SSL limitations by using an "electronic wallet" that can identify the user and validate the transaction. An electronic wallet is a type of software application used by the consumer for securely storing purchasing information. Furthermore, SET-based systems have an advantage over other mechanisms, in that SET adds digital certificates that associate the cardholder and merchant with a particular financial institution and the Visa or MasterCard payment system.

The **Payment Card Industry (PCI)** data security standard was developed by the major credit card companies as a guideline to help organizations processing card payments to prevent credit card fraud, hacking, and other security issues.

SET and E-Commerce

There was a requirement for an open encryption and security specification to protect credit card transactions on the Internet. SET enables users to employ the existing credit card payment infrastructure on an open network, such as the Internet, in a secure fashion. SET provides the following three services:

- Ensures privacy.
- Provides trust.
- Provides a secure communications channel.

The business requirements provided to participants in SET transactions are summarized as follows:

- Provide authentication that a cardholder is a legitimate user of a credit card account.
- Provide authentication that a merchant can accept credit card transactions through its relationship with a financial institution.
- Provide confidentiality of payment and ordering information.
- Ensure the integrity of all transmitted data.
- Ensure the use of the best security practices and system design techniques to protect all legitimate parties in an electronic commerce transaction.
- Create a protocol that neither depends on transport security mechanisms nor prevents their use.
- Facilitate and encourage interoperability among software and network providers.

The key features realized from SET are:

- Cardholder account authentication.
- Merchant authentication.
- Integrity of data.
- Confidentiality of information.

WIRELESS LAN

A **wireless LAN (WLAN)** is a type of LAN that uses high-frequency radio waves rather than wires to communicate between nodes. There are a number of IEEE specifications that have been developed or are under development to facilitate wireless transmissions. IEEE 802.11 refers to a family of specifications developed for wireless LAN technology, providing 1- or 2-Mbps transmission in the 2.4-GHz band. It specifies an over-the-air interface between a wireless client and a base station or between two wireless clients. Specifications include 802.11a, b, g, and i [Standards]:

802.11a—an extension to 802.11 that applies to wireless LANs and provides up to 54 Mbps in the 5-GHz band.

802.11b (also referred to as 802.11 High Rate or Wi-Fi)—an extension to 802.11 that applies to wireless LANS and provides 11-Mbps transmission in the 2.4-GHz band.

802.11g—applies to wireless LANs and provides up to 54 Mbps in the 2.4-GHz band.

802.11i (also sometimes called Wi-Fi Protected Access 2 [WPA 2])—ratified in June 2004. WPA 2 supports the 128-bit-and-above Advanced Encryption Standard, along with 802.1x authentication and key management features.

Service Access Points

A **service access point (SAP)** is a hardware device or a computer's software that acts as a communication point for users of a wireless device to connect to a wired LAN. Multiple access points, set up in locations around a facility, allow users to roam around the premises while remaining connected to the network. Access points are important for providing heightened wireless security and for extending the physical range of service for wireless user access. **FIGURE 8-2** depicts two SAPs allowing access to a server from the portable wireless devices.

Hotspot

A **hotspot** is a specific geographic location in which an access point provides public wireless network services to mobile visitors through a WLAN. Hotspots are often located in heavily populated places such as airports, bus and train stations, convention centers, and hotels. Hotspots typically have a short access range, effectively controlling the physical proximity of the user. As might be suspected, network transmissions can be intercepted in these hotspots, making it necessary to activate the security provisions on portable computing devices.

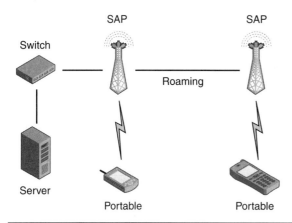

FIGURE 8-2 Service Access Points for Wireless Devices

Wireless Application Protocol

The **wireless application protocol (WAP)** is a worldwide standard for providing Internet communications and advanced telephony services on digital mobile phones, pagers, personal digital assistants (PDAs), and other wireless devices. The WAP Forum has developed the protocol as a means of transferring information to mobile wireless devices using a standard interface and display format. The WAP specification incorporates digital data networking standards and Internet technologies such as HTTP, IP, SSL, URLs, XML, scripting, and other content formats. It was also written to address the challenges of traditional wireless data access within the design objectives of the WAP Forum. The major benefits are outlined as follows:

- Powerful user interface.
- Fast access.
- Optimized protocols.
- Secure connections.
- Application access.
- Increased functionality.
- Efficient components.
- Standards adaptation.

Of particular interest is the provision for a secure wireless broadband connection. Many applications on the Web require a secure connection between the client and application server. The WAP specification ensures that a secure protocol is available for these transactions of a wireless broadband handset.

Wireless Transport Layer Security (WTLS) is the security layer of the WAP providing privacy, data integrity, and authentication for WAP services. WTLS, designed specifically for the wireless environment, is needed because the client and the server must be authenticated in order for wireless transactions to remain secure and because the connection needs to be encrypted. For example, a user making a transaction with a bank over a wireless device needs to know that the connection is secure and private and not subject to a security breach during transfer (sometimes referred to as a man-in-the-middle attack). WTLS is needed because mobile networks do not provide complete end-to-end security.

Wired equivalent privacy (WEP) is designed to provide the same level of security as that of a wired LAN. LANs are inherently more secure than WLANs because LANs are somewhat protected by the physical nature of their structure, having some or all of the network inside a building that can be protected from unauthorized access. WLANs, which are over radio waves, do not have the same physical structure and are therefore more vulnerable to tampering. WEP aims to provide security by encrypting data over radio waves so that it is protected as it is transmitted from one endpoint to another. However, it has been found that WEP is not as secure as once believed. WEP and WTLS standards are described in Chapter 13.

War Driving

War driving is term used to describe the act of driving around in a vehicle with a laptop computer, an antenna, and an IEEE 802.11 wireless LAN adapter to exploit existing wireless networks. Set on "promiscuous mode," the wireless adapter, typically a network interface card (NIC), will receive packets within its range. War driving exploits wireless networks that have ranges that extend outside the perimeter of buildings in order to gain free Internet access or illegal access to an organization's data. One safeguard against war driving is using the WEP encryption standard.

War Chalking

War chalking is the act of making chalk marks on outdoor surfaces (walls, sidewalks, buildings, sign posts, trees) to indicate the existence of an open wireless network connection, usually offering an Internet connection so that others can benefit from the free wireless access. The open connections typically come from the access points of wireless networks located within buildings to serve enterprises. The chalk symbols indicate the type of access point that is available at that specific spot.

There are three basic designs currently used: a pair of back-to-back semicircles, which denotes an open node; a closed circle, which denotes a closed node; and a closed circle with a "W" inside, which denotes a node equipped with WEP. War chalkers also draw identifiers above the symbols to indicate the password that can be used to access the node, which can easily be obtained with sniffer software. As a recent development, the debate over the legality of war chalking is still ongoing.

Cell Phone Security

The wireless application protocol (WAP) and Wireless Transport Layer Security (WTLS) can be attacked using various methods. Poor protocol design and implementation usually cause these problems. The attacker must be familiar with the WTLS protocol and its cryptography features to successfully launch an attack. The purpose of WTLS is to protect the data transferred between a cellular phone and the WAP gateway. These attacks can include the following:

- Key-search shortcut.
- Message forgery.
- Datagram truncation.
- Chosen plain text data recovery.

It is essential that the wireless network be configured properly and security provisions deployed at other layers of the network. There are four levels of voice privacy, which are used to identify security and privacy requirements. These four privacy levels are as follows:

- Level 0—no privacy.
- Level 1—equivalent to wireline.
- Level 2—commercially secure.
- Level 3—military and government secure.

The security and privacy requirements for these four levels include the following categories:

- Radio system performance.
- Theft resistance.
- Physical requirements.
- System lifetime.
- Privacy requirements.
- Law enforcement needs.

When a cryptographic system is designed for wireless systems, it must function in a hostile radio environment characterized by a number of impediments, including interference, thermal noise, multipath fading, and jamming. Performance can also be affected by hand-off activities. The system operator may or may not care if a call is placed from a stolen personal station as long as the call is billed to the correct account. The owner of a personal station, however, will care if the unit is stolen. Requirements needed to accomplish the reduction of theft are:

- Unique user ID.
- Unique personal station ID.
- Clone-resistant design.
- Eliminate repair and installation fraud.

Any cryptographic system used in a personal station must work in a mass-produced consumer product. The cryptographic system must meet basic handset and import/export requirements. It must also be low-cost, wireline compliant. It has been estimated that computing power doubles every two years, which means that a cryptographic algorithm that is secure today may be breakable in 5 to 10 years. A reasonable security requirement is that procedures must be viable for many years. It is necessary for the security designers to consider the best cracking algorithms today and have provisions for field upgradeability in the future.

A user of a personal computer services (PCS) station needs privacy in the following areas:

- Call setup information.
- Speech.
- Data.
- User location.
- User identification.
- Calling patterns.

All uses of PCS communications need to be private so that the user can send information on any channel—whether it is voice, data, or control—and be assured that the transmission is secure.

WIRELESS LAN SECURITY

Both wireless and wired networks are subject to the same security risks and issues. These include threats to the physical security of the resource, unauthorized access and eavesdropping, and attacks from within the authorized users. There are, however, two physical security concerns that must be addressed in a wireless implementation: the interception and reconstruction of radio transmissions and the theft or loss of system devices. These situations can result in eavesdropping episodes and unauthorized access and use of the wireless resources. While second- and third-generation (2G and 3G) wireless technologies continue to evolve and a security rating might be assigned to a specific network component, implementation-specific parameters remain key factors in defining the level of security actually achieved. To ensure the security of information stored or transmitted by a wireless device, compliance with an information security policy and associated standards is essential.

When a WLAN is part of an enterprise network, it provides an interface to a potential intruder that requires no physical intervention or mechanism. The basic security principles applicable to the wired networks also apply to the wireless environment; however, there are unique issues that must be addressed: unauthorized access, integrity, denial of service, inference and deception, and vulnerabilities.

Unauthorized Access

Wireless systems provide opportunities for a number of vulnerabilities in confidentiality. These include browsing, eavesdropping, inference, leakage, masquerading, and traffic analysis. Each of these activities can have a negative impact on the organization's assets.

Eavesdropping is the ability of an intruder to intercept a message without detection. One of the most challenging security issues associated with wireless is the radio-frequency (RF) emanation. Denying access to these signals is difficult, because the distance they travel often exceeds the physical control of the organization. This can allow passive interception by anyone with the proper equipment and a position that allows line of sight of the emitted signals. Eavesdropping on these radio transmissions is relatively simple. When a transmission occurs over the frequency range, anyone with a receiver that can tune that frequency can eavesdrop. These devices are available on the open market and are reasonably priced. Neither sender nor receiver is aware that someone is listening to the transmission, because the interception of the signal is entirely passive.

The wireless intruder can masquerade as a user, a serving network, or a home environment and can misuse privileges of each. Intruders may impersonate a user to utilize services authorized for that user. The intruder may have received assistance from other entities such as the serving network, the home environment, or even the user. This could include part of the serving network's infrastructure, where the intruder uses an authorized user's attempts to gain access to the resource. Users can abuse their privileges to gain unauthorized access to services or intensively use their subscriptions without any intention of paying. This abuse of privileges can also extend to the serving network. The serving network could misuse authentication data for a user, which could allow an accomplice to masquerade as that user.

Integrity

A number of activities can affect the integrity of the system's data and applications. These take the form of manipulations of user network traffic, control data, messages, stored data, and software. An intruder can modify, insert, replay, or delete user traffic on the radio interface. (*Note that this can also occur accidentally by a legitimate user.*) These same activities can also occur with control data. It is also possible that access to system entities can be obtained either locally or remotely and may involve breaching logical or physical controls.

Denial of Service

Wireless radio transmissions are vulnerable to denial of service (DoS) attacks. An intruder with a powerful transceiver can generate sufficient radio interference to interrupt WLAN communication. This attack can be conducted from beyond the perimeter or control of the organization. Equipment and components necessary to conduct this type of attack can be acquired from a number of sources. Protection against this threat is difficult and expensive, but it can be easily detected with the proper equipment. DoS attacks may include physical intervention, protocol intervention, masquerading, and abuse of emergency services.

There are several methods of disrupting a network by physical means. Cables can be cut on wireless and wired networks. Signal jamming can interrupt the wireless interface. Power supplies to transmission equipment can be disconnected or damaged. Physical intervention can cause delayed transmissions on both wired and wireless networks. These situations are usually easy to fix, but they can be difficult to locate.

Intruders can prevent the transmission of user and signaling traffic by introducing protocol failures. These protocol failures might be introduced by physical means. It is also possible for an intruder to masquerade as a network element that can intercept and block user traffic, signaling, or control data. Intruders may prevent access to services by other users and cause serious disruption to emergency services facilities by abusing the ability to make Universal Subscriber Identity Module (USIM)-less calls to emergency services from 2G and 3G terminals.

Inference and Deception

In wired networks, the wire can be traced to a particular device; this is not possible in the wireless environment, which means that an effective authentication mechanism is crucial for WLAN security. Both parties must be able to authenticate identities and provide authorizations.

Wireless can be used as the initial point for a transitive trust attack if the intruder can fool the WLAN to trust the intruder's device. If successful, the intruder's mobile device becomes a network node, and may actually have access behind the firewall. This type of attack can be accomplished by using any device compatible with the WLAN from a location beyond the perimeter of the organization. The only real protection against this attack is to ensure that there is a strong authentication mechanism for mobile devices accessing the network.

Discovery of the unsuccessful attacks depends on logging unsuccessful logon attempts; however, these can be misleading because of normal unsuccessful logon attempts due to radio path problems.

Vulnerabilities

The 802.11b standard offers wired equivalent privacy (WEP) as a simple method to protect over-the-air transmissions between WLAN access points and network interface cards. WEP operates at the data link and physical layers (OSI layers 1 and 2) and requires a secret key. This standard may provide sufficient security to discourage experimenters and casual eavesdroppers, but it will not stop a determined attack.

Several methods can be utilized to protect the access point from theft and tampering. Because the access point is located in an open area, it is important to ensure its physical security. It can be mounted high on a wall or in the ceiling to discourage unauthorized tampering. It can be installed in a secure wiring closet; it might be necessary to add an optional range extender antenna. Some access point devices can be optioned so that only authorized administrators can view or change settings.

It is also possible to limit the ability of stations to associate with the WLAN. A WLAN must initiate an association process of communicating with the access point before a station can become accepted as part of the network. Prohibiting an active scanning response can solve this problem.

A wireless network can be compromised by a trivial method of wandering around. The attacker needs a laptop, a wireless network card, antenna, and a wireless network-sniffing program. The sniffer is looking for the service set identifier (SSID), which is the network name of the wireless LAN. The attacker then uses this SSID to gain access through a dynamic host configuration protocol (DHCP)-assigned IP address. This situation can be mitigated by an internal firewall or by utilizing a security protocol such as Internet Protocol Security (IPSec). More drastic measures require implementing building facilities that block radio waves from leaving the premises.

Finally, some access points allow for the creation of an access control list (ACL), which is a method of authenticating legitimate WLAN users. A list of preapproved MAC addresses can be entered in the access point ACL table, which rejects all users who are not in the list.

SECURITY PROTOCOLS

Security protocols for e-commerce provide authentication by using public-key methods and by implementing encryption of communications between senders and receivers. Discussed in this section are public- and private-key methods; digital certificates; and SSL, IPSec, and AES protocols because they can be applied to the e-commerce environment. Specifications for these protocols are described in Chapter 13.

A public-key infrastructure (PKI) enables users of a public network such as the Internet to securely and privately exchange data and funds through the use of cryptographic keys that are obtained and shared through a trusted authority. The PKI provides digital certificates that can identify individuals or organizations and directory services that can store and revoke certificates. It uses public key cryptography to authenticate message senders and recipients and to encrypt and decrypt messages.

A digital certificate includes the certificate's name, a serial number, expiration dates, a copy of the certificate holder's public key, and the digital signature of the certificate-issuing authority so that a recipient can verify that the certificate is legitimate.

A private key can also be used to authenticate the source of the message. When a digital certificate is encrypted with a private key, the certificate can only be decrypted by using the matching public key, which identifies the certificate's source.

It is a time-consuming and complex effort building and maintaining a PKI to distribute digital certificates. It may be more appropriate to contract with a third-party organization like VeriSign to provide for general Internet e-commerce authentication services.

Protocols that can be deployed to provide security services in the e-commerce environment include SSL, IPSec, and AES. SSL provides for privacy, authentication, and message integrity and is a standard for securing Web traffic. IPSec secures each packet of data by encrypting it inside another packet that is then sent over the Internet. At the receiving end, the message is unpacked and decrypted. AES is in development and will provide a more robust encryption method using 128-bit keys instead of the 56-bit DES key.

IPSec and E-Commerce

IPSec provides the capability to secure communications across a LAN, private and public WANs, and the Internet. Functions that allow e-commerce systems to operate with a high degree of integrity and security include the following:

- Enhanced e-commerce security provisions.
- Secure remote access over the Internet.
- Secure branch office connectivity over the Internet.
- Extranet connectivity with partners over the Internet.
- Intranet and extranet connectivity to the Internet.

The principal feature of IPSec that enables it to support these varied applications is that it can encrypt and/or decrypt all traffic at the OSI IP level. This means that all distributed applications—which make e-commerce work—can be secured. These applications include remote logon, e-mail, file transfer, Web access, and client/server access. OSI, IPSec, SSL, PKI, and AES protocol details are provided in Chapter 13.

E-COMMERCE SYSTEM DESIGN CONCERNS

The primary concern of many information system and audit professionals is the profitability of e-commerce systems. E-commerce installations are often rushed into production based on competitive reasons, without much thought given to security systems. Security measures must be a part of the basic systems design and implementation plan, which should be a requirement of any automated system. Designing e-commerce systems that afford low vulnerability to attacks requires a rigorous approach based on the advice of security experts.

E-commerce systems are based on Internet use, which provides open and easy communications on a global basis. However, because the Internet is unregulated, unmanaged, and uncontrolled, it poses a wide range of risks and threats to the systems operating on it. The use of the Internet means that internal IT and e-commerce systems are potentially accessible by anyone, irrespective of their location.

Security Issues

Often, organizations engaged in e-commerce tend to overestimate the effectiveness of the security measures that have been deployed. E-commerce systems may show little correlation between satisfaction with security by systems managers and the actual existence of effective security policies. It requires an actual breach of security before many systems managers become concerned enough to spend significant resources on security measures.

Many companies engaged in e-commerce are not cognizant that they are e-consumers of other e-companies, and they fail to consider security issues that occur when engaging in e-commerce provided by these vendors. The bottom line is simple: security must be part of the initial development cycle of an e-commerce system and not an afterthought. E-commerce systems that are well organized, documented, and managed have the best opportunity of maintaining an acceptable security level. Security must be a part of the overall e-commerce strategy and not a reactive response after a breach has occurred.

According to *Businesslink*, some of the more common threats that hackers pose to e-commerce systems include [Businesslink]:

- Carrying out denial-of-service (DoS) attacks that stop access to authorized users of a Web site, so that the site is forced to offer a reduced level of service or, in some cases, cease operation completely.
- Gaining access to sensitive data—such as price lists, catalogs, and valuable intellectual property—and altering, destroying, or copying it.

- Altering the Web site, thereby damaging image or directing customers to another site.
- Gaining access to financial information about business or customers, with a view to perpetrating fraud.
- Using viruses to corrupt business data.

These risks can have a significant effect on a business running an e-commerce service. The potential business implications of a security incident include the following:

- Direct financial loss as a consequence of fraud or litigation.
- Subsequent loss as a result of unwelcome publicity.
- Criminal charges if found to be in breach of laws.
- Loss of market share if customer confidence is affected by a DoS attack.

The image presented by the business, together with the brands under which they are traded, are valuable assets. It is important to recognize that the use of e-commerce creates new ways for both image and brands to be attacked.

E-commerce servers should be behind a firewall, which will isolate the internal network from the outside, untrusted world, and allow only legitimate exchanges between e-consumers and e-commerce services. These firewall mechanisms are effective for external threats, but remember that most fraud occurs from internal tampering.

The computer resources and servers must be configured to handle volume spikes. There are busy hours when the transaction load might exceed the capacity of the system. Customers can be lost if access to the system is not available, but idle resources will not be productive to the organization. Market research on buying patterns would assist in determining the best mix of resources to deploy. A bonus can be realized with excessive capacity, which could make the system less vulnerable to hackers who could try to flood the system and shut it down.

Server Access

Commercial Web servers support authentication and authorization methods to establish legitimate users. These basic methods, coupled with SSL and IPSec protocols, should provide a sound security foundation. Servers connected to the Internet and other accessible networks are vulnerable to many different types of attacks. Prices can be changed on items added to e-commerce shopping carts, bogus overflow character inputs can be used to penetrate password barriers, and Web cookies can be altered to access unauthorized accounts.

Steps should be taken to limit physical and administrative access to e-commerce computer, database, and server resources. The fewer people, both employees and otherwise, who can access the systems, the safer they will be. Each person with authorized access should possess a unique ID, and there should be some method of ID tracking.

Credit Cards

If credit card usage is implemented on the e-commerce site, and it usually is, safeguards must be in place to prevent unauthorized use. There are a number of actions that can be taken to minimize unauthorized credit card use:

- Obtain real-time authorization from a credit card company.
- Use credit card verification codes from the card's face.
- Use address verification systems for customers' billing addresses.
- Implement rule-based detection software for transaction criteria.
- Use predictive statistical models for fraudulent transactions.

Maintenance and Upgrades

Regular system maintenance and upgrades should be performed on a scheduled basis. This means that server and computer operating systems have had security patches applied and that the systems are configured properly. This process must also apply to the e-commerce application software. Regular audits must be performed to verify the configuration and usage patterns. Audits must also monitor intrusion systems to ensure they are working properly. An administrator must be assigned the responsibility of assessing and correcting security deficiencies. This creates a centralized responsibility and ensures that someone is maintaining acceptable security levels.

DISTRIBUTED SECURITY AND PRIVACY ISSUES

A well-devised and implemented security program needs to be in place to thwart the efforts of unwanted visitors. Security software alone cannot stop a security breach if people have a valid ID and password. The following are recommendations to consider when creating a secure networking environment:

- Set and keep policies for maintaining network security.
- Determine the security levels required for each area of the organization.
- Work toward an acceptable level of security without inhibiting network access and use.
- Be vigilant, and keep a lookout for security holes.
- Protect vital areas under several levels of security.
- Maintain software for recording activity and user identities.
- Develop good passwords, and keep them secure.
- Do not allow the sharing of passwords.
- Use a virtual network with security features.

Wireless Networks

The use of wireless systems and devices is permeating all aspects of the telecommunications environment. In the past, communication devices and end-users were fixed in one location. Wireless communications breaks that barrier by allowing communication to and from a mobile communications device. Wireless, however, requires an infrastructure of wires in conjunction with the wireless system. It is becoming increasingly popular to interconnect computer equipment and to transmit data over wireless links rather than over conventional telecommunications circuits. Wireless transmission can be used to implement either long-distance WAN links or short-distance LAN links. There must be a way of interconnecting physically disjointed LANs and other groups of mobile users with stationary servers and resources. Networks that include both wired and wireless components are called *hybrid networks*. The ongoing development of a wireless network will allow its users to communicate with anyone, anywhere, and at any time.

The wireless network gives the impression of allowing the exchange of messages without plugging into a wire-based phone line. This is, however, a misconception, because most wireless systems do actually interface with some type of wire-based network.

Unauthorized persons can easily receive wireless transmissions, including both terrestrial radio and satellite signals. The carrier-switched network does not have this problem because many different signals are multiplexed into large transmission pipes and are not accessible or readable. Although it is illegal to intercept messages intended for others, enforcement is almost nonexistent, and scanners are readily available to enable eavesdroppers to monitor conversations.

Security and Privacy in Wireless Systems

Any user of the media can intercept communications on shared media, and anyone with access to the media can receive or transmit on the media. When the media are shared, privacy and authentication are lost unless some method is established to regain it. Cryptography is a method that provides the means to regain control over privacy and authentication. Some of the cryptographic requirements are in the air interface between the personal station (PS) and the radio system (RS). Other requirements are on databases stored in the network and on information shared between systems in the process of hand-offs or of giving service for roaming units. Generally speaking, a secure wireless system can be realized if the following functions are addressed:

- The identity of the user can be validated through an authentication technique.
- Eavesdroppers on a data conversation can be blocked via an encryption process.
- Information is restricted to authorized participants through some type of access control.
- A stolen or lost wireless device can be disabled from some central location.

IMPLEMENTATION ISSUES

Implementing a thorough security system is not as simple as installing technologies and forgetting them. There are a number of challenges that must be addressed for a security plan to work effectively. These include the following issues:

- *Ease of use*—requiring a user to jump through hoops to access a system or complete a transaction will negate the value of security.
- *Cost versus risk*—consideration must be given to the dollar amount of the transaction that is being protected.
- *Lack of standards*—standards are not yet developed that ensure technologies work together seamlessly.
- *Internal security risks*—there is a possibility that an internal breach will occur.
- *System defaults*—system defaults are usually set at the low end of security coverage.

Additionally, regulations such as the Gramm-Leach-Bliley Financial Services Modernization Act make implementing security systems difficult. It requires a notice to consumers and an opportunity to "opt-out" of sharing of nonpublic, personal information with nonaffiliated third parties subject to certain limited exceptions [Gramm-Leach-Bliley]. State regulators can further complicate security issues for financial services firms. The implementation strategy for financial security systems can be subdivided into four separate stages:

- *Security audit*—the audit examines processes, infrastructure, and applications to determine if security weaknesses exist.
- *Technology audit*—this audit measures the available technologies and applications against those that are needed.
- *Planning and implementation*—planning and implementation should consider the organization's business processes and those employees who use them.
- *Training and monitoring*—users must be thoroughly trained and monitored for acceptance of the security provisions.

E-Security and E-Thieves

E-merchants must evaluate the steps being taken to prevent online fraud, security and privacy violations, and intruder attacks. Although the cost of implementing these e-security measures can be significant, the alternative is even more costly. There are actions that can be taken to prevent theft, protect sensitive information, and foil destructive attacks.

Online fraud can occur in a number of ways; identification fraud and electronic price tag alteration are the most predominant forms. Identification fraud occurs when e-thieves use a consumer's credit card to make online purchases or when consumers make an online purchase and then later deny the transaction. E-merchants often have little to no recourse and are held liable when transactions conducted at their sites are later determined to be fraudulent. This means that the merchants must pay higher discount rates and fees and higher penalties based on their charge-back percentages. Electronic price tag alteration occurs when hackers manipulate the shopping cart software code and alter prices. It is estimated that one-third of all shopping cart applications have software holes.

Traditional password protection, which is used to control system and database access, is not sufficient for e-commerce security. Secure e-commerce requires that both parties to a transaction be positively mutually identified. This mutual authentication process prevents intruders from acquiring valuable information or goods under false pretenses. It is also essential that e-commerce transaction information be secured against theft. Encrypting the information before it is sent, then decrypting it when received can protect transaction communications. This security technique is designed to foil intruders who may intercept the transaction somewhere in the transmission path.

E-commerce transaction information, which is stored on computer systems and servers, must be carefully protected. This is usually accomplished by defensive hardware and software, which can include firewall and intrusion detection mechanisms. The goal is to keep systems safe from external and internal theft attempts. Confidential data, such as credit card numbers and account information, should be encrypted. Encryption can make the information unusable in the event e-thieves gain access to the system.

Attacks that use destructive techniques such as denial of service and viruses also pose a threat to e-commerce. Interruption of service caused by such attacks can be very costly to an e-commerce organization. Because access to the site may be blocked, both immediate customers and potential customers may be lost. A number of security measures can be effective in mitigating these types of attacks. Anti-virus software and the same measures used to foil theft are useful against these threats.

🔒 CHAPTER SUMMARY

E-commerce involves Internet use for purchases of such items as airline tickets, computer hardware and software, books, and miscellaneous products. It involves a number of methods for securing transactions, authorizing payments, and moving money between accounts. B2B is defined as e-commerce where both the buyers and sellers are organizations. B2C is a business selling online to individual consumers. Lastly, C2C involves individuals buying and selling over the Internet.

EDI is a process whereby standardized forms of e-commerce documents are transferred between remotely located computer systems, usually to and from organizations providing some product or service. These computerized forms include purchase orders and invoices.

SET is a specification for handling credit card transactions over a network, with emphasis on the Web and Internet. A digital certificate is a digital signature that can be used for authentication, to ensure the sender is validated, and to ensure the message has not been altered in transit. Secure transactions are critical for e-commerce on the Internet. Additional security mechanisms include SSL, SHTTP, and PCT.

Two types of keys are utilized in the security environment. A public key is used in an asymmetric encryption system. It is used in conjunction with a corresponding private key. A private key is also known as a symmetric key. Private-key encryption utilizes a shared secret key between one or more parties. The use of a public and private key, where two keys are utilized, is called an asymmetrical system. A third method of encryption is called the hash function. A hash function maps a variable-length data block or message into a fixed-length value called a hash code.

Networks that require a high level of security can use a method called encryption. Encryption is the conversion of plain text or data into an unintelligible form by means of a reversible translation, based on some algorithm or translation table. These include both symmetric and asymmetric key algorithms.

Four cornerstones of secure electronic commerce include (1) preventing unauthorized monitoring of traffic, (2) preventing the content of messages from being altered, (3) ensuring that the transmission is from an authentic source, and (4) preventing nonrepudiation.

A well-devised and implemented security program needs to be in place to thwart attacks and frauds. Security software and hardware alone cannot stop a security breach when users possess valid IDs and passwords.

 KEY TERMS

access point	electronic data interchange (EDI)	secure electronic transaction (SET)
asymmetric encryption	encryption	service access point (SAP)
business-to-business (B2B)	eTRUST	smart card
business-to-consumer (B2C)	hash function	symmetric encryption
certificate	hotspot	war chalking
certificate authority (CA)	IPSec	war driving
consumer-to-consumer (C2C)	key	wireless application protocol (WAP)
digital certificate	Payment Card Industry (PCI)	wireless local are network (WLAN)
digital envelope	private key	Wireless Transport Layer Security (WTLS)
e-business	public key	
electronic commerce	secret key	wired equivalent privacy (WEP)

🔒 SECURITY REVIEW QUESTIONS

1. Compare and contrast B2B, B2C, and C2C e-commerce transactions.
2. _____ is an open specification for handling credit card transactions over a network, with emphasis on the Web and Internet.
3. A _____ is a unique collection of information, transformed into un-forgeable form, used for authentication of users.
4. _____ provides digital signatures that are critical for verifying the authenticity of cardholders and others involved in the transactions.
5. _____ is the conversion of plain text or data into unintelligible form by means of a reversible translation, based on some algorithm or translation table.
6. A _____ is about the size of a credit card and contains a micro-processor for performing a number of functions.
7. The _____ data security standard was developed by the major credit card companies as a guideline to help organizations processing card payments prevent credit card fraud, hacking, and other security issues.
8. An _____ or _____ is a hardware device or a computer's software that acts as a communication point for users of a wireless device to connect to a wired LAN.
9. _____ is a term used to describe the act of driving around in a vehicle with a laptop computer, an antenna, and an IEEE 802.11 wireless LAN adapter to exploit existing wireless networks.
10. _____ provides the capability to secure communications across a LAN, private and public WANs, and the Internet.

🔒 RESEARCH ACTIVITIES

1. Describe how e-commerce can be used in selected marketing environments.
2. Compare the various 802.11 wireless specifications.
3. Provide an overview of the various encryption/decryption standards.
4. Provide an overview of the SSL and SHTTP protocols.
5. Research the subject of symmetric and asymmetric encryption systems. Identify systems that utilize these techniques.
6. Describe the differences between SHA1 and MD5 hashing functions. Look at the CRC16/32 function.
7. Research the 802.11n protocols, and provide an overview of each and a comparison matrix.
8. Identify vendors that provide security services for e-commerce applications and systems.
9. Develop an overview of DES, IDEA, and 3DES symmetric algorithms.
10. Develop an overview of DSS and RSA asymmetric algorithms.
11. Provide and overview of the Gramm-Leach-Bliley Financial Services Modernization Act.

PART THREE

SECURITY AND OPERATIONS ADMINISTRATION

CHAPTER 9

Business Continuity and
Disaster Recovery Planning

🔒 CHAPTER CONTENTS

- Identify the threats and vulnerabilities that could impact the network.
- See how to protect computer and network assets.
- Understand issues and identify techniques for access control.
- Identify hardware and software solutions used in BCP and DRP.
- Learn how to protect data and DBMS assets.
- Describe the business continuity planning process.
- Look at the process of disaster planning and recovery.
- Describe the alternatives, options, and responses for various disasters and incidents.

INTRODUCTION

Network security includes the development and implementation of methods and techniques for protecting the organization's networking assets. A primary goal is to ensure the network is as secure as possible against unauthorized access or use of network resources. Internal personnel are responsible for the majority of network intrusions that result in lost, compromised, or stolen resources and assets.

The first step in establishing network security is the development of written policies covering all aspects of network security in the organization. These policies must include both acceptable and unacceptable uses of computer and networking resources. Included would be policies relating to hardware and software components and employee time. The policy would also delineate the consequences for violating user policies. These policies are contained in documents titled business continuity planning (BCP) and disaster recovery planning (DRP).

To be effective, the organization's management at all levels must buy into these network security policies and make a serious commitment to them. Security policies must meet the organization's concerns without conflicting with other policies or limiting users' access to necessary resources.

Most importantly, rules and procedures can be followed only if the users are aware of and understand them. They cannot be effectively implemented without some type of notification and explanation. Training and awareness sessions must be part of ongoing personnel management. While security concerns are burning issues to the information technology (IT) department, many other departmental employees may not be too concerned.

SECURITY GOALS AND OBJECTIVES

This section is devoted to the goals and objectives of secure computing. The two main goals discussed include availability and confidentiality. These components are subsets of resource integrity. As any IT manager will attest, the inability of network users to access their data resources or e-mail will cause a "bad hair day."

Availability

Availability means the network resources are accessible to authorized users; however, they may also be available to illegitimate users. Authorized parties must not be prevented from accessing system resources. It is possible to make the resource so secure that it is difficult even for authorized users to access. System compromises can result from this security strategy. Availability is sometimes known by its opposite, which is denial of service. As stated in Chapter 1, the goals of availability are:

- Controlled concurrency.
- Fair allocation.
- Fault tolerance.
- Timely response.
- Usability.

Confidentiality

Confidentiality describes security and secrecy, meaning only authorized people can see protected data or resources. Someone must decide what resources are confidential and who has the right to access them. Confidentiality is probably the best understood of the security properties. Setting resource access "rights" for individual users usually enforces this process. Confidentiality includes the following issues:

- Determining what resources are confidential.
- Identifying those who can access the resource.
- Deciding how often the resource can be accessed.
- Identifying who can modify or delete the resource.
- Stating whether the resource status can be changed.

A good place to start this discussion is with the various types of threats that are posed and to continue with various attacks that can be expected. These threats and attacks will manifest themselves in numerous vulnerabilities. Remember that vulnerability is a weakness in a system that can be exploited by a threat.

PROTECTING ASSETS AND RESOURCES

The primary mission of this chapter is to present options and alternatives that can be utilized to protect the organization's computer and networking assets. Various techniques are required for providing access control using the **triple-A** technique of *authentication, authorization,* and *accounting.* A major topic to network managers is the issue of firewall implementations in the computer networking environment. As described in Chapter 5, a *firewall* is hardware or software that uses various filtering and screening methods to determine if a user will be allowed access to the resources of an organization. A firewall's function is to protect the organization's assets from the unsecured and untrusted Internet and ensure that only legitimate users are allowed access.

The fundamental purpose of triple-A mechanisms is to maintain security by preventing unauthorized use of the network. A number of authentication and access control mechanisms are employed to accomplish this task. **Authentication mechanisms** include the following:

- Biometric techniques.
- Certificates.
- Challenge–response handshakes.
- Kerberos authentication.
- One-time passwords.
- Passwords and PINs.
- RADIUS.
- Security tokens.

Access control mechanisms include following:

- Access control by authentication servers.
- Access control lists.
- Intrusion detection.
- Physical access control.
- Policy filters.
- Traffic filters.

INFRASTRUCTURE SECURITY AND CONTROL

Efforts to secure the computer, database, and network resources are in vain if the physical plant that houses them is not protected. This section provides an overview of the issues involved and presents various alternatives to counter these incidents, situations, and threats.

Every organization should assume that it will be a target of some kind, and as many barriers as feasible should be erected to counter these undesirable activities. Although sometimes expensive and troublesome, it is fairly easy to erect barriers against physical access. Equipment rooms and network demarcation closets can be kept locked. Note that a **demarcation** is the physical point at which a regulated service or network cabling is provided to the user. Access can be restricted to only those with a specific, legitimate need.

As concentration points for large numbers of circuits, equipment rooms and telecommunications closets are particularly vulnerable. They should be kept locked and the keys given only to authorized personnel. Circuit records and wiring schematics and other communications master records should not be kept in these rooms. As cabling and wiring come closer to the workstation or PC, it becomes increasingly easy to determine which one to tap. It is essential that these connections that attach to sensitive computer and network devices not show conspicuous tags. Most organizations are also vulnerable to malicious activities in these locations, which means that access to these areas must be monitored and restricted. Physical access to a network link would allow someone to tap into that link, jam it, or inject network traffic into it. An important concept that applies to the network world is to avoid the "single point of failure." It would be possible for a saboteur to disrupt an entire organization's network by destroying or incapacitating its network demarcation point.

In addition to accessing networks through computers and terminals, it is possible for intruders to physically break into network cabling systems. Fiber-optic cable is considerably more difficult to tap than copper wire because it does not radiate signals that can be collected through surreptitious means. An intruder might resort to tapping copper connectors in a wiring closet or at cable outlets. Physical security measures at plants and offices are the primary means to prevent such break-ins.

Physical access to a building or data center can be controlled via locks and access control mechanisms. Enterprise physical security can be based on security guards, closed-circuit television, and card-key entry systems. Data centers and limited-access buildings may employ the double door system, which requires anyone entering the facility to pass through two sets of security checkpoint doors, one door at a time. With these security measures in place, organizations can feel confident that the assets are protected and high user productivity is maintained.

PHYSICAL SECURITY

The primary emphasis of physical security is to prevent unauthorized access to the computing facility that includes the computer room, the communications room, network control center, and network infrastructure. Efforts are directed at preventing malicious vandalism or subtle tapping of communications circuits. Physical security can be thought of as the lock and key part of security because the primary protection mechanism is a lock of some type. Equipment rooms that house sensitive equipment are normally locked, workstations contain locking mechanisms, and doors into various sensitive areas are locked. In lieu of actual physical locks and keys, magnetically encoded cards are used to activate workstations and open doors. These methods of entry are also used as personal employee identification.

Physical security planning includes addressing a number of emergency situations, such as floods, storms, earthquakes, power failures, and fires. Disasters can occur from both fire and water damage originating from inside and outside sources. There are a number of proactive measures that can be taken to reduce the damage caused by these natural and man-made disasters.

Physical intrusion detection is the art of detecting and responding to computer and network misuse. The benefits include attack anticipation, deterrence, detection, response, damage assessment, and prosecution support. Facility access control devices include biometric devices, detectors, alarms, and sensors. The security administrator must evaluate the potential risks and implement the appropriate system for the maximum protection.

ACCESS SECURITY OF COMPUTER AND NETWORK RESOURCES

All efforts to secure the organization's resources will be in vain if the facilities that house them are not protected. Access control into computer and network facilities—and buildings—has become a priority issue with many organizations. This is particularly true if the asset is expensive and replacing or recreating it would be difficult and cost-prohibitive. This section looks at the issues relating to egress and ingress to buildings that house computer and network resources.

It is essential that only authorized personnel be allowed, unattended, into a facility. Not only is ingress an issue, egress can be just as important; hardware, software, and documentation tend to disappear if management controls are not present. Unauthorized people can cause several problems, including theft of equipment or data, destruction of equipment or data, and viewing of sensitive data and information.

Controls are implemented to reduce risk and loss. Controls can be preventive, detective, or corrective. These can be used to inhibit and discover harmful occurrences and restore those that have been harmed. An access control program must be in place that includes internal personnel, maintenance workers, contractors, vendors, and visitors. Smart cards or security cards are some devices that can utilized in the organization's access control program.

Access Control for Internal Personnel

The size of the office and staff can have an impact on the level of security access to resources. In small offices, with limited computer and networking resources, everyone may have access to everything. If this is a stand-alone entity, security implications might be limited; however, if this small office is part of a larger enterprise network, the situation changes. A list of questions that should be answered includes the following:

- Is the computer system stand-alone?
- Is the computer system networked? What is the method of communication, and where is the communication device located?
- Is the system in a secure room? Who has the keys?
- Who should have access to the processor and console?
- Do employees perform minor maintenance?

- Is other equipment or supplies located with the computer or networking components?
- Where is the office entrance? Is it in a larger building with multiple tenants?
- Is the facility located on the ground floor?
- Are data files stored off-campus? If so, who has access?
- Do employees access the facility after hours and on holidays?

Access Control for Contractors

There are a number of support organizations, vendors, and suppliers that might need access to the physical facility. Maintenance personnel will probably require frequent access to the computer and network components. Software engineers and other specialists may also require access during all hours of the day. Communication suppliers and vendors often have a requirement to access the demarcation closet. The demarcation point is a critical location in the network and access must be adequately controlled. Telephone and network technicians often require some access. Different groups may require a different level of access control. Very few of these people should be allowed unescorted access into sensitive areas. Someone must be responsible for providing authorization for these personnel to access computer equipment and networking facilities.

Activities that might be performed by external organizations include the following:

- Installation and maintenance of network services.
- Electrical and communication circuit wiring.
- Installation of network and computer devices and components.
- Maintenance of computer systems.
- Software upgrades.
- Office rearrangements.
- Furniture additions.
- Construction.
- Inspections.
- Hands-on training.
- Cleaning crews.

Access Control for Visitors

Visitors can fall into a number of different categories, including relatives of employees, tour groups, competitors, sales representatives, trainers, and others. None of these visitors should be allowed to roam freely throughout the organization. Trainers and education providers fit in a different category than the others as they may require access to both computer and networking components as part of a training session. The following suggestions may provide some guidance concerning access for the various classes of visitors.

- A clear and concise policy must identify security access requirements.
- An employee must accompany all nonemployees.
- Tour groups must be controlled and monitored by a tour guide.
- A supervisor must accompany sales representatives and competitors.
- Trainers must have a clearance to view and access corporate systems.

THEFT PREVENTION TECHNIQUES

The most successful method of preventing theft of computer and networking resources is to control access. Access control devices can prevent access by unauthorized individuals and record access by those authorized. Mainframes, client/servers, and other large devices are difficult to get past the front door, but there are a number of devices and software that are easy to conceal. There are several approaches that can be taken to reduce the incidence of theft of these resources, including preventing access, restricting portability, and detecting exit. (*Note that multifactor security will provide for a higher level of access security; multifactor authentication requires more than one authentication factor [i.e., password, smart card, or fingerprint]*).

Guard Solution

A common approach is to employ a human guard, but there are situations in which guard dogs are deployed. Guards are traditional, well understood, and adequate in many situations. There are a number of security services that offer guard solutions. To be effective, human guards must be continually on duty, which implies 24 hours a day, seven days a week (24/7). A guard must personally recognize a person or some identification, such as a badge. People often lose or forget badges, and badges can be forged. Employees and contractors who no longer have authorized access may still have their badges. The guard must make a record of everyone entering and leaving a facility, if any tracking is required. This guard service can be expensive, and it is essential to establish the credibility of the guards, who can also be a source of theft.

There are both advantages and disadvantages to using security guards. A guard can apply human judgment to situations; provide a visible deterrence, response, and control capability; and also provide escort services. The downside is the unpredictability of someone's reliability and integrity, human judgment errors, and the obvious expense of a full-time guard.

Lock Solution

The simplest technique to prevent theft is to lock the room or closet that contains the equipment or resource. The lock is easier, cheaper, and simpler to manage than employing a guard. It, however, does not provide a record of entries and exits, and there are difficulties attributed to lost and duplicated keys. There is the possibility that an unauthorized person can walk through a door that has been unlocked by another. There is also the inconvenience of fumbling for a key with an armload of something. A lock-and-key solution requires that someone be the "keeper of the keys." This person is not always available when someone needs access to a locked room.

Electronic Solution

More exotic access control devices employ magnetic strip cards, cards with radio transmitters, and cards with electronic circuitry that makes them difficult to duplicate. Because each of these cards interfaces with a computer, lists can be produced of those entering and exiting a secured location, along with date and time stamps. Some devices operate by proximity so that a person can carry it in a pocket or on a neck rope. It is also easy to update the access list of authorized personnel when someone is added or deleted from the list. New employees, dismissed employees, and lost or stolen cards can be readily noted on the access list.

An electronic solution can also be applied to alerting when a resource is removed from a secure location. A theft can be detected when someone tries to leave a protected area with a protected object. This special label is small and unobtrusive and is used by a number of libraries. It looks like a normal pressure-sensitive label; however, sensors at the entrance and exit can detect the security tag. These tags are available for vehicles, machinery, equipment, electronics, software, and other documents. The detector sounds an alarm, and someone must approach the person trying to leave with a protected object. This may require the addition of a human guard, which can add to the security cost.

Biometric Access Control

Biometric identification devices use individual physical attributes such as fingerprints, palm prints, voice attributes, iris and retina patterns, and signature dynamics to identify authorized users (**FIGURE 9-1**). Biometrics is currently used as a network security technique in a limited number of U.S. companies. Biometric solutions can be applied to both physical facility access and computer access. Fingerprint identification is the most popular biometrics technique, and retina scanning is the most accurate. Biometric identification has been expensive

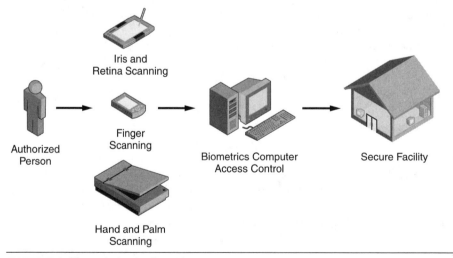

FIGURE 9-1 Biometric Access Control

to implement; costs are coming down, however. There is considerable end-user resistance to fingerprinting, which is associated with criminal activity. While biometrics promises more secure identification of authorized users than that of passwords, it also can be circumvented. An overview of biometric techniques was presented in Chapter 1.

The performance of a biometric system may be characterized by assessing how frequently the system commits errors of false acceptance and false rejection. System designers and assessors use two numbers for this purpose: **false acceptance rate (FAR)** and **false rejection rate (FRR)**. The FAR is the probability that the system accepts an impostor as a legitimate individual. The FRR is the probability that the system rejects a legitimate individual as an impostor.

Biometric systems designed for high-security access applications, where break-in concerns are great, operate at a small FAR. As a result, the number of people who are falsely rejected is greater in these systems. Biometric systems designed for police applications operate at a high FAR. In these applications, the desire to catch a criminal outweighs the inconvenience of investigating a large number of falsely identified individuals.

SECURITY COST JUSTIFICATION

Because network security measures can require a substantial investment, it is imperative they are made with some confidence that the investments are warranted. One national study has found that large companies and government agencies were able to quantify an average loss of $1 million from security breaches. Security programs and measures, however, can also be very expensive.

One method of determining the degree of security needed is to assess the value of the database element that may be placed at risk. This value would include the cost of collecting the data and re-creating the database. The possibility exists that the original data are no longer available, which means that the database could not be reconstructed. This scenario assumes that the database was not backed up, which is also a possibility. The organization's return on investment in network security would depend on the monetary value assigned to the data and database. This exercise is not a trivial pursuit.

Another method of determining costs of security is to conduct an in-depth threat and vulnerability assessment. A search of possible providers that could conduct such an analysis reveals a cost of less than $20,000. Modern technology is enabling business communication in ways never before imagined; however, advances come with new internally and externally devastating threats. Many organizations make the mistake of concentrating on technical areas before examining the foundations of their information security program. A threat and vulnerability evaluation would look at the most critical areas of the organization.

Organizational elements and areas that could be analyzed include the following:

- Policies and procedures, auditing, awareness, IT change controls.
- Network device security, communications security, network access controls, Internet/Web security, intrusion detection, vulnerability testing, PBX/voice system security, network change controls, firewalls and proxy servers, dial-up access security, encryption, e-mail security, wireless controls.

- Workstation and computer operating system access controls, including user authentication, data access authorization, audit logs, application security.
- Fault tolerance and redundancy, data backup, recovery/continuity planning.
- Facilities access control.
- Disaster and interruption avoidance, air conditioning and temperature controls, electrical power and utilities (HVAC).
- Protection of all forms of physical storage media, including paper documents.
- Hardware maintenance and change controls, anti-theft, anti-tampering.
- Software maintenance and change controls, anti-virus and related malicious software safeguards, database security.
- Training, professional development.

Managers and security administrators must compare the cost of analyses such as this against the cost of a major disaster. This goes back to the old saying of "pay me now or pay me later."

SECURITY SYSTEMS DESIGN

An important aspect of security systems is the design of the perimeter network and the security policies that must be included in this development. It is essential that the administrator and security manager know how the components function and interact with both internal and external networks. It is also important for top management to understand that security must be designed into systems and not added later. A number of issues must be addressed to successfully protect the organization's computer and networking assets. These include the following:

- Identify and understand the enemy.
- Measure the cost of security or lack of.
- Identify security assumptions.
- Look at the human factors.
- Identify the organization's weaknesses.
- Limit the scope of system access.
- Understand the computer and network environment.
- Limit trust in software.
- Look at physical security.
- Make security part of the normal operating procedures.

This process can be initiated by conducting a security audit of the organization (Appendix A).

SECURITY EVALUATION

How does an administrator know that the security system deployed will perform as promised? Reliance can be placed on the word of the service provider or on an independent, impartial evaluator. The process of security evaluation involves an assessment of the security properties of a particular computer system or communications network. A standard set of requirements is used, as a metric, for determining and comparing how effectively different systems will respond in mitigating the effects of malicious attacks. This determination and comparison is usually performed by an independent organization, which has no vested interest in the outcome of the assessment.

Comparing the security effectiveness of different systems is difficult if varied approaches are taken to mitigating attacks. Security evaluation that includes a standard, well-defined set of security requirements provides a means of comparing the effectiveness of different security approaches. To achieve this goal of uniformity, security requirements that require subjective judgment to determine compliance must be minimized.

A security evaluation offers the opportunity for an independent organization to provide an assessment of the security properties of a system. This will remove the inherent biases that can occur if a development organization performs an evaluation on its own product. The security evaluation process can be viewed as part of quality assessment processes that are common in typical software and system engineering efforts.

When a standard metric is established for determining security effectiveness, computer systems and network vendors will desire to meet these requirements in the development efforts. These requirements must be balanced by resources and cost considerations. If the security specifications are too stringent, the vendors will ignore them.

System tests, formal methods, and other life-cycle activities can be used as evidence that a particular system is secure. Security evaluation can be used as additional evidence that a system is secure. Security evaluation may provide the most convincing assurance, because it serves as a means for reviewing, assessing, and summarizing the results of all other assurance activities.

Internetworks may involve large-scale, multi-protocol networks that span multiple time zones or may involve simple single-protocol, point-to-point connections in a local environment. The trend is toward an increasingly complex environment, which involves multiple media types, multiple protocols, and often some connectivity to a private network service or an ISP. It is, therefore, possible that control of the components, throughput, and management of these networks is in someone else's hands. More complex network environments mean that the potential for performance and availability issues in internetworks is high, and the source of problems is often elusive. The keys to maintaining a secure, problem-free network environment, as well as maintaining the ability to isolate and fix a network fault quickly, are documentation, planning, and communication. This requires a framework of procedures and personnel in place before the requirement for problem solving and recovery occurs.

Network problems can typically be resolved in one of two ways: proactive prevention or after-the-fact reaction. It is possible to prevent problems from occurring by a program of computer and network resource planning and management. The alternative is repair and control of damage that can be accomplished by reactive responses. Network management and planning should combine to form an overall security plan. This network plan combination should include:

- Cable diagrams.
- Cable layouts.
- Documentation on computer and network device configurations.
- Important files and their layouts.

- Listing of protocols and network standards in use.
- Network capacity information.
- Software.

Security troubleshooting is often characterized as an art that can only be gained from experience in the trenches. This experience, along with some documented methodology, allows the administrator to successfully solve difficult network issues. The methodology keeps the troubleshooter from skipping or overlooking the obvious, and the experience helps draw appropriate conclusions and check for obscure problems.

Before someone starts this troubleshooting process, it is essential for the network professional to establish a baseline or reference point for system comparisons. Information should be gathered and documented on the network devices, software elements, facility components, network traffic, performance levels, and security systems. This information will prove invaluable later when a problem develops in the network.

Establishment of policies and procedures that apply to the enterprise network must be developed during its planning stages and continue throughout the network's life. Such policies should include security, hardware and software standards, upgrade guidelines, backup methods, and documentation requirements. Through careful planning, it is possible to minimize the damage that results from most predictable events and control and manage their impact on the organization.

ADMINISTRATION

It is essential that someone at the management level be responsible for computer and network security administration. This responsibility is often assigned to the network administrator because many of the duties required fall under the auspices of network management. This position should not be taken lightly—the success or survival of the organization may depend on this person.

Common duties for a network administrator's office include the following:

- Software installation and upgrades.
- Database access approval and maintenance.
- Login script and menu creation and maintenance.
- Login IDs and password assignment.
- Backup and restoral processes.
- Training and documentation support.
- Facilities monitoring and other audits.
- Future expenditure requests and justifications.

The security administrator should participate in the organization's planning council activities.

CORPORATE PLANNING

Enterprise security goals must be set and supported by the organization's upper management. The "real" leadership must define the vision and allocate sufficient resources to completely and successfully implement all of the security elements necessary to protect the organization's assets. A clear message must be sent to all personnel and users that the computer and network resources are valuable and must be properly protected.

Contingency planning scenarios should be a part of the development of a security program. As an example, a plan must be in place if a laptop capable of accessing sensitive corporate resources is stolen. It is necessary to look at different security-oriented events and develop a solution to counter particular threats and attacks.

The entire organization must be aware of the need for a security plan. By making employees aware of the ramifications of leaving a workstation unattended or writing a password on a sticky note on the monitor, awareness and compliance are more likely to occur. Security must be part of the hiring process. If security is emphasized from the first day, employees are more likely to develop habits conducive to a secure operation. It should not be a surprise that the IT department is the most sensitive area of the organization. IT personnel have access to all levels of information, so it is incumbent on management to monitor activities in this area.

In any security system there will be a weak link that is human and not technological. A common problem is personnel turnover. Former employees' network access must be denied promptly to avoid possible security violations. There must be a process in which the human resources department notifies IT of an employee's departure so that network access can be removed. Delays can result in data theft or corruption. It is common practice in many organizations to escort former employees to the door and collect all corporate items such as smart cards and credit cards. Having security measures in place means that someone must administer those measures. This task is usually the responsibility of the IT department, which means that these employees must be trustworthy, competent, and conscientious.

With today's heterogeneous networking environments, it is necessary to know whether security protocols and software work together. It is useless to have only part of the network secure—the entire network must be secure from both internal and external threats. A successful computer network security system requires a marriage of technology and process, which is part of a security requirement assessment.

SECURITY REQUIREMENTS ASSESSMENT

As with any assessment program, a formalized process must be followed to accomplish the stated goals. This usually takes the form of an iterative process in which a number of steps are executed many times until the process has been refined. Each of these steps must be clearly defined, including roles and responsibilities for computer operations processes and network-related activities. This means that process definition and setting of the organization's security goals and standards must precede technology evaluation, selection, and implementation.

There is a simple and straightforward life-cycle approach that can be utilized to accomplish this task. The application of this structured process ensures that all potential user group and information combinations have been considered. When successfully completed, this implies that appropriate security processes and technology have been determined that allow legitimate access into any of the organization's computer and network resources. These include the following steps that are processed repetitively until an evaluation is successful:

- Identify the organization's security issues.
- Analyze security risks, threats, and vulnerabilities.
- Design the security architecture and the associated processes.
- Audit the impact of the security technology and processes.
- Evaluate the effectiveness of current architectures and policies.

Note that evaluation processes validate the effectiveness of the original analysis steps, and feedback from these evaluation steps causes a renewed analysis with possible ripple effects of changes in architecture or implemented technology.

MAINTAINING NETWORK INTEGRITY

Protecting network assets and operations is a continuing task with results that can never be certain. When intelligently applied, protective efforts can reduce, but never completely eliminate, the chances of losses due to security breaches. Although most network security violations take place within corporate networks and are initiated by authorized users, most funding for security programs is allocated to measures that guarantee that only authorized users are allowed to access the network. These funds are also allocated to prevention and detection of external invasions.

A primary task of maintaining network **integrity** involves troubleshooting the network environment. Past results indicate that a systematic approach is the most effective. The administrator should be able to identify problems from symptoms and initiate corrective action based on this systematic approach. If change is not managed, a great deal of time will be spent fire-fighting instead of fire-preventing. A major part of this structured approach is network management and planning, which can be accomplished by addressing the following issues:

- Data backup.
- Documentation procedures and methodology.
- Hardware and software standards.
- Network baseline.
- Preemptive troubleshooting.
- Security policies.
- Upgrade guidelines.

Network Baseline

A baseline for network performance must be established if network monitoring is going to be used as a preemptive troubleshooting tool. A **baseline** defines a point of reference against which to measure network performance and behavior when problems occur. This baseline is established during a period when no problems are evident on the network. A baseline is useful when identifying daily network utilization patterns, possible network bottlenecks, protocol traffic patterns, and heavy-user usage patterns and time frames. A baseline can also indicate whether a network needs to be partitioned or segmented or whether the network access speed should be increased. The three components that must be created to establish a baseline are:

- Current topology diagrams.
- Response time measurements of regular events.
- Statistical characterization of the critical segments.

These three components require some effort in developing; however, the payoff comes when a problem occurs in the network. A small amount of time spent each week by a number of personnel who are assigned portions of the network can accomplish this task in a relatively short time.

Security Policies

All security policies set forth in a network plan should be detailed and followed closely. The security policies depend on the network size, the organization's security standards, and the value and sensitivity of the data. The security plan must include physical, network, and computer security. The five most significant issues involving security of a computer network, that should be addressed, include the following:

- *Identification/authentication*—users are accurately identified.
- *Access control/authorization*—only legitimate users can access a resource.
- *Privacy*—eavesdropping is not an issue, and transmissions are private.
- *Data integrity*—activities on a database are controlled and protected.
- *Nonrepudiation*—users cannot deny any legitimate transactions.

Network security can be enhanced by a number of username and password requirements and resource access requirements. Standards for username and passwords include the following suggestions:

- Establish minimum and maximum password lengths for user accounts.
- Provide the users with the details in reference to character restrictions.
- Determine the frequency for changing passwords.
- Decide if and when passwords can be reused.
- Decide if there will be exceptions to the policy.

Resource access is generally granted only to those who specifically require it. It is always easier to grant new access to users than to take it away. For dial-in users, special security arrangements are probably necessary. Many organizations require a security card, which provides a code that must be entered for dial-up access. It is essential that the number of users who perform network administration tasks be limited to the absolute minimum. The more users with access to administrative functions, the more likely security problems will occur.

Another user issue that can cause a security breach is leaving the work area without logging out of the system: this not only allows anyone to utilize that person's access rights, but could also put that employee's job in jeopardy. The system can assist operators by logging off any user who has not entered a transaction within a certain time period, such as five minutes. Users who leave their workstations for more than five minutes would have to go through the triple-A process again. This can become a performance issue if transaction-processing time is sporadic and the workstation is frequently logged off. A transaction log can be utilized to identify the optimum automatic logoff value.

Access to many enterprise systems is via dial-up using modems. Because this technique is available to everyone in the world with a dial-up modem, special attention must be devoted to limiting the access to legitimate users. A security policy that is both usable and enforceable is a requirement in all enterprise computer networking systems. This policy should include some, if not all, of the following elements:

- Provide protection for analog telephone numbers. Don't advertise them to the world. Use numbers that are different from regular enterprise telephone numbers.
- Maintain an inventory of all dial-up telephone lines. If the line is not being utilized, make sure that it is not connected to a modem.
- Don't have modems scattered around the premises. Home all modems into a central rack where they can be controlled. Use a modem pool to consolidate them into a controlled environment.
- Dial-up lines and modems must be located in a secure closet. These lines and modems must be tagged with circuit IDs.
- Monitor all dial-up activity. Look for failed login attempts. Caller ID may be useful for identifying calling telephone numbers.
- Don't display any banner information that is presented upon connect. This is a place where a warning message can be displayed to callers.
- Require a dial-back authentication procedure if feasible. This may be impractical with roving users.
- Provide help desk and PBX employees with specific instructions about social engineering tactics. Remote access credentials cannot be reset without the approval of a supervisor.
- Connectivity for all analog facility activity, including fax and voicemail, must be controlled by a central authority. This includes the standard plain old telephone service (POTS) line.
- Provide for an audit activity that monitors all of the preceding elements.

Hardware and Software Standards

To make hardware and software easier to manage, all network components should follow established standards. Several different levels of configurations can be established, depending on the requirements of the desktop users. These standards should cover both hardware and software configurations.

Standards should also be established for networking devices (including manufacturers) and operating systems (including versions). This also includes standards for server configurations and server types.

Keep in mind the pace of industry change and obsolescence when establishing hardware and software standards. Regular evaluations of network standards are required to ensure that the network remains current.

Upgrade Guidelines

Upgrades for hardware and software and new networking products are a fact of life. It is necessary to establish guidelines for handling these upgrades. They can be handled more easily if the user community has advance notice of such an upgrade, and they should not be performed during normal working hours.

It is a good idea to test upgrades through stand-alone platforms or through a group of technically astute network users. Always have a plan for backing out of an upgrade if it fails to perform as expected. Through careful planning and testing, the upgrade process can be relatively painless.

Security Threats

Security is concerned with protecting data and data systems and includes security techniques for both physical facilities and software. It is also concerned with ensuring the integrity of the network operating system (NOS). The NOS contains the software that runs on a server and controls access to files and other resources from multiple users. Physical security is concerned primarily with providing secure access, while software security includes authentication, authorization, access controls, and user logon. This section addresses security controls for operating and networking systems.

Threats are the reason it is necessary to be concerned about security. These include the following destructive activities:

- Internal users may try to access unauthorized data systems.
- Internet users may try to attack systems available to the network.
- Unauthorized users may try to access personal user accounts.
- Attackers may gain access to an account and lock out or restrict the legitimate users.
- Attackers may modify data values or destroy data.
- Proprietary information may be copied for resale to competitors.

A number of these security attacks can be attributed to hackers. Historically, a *hacker* was defined as a person who "hacks" away at a computer until access is gained or until the attack was successful. Students initially performed these activities, primarily for fun and sport. Today, the term has a more positive meaning and has been replaced with the term *cracker*, which is reserved for the individual who willfully breaks into computer systems with the purpose of wreaking havoc.

The most common security breach is access to unauthorized user accounts. This activity occurs when the attacker impersonates or masquerades as the legitimate user by obtaining a userid and password. These can often be obtained from posted notes, shoulder surfing, or a network monitor. Because some users may use some personal object or a relative's name as a password, the possibility exists for a password cracker to guess usernames and passwords. Another technique that is successful is the dictionary attack, where the cracker has access to a very large dictionary of words commonly used for passwords. This threat can be countered by locking a user account after a number of failed logon attempts, usually three.

The most serious attack, however, is when someone gains access to an administrator or superuser account. A *superuser* is a system administrator with high-level access privileges. With this access, attackers may lock out the legitimate account owner and perform destructive activities on the system or databases.

Another technique that can have significant repercussions is eavesdropping. Network traffic can be monitored with sniffers or wiretaps. A *sniffer* is a LAN protocol analyzer that supports a variety of hardware to include Ethernet and token ring topologies. The attacker may monitor the network for long periods of time and record valuable or sensitive information that can be used for future attacks. Information captured can be re-sent in a replay attack, which results when a service already authorized and completed is forged by another duplicate request in an attempt to repeat authorized commands. It is possible for an attacker to replay an authentication routine to gain illegal access to a system or network. Sequencing and time-stamping packets can avoid these situations. An eavesdropper might capture packets, modify them, and reinsert them into the data stream, which can be unknown to the legitimate sender and receiver.

The last threat discussed in this section concerns the denial of service attack, which involves an attempt to deny corporate computing resources to legitimate users. The attacker can cause a server or processor to slow or stop operations using techniques that overwhelm it with some useless task. It is also possible to corrupt the operating system of the processor. This type of attack is becoming commonplace across the Internet.

Securing Data Systems

Network security features such as access controls can be used to protect resources from unauthorized access. Many directories and network resources contain access control lists that contain entries that specifically identify access parameters. These lists identify which users and groups have object access and the respective permissions for that access. An *object* is an entity or component, identifiable by the user, which may be distinguished by its properties, operations, or relationships. These objects can have specific access levels, which include read, write, and execute functions. These functions are discussed later in more detail.

Most network operating systems have an auditing system designed to record network activities. These systems can be available for real-time or almost-real-time network traffic monitoring. The auditing records can be reviewed on a regular basis to determine if the system is being compromised. This auditing system can record activities such as logons, file access, network traffic, and account access. It is essential that auditing records be protected to prohibit an attacker from modifying them, which could effectively cover up an illegal activity.

AUTHENTICATION TECHNIQUES

Authentication methods identify users. Once users are identified and authenticated, it becomes possible to access resources based on an authorization. An authentication system may be the most important part of an NOS; it requires that a user supply some identification, such as a username and password. Simple password systems may be sufficient for small systems; however, if a higher level is required, then more advanced security may be necessary. These systems may provide dial-back capabilities or use biometric or token authentication devices. Each of these systems is discussed in detail.

Dial-Back Systems

An increasingly mobile workforce often requires remote access to the computer resource. Remote network access can assist employees in gaining access to databases, facilitate a telecommuting system, or help traveling executives maintain contact with corporate headquarters. This type of dial-up access should be granted cautiously and judiciously—and only to those that require it—because network resources are easily comprised by this access method. This type of doorway into the network invites other nonemployees to try the locks on the door. There are many technical solutions that can be implemented to provide the required level of security and ensure that only authorized individuals gain access to the corporate network using such a door.

A dial-back system is a solution that can provide some level of protection for these remote dial-in users. Using a dial-back modem, the remote user calls the computer resource, and the dial-back modem calls the user back at a predefined telephone number to make the connection. The normal identification and authentication process occurs over this connection.

Biometrics

As previously stated, biometrics is the process of using hard-to-forge physical characteristics of individuals, such as fingerprints, voiceprints, and retinal patterns to authenticate users. This is called a biometric-based authentication or third-factor authentication, which is "something you are." Minute measurements such as the timing of a pattern of keystrokes or a written signature can be used to differentiate users.

Because a scanner or sensor is used to capture biometric data, there is a possibility of obtaining incomplete or incorrect data for authentication. The performance of biometric methods is based on the percentage of false rejection and false acceptance. A false acceptance occurs when the authentication process accepts an invalid user. A false rejection occurs when the process rejects a valid user. Biometric authentication over a network can still be subject to capture, and replay of additional encryption is not used for the biometric data.

Token Authentication

Token-based authentication is a security technique that authenticates users who are attempting to log in to some secure computer or network resource. This method helps eliminate insecure logons (logons that send users' passwords across the network where they can be observed in the clear). Someone capturing the password could use it to repeatedly masquerade as the legitimate user and access a secure system resource. This situation can be countered by not sending passwords in any form across an insecure channel. An alternative process is to use a token, which resembles a credit card.

Token devices are microprocessor-controlled smart cards, which are used to implement two-factor authentication. The user supplies the logon password and the one-time value generated by the smart card. The smart card generates one-time passwords that are good for only one logon attempt. Two-factor authentication identifies a user and then authenticates the user. Organizations often assign tokens to remote and mobile users who need to access internal network resources from outside locations.

Security Dynamics offers a token called **SecurID** that uses a time-based technique for displaying a number that changes every minute. This card (token) is synchronized with a security server at the corporate location. When users log in, they are prompted for a value from the SecurID card. Because the value changes every minute, someone who manages to capture it online cannot reuse it.

Software-based token devices that run on portable computers are also available that provide much the same functionality as hardware tokens. It has been suggested that software tokens are less secure than hardware ones and can be more easily compromised.

The use of an authentication device, which is protected by a password, is superior to a single password because the loss of one of the authentication factors will not allow system access. The likelihood of losing both factors is remote.

DATA MANAGEMENT

Data management is concerned with the distribution of data to users and the protection of that data from theft, unauthorized access, or destruction. Elements covered under the data management umbrella are data backup, archiving, data migration and warehousing, database management systems, and security. The major components of resource security, which are integrity and safety, apply to all of these elements. Database management is described in Chapter 11.

Data Backup and Archiving

A comprehensive backup program can prevent significant data losses. A backup plan is an important part of the network plan and should be revised as the needs of the network grow. There are six major action parts of this plan:

- Determine what data should be backed up and how often.
- Develop a schedule for backing up the data.
- Develop a plan for storing data in a secure location.
- Identify the personnel responsible for performing backups.
- Maintain a backup log listing what data are backed up.
- Test the backup system regularly.

Types of backups include the full backup, copies of files, incremental backups, daily copies, and differential (changed) backups. Each of these methods has advantages and disadvantages, so the administrator may elect to use different methods for different data files.

Mirrored servers provide real-time backup for the current state of all files. All files are transported to the backup server, which can be used to restore the mirrored servers. Files on the backup server are moved to the archival drive on a scheduled basis. These files are then stored on some media for off-site storage. An important part of this system is an inventory of the off-site storage media.

Data Migration and Warehousing

Data migration is an archiving process that moves stagnant files to a secondary storage system, such as optical disk, zip disks, or streaming tapes. The files may be imaged documents or historical information that will be required at some future date. Migration works in conjunction strategies, and regular backups are still required. These files remain available offline, but they are accessible to users over the computer network.

Data Resource Security

The data resource is a very important asset to most organizations. In many cases, data cannot be replaced once lost. This is a primary reason for backing up the data asset on a regularly scheduled time frame. If the proper backups are not available and a disaster occurs, the organization could lose a considerable amount of money and/or prestige. In addition to protecting current data, many organizations must store the data on a permanent basis for legal reasons. There are a number of measures that can be taken to lessen the chance of data loss. These losses can be caused by intruders, malicious employees, or contractors, or they can be caused by nature or accidents.

PROTECTION AGAINST INTRUDERS

Intruders can be described as unauthorized visitors who are not members of the normal user community. These people can cause three problems, namely:

1. Theft.
2. Destruction of equipment, software, or data.
3. Viewing of sensitive data and information.

Intruders can use various methods to gain access to a computer or network facility. Access can be physical or electronic, and there are methods to counter both. Intruders can be prevented from accessing a LAN by ensuring that users protect passwords, log off when not at the workstation, and take security seriously. There are operating system parameters that can be set to limit time-of-day access and device-specific logons. Users must be trained to take security seriously. They should be aware of the consequences of leaving a workstation logged on. Most workstations allow for a screensaver login. User accounts can be set to require a scheduled changing of passwords.

Theft Protection

Theft can be the result of espionage by competitors, other governments, internal personnel, partners, and contractors. The bottom line is the asset must be protected from theft from any source, because the alternative could be devastating to the organization's operations. This protection must include the data and the hardware that is used to store that data. Not only is the equipment valuable, but it can take a long time to acquire new hardware and reload the data. Reloading databases and verifying the integrity of the data can be very time-consuming. There are a number of obvious solutions to the theft problem; however, the solution should not cost more than the resource is worth, and the value may not be in real dollars.

It is necessary for the administrator to keep track of users. The administrator must know when users leave the company's employ or when they change roles. The accounts need to be modified to reflect the current access levels. Audit trails must be maintained that can identify system disruptions. Theft of storage devices can be detected if they are removed from the network. There are a number of software surveillance tools that can accomplish this task. It may not be popular, but surveillance cameras are an option at entrance points.

Natural Disaster Protection

There are some natural disasters where, due to the magnitude of the disaster, a good plan is worthless. The best plan is to allocate sufficient protection based on normal circumstances. It is possible to determine where flood and earthquake zones exist. Hurricanes and tornadoes cannot be predicted, but there are locations that are prone to both of these natural occurrences. The physical construction of the facility should be a consideration. Computer rooms and network demarcations can be located on second floors. Fire detection and suppression devices can be installed. Electrical failures should be considered, and backup systems can be installed. The bottom line is to spend no more than the asset is worth or the cost to replace it. Last but not least, off-site backup of data is a must.

Database and DBMS Protection

Access to a database or the database management system can be controlled by the use of access rights. Logon restrictions and directory or file access rights are important techniques administrators and supervisors use to protect data against malicious or accidental loss or corruption. Users should never be given more access rights than needed to handle the task at hand. Many users only need the right to access and read in a program directory. Excessive or blanket rights permissions can lead to problems, such as overwrites, corruption, and virus attacks on the database. This might get old; an off-site backup program is required for database restoration, in the event of some security breach.

DOCUMENTATION

A well-documented network includes everything necessary to review history, understand the current status, plan for growth, and provide comparisons when problems occur. The following list outlines a set of documents that should be included in a network plan.

- Address list.
- Cable map.
- Contact list.
- Equipment list.
- Network history.
- Network map.
- Server configuration.
- Software configuration.
- Software licenses.
- User administration.

It is essential to take the time during installation to ensure that all hardware and software components of the network are correctly installed and accurately recorded in the master network record. This documentation also applies to the hardware and software configurations for each of the network components. Being able to quickly find faulty network components and have documentation on the configuration will save a considerable amount of personnel effort and time.

Documentation should be kept in both hard-copy and electronic form so that it is readily available to anyone who needs it. Complete, accurate, and up-to-date documentation aids in troubleshooting the network, planning for growth, and training new employees.

THREAT ASSESSMENT

A challenge for the administrator is to determine the proper level of security that is required to protect the organization's assets. This concept, called **threat assessment**, identifies the organization's assets and resources and the accessing entities. Organizations can best assess computer and network threats by using a structured approach. These threats can be directed at hardware, software, data and information, systems, and/or security measures. After the administrator has assessed the various vulnerabilities, the organization will be in a good position to protect its assets and resources. There are five requirements in this threat assessment process: identifying critical assets, identifying possible sources of the threat, developing the risk analysis, prototyping the solution, and documenting the results of the threat assessment.

Identifying Critical Assets

The first step in threat assessment is to decide which assets are critical. A number of organizations maintain a significant amount of sensitive and critical information that is vital to their survival. This information could include customer order information, sales figures, supplier contracts, customer lists, and many other proprietary assets. If this database was compromised, the business or organization `might fail, or there could be other serious ramifications that could even affect national security. This means that considerable attention should be devoted to seriously determining which elements are crucial and how these security lapses would damage the organization.

Identifying Threat Sources

After determining the critical elements of the organization, the next step is to identify any possible threat sources. Threats can originate from inside and outside the organization, from competitors, from terrorists, and from the hacker community. The object of this analysis is to determine who would benefit from the use of your resources and assets. It should be noted that some threat sources are not after financial gain. A good starting point is to list all possible assets and create a matching list of every entity that might receive some benefit from breaking into the asset. Determining who might benefit from the asset theft helps identify potential threat candidates and locations of attack.

Historically, break-ins occur from inside the computer network. Employees and contractors have ready access, both physically and through the network access, to the organization's resources. Most organizations do not take sufficient precautions to protect their assets from internal personnel and contractors. A list of potential insider actions that should be considered as a threat includes the following:

- Hamper corporate operations.
- Sell to a competitor.
- Hurt customer relations.
- Cause internal strife.

- Cause asset loss.
- Create physical damage.
- Cause internal outage of resources.
- Compromise customer information.
- Reduce the organization's ability to function.

The activities listed are not that difficult to initiate, given access to the appropriate resources. (*Note that this list would not only apply to internal users, but to anyone who could access the computer and networking asset.*) If the administrator can proactively identify the sources of potential threats, actions can be taken to limit the possibilities of a threat occurring.

Developing the Risk Analysis

Risk analysis is the process of understanding how the loss of an asset will affect an organization. This process can be quite formidable if the resources are significant, but performing some simple calculations will produce a ballpark figure. A look at such elements as replacing, repairing, upgrading, and managing a threat can assist in this endeavor. It is often cheaper to proactively fix a potential problem than to respond to a threat. After-the-fact problems can include negative publicity, a reduction in sales, loss of customers, and loss of credibility (particularly if this is an e-commerce operation). This means that even a minor security breach can cause major repercussions that would be expensive to correct. Funds might be well spent to properly plan for all identified threats.

Prototyping the Solution

Prototyping involves developing a scenario concerning a security violation and determining the effect on the organization. This is similar to role-playing, where someone tries to breach security and another group tries to detect and defeat it before any harm is done. Role-playing in security terms is essential to understanding the threat environment and making sound decisions on what can and cannot be protected. In a computer and network attack, efforts must be made to identify all the potential points of attack and then attempt to identify countermeasures. These measures include methods to identify, correct, and handle the repercussions of the various attacks. Actions for a proper defense include the following elements:

- Setting up information defenses.
- Monitoring for information attack.
- Delaying the attack until assessment and reinforcements are available.
- Counterattacking.
- Capturing and destroying the intruder.
- Cleaning up problems discovered.

By deploying some role-playing or simulation in the environment, threats can be identified and proper defenses planned.

Documenting the Results

Documentation is the final phase of threat assessment. Without documentation, many of the efforts previously discussed will be in vain. Not only should these threat methods and procedures be documented, but updates must follow that represent the current situation. Documentation can take a considerable number of hours to complete, but this time and effort is an essential part of any plan for threat management.

GAP ANALYSIS

A logical follow-up to threat assessment is called *gap analysis*. All of the known threats and problems have been identified, and suggested solutions and countermeasures have been identified—or have they? Ensuring confidentiality, integrity, and availability of information is a major goal of a computer system. Conducting regular reviews of day-to-day practices and comparing them with threat assessment documentation can reveal gaps in security precautions.

This **gap analysis** is an effective methodology for testing the authenticity, integrity, and confidentiality of an organization's hardware and software systems and can provide assurance that security implementations are consistent with the real requirements. Not all gap analyses are the same. Factors that influence the analysis include the size of the organization, the industry, the cost involved, efforts involved, and the depth of the analysis. A number of common steps are employed when conducting a gap analysis:

- Identify the applicable elements of the organizational standards.
- Collect methods and procedures and policy documents.
- Assess the implementation of the policies and procedures.
- Conduct a physical inventory of all computer and network hardware and software components.
- Interview users to determine compliance levels of policies.
- Compare current security environment to policies.
- Prioritize the identified gaps in policies versus actual.
- Implement the remedies to conform to policies.

Analysts may frequently overlook the human elements of security, but most security gaps are the result of human causes.

AUDITING

Auditing involves the process of collecting and monitoring all aspects of the computer network to identify potential holes and flaws in the systems. It is also used to keep track of system utilization and usage. This information becomes part of contingency planning and disaster recovery efforts.

A network auditing system also logs details of user transactions on the network so that malicious or unintended activities can be tracked. When auditing is implemented, vast amounts of data may be recorded and archived for future reference. Some audit systems provide event alarms to warn administrators when certain conditions or levels are met.

Auditing records can be viewed using special filters to produce reports that show specific activities. Filters can be applied to show specific date and time ranges, file and directory activities, and user events. Administrators should look for a large number of failed logon attempts and logins that take place at odd hours, which could indicate that someone is attempting an unauthorized access to the system.

An auditor can use software to set up auditing features, view audit logs, and look at designated directories. A record can be kept for every activity designated for tracking. Events that can be tracked include the following:

- Logon and logoff.
- Connection establishment and termination.
- Space restrictions.
- Granting of trustee rights.
- Dismounting volumes.
- File creation and modification.
- Directory creation and deletion.
- Server commands and queue activities.
- Changes in the security environment.

An additional step taken by operations management is to monitor the activities of the network or systems administrator. The auditing system can be used to verify the integrity of this person, who basically has unlimited rights to the system.

SECURITY POLICY

Official corporate security policies and guidelines have been in place for many years. These guidelines usually covered the rules associated with the security of confidential information, intellectual property, and corporate secrets. There were also rules and procedures for physical security, such as access to computer assets. With the advent of networking and the accessibility of the Internet, security has moved to a position of prominence. The ramifications of not having a corporate security policy are significant, due to the costs that can be incurred. Corporations have responded to this need by establishing a code of conduct that employees are required to sign.

The corporate code of conduct should clearly set forth the standards of conduct that are expected from all employees. Rules must be established that identify the corporate elements that must be protected. Finally, it is necessary to state the repercussions from failure to adhere to these standards. A corporate code of conduct should accomplish the following:

- *Provide the scope of coverage*—the scope of the security policy should state the audience affected and the components of the organization covered under the rules. It should also provide some detail as to the specific objects covered under the policy.
- *Identify the professional responsibility*—employees have a responsibility to support the goals and mission of the corporation. Employees are expected to perform in an acceptable professional manner.

- *Set forth a confidentiality policy*—confidentiality of privileged information and communications is set forth. Levels of security must be set forth as they apply to each specific entity. Employees are expected to comply with and advise others of the policies.
- *Address conflict of interests*—corporate interests and personal interests must be kept separate. This means that private interests, obligations, and transactions must not be in conflict with the corporate mission. Employees must perform duties and responsibilities in a fair and just manner in the best interests of the corporation.
- *Present the legal ramifications*—this is a statement of penalties resulting from failure to comply with the corporate security policy. Employees are expected to refrain from unlawful and dishonest conduct.

Employees in the organization and other authorized users are the source of most breaches of network security. Measures that minimize these breaches can include passwords and other means to identify authorized users. Networks can be monitored for abnormal patterns, and employees can be educated in security practices.

One major challenge to the organization is to balance the cost of security against the risks being addressed. The cost of providing solutions and controls should be in proportion to the value of the assets being protected. It makes no sense to spend more to protect an asset than the asset is worth. An analysis of the situation must prove the feasibility and viability of the proposed security controls. This analysis needs to look at the criticality of the systems to the business. What is the exposure of the systems to fraud and illegal disclosure of information? The risk to assets from both internal and external sources must be explored. One of the first steps toward securing the organization's assets is to develop a site security policy.

Site Security Policy

A **security policy** is a formal statement of rules by which users who have access to an organization's technology and database assets must abide. This policy must be formulated by key organizational individuals, who have authority to enforce the policies developed and who understand the ramifications of these policies. A site security policy is developed for the following reasons:

- It enables security implementation and enforcement.
- A basis is created for legal action.
- A process is developed for conducting security audits.
- Formalized step-by-step procedures are developed.

There are a number of key characteristics of an acceptable security policy. Primarily, it must be capable of being implemented both organizationally and technically. It must be flexible to allow for changing conditions. The policy must clearly define the areas of responsibility for the users, both inside and outside the organization, and for corporate and site management. Lastly, it must be enforceable with a security management system or set of security tools. It is important to note that a security policy should not determine how a business operates. A policy should be chosen to fit the current organization operation and structure. This policy should meld with the hardware, software, and network environment.

CONTINGENCY PLANNING/DISASTER RECOVERY

Many organizations develop a business continuity plan or disaster recovery plan in the event of some natural or man-made catastrophe. Whether a natural disaster such as a storm or flood or a man-made virus occurs, no organization is immune to the costs and disruptions that result.

Security awareness programs are efforts necessary to educate the employee and user community as to the importance of physical security. Many users are not aware of the consequences of simple lapses in security, which could cost the organization millions of dollars in computer and network damages.

Continuity Plan

A **business continuity plan (BCP)** is a strategic instrument aimed at mitigating the threats to critical functions and ensuring continuous operation. This plan is concerned primarily with the processes, resources, equipment, and devices needed to continue operating critical activities of a business when a disaster has occurred.

In a business environment that is increasingly dominated by electronic commerce, reliable network and computer connectivity are a must. The cost for system downtime for these companies is staggering. Cost categories include the following [Greene, 2006]:

- Lost customers.
- Lost revenue.
- Lost market share.
- Increased expense.
- Tarnished reputation.

The scope of the plan depends on a number of characteristics, including company size, product, number of employees, and site locations. Objectives that must be considered are as follows:

- Guarantee safety of all employees, customers, and partners.
- Coordinate the activities of recovery personnel.
- Recover critical functions quickly.
- Limit any disaster-related damages.
- Mitigate financial losses and legal liabilities.
- Minimize cost of recovery operations.

Note that a function is defined as critical if it affects a high-profile client, generates significant revenue, or satisfies a legal or regulatory requirement. Note that the highest priority is employee safety.

Many organizations believe they can solve security issues by buying a solution. This might be a false assumption, because security should be embedded in the core operations of the organization and not applied to the surface. System design should incorporate security as the system is being developed—and not included as an afterthought.

The proper location for implementing asset security is the organization itself, starting with the employees who need access to computer and networking resources in order to perform their functions. The most powerful security measure is to obtain and maintain the loyalty of these employees. Security measures should be designed and implemented so they protect the organization's assets without unduly interfering with legitimate uses of the network.

Organizations must address contingency and recovery plans in a comprehensive manner. This comprehensive plan must address the risks an organization faces and the business impacts of those risks. Elements that must be addressed include the following:

- Emergency response and life and safety protection.
- Situation and damage assessment.
- Asset salvage and recovery.
- Alternate facilities for emergency operation and business recovery.

Disaster Planning

A process missing from many organizations is a disaster plan. The overall process of systems management, which includes database backup and the steps necessary to protect the organizations' resources, is essential. System backups must be conducted on a scheduled basis, and there must be off-site database storage. Use of early detection and loss mitigation systems can help in this area. A program must be in place to detect problems early, which can help avoid a major crisis.

Disaster recovery is the activity that occurs if the organization has developed a disaster plan. This plan should cover local area network (LAN), metropolitan area network (MAN), wide area network (WAN), and private branch exchange/automatic call distributor (PBX/ACD) resources. It should also include computer systems, servers, and local network service. The plan should identify the most common hazards and assess their potential impact if there is a catastrophic event. The security section of the plan should describe how to limit access to critical facilities. Many organizations have developed formal disaster recovery plans to guide them through service restoration following a natural disaster or civil disturbance. The key to disaster planning is to prevent damage from occurring in the first place. A service loss can occur as a result of fire, water, snow, earthquake, landslide, lightning, or human activities. There are a number of precautions that can be taken to prevent or minimize damage from these causes when damage does occur. Contingency planning can be utilized to address these issues.

Contingency Planning

A **contingency** is defined as an event that might occur, but is not likely or intended; however, there is a possibility that it may occur. The key to a successful recovery from a disaster is adequate preparation. Seldom does a crisis destroy irreplaceable hardware and software resources. Most of these computer and networking components are available from many suppliers and are readily available at a cost. Databases, specialized software, and application software, however, are another story. Locally developed software is more vulnerable because it cannot be quickly substituted from another source. The requirement is to continue work after and during a crisis.

Preemptive Precautions

Taking preemptive precautions may be costly in the short term, but they save time and resources when problems arise, prevent equipment problems, and ensure data security. A preemptive approach can prevent additional expense and frustration when trying to identify the causes of failures.

DISASTER RECOVERY

Disaster recovery is an extension of planning for normal computer, database, and network systems outages. A disaster may possibly occur where immediate repair is not possible and the computer facility and equipment are no longer usable. Having a computer in an alternate site and having the ability to switch the telecommunications lines to this alternate are viable alternatives in many situations. It may also be possible to quickly obtain a new system from a computer vendor, because many vendors have the capability to provide a new system and all of its components on a short notice. This solution requires a place to install this system that is equipped with suitable power and air conditioning. Of equal importance in the ability to switch the telecommunications network to the new computer location promptly. Telephone companies are developing techniques and facilities to allow network switching to alternate locations; it is essential to determine if the broadband network in the alternative location supports the protocols utilized on the organization's networking system.

It is beneficial to work out a mutual aid pact with another company, where both organizations agree to provide backup in the event of a disaster. This assistance could be in the form of after-hours computer time or space to house a temporary operations center. A common problem with backup operations is the requirement of telecommunications facilities, which can be difficult to install on short notice. A backup location that might be in close proximity could be problematic in that both could suffer similar disasters simultaneously. An earthquake, hurricane, or tornado could destroy both locations and effectively neutralize any recovery plans.

There are several companies whose sole purpose is to provide disaster recovery plans and facilities. These companies have a significant investment in computer hardware, which can be used in disaster situations. These services are not cheap—but often result in a "pay me now or pay me later" position. Subscribing to such a service is like buying insurance. Whatever plan is developed must provide for a specific disaster type, because the response to a fire is different than the response to a flood. A short list of organizations that supply alternative site support is as follows:

- Agility Recovery Solutions.
- DPS Management Consultants.
- Hewlett-Packard Business Continuity & Availability Services.
- IBM Business Resilience and Continuity Services.
- Sunguard Availability Services.

Some organizations develop a disaster recovery plan and never validate it for effectiveness and completeness. Rarely will all of the problems and issues of a real disaster be covered when a recovery plan is created. The recovery plan must be tested to identify weaknesses, and a disaster recovery firm can provide this capability. Tests usually involve transferring software systems between computer systems and ensuring that communications can be established in the event of a disaster.

As an organization becomes increasingly reliant on telecommunications and computer networks, it must constantly reassess how much downtime can be afforded. One way to accomplish this is to get users involved in assessing the impact of an extended outage caused by a disaster. This can result in building a case for additional funds for supporting and maintaining disaster recovery procedures.

Disaster Recovery Plan

A **disaster recovery plan (DRP)**—sometimes referred to as a business continuity plan (BCP) or business process contingency plan (BPCP)—describes how an organization is to deal with potential disasters. Just as a disaster is an event that makes the continuation of normal functions impossible, a disaster recovery plan consists of the precautions taken so that the effects of a disaster are minimized and the organization is able to either maintain or quickly resume mission-critical functions. Typically, disaster recovery planning involves an analysis of business processes and continuity needs; it may also include a significant focus on disaster prevention.

Disaster recovery is becoming an increasingly important aspect of enterprise computing. As devices, systems, and networks become ever more complex, there are simply more things that can go wrong. As a consequence, recovery plans have also become more complex. For example, 15 or 20 years ago, if there was a threat to systems from a fire, a disaster recovery plan might consist of powering down the mainframe and other computers before the sprinkler system came on, disassembling components, and subsequently drying circuit boards in the parking lot with a hair dryer. Current enterprise systems tend to be too large and complicated for such simple and hands-on approaches, however, and interruption of service or loss of data can have serious financial impact, whether directly or through loss of customer confidence.

Appropriate plans vary from one enterprise to another, depending on variables such as the type of business, the processes involved, and the level of security needed. Disaster recovery planning may be developed within an organization or purchased as a software application or a service. It is not unusual for an enterprise to spend 25 percent of its information technology budget on disaster recovery (Whitman, 2007).

Nevertheless, the consensus within the DR industry is that most enterprises are still ill-prepared for a disaster. Despite the number of very public disasters since 9/11, many companies do not have a disaster recovery plan. Of those that do, nearly half have never tested their plan, which is tantamount to not having one at all.

Organizations must implement precautionary measures with an objective of preventing a disaster situation in the first place. These may include some of the following:

- Local mirroring of systems and/or data and use of disk protection technology such as redundant array of inexpensive disk (RAID).
- Surge protectors to minimize the effect of power surges on delicate electronic equipment.

- Uninterruptible power supply (UPS) and/or a backup generator to keep systems going in the event of a power failure.
- Fire prevention, including more alarms and accessible fire extinguishers.
- Anti-virus software and other security measures.

Service Level Agreement

Most organizations depend on services or products provided by others. This can be an Achilles' heel as far as continuity is concerned. However, the situation can be mitigated via the use of a binding service level agreement that stipulates expectations and requirements clearly for both parties.

A **service level agreement (SLA)** is a formal agreement between a service provider and customers to provide a certain level of service. Penalty clauses might apply if the SLA is not met. As with the disaster recovery plan, the SLA should be carefully crafted to suit a particular situation.

Service level agreements can be established for availability (24/7 and 98 percent during scheduled hours), for performance (response time for 95 percent queries in one minute or less), and for timeliness.

Techtarget has identified several metrics that SLAs may specify:

- The percentage of the time services will be available.
- The number of users that can be served simultaneously.
- Specific performance benchmarks to which actual performance will be periodically compared.
- The schedule for notification in advance of network changes that may affect users.
- Help-desk response time for various classes of problems.
- Dial-in access availability.
- Usage statistics that will be provided.

🔒 CHAPTER SUMMARY

Primary goals of an organization include availability and confidentiality of the computer and network assets and resources. Business continuity planning and disaster recovery planning address the preservation of the organization in the face of major disruptions to normal operations.

Organizations must establish a baseline for network performance, integrity, and security. A baseline defines a point of reference against which to measure network performance and behavior when problems occur.

Authentication and access control mechanisms are employed to ensure that only authorized users are allowed into the network. Authentication mechanisms include biometric techniques, certificates, passwords, PINs, tokens, and other technical solutions. Access control mechanisms include access control lists, intrusion detection, physical access control, and various network traffic filters.

Physical security planning includes addressing a number of emergency situations, such as floods, storms, earthquakes, power failures, and fires. There are a number of proactive measures that can be taken to reduce the damage caused by both natural and man-made disasters.

Intrusion detection is the art of detection and responding to computer and network misuse. Security elements include deterrence, detection, and response. Intrusion detection systems allow for damage assessment, attack anticipation, and prosecution support. Security cards, biometric systems, alarms, and sensors can affect facility access control.

Various documents attempt to address network security concepts and terminology. ISO17799 provides information concerning compliance and implementing audit data and procedures, maintaining security awareness, and conducting post-mortem analysis. The Government Information Security Reform Act, also called the Security Act, focuses on program management, implementation, and evaluation aspects of the security of unclassified and national security systems.

 KEY TERMS

access control mechanisms	data migration	prototyping
auditing	demarcation	risk analysis
authentication mechanisms	disaster recovery	SecurID
availability	disaster recovery plan (DRP)	security policy
baseline	false acceptance rate (FAR)	service level agreement (SLA)
business continuity plan (BCP)	false rejection rate (FRR)	threat assessment
confidentiality	gap analysis	triple-A
contingency	integrity	

SECURITY REVIEW QUESTIONS

1. _____ means the network resources are accessible to authorized users; however, they may also be available to illegitimate users.
2. Describe the goals of availability.
3. _____ describes security and secrecy, meaning only authorized people can see protected data or resources.
4. _____ techniques include authentication, authorization, and accounting.
5. Identify the various authentication mechanisms that are available.
6. A(n) _____ is the physical point where a regulated service or network cabling is provided to the user.
7. A(n) _____ defines a point of reference against which to measure network performance and behavior when problems occur.
8. _____ is an archiving process that moves stagnant files to a secondary storage system, such as optical disk, zip disks, or streaming tapes.
9. _____ is the process of understanding how the loss of an asset will affect an organization.
10. _____ involves developing a scenario concerning a security violation and determining the effect on the organization.

RESEARCH ACTIVITIES

1. Provide an overview of the various biometric system features and operations.
2. Identify physical security devices that could be installed to protect a secure computer and network location.
3. Identify the relevant issues associated with the Government Information Security Reform Act.
4. Identify vendors who provide security contracting and services for data centers.
5. Collect a baseline document that has been created for some organization, and review it for any discrepancies or shortcomings.
6. Create a hypothetical computer disaster scenario, and develop a recovery plan.
7. Identify companies that provide for disaster recovery alternate sites. Describe their capabilities.
8. Develop a service level agreement for some organization.
9. Identify companies that provide data backup and archiving capabilities.
10. Identify an organization that has experienced a disaster, and prepare an overview of the situation and the response generated to recover.
11. Identify those organizations that provide vulnerability assessment services. Develop a cost matrix based on the various categories of review.

CHAPTER 10

Intrusion Detection and Prevention

🔒 CHAPTER CONTENTS

- Understand the use of intrusion detection and prevention technologies.
- Evaluate intrusion detection and prevention methods and solutions.
- Become familiar with the various IDS and IPS configurations and options.
- Look at the benefits realized from installing IDS and IPS.
- See why network detection and prevention systems are necessary.
- Identify the differences between host-based and network-based systems.

INTRODUCTION

Access to the Internet by everyone in the world and the increase of e-commerce activities has provided an increased opportunity for illegal and destructive attacks on IT resources. The interconnectivity of computers for large and small organizations includes customers, suppliers, partners, and contractors. Organizations must develop and possess a high degree of trust based on computer system and digital asset security controls.

Presentations in this chapter include information directed at three disciplines of computer security and address the fundamental needs of detection, prevention, and response for digital assets. Numerous organizations are active and provide a wealth of information concerning these types of security systems.

Historically, installed security systems have been devoted to disaster detection and response—and not disaster prevention. Obviously, it is better to prevent some intrusion or occurrence than planning to plan for a loss. If all threats are prevented, then detection and response activities are moot.

Both intrusion detection and intrusion technologies and systems are described. There are numerous issues that must be addressed before implementing any type of security system. Comparisons of the various alternatives are presented.

COMPUTING SECURITY ISSUES

With the explosion in Internet connectivity and the mainstream use of broadband and mobile technologies, there has been a huge increase in the number of computer systems and storage devices connected to the public network. With an ever-increasing reliance on computing infrastructure, critical IT assets, confidential data, and intellectual property are more susceptible to cyber attack than ever before. In response to the changing threat landscape, systems are being developed to provide advanced protection beyond that offered by firewalls and routers.

Despite all the progress that has been made in network security over the past 10 years, enterprise organizations continue to struggle with how best to protect information from attack or misuse. In particular, firewalls, and anti-virus and intrusion detection/prevention systems work well at the network perimeter, but they are wholly inadequate for defending internal or highly meshed networks. These technologies add expensive complexity to internal IT infrastructure, introduce significant performance bottlenecks, and miss most of the threats they are intended to stop.

In addition, most security technologies do not cooperate easily with network management and optimization applications. Security operations that block access to services or drop suspicious packets raise unexpected alarms in IT. Likewise, changes in IT infrastructure often carry significant security implications that do not become apparent until too late. Each event requires significant time to identify what happened, analyze the severity of the incident, and determine how best to respond—and time is what is least at hand during a crisis.

INTRUSION DETECTION

In the information technology arena, an **intrusion** is an unauthorized access to, and/or activity in an information system. **Intrusion detection (ID)** is the art of detection and responding to situations involving computer, database, and network misuse. The benefits of intrusion detection capabilities to an organization include the following security elements [Proctor, 2001]:

- *Deterrence*—prevent or discourage from acting by some fear or doubt.
- *Detection*—discover or discern the existence of some situation or event.
- *Response*—a reaction to a specific stimulus.
- *Damage assessment*—establish a value of some incident.
- *Attack anticipation*—prepare for some potential event.
- *Prosecution support*—evidence and forensic investigation.

Different intrusion detection techniques provide different types of benefits for a variety of environments; therefore, it is essential to select and implement the most viable one. The key to selecting the correct detection system is to define the environment-specific requirements that best satisfy the organization's security needs.

The intrusion detection industry supplies tools with capabilities and features that go far beyond detecting intruders from outside the organization. Intrusion detection systems may provide the following capabilities:

- Event log analysis for insider threat detection.
- Network traffic analysis for perimeter threat detection.
- File and database integrity checking.
- Security configuration management.

Many products provide only one of these capabilities; however, hybrid systems are available that are multifunctional. A hybrid system includes functionalities and elements from multiple security technologies and applications. A hybrid system may contain the following components:

- Alert notification.
- Command console.
- Database.
- Network tap.
- Network sensor.
- Response subsystem.

False Positives and False Negatives

There is a requirement to measure predefined thresholds between referenced and current templates for similarities. The result of these comparisons can result in a false positive or a false negative response. A **false positive** results when the system accepts the wrong user, causing a security concern. A **false negative** means a legitimate user could be rejected, resulting in embarrassment and potential availability issues.

The system threshold can be set at various levels to ameliorate these false positive and false negative issues. These settings can result in a lower *false acceptance rate* (*FAR*) and/or a higher *false rejection rate* (*FRR*). The task for system administrators is to create the right balance between these two errors. (*Note that these terms were further defined and discussed in Chapter 9.*)

INTRUSION DETECTION SYSTEM

An **intrusion detection system (IDS)** generally detects unwanted manipulations of computer systems, mainly through the Internet, but also functions in a corporate internetwork environment. The manipulations may take the form of attacks by hackers or crackers. An IDS is used to detect several types of malicious behaviors that can compromise the security and trust of a computer system. These include network attacks against vulnerable services, data-driven attacks on applications, host-based attacks such as privilege escalation, unauthorized logins and access to sensitive files, and malware (viruses, Trojans, and worms). These security systems are normally composed of several components:

- *Sensor*—sniffs packets off the network.
- *Console*—monitors events and alerts and control the sensors.
- *Engine*—records events logged by the sensors in a database and uses a system of rules to generate alerts from security events received.

FIGURE 10-1 depicts a possible IDS configuration that includes various network security devices. Taps are distributed to the various mission-critical segments of the network, usually one per segment. There are several ways to categorize an IDS, depending on the type and location of the sensors and the methodology used by the engine to generate alerts. In many simple IDS implementations, all three components are combined in a single device or appliance. The general steps that occur in an IDS implementation are as follows:

1. A packet is generated in the network.
2. A sensor reads the packet.
3. The detection engine identifies a predefined pattern or signature.
4. A security component or person is notified.
5. A response is generated to the system.
6. The alert is stored for later review and correlation.
7. Summary reports of alert activities are generated.
8. The original traffic may be archived.
9. Data forensics are employed for trends.

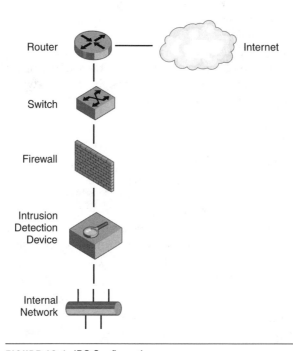

FIGURE 10-1 IDS Configuration

An IDS inspects all inbound and outbound network activity and identifies suspicious patterns that may indicate a network or system attack from someone attempting to break into or compromise a system. There are several ways to categorize an IDS:

- Misuse detection versus anomaly detection.
- Network-based versus host-based systems.
- Passive system versus reactive systems.

This section is devoted to providing a description and overview of each of these categorizations of IDS.

Misuse Detection Versus Anomaly Detection

An **anomaly-based intrusion detection system** is a system for detecting computer intrusions and misuse by monitoring system activity and classifying it as either *normal* or *anomalous*. The classification is based on heuristics or rules, rather than patterns or signatures, and will detect any type of misuse that is identified during normal system operation. This is different than signature-based systems that only detect attacks for which a signature has previously been created.

An **anomaly** is defined as a deviation, irregularity, or an unexpected result. A data anomaly may occur when a data field defined for one purpose is used for another. The anomaly detector monitors network segments to compare their state to the normal baseline and look for anomalies.

Misuse generally involves at least one of the following activities:

- Data are read or accessed by some unauthorized person or entity.
- Data are modified or deleted by some unauthorized person or entity.
- Self-inflicted denial of service occurs.

Security policies must identify data and files that are sensitive and should be protected from unauthorized access, modification, deletion, or disclosure. Operational components that are required for the business operation must also be identified. These components are identified during the development of the unit's baseline.

To determine legitimate attack traffic, the system must be taught to recognize normal system activity. This can be accomplished in several ways, most often with artificial intelligence–type techniques. Systems using neural networks have been used to great effect. Neural computing involves the ability to recognize patterns based on experiences. Another method is to define what normal usage of the system comprises, using a strict mathematical model, and flag any deviation from this as an attack. This is known as *strict anomaly detection*.

There are very few reliable and trusted commercial anomaly-based intrusion detection systems. One such system, Manhunt, purchased by Symantec in 2001, uses anomaly-based protocol inspection. Another system, StealthWatch by Lancope, is a network behavior analysis solution that combines behavior-based anomaly detection with network performance monitoring.

Network behavior analysis (NBA) is a method of enhancing the security of a proprietary network by monitoring traffic and noting unusual actions or departures from normal (behavior) operation. An NBA solution offers protection for a network in addition to that provided by traditional anti-threat applications such as firewalls, anti-virus software, and spyware detection programs.

An NBA program passively monitors the communications between hosts and clients in real time and flags unknown, new, or unusual patterns that could indicate the presence of threats. An NBA program can also monitor and record trends in bandwidth and protocol use. These functions can minimize the time and labor involved in locating and resolving problems. An effective NBA solution may proactively forestall serious security breaches and render complex and time-consuming disaster recovery procedures unnecessary.

An NBA solution is not effective on its own. It should be used in addition to conventional firewalls and solutions for the detection, blocking, and removal of malware.

Passive System Versus Reactive System

In a **passive system**, the intrusion detection system (IDS) sensor detects a potential security breach, logs the information, and signals an alert on the console and/or owner. In a **reactive system**, also known as an intrusion prevention system (IPS), the IDS responds to the suspicious activity by resetting the connection or by reprogramming the firewall to block network traffic from the suspected malicious source. This can happen automatically or at the command of an operator.

Although they both relate to network security, an IDS differs from a firewall in that a firewall looks outwardly for intrusions in order to stop them from happening. Firewalls limit access between networks to prevent intrusion and do not signal an attack from inside the network. An IDS evaluates a suspected intrusion once it has taken place and signals an alarm; it also watches for attacks that originate from within a system. This is traditionally achieved by examining network communications, identifying heuristics and patterns (often known as signatures) of common computer attacks, and taking action to alert operators. A system that terminates connections is called an intrusion prevention system and is another form of an application-layer firewall.

Honeypot

In computer terminology, a **honeypot** is a trap set to detect, deflect, or in some manner counteract attempts at unauthorized use of information systems. Generally it consists of a computer, data, or a network site that appears to be part of a network but that is actually isolated, (un)protected, and monitored and that seems to contain information or a resource that would be of value to attackers.

A honeypot is valuable as a surveillance and early-warning tool. While it is often a computer, a honeypot can take on other forms, such as files or data records or even unused IP address space. Honeypots should have no production value and hence should not see any legitimate traffic or activity. Whatever they capture can then be surmised as malicious or unauthorized.

INTRUSION DETECTION SYSTEM CONFIGURATIONS

An IDS consists of a conglomeration of capabilities to detect and respond to threats. Intrusion detection systems are available that provide the following functions:

- Event log analysis for insider threat detection.
- File integrity checking.
- Network traffic analysis for perimeter threat detection.
- Security configuration management.

Note that intrusion detection systems can be utilized for both physical facilities and computer and network elements.

The two categories of intrusion detection systems are network based and host based. **Host-based technologies** examine events relating to file and database access and applications being executed. **Network-based technologies** examine events such as packets of information exchanged between networked computers. A hybrid system that includes components from both host- and network-based detection systems offers the best solution.

The explosive growth of the Internet, and the pressure of more companies to be part of this development, opened a whole new aspect of network security. Unfortunately, as the Internet grows exponentially, so does the potential damage from people who are not security conscious. Solutions to overcome these problems include firewall components such as packet filters and proxy firewalls.

Today, however, such solutions are no longer enough. Firewalls cannot detect unintentional backdoors around the firewall, especially if you're not using a proxy firewall. Articles and statistics suggest that more than 50 percent of all recorded breaches today originate from someone legitimately behind the firewall. Therefore, people started deploying intrusion detection (ID) systems as an additional part of a network's security architecture.

Network-based intrusion detection is effective at detecting outsiders attempting to penetrate the enterprise network defenses. The two intrusion detection architectures include traditional sensor and distributed systems. The traditional sensor architecture is easy to deploy and operate; however, it is limited by high-speed, switched, or encrypted networks. The distributed architecture addresses these issues but is significantly more difficult to deploy and manage.

The process is straightforward. A network monitor watches live network packets and looks for signs of network attacks, anomalies, and misuse. When the system observes an event, the sensor can send pages, e-mail messages, take action to stop the event, and record it for future forensic analysis. (*Note that sensors usually run in a promiscuous, indiscriminate mode.*)

NETWORK-BASED INTRUSION DETECTION SYSTEM

A **network-based intrusion detection system (NIDS)** is an intrusion detection system that contains capabilities to detect malicious activity such as denial of service attacks, port scans, or even attempts to crack into computers by monitoring network traffic. The NIDS does this by reading all the incoming packets and attempting to identify suspicious patterns. If, for example, a large number of TCP connection requests to a very large number of different ports are observed, it could be assumed that there is someone committing a "port scan" at some of the computer(s) in the network. It also attempts to detect incoming shellcodes in the same manner that an ordinary intrusion detection system does. A **shellcode** is a relocatable piece of machine code used as the payload in the exploitation of a software bug. It is called *shellcode* because it typically starts a command shell from which the attacker can control the compromised machine.

A NIDS is not limited to only inspecting incoming network traffic. Often valuable information concerning an ongoing intrusion can be learned from outgoing and/or local traffic. Some attacks might even be staged from the inside of the monitored network or network segment and are, therefore, not regarded as incoming traffic. Often, network intrusion detection systems work with other systems as well. They can, for example, update some firewalls' blacklists with the IP addresses of computers used by suspected crackers.

In a NIDS the sensors are located at choke points in the network to be monitored, often in the demilitarized zone (DMZ) or at network borders. The sensor captures all network traffic and analyzes the content of individual packets for malicious traffic. In systems, Perimeter IDS and Application Protocol-Based IDS are used to monitor the transport and protocols' illegal or inappropriate traffic or constructs of a computer language (i.e., SQL). In a host-based system, the sensor usually consists of a software agent that monitors all activity of the host on which it is installed.

A NIDS is an independent platform that identifies intrusions by examining network traffic and monitoring multiple hosts. NIDSs gain access to network traffic by connecting to a hub, network switch configured for port mirroring, or network tap. An example of a NIDS is Snort.

A protocol-based intrusion detection system component consisting of an agent would typically sit at the front end of a server, monitoring and analyzing the communication protocol between a connected device, such as a user/PC or system. For a Web server this would typically monitor the SHTTP protocol stream and understand the HTTP protocol relative to the Web server/system it is trying to protect. Where SHTTP is in use, then this system would need to reside in the interface between where SHTTP is unencrypted and immediately prior to it entering the Web presentation layer.

Intrusion detection techniques can be used to monitor network traffic, looking for patterns that suggest known types of computer attacks. An alternative approach, designed to discover previously unknown types of attacks, requires monitoring network statistics for unusual changes that might indicate attack activity. Intrusion detection monitoring may be accomplished using a network host computer, or detection facilities may be distributed at various points throughout the network. These systems often employ both pattern and statistical methods and use both host-based and distributed monitoring.

The most effective intrusion detection monitoring occurs dynamically as information packets travel through the network. If this activity is in-band, network traffic could experience slow throughput. To meet intrusion detection needs, vendors are now offering security chips capable of examining as many as 20 million packets per second.

Attackers often turn to scanning systems to gather information on the target network. Scanning tools have the ability to automatically check a target network for possible computer and network vulnerabilities. These tools employ a database of known configuration errors, system bugs, and other problems that can be used to infiltrate a system. Defending against vulnerability scanners requires the administrator apply system patches on a regular basis and periodically conduct internal vulnerability scans.

Testing to assess the network intrusion vulnerability may help administrators discover security weaknesses. Such testing can be performed in-house or through a security consultant. When holes in network security are discovered through vulnerability testing, proactive action can be taken to close them.

A security scanner consists of software that will audit remotely a given network and determine whether bad guys may break into it, or misuse it in some way. Nessus is an example of a vulnerability scanner that might be used to improve the security of the enterprise.

HOST-BASED INTRUSION DETECTION SYSTEM

A **host-based intrusion detection system (HIDS)** is an intrusion detection system that monitors and analyzes the internals of a computing system rather than on its external interfaces of the NIDS.

HIDSs are distributed systems that gather and process event logs and other data from computers in an organization. The process is simple: a host monitor looks at system logs for evidence of malicious or suspicious application activity in real time. It also monitors key system files for evidence of tampering.

The data may be processed locally at the target location or transported to a centralized site for processing. Operationally, host-based systems can be effectively utilized for surveillance, damage assessment, intelligence gathering, and compliance.

Managing a host-based system is considerably more difficult than managing a network-based system. It is critical to have developed a good management policy and an efficient audit policy before implementing either system, which can significantly reduce the operational performance overhead. An in-depth understanding of the issues regarding intrusion detection can be gained by reading *The Practical Intrusion Detection Handbook* [Proctor, 2001].

Implementing host-based intrusion detection involves installing/loading software on the system to be monitored. The loaded software uses log files and/or the system's auditing agents as sources of data. In contrast, a network-based IDS monitors the traffic on its network segment as a data source. Both network-based and host-based IDS sensors have pros and cons; in the end, administrators will probably want to use a combination of both. The person responsible for monitoring the IDS needs to be an alert, competent system administrator who is familiar with the host machine, network connections, users and their habits, and all software installed on the machine. This doesn't mean that they must be an expert on the software itself, but rather must have a feel for how the machine is supposed to be running and what programs are legitimate. Many break-ins have been contained by attentive system administrators who have noticed something "different" about their machines or who have noticed a user logged on at an atypical time.

Host-based intrusion detection involves not only looking at the communications traffic in and out of a single computer, but also checking the integrity of the system files and watching for suspicious processes. To get complete coverage at the computer site with host-based ID, administrators need to load the ID software on every computer. There are two primary classes of host-based intrusion detection software: personal firewalls (host wrappers) and agent-based software. Either approach is much more effective in detecting trusted-insider attacks (so-called anomalous activity) than is network-based ID, and both are relatively effective for detecting attacks from the outside.

Personal firewalls or host wrappers can be configured to look at all network packets, connection attempts, or login attempts to the monitored machine. This can also include dial-in attempts or other non-network-related communication ports. Personal firewalls can also detect software on the host attempting to connect to the network.

In addition, host-based agents may be able to monitor accesses and changes to critical system files and changes in user privilege. In addition, UNIX has a rich set of software tools to perform intrusion detection. No single package will do everything, and the software should be tailored to the individual computer that is being monitored. For example, if a machine has only a handful of users, perhaps only the connections from the outside and the integrity of the system files need to be monitored, whereas a machine with numerous users or network traffic may need more stringent monitoring. Types of software that help monitor hosts include:

- System and user log files.
- Connectivity monitoring.
- Process monitoring, process accounting.
- Disk usage monitoring (quotas).
- Session monitoring.
- System auditing.

UNIX host-based intrusion detection is only as good as the system logging process. Programs can be written to analyze log files and alert the system administrator via e-mail or pager when something is amiss. System logging data can be sent to a remote site or modified so that the log files are stored in nonstandard places to prevent hackers from covering their tracks. With the prevalence of hacking scripts, locally built monitoring can be set up to watch for specific instances of break-ins.

BENEFITS OF AN INTRUSION DETECTION SYSTEM

Networks are often large and complex and difficult to monitor. An intrusion detection system can help reveal potential security problems on the network by documenting them. ID systems add the ability to verify the firewall configurations. In case of an incident, the probability of tracking down the attacker is increased by the chronological record of events generated by the IDS.

With an intelligent ID system configuration, administrators can trace suspicious occurrences by reconstructing the chain of events. This can be used as a proof of concept or to explain malicious traffic. An ID system, in contrast to a firewall, is a passive system; it does not influence the network traffic. Thus, most people attacking or trying to circumvent a system won't recognize the intrusion detection node, and incidents can be logged without interruption.

INTRUSION DETECTION SYSTEMS AND VENDORS

There are a number of providers of intrusion detection systems. There are different levels of support for acquisition, deployment, and maintenance that can be provided by these companies. Examples of these system providers are as follows:

- AXENT (*www.axent.com*).
- Cisco Systems, Inc.
- Computer Associates.
- CyberSafe (*www.cybersafe.com*).
- Internet Security Systems.
- Intrusion.
- ISS (*www.iss.net*).
- Lancope.
- Network Security Wizards.
- Pentasafe.
- Polycenter.
- Symantec.
- Tripwire (*www.tripwiresecurity.com*).

There are many Web sites that provide information on both intrusion detection and prevention products and services.

Intrusion Detection Tools

Insecure.org has developed a list of the top five intrusion detection tools. Additional details are available at *http://insecure.org/*. Each tool is described by one or more attributes and did not appear on a previous list. The rating criteria are as follows [IDS]:

- Generally costs money. A free limited/demo/trial version may be available.
- Works natively on Linux.
- Works natively on OpenBSD, FreeBSD, Solaris, and/or other UNIX variants.
- Works natively on Apple Mac OS X.
- Works natively on Microsoft Windows.
- Features a command-line interface.
- Offers a GUI (point and click) interface.
- Source code is available for inspection.

TABLE 10-1 identifies the top five tools that were identified using the aforementioned criteria.

These tools and other security systems that provide IDS capabilities are included in Chapter 12.

TABLE 10-1   Top Five Tools

Rank	Product	Explanation
1	Snort	Everyone's favorite open-source IDS
2	OSSEC HIDS	An open-source host-based intrusion detection system
3	Fragrouter	Network intrusion detection evasion toolkit
4	BASE	The Basic Analysis and Security Engine
5	Sguil	The Analyst Console for Network Security Monitoring

INTRUSION DETECTION DECISIONS

Administrators need to educate themselves on the subject of intrusion detection and must understand the differences between IDS and IPS and the benefits of each system. Questions concerning standards, installation, and ongoing maintenance must be addressed, such as:

- What is a honeypot, and how is it used?
- Are there limitations of intrusion signatures?
- How is a tool like an integrity checker used in intrusion detection?
- How are network-based intrusion detection systems deployed in a switched network?
- Can a MAC address be used in intrusion detection?
- Should communication between a sensor or agent and the monitor be encrypted?
- Should network mapping attempts cause concern?
- Can the volume of network traffic get high enough to exceed the capability of the detectors?
- If hackers break into the network, how would the press ever find out, and why would anybody else care?
- What is the risk to Windows 9x from dedicated Internet connections?
- Why are switched networks insecure?
- What occurs after deploying the intrusion detection system?

Intrusion detection system evasion techniques can bypass detection by creating different states on the IDS and on the targeted computer. The adversary accomplishes this by manipulating either the attack itself or the network traffic that contains the attack.

INTRUSION PREVENTION

Intrusion prevention is a preemptive approach to network security used to identify potential threats and respond to them swiftly. Like an intrusion detection system (IDS), an intrusion prevention system (IPS) monitors network traffic. However, because an exploit may be carried out very quickly after the attacker gains access, intrusion prevention systems also have the ability to take immediate action, based on a set of rules established by the network administrator. For example, an IPS might drop a packet that it determines to be malicious and block all further traffic from that IP address or port. Legitimate traffic, meanwhile, should be forwarded to the recipient with no apparent disruption or delay of service.

INTRUSION PREVENTION SYSTEMS

The inadequacies inherent in current defenses have driven the development of a new breed of security products known as intrusion prevention systems, a term that has provoked some controversy in the industry since some firewall and IDS vendors think it has been "hijacked" and used as a marketing term rather than as a description for any kind of new technology. These systems signaled a shift in approach away from passive detection of computer network incidents and attacks. They are supposed to include a more reactive approach built on both the ability to respond to known methods of attack and an ability to create adaptive responses to previously unknown attacks.

While it is true that firewalls, routers, IDS devices, and even gateways all have intrusion prevention technology included in some form, there are sufficient grounds to create a new market sector for true intrusion prevention products. These systems are proactive defense mechanisms designed to detect malicious packets within normal network traffic, which is something that the current breed of firewalls do not actually accomplish. The objective is to stop intrusions dead, blocking the offending traffic automatically before it does any damage, rather than simply raising an alert as, or after, the malicious payload has been delivered.

An **intrusion prevention system (IPS)** is a computer security device that monitors network and/or system activities for malicious or unwanted behavior and can react, in real time, to block or prevent those activities. Network-based IPS, for example, will operate in-line to monitor all network traffic for malicious code or attacks. When an attack is detected, it can drop the offending packets while still allowing all other traffic to pass. Intrusion prevention technology is considered by some to be an extension of intrusion detection technology.

Intrusion prevention systems were invented in the late 1990s to resolve ambiguities in passive network monitoring by placing detection systems in-line. A considerable improvement upon firewall technologies, IPSs make access control decisions based on application content, rather than IP address or ports as traditional firewalls had done. Because IPSs were originally a literal extension of intrusion detection systems, they continue to be related.

The first commercial/retail IPS was the BlackICE product from NetworkICE Corporation. It debuted in 1998 with a business and personal version of the product. It provided host and in-line network IPS capabilities using protocol analysis as its core detection technique. This system is described in Chapter 12. Intrusion prevention systems may also serve secondarily at the host level to deny potentially malicious activity. There are advantages and disadvantages to host-based IPS compared with network-based IPS. In many cases, the technologies are thought to be complementary.

An intrusion prevention system must also be a very good intrusion detection system to enable a low rate of false positives. Some IPSs can also prevent yet-to-be-discovered attacks, such as those caused by a **buffer overflow**, which can occur when a value assigned to a variable exceeds the size of the buffer allocated and memory locations not allocated to this variable are overwritten.

IPS and Application Firewalls

The role of an IPS in a network is often confused with access control and application-layer firewalls. There are, however, some notable differences in these technologies. While all share similarities, how they approach network or system security is fundamentally different. An IPS is typically designed to operate completely invisibly on a network. IPS products do not have IP addresses for their monitoring segments and do not respond directly to any traffic. Rather, they merely silently monitor traffic as it passes. While some IPS products have the ability to implement firewall rules, this is often a mere convenience and not a core function of the product. Moreover, IPS technology offers deeper insight into network operations providing information on overly active hosts, bad logons, inappropriate content, and many other network and application-layer functions.

Application firewalls are a very different type of technology. An application firewall uses proxies to perform firewall access control for network and application-layer traffic. Some application-layer firewalls have the ability to do some IPS-like functions, such as enforcing RFC (Request for Comments) specifications on network traffic. Some application-layer firewalls have also integrated IPS-style signatures into their products to provide real-time analysis and blocking of traffic. Application firewalls do have IP addresses on their ports and are directly addressable. Moreover, they use full proxy features to decode and reassemble packets. Not all IPSs perform full proxy-like processing. Also, application-layer firewalls tend to focus on firewall capabilities, with IPS capabilities as add-ons. While there are numerous similarities between the two technologies, they are not identical and are not interchangeable. (*Note that a* **proxy** *is an application running on a gateway that relays network packets between a trusted client and an untrusted host.*)

Intrusion Detection and Prevention

Intrusion detection and prevention include the process of monitoring the events occurring in a computer system or network, analyzing them for signs of possible incidents, and attempting to stop detected possible incidents. An effective IDS and IPS will use a combination of network- and host-based intrusion detection configurations. Determining where to use each type and how to integrate the data is a real and growing concern. **FIGURE 10-2** provides an example of a host-based intrusion detection/prevention system (IDPS). **FIGURE 10-3** provides an example of a network-based IDPS sensor configuration. Additional details are available in the NIST special publication 800–94 titled "Guide to Intrusion Detection and Prevention Systems (IDPS) [NIST 2007]."

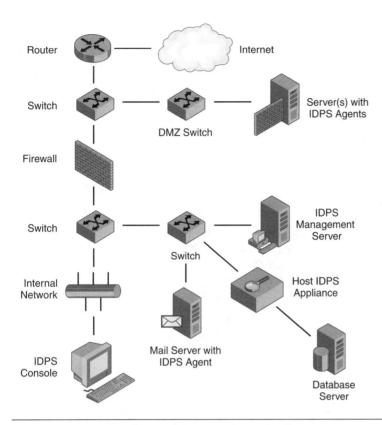

FIGURE 10-2 Host-Based Intrusion Detection/Prevention System

SYSTEM PROCESSES

System processes include stateful inspection, deep packet inspection, and protocol analysis.

Stateful Inspection

Stateful inspection and deep packet inspection are necessary capabilities when selecting an IPS solution. **Stateful inspection** is a firewall architecture that works at the network layer and is also referred to as *dynamic packet filtering*. Unlike static packet filtering, which examines a packet based on the information in its header, stateful inspection tracks each connection traversing all interfaces of the firewall and makes sure they are valid. A stateful firewall may examine not just the header information, but also the contents of the packet up through the application layer in order to determine more about the packet than just information about its source and destination. A stateful inspection firewall also monitors the state of the connection and compiles the information in a state table. Because of this, filtering decisions are based not only on administrator-defined rules (as in static packet filtering), but also on context that has

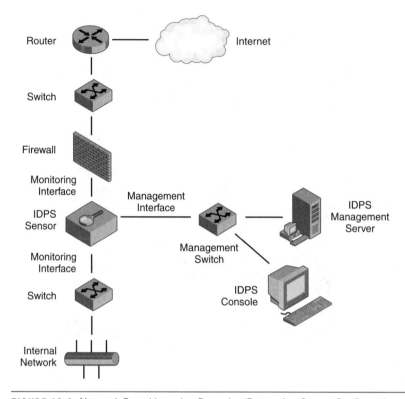

FIGURE 10-3 Network-Based Intrusion Detection/Prevention Sensor Configuration

been established by prior packets that have passed through the firewall. As an added security measure against port scanning, stateful inspection firewalls close off ports until connection to the specific port is requested.

Deep Packet Inspection

Deep packet inspection (DPI) is a form of computer network packet filtering that examines the data and/or header part of a packet as it passes an inspection point, searching for non-protocol compliance, viruses, spam, intrusions, or predefined criteria to decide if the packet can pass or if it needs to be routed to a different destination or for the purpose of collecting statistical information. It also called *content inspection* or *content processing*. This is in contrast to shallow packet inspection (usually called just *packet inspection*), which just checks the header portion of a packet.

An issue with signature-based (content) techniques is there will be a lag between a new threat being discovered in the wild and the signature for detecting that threat being applied to the IDS. During that lag time, an IDS would be unable to detect the new threat.

Protocol Analysis

A key development in IDS/IPS technologies was the use of protocol analyzers. **Protocol analyzers** can natively decode application-layer network protocols, like HTTP or FTP. Once the protocols are fully decoded, the IPS analysis engine can evaluate different parts of the protocol for anomalous behavior or exploits. For example, the existence of a large binary file in the User-Agent field of an HTTP request would be very unusual and likely signal an intrusion. A protocol analyzer could detect this anomalous behavior and instruct the IPS engine to drop the offending packets.

Not all IPS/IDS engines are full protocol analyzers. Some products rely on simple pattern recognition techniques to look for known attack patterns. While this can be sufficient in many cases, it creates an overall weakness in the detection capabilities. Many system vulnerabilities have dozens or even hundreds of exploit variants, so pattern recognition–based IPS/IDS engines can be evaded. For example, some pattern recognition engines require hundreds of different signatures (or patterns) to protect against a single vulnerability. This is because they must have a different pattern for each exploit variant. Protocol analysis–based products can often block exploits with a single signature that monitors for the specific vulnerability in the network communications.

INTRUSION PREVENTION SYSTEM TYPES

As with IDS, IPS configurations include both host-based IPS and network-based IPS implementations. IPSs have some advantages over intrusion detection systems (IDSs). One advantage is they are designed to sit in-line with traffic flows and prevent attacks in real time. In addition, most IPS solutions have the ability to look at (decode) OSI layer 7 protocols like HTTP, FTP, and SMTP, which provides greater awareness. When deploying NIPS, however, consideration should be given to whether the network segment is encrypted because many products are unable to support inspection of such traffic. A short description for each type of IPS is as follows:

- **Host-based**—a host-based IPS (HIPS) is one in which the intrusion prevention application is resident on that specific IP address, usually on a single computer.
- **Network-based**—a network-based IPS is one in which the IPS application/hardware and any actions taken to prevent an intrusion on a specific network host(s) are performed from a host with another IP address on the network.
- **Signature-based**—a signature-based IDS will monitor packets on the network and compare them against a database of signatures or attributes from known malicious threats. This is similar to the way most anti-virus software detects malware.
- **Rate-based**—rate-based IPS (RBIPS) is primarily intended to prevent denial of service and distributed denial of service attacks. They work by monitoring and learning normal network behaviors.

Host-Based Intrusion Prevention Systems

As with host-based IDS systems, the host-based IPS (or HIPS) relies on agents installed directly on the system being protected. It binds closely with the operating system kernel and services, monitoring and intercepting system calls to the kernel or application programming interfaces (APIs) in order to prevent attacks as well as log them. It may also monitor data streams and the environment specific to a particular application, such as file locations and registry settings for a Web server, in order to protect that application from generic attacks for which no "signature" yet exists.

One potential disadvantage with this approach is that, given the necessarily tight integration with the host operating system, future OS upgrades could cause problems. Because a host-based IPS agent intercepts all requests to the system it protects, it has certain prerequisites: it must be very reliable, must not negatively impact performance, and must not block legitimate traffic. Any HIPS that does not meet these minimum requirements should never be installed in a host, no matter how effectively it blocks attacks.

Network-Based Intrusion Prevention Systems

Network intrusion prevention systems (NIPSs) are purpose-built hardware/software platforms that are designed to analyze, detect, and report on security-related events. NIPSs are designed to inspect traffic and, based on their configuration or security policy, can drop malicious traffic.

The network-based IPS combines features of a standard IDS, an IPS, and a firewall and is sometimes known as an in-line IDS or gateway IDS (GIDS). The next-generation firewall—the deep inspection firewall—also exhibits a similar feature set, but it is not yet ready for mainstream deployment.

As with a typical firewall, the NIPS has at least two network interfaces: one designated as internal and one as external. As packets appear at either interface, they are passed to the detection engine, at which point the IPS device functions much as any IDS would in determining whether the packet being examined poses a threat.

However, if it should detect a malicious packet, in addition to raising an alert, it will discard the packet and mark that flow as bad. As the remaining packets that make up that particular TCP session arrive at the IPS device, they are discarded immediately.

Legitimate packets are passed through to the second interface and on to their intended destination. A useful side-effect of some NIPS products is that as a matter of course—in fact, as part of the initial detection process—they will provide "packet scrubbing" functionality to remove protocol inconsistencies resulting from varying interpretations of the TCP/IP specification or intentional packet manipulation. Thus, any fragmented packets, out-of-order packets, or packets with overlapping IP fragments will be reordered and "cleaned up" before being passed to the destination host, and illegal packets can be dropped completely.

Some "reactive" IDS vendors may state they have intrusion prevention capabilities just because they can send TCP reset commands or reconfigure a firewall when they detect an attack. The problem here is that unless the attacker is operating on a 56,000 bps modem, the likelihood is that by the time the IDS has detected the offending packet, raised an alert, and transmitted the TCP resets, the payload of the exploit has long since been delivered, and the game is over! There are not many crackers using 56,000 bps modems these days.

A true IPS device, however, is sitting in-line, and all the packets have to pass through it. Therefore, as soon as a suspicious packet has been detected, and before it is passed to the internal interface and on to the protected network, it can be dropped. Not only that, but now that flow has been flagged as suspicious, all subsequent packets that are part of that session can also be dropped with very little additional processing. Some products are also capable of sending TCP resets or Internet group message protocol (ICMP) unreachable messages to the attacking host.

When deploying a network-based IPS, consideration should be given to whether the network segment is encrypted because many products are unable to support inspection of such traffic.

Rate-Based Intrusion Prevention Systems

Rate-based IPSs (RBIPSs) are primarily intended to prevent denial of service and distributed denial of service attacks. They work by monitoring and learning normal network behaviors. Through real-time traffic monitoring and comparison with stored statistics, RBIPSs can identify abnormal rates for certain types of traffic. These include TCP, UDP, or address resolution protocol (ARP) packets, connections per second, packets per connection, packets to specific ports, and so forth. Attacks are detected when thresholds are exceeded. The thresholds are dynamically adjusted based on time of day, day of the week, and so on, and draw on stored traffic statistics.

Unusual but legitimate network traffic patterns may create false alarms. The system's effectiveness is related to the granularity of the RBIPS rule base and the quality of the stored statistics. Once an attack is detected, various prevention techniques may be used such as:

- Rate-limiting specific attack-related traffic types.
- Source or connection tracking.
- Source-address, port or protocol filtering (black-listing) or validation (white-listing).

Host-Based Versus Network-Based IPS Comparisons

There are a number of differences between host-based IPS and network-based IPS configurations. Administrators and security managers must determine the system most appropriate for the installation being secured.

The HIPS can handle encrypted and unencrypted traffic equally, because it can analyze the data after it has been decrypted on the host.

The NIPS does not use processor and memory on computer hosts, but uses its own CPU and memory.

NIPS is a single point of failure, which is considered a disadvantage; however, this property also makes it simpler to maintain. This attribute also applies to all network devices like routers and switches and can be overcome by implementing the network accordingly (failover path, etc.). A bypass switch can be implemented to alleviate the single point of failure disadvantage, though. This also allows the NIPS appliance to be moved and taken off-line for maintenance when needed.

NIPS can detect events scattered over the network (e.g., low-level event targeting many different hosts, like HostScan, worm) and can react, whereas with a HIPS, only the host's data are available to make a decision; it would take too much time to report it to a central decision-making authority. (*Note that HostScan is very powerful network scanner software that includes an IP scanner, port scanner, and network service scanner.*)

IMPLEMENTATION CHALLENGES

There are a number of challenges to the implementation of an IPS device that do not have to be faced when deploying passive-mode IDS products. These challenges all stem from the fact that the IPS device is designed to work in-line, presenting a potential choke point and single point of failure.

If a passive IDS fails, the worst that can happen is some attempted attacks may go undetected. If an in-line device fails, however, it can seriously affect the performance of the network. Perhaps latency rises to unacceptable values, or perhaps the device fails closed, in which case you have a self-inflicted denial of service condition on the system. On the bright side, there will be no attacks getting through! But that is of little consolation if none of your customers can reach an e-commerce site.

Even if the IPS device does not fail altogether, it still has the potential to act as a bottleneck, increasing latency and reducing throughput as it struggles to keep up with up to a gigabit or more of network traffic. Devices using off-the-shelf hardware will certainly struggle to keep up with a heavily loaded gigabit network, especially if there is a substantial signature set loaded. This situation could be a major concern for both the network administrator, who could see carefully crafted network response times go through the roof when a poorly designed IPS device is placed in-line, and the security administrator, who will have to fight tooth and nail to have the network administrator allow placing this unknown quantity among the high-performance routers and switches.

As an integral element of the network fabric, the network-based IPS device must perform much like a network switch. It must meet stringent network performance and reliability requirements as a prerequisite to deployment, because very few customers are willing to sacrifice network performance and reliability for security. A NIPS that slows down traffic, stops good traffic, or crashes the network is fairly useless.

Dropped packets are also an issue: if even one of those dropped packets is one of those used in the exploit data stream, it is possible that the entire exploit could be missed. Most high-end IPS vendors will get around this problem by using custom hardware, populated with advanced FPGAs and ASICs. An FPGA is a *semiconductor* device containing *programmable logic* components and an ASIC is an integrated circuit customized for a particular use, rather than intended for general-purpose use. However, it is necessary to design the product to operate as much as a switch as an intrusion detection and prevention device.

It is very difficult for any security administrator to be able to characterize the traffic on a network with a high degree of accuracy. Questions that might need addressing include:

- What is the average bandwidth?
- What are the peaks?
- Is the traffic mainly one protocol or a mix?
- What is the average packet size and level of new connections established every second? Are they both critical parameters that can have detrimental effects on some IDS/IPS engines?

If the IPS hardware is operating "on the edge," all of these are questions that need to be answered as accurately as possible in order to prevent performance degradation.

Another potential problem is the old false positive. The bane of the security administrator's life, the false positive rears its ugly head when an exploit signature is not crafted carefully enough, such that legitimate traffic can cause it to fire accidentally. While merely annoying in a passive IDS device, consuming time and effort on the part of the security administrator, the results can be far more serious and far reaching in an in-line IPS appliance.

Once again, the result is a self-inflicted denial of service condition, as the IPS device first drops the "offending" packet, and then potentially blocks the entire data flow from the suspected hacker. If the traffic that triggered the false positive alert was part of a customer order, the customer will not wait around for long as the entire session is torn down and all subsequent attempts to reconnect to the e-commerce site are blocked by the well-meaning IPS.

Another potential problem with any gigabit IPS/IDS product is, by its very nature and capabilities, the amount of alert data it is likely to generate. On such a busy network, how many alerts will be generated in one working day—or even one hour? Even with relatively low alert rates of 10 per second, this translates to about 36,000 alerts every hour. That is 864,000 alerts each and every day! The ability to tune the signature set accurately is essential in order to keep the number of alerts to an absolute minimum. Once the alerts have been raised, however, it then becomes essential to be able to process them effectively. Advanced alert handling and forensic analysis capabilities—including detailed exploit information and the ability to examine packet contents and data streams—can make or break a gigabit IDS/IPS product.

Of course, one point in favor of IPS when compared with IDS is that because it is designed to prevent the attacks rather than just detect and log them, the burden of examining and investigating the alerts—and especially the problem of rectifying damage done by successful exploits—is reduced considerably.

Unified threat management (UTM), sometimes called "next-generation firewalls," are an entirely different breed of products. UTM products bring together multiple security capabilities onto a single platform. A typical UTM platform will provide firewall, VPN, anti-virus, Web filtering, intrusion prevention, and anti-spam capabilities. Some UTM appliances are derived from IPS products such as 3Com's X-series products. Others are derived from firewall products, such as Juniper's SSG or Cisco's ASA appliances. And still others were derived from the ground up as a UTM appliance such as those provided by Astaro or Fortinet. The main feature of a UTM is that it includes multiple security features on one appliance. IPS is merely one feature.

Access control is also an entirely different security concept. Access control refers to general rules allowing hosts, users, or applications access to specific parts of a network. Typically, access control helps organizations segment networks and limit access. While an IPS has the ability to block access to users, hosts, or applications, it does so only when malicious code has been discovered. As such, IPS does not necessarily serve as an access control device. While it has some access control abilities, firewalls and network access control (NAC) technologies are better suited to provide these features.

REQUIREMENTS FOR EFFECTIVE PREVENTION

There are a number of generic requirements for effective prevention of potential pitfalls facing anyone deploying these security systems and for identifying the features and capabilities that will help administrators avoid these problems and situations. Only by operating in-line can an IPS device perform true protection, discarding all suspect packets immediately and blocking the remainder of that flow. These generic requirements include:

- Unquestionable detection accuracy.
- Reliability and availability.
- Resilience.
- Low latency.
- High performance.
- Fine-grained granularity and control.
- Advanced alert handling and forensic analysis capabilities.

Unquestionable Detection Accuracy

It is imperative that the quality of the signatures is beyond question, because false positives can lead to a denial of service (DoS) condition. The user must be able to trust that the IDS is blocking only the user-selected malicious traffic. New signatures should be made available on a regular basis, and applying them should be quick (applied to all sensors in one operation via a central console) and seamless (no sensor reboot required).

Reliability and Availability

Should an in-line device fail, it has the potential to close a vital network path and thus, once again, cause a DoS condition. An extremely low failure rate is thus very important in order to maximize up-time, and if the worst should happen, the device should provide the option to fail open or support fail-over to another sensor operating in a fail-over group. In addition, to reduce downtime for signature and protocol coverage updates, an IPS must support the ability to receive these updates without requiring a device reboot. When operating in-line, sensors rebooting across the enterprise effectively translate into network downtime for the duration of the reboot.

Resilience

As mentioned earlier, the very minimum that an IPS device should offer in the way of high availability is to fail open in the case of system failure or power loss (some environments may prefer this default condition to be "fail closed" as with a typical firewall; however, the most flexible products will allow this to be user-configurable). Active-active stateful fail-over with cooperating in-line sensors in a fail-over group will ensure that the IPS device does not become a single point of failure in a critical network deployment.

Low Latency

When a device is placed in-line, it is essential that its impact on overall network performance is minimal. Packets should be processed quickly enough such that the overall latency of the device is as close as possible to that offered by an OSI layer 2/3 device, such as a switch, and no more than a typical OSI layer 4 device such as a firewall or load balancer.

High Performance

Packet processing rates must be at the rated speed of the device under real-life traffic conditions, and the device must meet the stated performance with all signatures enabled. Headroom should be built into the performance capabilities to enable the device to handle any increases in size of signature packs that may occur over the next three years. Ideally, the detection engine should be designed in such a way that the number of "signatures" (or "checks") loaded does not affect the overall performance of the device.

Fine-Grained Granularity and Control

Fine-grained granularity is required in terms of deciding exactly which malicious traffic is blocked. The ability to specify traffic to be blocked by attack, by policy, or right down to individual host level is vital. In addition, it may be necessary to only alert on suspicious traffic for further analysis and investigation.

Advanced Alert Handling and Forensic Analysis Capabilities

Once the alerts have been raised at the sensor and passed to a central console, someone must examine them, correlate them where necessary, investigate them, and eventually decide on an action. The capabilities offered by the console in terms of real-time and historic alert viewing and reporting are key in determining the effectiveness of the IPS product.

MANAGEMENT AND ADMINISTRATION CONSIDERATIONS

Management and security personnel must become familiar with the intrusion detection and prevention environment before embarking on a quest for a security solution. A number of questions have been assembled to assist in the decision to implement a security system. Some of these questions are systems management–related and some are oriented toward product technical features and capabilities. A checklist could assist management in selecting a product that would provide an acceptable and cost-beneficial security solution [Networkworld].

- Where is this product designed to sit on the network?
- Is this product primarily designed to mitigate attacks with rate-based mechanisms or content/anomaly-based mechanisms?
- What additional content-based and rate-based features does this product offer?
- Does the product have a learning mode, and how long does it take to learn it?
- How easily can you run this product in an alert-only mode?
- Does the product provide centralized configuration and/or management capabilities?
- What is the overall strategy for alerting for both malicious activity and blocked traffic?
- What are the product reporting capabilities?
- Does this product have the ability to connect to a security event management system via some event-reporting mechanism?
- If this device's log fills, will it continue to operate without logging?
- Does the vendor offer log analysis tools for forensics and capacity planning?
- What are the latency, throughput, and jitter claims made regarding this product, and how are those numbers derived?
- What tools does this product offer that measure baseline traffic norms? What is the underlying IDS system in this product?
- How granularly can administrators define which incoming traffic the IPS is going to examine and, eventually, limit or block? How big is the signature database? Which of those signatures are turned on by default? What is the update mechanism for new signatures?
- How sophisticated are the rate detection and control mechanisms offered? (For example, can they detect just a flood, or can they track potentially malicious single connections over time?) How do administrators see, enable, disable, and modify attributes of bad traffic signatures?
- How does this product discover machines and services running on the network that need IPS protection?
- What kinds of traffic can this product block (e.g., DoS attack, UDP protocol attacks, buffer overflow attacks, fragmentation attacks, spoofing attacks [inbound/outbound], application-layer attacks)?
- What are the action options offered by this product once malicious traffic is discovered (e.g., drop-only, pass and track, pass and alert, pass but limit)?
- What kind of communication happens between this IPS device and either an installed firewall or a built-in one?
- What are the configuration options (e.g., rules per port, per system)?
- What secure management access methods does this device support, such as SNMPv3 or SSHv2? Are these the only methods enabled by default?

After a decision has been made concerning the type and variety of IDS/IPS required, the procurement and project management phases must be initiated. Security managers and administrators already know the offerings for these systems are endless and vendor sales personnel are circling the installation. The product procurement process is important; however, the project management of the installation and implementation is a critical part of the success or failure of the initiative. Chapter 12 identifies the necessary steps for security system procurement and project management. Someone from the organization and the supplier must be allocated full-time to this project. This is not a part-time endeavor if success is part of the criteria.

ORGANIZATIONS AND STANDARDS

Numerous organizations and user groups are involved in the development of standards for intrusion detection and prevention systems. Specific organizations are described in this section. These and other organizations are further described in Chapter 13.

Organizations

A short list and description of the major players include the following:

- *ICSA*—the International Computer Security Association's mission is to continually improve commercial computer security through certification of firewalls, anti-virus products, and Web sites. ICSA also shares and disseminates information concerning information security.
- *SANS*—the SysAdmin, Audit, Network, Security group is the most trusted and by far the largest source for information security training, certification, and research in the world.
- *IETF IDWG*—the Internet Engineering Task Force (IETF) is the body that defines standard Internet operating protocols such as TCP/IP. This document defines a proposed data model for the Intrusion Detection Exchange Format (IDEF), which is the intended work product of the Intrusion Detection Exchange Format Working Group (IDWG).
- *CIDF*—the Common Intrusion Detection Framework (CIDF) is an effort to develop protocols and application programming interfaces so that intrusion detection research projects can share information and resources and so that intrusion detection components can be reused in other systems.
- *CVE®*—this resource is international in scope and free for public use. CVE is a dictionary of publicly known information security vulnerabilities and exposures. CVE's common identifiers enable data exchange between security products and provide a baseline index point for evaluating coverage of tools and services.
- *GIAC*—this worldwide benchmark of excellence validates that GIAC is a responsible, fair, and quality-oriented testing and certification-granting organization within the high-stakes testing and certification industry. By achieving this accreditation, GIAC demonstrates a commitment to process and procedures that adhere to an international standard of excellence.

🔒 CHAPTER SUMMARY

An IDS generally detects unwanted manipulations of computer systems, mainly through the Internet. The manipulations may take the form of attacks by crackers. An intrusion detection system is used to detect several types of malicious behaviors that can compromise the security and trust of a computer system.

In a network-based system, or NIDS, the individual packets flowing through a network are analyzed. The NIDS can detect malicious packets that are designed to be overlooked by a firewall's simplistic filtering rules. In a host-based system, the IDS examines the activity on each individual computer or host. It also monitors and analyzes the internals of the computer system.

Intrusion prevention is a preemptive approach to network security used to identify potential threats and respond to them swiftly. Like an intrusion detection system (IDS), an intrusion prevention system (IPS) monitors network traffic.

An intrusion prevention system is a computer security device that monitors network and/or system activities for malicious or unwanted behavior and can react, in real time, to block or prevent those activities. Network-based IPS, for example, will operate in-line to monitor all network traffic for malicious code or attacks.

There are a number of challenges to the implementation of an IPS device that do not have to be faced when deploying passive-mode IDS products. These challenges all stem from the fact that the IPS device is designed to work in-line, presenting a potential choke point and single point of failure.

 KEY TERMS

anomaly	host-based technologies	network behavior analysis (NBA)
anomaly-based intrusion detection system	intrusion	passive system
	intrusion detection (ID)	protocol analyzer
buffer overflow	intrusion detection system (IDS)	proxy
deep packet inspection (DPI)	intrusion prevention	rate-based IPS (RBIPS)
false negative	intrusion prevention system (IPS)	reactive system
false positive	misuse	shellcode
honeypot	network-based IDS (NIDS)	signature-based IDS
host-based IDS (HIDS)	network-based IPS (NIPS)	stateful inspection
host-based IPS (HIPS)	network-based technologies	

SECURITY REVIEW QUESTIONS

1. _____ is the art of detection and responding to situations involving computer, database, and network misuse.

2. A(n) _____ generally detects unwanted manipulations of computer systems, mainly through the Internet, but also functions in a corporate internetwork environment.

3. Provide a list of intrusion detection capabilities available to an organization.

4. A(n) _____ is an intrusion detection system that contains capabilities to detect malicious activity such as denial of service attacks and port scans.

5. A(n) _____ is an intrusion detection system that monitors and analyzes the internals of a computing system rather than its external interfaces with the NIDS.

6. _____ is a method of enhancing the security of a proprietary network by monitoring traffic and noting unusual actions or departures from normal (behavior) operation.

7. A(n) _____ is based on heuristics or rules, rather than patterns or signatures.

8. _____ is a preemptive approach to network security used to identify potential threats and respond to them swiftly.

9. A(n) _____ is a computer security device that monitors network and/or system activities for malicious or unwanted behavior and can react, in real time, to block or prevent those activities.

10. _____ is a form of computer network packet filtering that examines a packet as it passes an inspection point, searching for non-protocol compliance, viruses, spam, intrusions, or predefined criteria to decide if the packet can pass.

RESEARCH ACTIVITIES

1. Develop a comparison of intrusion detection and prevention systems.

2. Identify vendors that provide intrusion detection systems. Create a spreadsheet of features and costs.

3. Identify those vendors that offer intrusion systems. Create a report describing features and functionalities.

4. Develop a graphic that depicts the flow of an intrusion detection scenario.

5. Identify several organizations that utilize either an IDS or IPS. Describe the products implemented.

6. Describe the differences between a HIPS and a NIPS.

7. Develop a list of the standards organizations that are involved in the IPS/IDS products. Provide a summary of the contents of the documents.

8. Using the checklist listed in the "Management and Administration Considerations" section, match these items against a real IDS/IPS product offering.

9. Describe the use of a honeypot as a passive detection tool.

CHAPTER 11

Problem Solving and Security Administration

🔒 CHAPTER CONTENTS

- Understand the need and content of a baseline.
- Identify the documentation required for network management.
- Look at the numerous administration, troubleshooting, and problem-solving issues.
- Review the requirements of a security audit.
- Become familiar with computer forensic issues.
- Look at the various types of situations that can affect the security and integrity of a network.
- Identify the various hardware and software tools used in network management.
- Understand the issues and options for network management and control.

INTRODUCTION

Network problems can typically be resolved in one of two ways, either *proactive prevention* or *reactive response*. It is possible to prevent problems from occurring by a structured program of computer and network resource planning and management. The alternative is repair and control of damage that can be accomplished by reactive responses. Once again, the old axiom of "pay me now or pay me later" comes into play. Network management and planning should combine to form an overall security plan. A baseline should be developed that includes all the components of both the computer and network infrastructure.

A major element of network management includes network management support systems and network management products and services. The tools are a must, particularly for large networks, in managing and troubleshooting the network assets. Network management and security are not "add-ons"; they must be considered in the design phase of the initial network design.

Computer and network security troubleshooting is often characterized as an art that can only be gained from experience in the trenches. This experience, along with some documented methodology, allows the administrator to successfully solve difficult network issues.

The methodology keeps the troubleshooter from skipping or overlooking the obvious, and the experience helps the troubleshooter draw appropriate conclusions and check for obscure problems.

Before someone starts this troubleshooting process, it is essential for the network professional to establish a *baseline*, or reference point, for system comparisons. If you don't know where you are, how can you determine where you are going? Information should be gathered and documented on the network devices, software elements, facility components, network traffic, performance levels, and security systems. This information will prove invaluable later when a problem develops in the network.

THE NEED FOR PROBLEM SOLVING

Business and government networks may involve large-scale, multi-protocol networks that span multiple time zones and countries or may involve simple, single-protocol, point-to-point connections in a local environment. The trend is toward an increasingly complex environment, which involves multiple media types, multiple protocols, and often some connectivity to a private network service or an Internet service provider. Quite possibly, control of the components, throughput, and management of these networks is someone else's responsibility.

More complex network environments mean that the potential for availability and performance issues in these internetworks is high, and the source of problems is often difficult to pinpoint. The keys to maintaining a secure, problem-free network environment, as well as maintaining the ability to isolate and fix a network fault or security breach quickly, are documentation, planning, and communication. This requires a framework of procedures and personnel in place before the requirement for problem solving and recovery occurs.

Establishment of policies and procedures that apply to the computer resource and network must be developed during its planning stages and continue throughout the network's life. Such policies should include security, hardware and software standards, upgrade guidelines, backup methods, network intrusions, and documentation requirements. These will take the form of contingency and disaster recovery planning development. Through careful planning, it is possible to minimize the damage that results from most predictable events and control and manage their impact on the organization.

THE SECURITY AUDIT

The tasks involved in maintaining a secure network and computer system can be both time-consuming and difficult. A **security audit** should be part of the ongoing operating processes in the organization. There are a number of questions that must be formulated and answered as to what resources need protection. The following list contains sample questions that can be used in the development process for such an exercise:

- Is security important to the organization?
- Are all users aware of security policies and procedures?
- Is there a security classification system for files and documents?
- What types of security breaches and attacks have occurred?

- Has the monetary or prestige loss been calculated?
- What elements of the organization have been compromised?
- What security tools are operational?
- Who have been the perpetrators?
- Where did the attacks originate?

Appendix A provides a guide for conducting such a security audit. It is essential that all computer and network assets be afforded some level of protection. These assets include the building, equipment rooms, wiring closets, computer and network devices, storage devices, software, and documentation.

Computer Security Audit

A **computer security audit** is a manual or systematic measurable technical assessment of a system or application. Manual assessments include interviewing staff, performing security vulnerability scans, reviewing application and operating system access controls, and analyzing physical access to the systems. Automated assessments include system-generated audit reports or using software to monitor and report changes to files and settings on a system. Systems can include personal computers, servers, mainframes, network routers, and switches. Applications can include Web Services, Microsoft Project Central, and an Oracle Database. Categories that should be addressed are included in the following list:

- Physical security.
- Network security.
- Protocols/services.
- Passwords.
- User security.
- Data storage security.
- System administration.

BASELINE

A well-documented network includes everything necessary to review history, understand the current status, plan for growth, and provide comparisons when problems occur. This is called a **baseline**. The following list outlines a set of documents and information that should be included in a network plan.

- Address list.
- Cable map.
- Capacity information.
- Contact list.
- Equipment list.
- Important files and their layouts.

- Network history.
- Network map.
- Server configuration.
- Software configuration.
- Software licenses.
- Protocols and network standards.
- User administration.

It is essential to take the time during installation to ensure that all hardware and software components of the network are correctly installed and accurately recorded in the master network record. This documentation also applies to the hardware and software configurations for each of the network components. A considerable amount of personnel effort and time can be saved by being able to quickly find a faulty network component and having documentation on the configuration.

Documentation should be kept in both hard-copy and electronic form so it is readily available to anyone who needs it. This includes information on systems that are accessed by the telecommunications network. Complete, accurate, and up-to-date documentation will aid in troubleshooting the network, planning for growth, and training new employees.

Network Management and Monitoring

Network management is a collection of activities that are required to plan, design, organize, control, maintain, and expand the communications network. There are many software solutions available to assist with network management. This software can help identify conditions that may lead to security and integrity problems, prevent network failures, and troubleshoot problems when they occur.

Activities that pertain to the operation, administration, maintenance, and provisioning of networked systems include the following:

- *Operation* deals with keeping the network—and the services that the network provides—up and running smoothly. It includes monitoring the network to spot problems and issues as soon as possible, ideally before users are affected.
- *Administration* deals with keeping track of resources in the network and how they are assigned. It includes all the "housekeeping" that is necessary to keep the network under control.
- *Maintenance* is concerned with performing repairs and upgrades. This includes equipment replacement, router patches for an operating system image, and addition of switches to a network. Maintenance also involves corrective and preventive measures to make the managed network run "better," such as adjusting device configuration parameters.
- *Provisioning* is concerned with configuring resources in the network to support a given service. For example, this might include setting up the network so that a new customer can receive voice service.

An initial step is to develop a baseline of the current state of the network and computer resources. After a baseline for the network has been developed, it will be possible to monitor the network for changes that could indicate potential problems. It is essential to establish what is "normal" in the network so "abnormal" situations can be readily identified. Network monitoring software can gather information on events, system usage statistics, and system performance statistics. Information gathered from these monitors can assist the network administrator in the following ways.

- Monitoring trends in network traffic and utilization.
- Developing plans to improve network performance.
- Providing forecasting information for growth.
- Identifying those network devices that create bottlenecks.
- Monitoring events that result from upgrades.

Management must also consider the implications of any IPS and IDS might be active in the network. These systems were discussed in Chapter 10.

SECURITY INVESTIGATIONS

Forensic analysis consists of a cycle of data gathering and processing of evidence that has been gathered from some incident. Data collected by intrusion detection systems, firewalls, and network devices such as switches, routers, gateways, and servers can be used to analyze and evaluate the extent to which a network has been compromised by an attack or intrusion. Logs are an essential source of information for this type of forensic examination. In addition, if equipment that has been the target of an attack can be secured at a crime scene, photographs and fingerprints can be taken, and the equipment can be thoroughly examined. Documentation is an important element used in a court of law if an attacker is to be prosecuted. It is essential that the evidence trail be preserved and secured. It is essential that the affected device be isolated so the evidence is not compromised. Hardware and software tools are available for isolating and imaging computer information. There are other packages that take this output and use information and computer forensic techniques to establish evidence of a criminal act.

Incident Response

Advance preparation must be accomplished before anyone can successfully prosecute a computer crime. **Incident response** processes and tactics must be developed for a successful reaction to some computer incident. The plan must be well documented and formally practiced. Law enforcement agencies have "first responders" whose job is to secure computer evidence. A number of computer forensic tools are available to forensic investigators and law enforcement first responders. A note is important here. If an incident is reported to law enforcement, the organization loses control of the situation—and it may become public knowledge.

Computer Investigations

A computer crime **investigation** would begin as soon as an incident report is provided to the authorities. Similar to personal and property crimes, a number of steps are required to determine if a crime has occurred and to protect evidence for prosecution if a crime has occurred. Six steps are summarized as follows:

- *Detection and containment*—review audit trails and preserve the evidence.
- *Notification of management*—report to limited number of supervisors.
- *Preliminary investigation*—determine if a crime has actually occurred.
- *Crime disclosure determination*—notify authorities if required or desired.
- *Investigation process*—identify potential suspects and witnesses; prepare for search and seizure.
- *Report generation*—provide documentation to management and law enforcement.

Evidence will be collected during the investigation phase of the incident. *Evidence* is defined as information that would be presented in a court of law to substantiate the charges. There are four general categories of evidence that might be presented in court:

- *Direct evidence*—oral testimony or written statements.
- *Real or physical evidence*—tangible objects such as tools and property.
- *Documentary evidence*—printouts and manuals.
- *Demonstrative evidence*—expert and non-expert witnesses.

Two other categories of evidence might be relevant to a computer crime or incident—corroborative and circumstantial evidence. *Corroborative evidence* supports or substantiates other case evidence, whereas *circumstantial evidence* is used for reasonable inferences to fact.

An important concept is termed the **hearsay rule**. Hearsay evidence is not based on firsthand knowledge of the witness. This information is usually obtained through some other source and is usually not admissible in court.

For evidence to be admissible in a court of law, it must pass several proofs or validations. It must be relevant, reliable, and legal. To be relevant, evidence must tend to prove or disprove facts and must be material to the case. To be reliable and acceptable, evidence must not be tainted from modifications, additions, or deletions. This problem can be resolved by creating a reliable image using a hashing process for storage devices. Lastly, evidence must have been obtained legally.

Two important processes that must be addressed when prosecuting criminal activities are the "chain of custody" and the evidence life cycle. These also apply to computer crimes. The chain of custody provides accountability and protection of evidence throughout its life cycle. Evidence must be secured in locked areas, and documentation must follow the entire trail, including information about who handled it and when. If this is not done, the evidence can become contaminated and ruled inadmissible in court. An evidence log would include the following information:

- Individuals involved.
- Evidence description.
- Evidence location.
- Evidence movement.

Any time evidence changes possession or location, a notation must be made in the evidence log. This activity might seem trivial, but cases can be lost because of sloppy handling of computer crime evidence. The evidence life cycle is intertwined with the chain of custody. It describes the phases of evidence from its initial discovery to its final disposition. There are six phases to the evidence life cycle:

- Collection.
- Identification.
- Examination.
- Logistics.
- Presentation.
- Return.

If everything has been handled properly and luck is on your side, a verdict for the plaintiff might be the result; however, computer crimes are difficult to prosecute, so don't be surprised if the defense wins. It should be obvious that considerable documentation is required, and a number of forms are available for this purpose. There are also a number of consulting organizations that provide computer forensic services if the resources are not available from local personnel.

Intrusion Detection

Intrusion detection techniques and equipment are utilized to detect and respond to computer and networking misuse. Different intrusion detection techniques provide different benefits for different situations and environments; therefore, it is essential that the security administrator deploy the security system that best matches the need. Unnecessary cost can be incurred for nonessential detection devices. The key to selecting the right security detection system is to define the specific security requirements first and then implement a system based on those requirements. In addition to detection, new products are being offered that provide for intrusion prevention capabilities. Solutions are presented in Chapter 12.

Monitoring

Internal staff can conduct network and physical monitoring; however, there are vendors that specialize in security monitoring and surveillance. Some providers deploy intrusion detection sensors at customer locations and provide security experts to monitor corporate resources such as routers and firewalls. Others place probes on the customer's networks to collect audit data from network devices. The data are transmitted in encrypted form back to the central facility, where the data are monitored continuously.

In the security monitoring application, a video camera can be mounted on top of a building, in a doorway or corridor, or in the corner of a room viewing the area being monitored. Black-and-white television is most often used, with the picture being updated every 30 to 90 seconds. This periodic refreshing of the picture is called "freeze-frame" television. It requires a much slower, less expensive telecommunications line than one that is transmitting full-motion pictures, which is similar to commercial-quality television. Video cameras are not prevention devices, but they do provide significant value in intrusion events. Investigation and prosecution can be aided with sufficient video evidence.

Some network-based intrusion detection systems consist of sensors deployed throughout a network that provide a data stream to a central console. Sensors may contain logic that collects network packets, searches for patterns of misuse, and then reports an alarm situation back to the console. Two types of sensor-based architectures include the traditional sensor design and the network node design. Sensor-based systems monitor whole network segments. They are not widely distributed because there are relatively few segments to monitor, as opposed to the sensor-based systems that are widely distributed onto every mission-critical target. Network-node systems place an agent on each managed network computer device in the network to monitor traffic bound only for that individual target.

Preemptive Activities

Network management and administration must be proactive in the fight against cybercrime threats and attacks. A considerable amount of information has been presented in this book that can be used as effective approaches to countering these situations. Incorporating the numerous suggestions will take time and resources, but not addressing the issues can cost a lot more. The following list of initiatives summarizes programs and activities that might be undertaken to counter the negative impacts of computer and network incidents. While this is a formidable list, not taking action is unacceptable. The categories include access controls, hardware, software, and management.

Access controls:
- User authentication.
- Properly defined user rights.
- Prompt removal of employee accounts upon separation.
- Require approval by management of user authorization.
- Proper registry permissions.

Hardware:
- Workstation screen locks.
- Computer keyboard locks.
- Firewalls.
- Screening routers.
- Properly configured routers.
- Properly configured modems.

Software:

- Anti-virus software.
- Anti-spyware software.
- Encryption.
- Prompt application of patches and updates.
- VPN tunneling.
- Checksums.

Management:

- Change control policy.
- Separation of duties.
- Audit logs and log reviews.
- Review open ports and service.
- Social engineering prevention.
- Employee training and awareness.

Computer Security Organizations

Computer security is a field of computer science concerned with the control of risks related to computer use. The following organizations offer tools and assistance that may be useful in conducting investigations into computer security or computer-related investigations.

- Established in 1988, the Computer Emergency Readiness Team (CERT®) Coordination Center (CERT/CC) is a center of Internet security expertise, located at the Software Engineering Institute, a federally funded research and development center operated by Carnegie Mellon University. US-CERT is a partnership between the Department of Homeland Security and the public and private sectors. Established to protect the nation's Internet infrastructure, US-CERT coordinates defense against and responses to cyber attacks across the nation.
- The High Technology Crime Investigation Association (HTCIA) is designed to encourage, promote, aid, and affect the voluntary interchange of data, information, experience, ideas, and knowledge about methods, processes, and techniques relating to investigations and security in advanced technologies among its membership.
- The International Association for Computer Information Systems (IACIS®) is an international volunteer nonprofit corporation comprised of law enforcement professionals dedicated to education in the field of forensic computer science. IACIS members represent federal, state, local, and international law enforcement professionals. Regular IACIS members have been trained in the forensic science of seizing and processing computer systems.
- The IEEE Computer Society is the world's leading organization of computer professionals. Founded in 1946, it is the largest of the 37 societies of the Institute of Electrical and Electronics Engineers (IEEE). The Computer Society's vision is to be the leading

provider of technical information and services to the world's computing professionals. The Society is dedicated to advancing the theory, practice, and application of computer and information processing technology.

- The Internet Crime Complaint Center (IC3) is a partnership between the Federal Bureau of Investigation (FBI) and the National White Collar Crime Center (NW3C).

NETWORK PROBLEM SOLVING

Many network problems can be solved by first verifying the status of the affected computers or networking components. Taking several initial steps can help the administrator in resolving network problems:

- Identify possible cockpit problems and user errors.
- Ensure that all physical connections are in place.
- Verify that the network interface card (NIC) is working.
- Warm-start the device (reload the software).
- Cold-start the device (power cycle off and on).

It is essential that a structured approach be taken when troubleshooting. These simple steps include the following:

- Prioritize the problem in relation to all other problems in the network.
- Develop information about the problem.
- Identify possible causes.
- Eliminate the possibilities, one at a time.
- Ensure that the fix does not cause other problems.
- Document the solution.

Collecting Information Methodology

The first step in solving a problem is to collect and document as much information as possible in order to have an accurate description of the situation. It is necessary to collect peripheral information that might not appear to have any impact on the situation. This includes environmental conditions that could contribute to the problem, such as heat, humidity, and possible sources of electromagnetic interference (EMI) and radio-frequency interference (RFI).

If the problem involves user interaction, it will be necessary to check the sequence of steps the user took. Before troubleshooting the physical devices and system software, attempt to recreate or confirm the problem to ensure that the problem is not user (cockpit) error.

From the information gathered for the trouble report, a structured approach can begin to list, prioritize, and examine possible causes of the reported incident. It is essential that the problem be logically evaluated, starting with the most basic causes. The first step would be to check if the network cable and power cable are connected. If they are, this would be the time to call a technician.

After checking the obvious, it would be very useful to have a troubleshooting device, such as a Flukemeter, that can be utilized to check the network cable, the NIC, the port (interface) of the device, and the wiring in the installation. Another option, if such a device is not available, is to troubleshoot the situation by using a replacement. Replacement can take longer to troubleshoot a situation because of the time necessary to remove and replace the components to see if this resolves the problem. Because it is necessary to make only one change at a time, this process could become time consuming and, likely, a replacement component is not readily available. (*Note that making multiple changes before checking the results of a single test will not reveal which change was effective.*) Both replacement and network management tools can solve problems, but the network management tool will probably allow for a quicker resolution.

Troubleshooting should progress logically. If a single device is malfunctioning, start troubleshooting with that device. If multiple devices are malfunctioning, look for a common cause, such as a centralized wiring hub. If the entire network is malfunctioning, check the network statistics against the baseline. In every case, start with the most basic and work toward the most complex. Once the problem is solved, ensure that documentation is completed and includes a list of the conditions observed, the steps taken to solve the problem, and a summary of the entire service call.

FIGURE 11-1 illustrates the process flow for troubleshooting and problem solving some network issue. This model assumes that the organization has formally established and documented all elements of the plan as presented in this chapter. This process flow is recursive in that the flow repeats until the problem is solved. The following steps detail the activities that occur at each element of the process flow:

- *Definition of the problem*—the problem should be defined in terms of a set of symptoms and potential causes. By using the baseline, it is possible to identify the location of the problem or at least know where to start the troubleshooting effort.
- *Details of the problem*—information can be collected from sources such as network management systems, protocol analyzer traces, network monitors, and network surveillance personnel.
- *Alternatives assessment*—now is the time to consider the possible problems based on the facts that have been gathered. The obvious non-issues can be eliminated at this time.
- *Problem-solving methodology*—an action plan can be developed and the most likely cause of the problem can be identified. The plan will allow for one variable to be changed at a time until all options are exhausted. Changing one variable at a time allows for the reproduction of a given solution for a specific problem. Also, if more than one change is made before a test is made, it will be impossible to determine which change made the problem disappear.
- *Results observation*—tests must be made at this module to ensure that the modifications are correcting the problem and not creating other problems. This process reiterates the process for each test and may require additional details for each cycle.
- *Problem resolution*—when the problem has been solved, the next and last step of the process flow is to document the situation. If the problem has not been solved, the process is repeated.
- *Documentation*—the final step is important because the problem may well occur again and it is essential that the troubleshooting efforts not be duplicated.

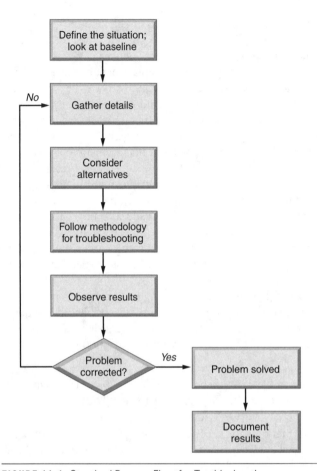

FIGURE 11-1 Standard Process Flow for Troubleshooting

Troubleshooting Documentation

Some type of electronic tracking or journal can be maintained to accumulate troubleshooting and problem-solving information, which will ensure that time is not wasted repeating work that has already been completed and that an audit trail is developed for each trouble. The information developed can also be utilized in requests for additional equipment, personnel, and training. It can also be a useful tool for training future network support personnel.

A typical method for administering such a database is to assign some unique identifier to each problem or trouble report. A trouble report would be generated for each incident and cross-referenced for recurring incidents to the same network element. The trouble report documents issues and requests for service from network users and can be used to ensure that a consistent troubleshooting methodology is being followed. A typical trouble report might include the following elements:

- A trouble report identifier.
- A preliminary description of the situation.
- Investigation and analysis of the situation.
- The service actions taken to resolve the issue.
- A summarization of the incident.

Another source of information that can be useful in troubleshooting the network is the data, usually in the form of traps or alerts, that are collected from the managed network devices. It is essential that data collected from the managed devices be stored so that problems can be tracked and trends can be analyzed. There are a number of trouble-tracking products for both voice and data communication systems available in the market today. Product solutions are described in Chapter 12. A sample list follows:

- Hewlett Packard Open View Network Node Manager (NNM 6.0).
- TAVVE Performance Reporting Module (PRM).
- Cisco Resource Management Essentials (RME).
- Remedy Action Request System (ARS) help desk ticket system.
- Remedy/Oracle–based change management system for SIO.
- Remedy/Oracle–based asset management system for SIO.
- Cisco TACACS (router access authentication security).
- Microsoft SMS tool (inventory and software distribution system).
- Cisco SYSNET (network modeling and design tool).
- Cisco Works 2000/Traffic Director (RMON Traffic Management Console).
- NetScout Fast Ethernet Probes (collect traffic data from network core).

NETWORK TESTING SUPPORT AND RESOURCES
Network Utilities and Software Routines

A number of aids are available for the network user to perform simple tests over the Internet. These include tracert and ping.

Trace route (tracert)

Tracert is a utility that traces a packet from your computer to an Internet host, showing how many hops the packet requires to reach the host and how long each hop takes. If you're visiting a Web site and pages are appearing slowly, you can use trace route to figure out where the longest delays are occurring.

The original trace route is a UNIX utility, but nearly all platforms have something similar. Windows includes a trace route utility called tracert. In Windows, you can run tracert by selecting *Start* → *Run . . .*, and then entering tracert followed by the domain name of the host. For example: *tracert www.pcwebopedia.com.*

Traceroute utilities work by sending packets with low time-to-live (TTL) fields. The TTL value specifies how many hops the packet is allowed before it is returned. When a packet can't reach its destination because the TTL value is too low, the last host returns the packet and identifies itself. By sending a series of packets and incrementing the TTL value with each successive packet, trace route finds out who all the intermediary hosts are.

PING

The utility **PING** uses ICMP messages to check the physical connectivity of the machines on a network. *Note that PING can be used in a network attack.* An example: *PING 10.10.10.1*

WHOIS

WHOIS searches across multiple registrar databases to provide registration information on millions of domain names with many different extensions, regardless of where they are registered.

IPCONFIG

IPCONFIG is a command line tool used to control the network connections on Windows 9x/ NT/2000/XP/Vista machines.

Port scan

A **port scan** is a series of messages sent by someone attempting to break into a computer to learn which computers the network services. These scans are associated with a "well-known" port number. Port scanning is a favorite approach of computer crackers and gives the assailant an idea of where to probe for weaknesses. Essentially, a port scan consists of sending a message to each port, one at a time.

Security Probes and Network Penetration Testing Tools

Instead of passively gathering network statistics like auditing tools, security probes actively test various aspects of enterprise network security and report results and suggest improvements. There are a number of security probes that perform vulnerability scanning. Three such products are SAINT, Retina, and SATAN.

SAINT® screens every live system on a network for TCP and UDP services. For each service it finds running, it launches a set of probes designed to detect anything that could allow an attacker to gain unauthorized access, create a denial of service, or gain sensitive information about the network. SAINT's vulnerability scanner provides links where you can download patches or new versions of software that will eliminate the detected vulnerabilities.

Retina® combines advanced scanning technology with the most comprehensive vulnerability database to deliver the strongest level of security protection for even the most complex environments. Retina's comprehensive network vulnerability assessment and prevention drives business continuity by identifying and prioritizing security threats arising from software vulnerabilities, system misconfigurations and policy noncompliance.

SATAN® is able to probe networks for security and weak spots. It was written to analyze UNIX and TCP/IP-based systems. Once it has found a way to get inside a network, it continues to probe all TCP/IP machines within that network. After all vulnerabilities have been identified, it generates a report that details the results. It also suggests methods for eliminating the vulnerabilities.

Although SATAN was developed as a tool for network managers to detect weaknesses in their own networks, it is widely available on the Internet and can easily be employed by hackers and crackers seeking to attack weaknesses in target networks.

Additional security tools available include the following:

- Portmap—converts RPC program numbers into Internet port numbers.
- Sara—third-generation network security analysis tool.
- Scanssh—supports scanning a list of addresses and networks for open proxies.
- Screend—Internet (IP) gateway screening daemon.
- Securelib—checks the address of the machine initiating a connection to ensure it is allowed to connect, based on the contents of the configuration file.
- TCP wrappers—a tool commonly used on UNIX systems to monitor and filter connections to network services.
- Xinetd—access control and other functions for stopping connections from evil bad guys.

SECURITY TOOLS

Network monitors, network analyzers, and cable testers each provide the network manager and technician with a different suite of tools. Security tools such as sniffers are also available in hardware instruments. A network-connected device operating in promiscuous mode can capture all frames on a network, not just frames addressed directly to it. A network analyzer operates in this mode to capture network traffic for evaluation and to measure traffic for statistical analysis. A hacker may also use such a device to capture network traffic for unscrupulous activities. Network traffic can be encrypted to protect against such eavesdropping. The capabilities of these devices are listed in the following sections. Different types of surveillance and test equipment can be utilized in this war against the various threats. These devices include sniffers, network analyzers, monitors, and protocol analyzers. These devices are available, in many configurations, capabilities, and price points from a multitude of vendors.

Sniffer

A **sniffer** is a program and/or device that monitors data traveling over a network. Sniffers can be used both for legitimate network management functions and for stealing information off a network. Unauthorized sniffers can be extremely dangerous to a network's security because they are virtually impossible to detect and can be inserted almost anywhere. This makes them a favorite weapon in the hacker's arsenal. On Internet (TCP/IP) networks, where they sniff packets, they're often called *packet sniffers*.

Protocol Analyzer

Historically, a **protocol analyzer** has been a great tool for troubleshooting network problems and monitoring for excessive bandwidth usage. Additionally, a protocol analyzer can also fight virus and hack attacks. Along with keeping track of network devices and up-time, this analyzer can also locate network security breaches and help identify and isolate virus-infected systems. It is possible to enhance network security by augmenting firewalls and other perimeter defenses with an analyzer. Often, protocol and network analyzer functions are available in the same test equipment.

A protocol analyzer displays and collects network activity by decoding the different protocols from devices on the network. These data are usually available in both binary and hexadecimal formats. The resulting activity can be presented in human-readable form. Most mature analyzers also include some statistical reporting functionality. By watching network traffic, understanding bandwidth utilization, and reviewing connection dynamics, administrators can easily determine what device is causing the problem and why. A network incident could be a simple configuration or traffic-volume problem, and not an attack.

Network Monitoring

Properly securing a network is less expensive than rebuilding a corrupted one. Network security tools protect the organization's networks from unauthorized users and hackers. There are several types of **network monitoring** security tools available to accomplish this task, including access control systems, data encryption, digital certificates, and vulnerability scanners. When selecting network security tools, it is important to determine which are best suited for the network being protected.

Encryption is ideal for protecting credit card numbers and other data. Firewalls provide good protection from the outside but provide little protection from internal threats. Access control helps secure a network from the inside. One tool will rarely get the job done, but a combination that includes all three of the aforementioned functions can provide an acceptable level of security.

There are a wealth of products and services that are available on the market for protecting the organization's computer and networking assets. Functions provided by these include the following:

- Access control.
- Anti-hacker.
- Audit trail.
- Authentication.
- Auto logoff.
- Cryptographic.
- Data encryption.
- Data integrity.
- Encryption.

- Filtering.
- Monitoring and reporting.
- Operating system security.
- Password protection.
- Risk analysis management.
- User account restrictions.
- Virus protection.

Network monitors provide capabilities of collecting network statistics, providing diagnostic tools, and processing of network packets. Another tool that is being used by hackers and network managers is a **keylogger**. This hardware or software component can capture all keystrokes from targeted devices. The legality of this method is suspect.

Network Analyzers

A **network analyzer** is a monitoring, testing, and troubleshooting device used by network administrators and technicians. This device is attached to a network for the purpose of capturing network traffic. Captured frames can be displayed in raw or filtered form. These devices are normally portable and can be inserted in many places in the network. The data obtained depend on the location of insertion in the network.

Network analyzers operate in promiscuous mode, as previously stated, and listen to all traffic on that particular portion of the configuration. The user can choose to capture frames transmitted by a particular network computer or frames that carry data or information for a particular application or service. The captured traffic is then monitored to evaluate network performance, locate bottlenecks, or track security breaches.

Analyzers are available in a number of configurations and possess many different features. Low-end analyzers are usually designed for traditional Ethernet and token-ring LANs. High-end devices are capable of addressing a variety of network types, including Frame Relay, ATM, and Fast Ethernet networks. WAN protocol analyzers are designed to handle a diversity of link configurations and a variety of data link protocols. (*Note that an analyzer product can consist of either hardware or software or both.*)

Some of the high-end network analyzers could cost tens of thousands of dollars. Software-based analyzers, however, are available as freeware. Many network analyzers are available on the Internet by the hacker community for the express purpose of capturing sensitive information on networks, such as passwords sent in the clear.

Network analyzers provide the following features:

- Collect network statistics.
- Use SNMP to query managed devices.
- Generate traffic for an analysis.
- Analyze network statistics.
- Analyze types of devices on the network.
- Analyze types of collisions.

- Analyze types of errors.
- Identify top broadcasting hosts.
- Provide diagnostic tools.
- Troubleshoot managed network devices.

Cable testers provide for the following measurements:

- *Wire map*—provides the basis for checking improperly connected wires, including crossed wires, reversed pairs, and crossed wire pairs.
- *Attenuation*—the loss of signal power over the distance of the cable. To measure attenuation on a cable, the cable tester must be assisted by a second test unit called a signal injector, or remote.
- *Noise*—refers to unwanted electrical signals that alter the shape of the transmitted signal on a network. Noise can be produced by fluorescent lights, radios, electronic devices, heaters, and air conditioning units.
- *Near-end crosstalk (NEXT)*—refers to a measure of interference from other wire pairs. The signal bleeds from one set of wires to the other, causing crosstalk.
- *Distance measurement*—specifies maximum cable lengths for network media. Cables that are too long can cause delays in transmission and network errors.

MANAGING THE NETWORK

As stated previously, network management is a collection of activities that are required when managing the communications network. Functions that are performed as part of network management accordingly include:

- Controlling.
- Planning.
- Allocating.
- Deploying.
- Coordinating.
- Network planning.
- Bandwidth management.
- Monitoring the resources of a network.
- Predetermined traffic routing to support load balancing.
- Cryptographic key distribution authorization.

Additional major management functions discussed later in this section include:

- Accounting management.
- Configuration management.
- Fault management.
- Security management.
- Performance management.

Network Management Tools

Network management tools allow for the performance of management functions such as monitoring network traffic levels, monitoring software usage, finding efficiencies, and finding bottlenecks. The following list identifies the top network management platforms currently used to support network management. Additional details are presented in Chapter 12.

- HP OpenView.
- IBM NetView (mainframe).
- Sun Soltice/SunNet Manager.
- Tivoli Enterprise.
- IBM NetView (AIX).
- CA Unicenter TNG.
- Compuware Ecotools.
- BMC Patrol.
- Boole & Baggage Command/Post.

Additional tools utilized to conduct network management operations are:

- CiscoWorks.
- Network General Sniffer.
- RMON Probes.
- Bay Optivity.
- Cabletron Spectrum.
- Locally developed software.

Network managers need a comprehensive set of tools to help them perform the various network tasks. Most tools can be classified as primarily hardware or software, and most hardware test instruments are supported by software. Network management software is categorized into three different types: device management, system management, and application management.

The most common categories of hardware tools for network management are cable testers, network monitors, and network analyzers. Other sophisticated network management tools can be used for daily network management and controls. These management tools typically have three components:

- *Agent*—the client software part of the management tool. The agent resides on each managed network device.
- *Manager*—a centralized software component that manages the network. The management software stores the information collected from the managed devices in a standardized database.
- *Administration system*—the centralized management component that collects and analyzes the information from the managers. Most administration systems provide information, alerts, traps, and the ability to make programmable modifications to the network components.

The two main management protocols used with network management systems are **simple network management protocol (SNMP)** and **common management information protocol (CMIP)**. SNMP allows management agents that reside on the managed devices to provide information to SNMP management software. SNMP utilizes a management information base (MIB) for maintaining the statistics and information that SNMP reports and uses. Typically stored measurement items include network errors, system utilization statistics, packets transmitted/received, and numerous other items of information that may be useful for a particular network component. Additional details concerning SNMP and CMIP are provided in Chapter 13.

Network administrators use SNMP to manage devices such as wiring hubs and routers. Management tasks might include:

- Network traffic monitoring.
- Remote management capabilities.
- Port isolation for testing purposes.
- Automatic disconnection of nodes.
- Automatic reconfiguration based on time of day.

Network managers can provide network topology maps, historical management information, traps and alerts, and traffic monitoring throughout the network.

Network Management System

Any network, whether it is a LAN, MAN, or WAN, is really a collection of individual components working together. Network management helps maintain this harmony, ensuring consistent reliability and availability of the network, as well as timely transmission and routing of data. A **network management system (NMS)** is defined as the systems or actions that help maintain, characterize, or troubleshoot a network. The three primary objectives to network management are to support systems users, to keep the network operating efficiently, and to provide cost-effective solutions to an organization's telecommunications requirements.

A large network cannot be engineered and managed by human effort alone. The complexity of such a system dictates the use of automated network management tools. The urgency of the need for such tools and the difficulty of supplying such tools increase if the network includes equipment from multiple vendors and manufacturers.

Network management can be accomplished by utilizing dedicated devices, by host computers on the network, by people, or by some combination of these. No matter how network management is performed, it usually includes the following key functions.

- Network control.
- Network monitoring.
- Network troubleshooting.
- Network statistical reporting.

These functions assume the role of network watchdog, boss, diagnostician, and statistician. These functions are closely interrelated and are often performed on the same device.

Network Management System Elements

This section begins with an overview of network management, with a focus on hardware and software tools, and organized systems of such tools, which aid the human network manager in this difficult task. Considerable information concerns the requirements for network management; the general architecture of a network management system; and SNMP, which is the standardized software package for supporting network management.

The term *network management* has traditionally been used to specify real-time network surveillance and control; network traffic management; functions necessary to plan, implement, operate, and maintain the network; and systems management.

Network management supports the users' needs for activities that enable managers to plan, organize, supervise, control, and account for the use of interconnection services. It also provides for the ability to respond to changing requirements, such as ensuring that facilities are available for predictable communications behavior and providing for information protection, which includes the authentication of sources and destinations of transmitted data.

The task of network management involves setting up and running a network, monitoring network activities, controlling the network to provide acceptable performance, and ensuring high availability and fast response time to the network users.

Network equipment manufacturers have developed an impressive array of network management products over the past several years. As with most telecommunications technologies, network management began as a proprietary system, but the real growth started when the Internet community introduced SNMP in the late 1990s.

An effective network management system requires trained personnel to interpret the results. An effective network management system will include most of the following elements:

- An inventory of circuits and equipment.
- A trouble report receiving and logging process.
- A trouble history file.
- A trouble diagnostic, testing, and isolation facility and procedures.
- A hierarchy of trouble clearance and escalation procedures.
- An activity log for retaining records of all major changes.
- An alarm reporting and processing facility.

Not every network management system will have all of these elements, but most systems will contain these functions to some degree. The more complex the network, the more likely the functions will be automated on a mechanized system.

Database and DBMS Protection

Access to a database or the database management system can be controlled by the use of access rights. Logon restrictions and directory or file access rights are important techniques administrators and supervisors use to protect data against malicious or accidental loss or corruption. Users should never be given more access rights than needed to handle the task at hand. Many users only need the right to access and read in a program directory. Excessive or blanket rights permissions can lead to problems such as overwrites, corruption, and virus attacks on the database. Although this might get old, an off-site backup program is required for database restoration, in the event of some security breach. Identify theft and fraud is often the end result of an attack on a database.

NETWORK MANAGEMENT AND CONTROL

Network management is a collection of activities that are required to plan, design, organize, maintain, and expand the network. LAN network management was introduced in Chapter 6. A network management and control system consists of a collection of techniques, policies, procedures, and systems that are integrated to ensure that the network delivers its intended functions. At the heart of the system is a database of information, either on paper or mechanized. The database consists of several related files that allow the network managers to have the information they need to exercise control over its functions. A network control system has five major functions:

- Managing network information.
- Managing network performance.
- Monitoring circuits and equipment on the network.
- Isolating trouble when it occurs.
- Restoring service to end users.

Network management is generally concerned with monitoring the operation of components in the network, reporting on the events that occur during the network operation, and controlling the operational characteristics of the network and its components. Taking pre-emptive precautions may be costly in the short term, but they save time and resources when problems arise, prevent equipment problems, and ensure data security. A preemptive approach can prevent additional expense and frustration when trying to identify the causes of failures. Functions include monitoring, reporting, and controlling. Additionally, three areas of protection should be addressed. These include intruders, theft, and natural disasters.

Monitoring

Monitoring involves determining the status and processing characteristics currently associated with the different physical and logical components of the network. Depending on the type of component in question, monitoring can be done either by continuously checking the operation of the component or by detecting the occurrence of extraordinary events that occur during the network operations.

Reporting

The results of monitoring activities must be reported, or made available, to either a network administrator or to network management software operating on some machine in the network.

Controlling

Based on the results of monitoring and reporting functions, the network administrator or network management software should be able to modify the operational characteristics of the network and its components. These modifications should make it possible to resolve problems, improve network performance, and continue normal operation of the network.

Protect Against Intruders

Intruders can be described as unauthorized visitors who are not members of the normal user community. These people can cause three problems: (1) theft of equipment, software, or data; (2) destruction of the same; and (3) the viewing of sensitive data and information.

Intruders can use various methods to gain access to a computer or network facility. Access can be physical or electronic, and there are methods to counter both. Intruders can be prevented from accessing a LAN by ensuring that users protect passwords, log off when not at the workstation, and take security seriously. There are operating system parameters that can be set to limit time-of-day access and device-specific logons. Users must be trained to take security serious. They should be aware of the consequences of leaving a workstation logged on. Most workstations allow for a screen-saver login. User accounts can be set to require a scheduled changing of passwords.

Theft Protection

Theft can be the result of espionage by competitors, other governments, internal personal, partners, and contractors. The bottom line is the asset must be protected from theft by any source because the alternative can be devastating to the organization's operations. This protection must include the data and the hardware that is used to store that data. Not only is the equipment valuable, but it can take a long time to acquire new hardware and reload the data. Reloading databases and verifying the integrity of the data can be very time-consuming. There are a number of obvious solutions to the theft problem; however, the solution should not cost more than the resource is worth, and the value may not be in real dollars.

It is necessary for the administrator to keep track of users. The administrator must know when users leave the company's employ or change roles. The accounts need to be modified to reflect the current access levels. Audit trails must be maintained that can identify system disruptions. Theft of storage devices can be detected if they are removed from the network. There are a number of software surveillance tools that can accomplish this task. It may not be popular, but surveillance cameras are an option at entrance points.

Natural Disaster Protection

There are some natural disasters in which a good plan is worthless because of the magnitude of the disaster. The best plan is to allocate sufficient protection based on normal circumstances. It is possible to determine where flood and earthquake zones exist. Hurricanes and tornadoes cannot be predicted; however, there are locations that are prone to each of these natural occurrences. The physical construction of the facility should be a consideration. Computer rooms and network demarcations can be located on second floors. Fire detection and suppression devices can be installed. Electrical failures should be considered, and backup systems can be installed. The bottom line is to spend no more than the asset is worth or the cost to replace it. Last but not least, off-site backup of data is a must.

COMMON MANAGEMENT INFORMATION PROTOCOL

The International Organization for Standardization's (ISO's) approach to network management is CMIP. This protocol defines the notion of objects, which are elements to be managed. The key areas of network management as proposed by the ISO are divided into five **specific management functional areas (SMFAs)**:

- *Accounting management*—records and reports usage of network resources.
- *Configuration management*—defines and controls network component configurations and parameters.
- *Fault management*—detects and isolates network problems.
- *Performance management*—monitors, analyzes, and controls network data production.
- *Security management*—monitors and controls access to network resources.

Accounting Management

Accounting management concerns the ability to identify costs and establish charges related to the use of network resources. In many enterprise networks, individual divisions or cost centers are charged for the use of network services. These are internal accounting issues rather than actual cash transfers, but they are important to the participating users. The network manager needs to be able to track the use of network resources to ensure that the network is functioning efficiently and effectively. Steps toward appropriate accounting management include:

- Measuring utilization of all important network resources.
- Analysis of the results for insights into current usage patterns.
- Setting of usage quotas.
- Corrections made to reach optimal access practices.
- Ongoing measurement of resource use to yield billing information.

Configuration Management

Modern data communications networks consist of individual components and logical subsystems that can be configured to perform many different applications. **Configuration management** is concerned with the ability to identify the various components that comprise the network configuration; to process additions, changes, or deletions to the configuration; to report on the status of components; and to start up or shut down all or any part of the network.

Each network device has a variety of versions associated with it. A workstation could have version information concerning the operating system, communications hardware and software, and network protocols. Configuration management subsystems store this information in a database for easy access. When a problem surfaces, this database can be searched for clues that may help solve the problem.

Fault Management

Fault management concerns the ability to detect, isolate, and correct abnormal conditions that occur in the network environment. Central to the definition of fault management is the fundamental concept of a fault. Faults are to be distinguished from errors. A *fault* is an abnormal condition that requires management attention to fix. A fault is usually indicated by a failure to operate or by excessive errors. It is usually possible to compensate for errors using the error-control mechanisms of the various protocols.

Because faults cause downtime or unacceptable network degradation, fault management is the most widely implemented of the ISO network management elements. Fault management involves:

- Determining symptoms and isolating the problem.
- Fixing the problem and testing the solution on all important subsystems.
- Recording the detection and resolution of the problem.

Performance Management

Data communications networks are composed of many and varied components, which must intercommunicate and share data and resources. **Performance management** concerns the ability to evaluate activities of the network and to make adjustments to improve the network's performance. Performance variables that might be provided include network throughput, user response times, and line utilization. Performance management involves three main steps:

- Performance data are gathered on variables of interest to network administrators.
- The data are analyzed to determine normal (baseline) levels.
- Appropriate performance thresholds are determined for each important variable so that exceeding these thresholds indicates a situation requiring attention.

Performance management of a computer network comprises two broad functional categories: monitoring and controlling. *Monitoring* is the function that tracks activities on the network. The *controlling* function enables performance management to make adjustments to improve network performance.

Management entities continually monitor performance variables. When a performance threshold is exceeded, an alert is generated and sent to the network management system. Performance management also permits proactive methods using network simulation software.

Such simulation can alert administrators to impending problems so counteractive measures can be taken.

Two measurements that are necessary in performance management are system effectiveness and system availability. A system is effective if it provides good performance, is available when needed, and is reliable when it is used.

Security Management

Security management concerns the ability to monitor and control access to network resources, including generating, distributing, and storing encryption keys. Passwords and other authorization or access-control information must be maintained and distributed. Security management is involved with the collection, storage, and examination of audit records and security logs.

Security management subsystems work by partitioning network resources into authorized and unauthorized areas. For some users, access to any network resources is inappropriate because such users are usually company outsiders. For internal users, access to information originating from a particular department, such as payroll, is inappropriate.

Security management subsystems perform several functions. They identify sensitive network resources and determine mappings between sensitive network resources and user sets. They also monitor access points to sensitive network resources and log inappropriate access to sensitive network resources.

NETWORK MANAGEMENT STANDARDS ORGANIZATIONS

Many organizations today deal with network management standardization. The roles played by these organizations range from setting the network management standards to promoting acceptance of the standards. The organizations that play a role in network management include:

- American National Standards Institute (ANSI).
- International Organization for Standardization (ISO).
- Institute of Electrical and Electronic Engineers 802 Committee (IEEE 802).
- Internet Activities Board (IAB).
- International Telecommunications Union Telecommunications Sector (ITU-T).
- National Institute of Standards and Technology (NIST).
- Open Systems Foundation (OSF).

The OSF was an organization founded in 1988 to create an open standard for an implementation of the UNIX operating system. These and other network management organizations are described in Chapter 13.

CHAPTER SUMMARY

The network administrator has a broad range of responsibilities that include network planning, monitoring, and maintenance. Typical activities revolve around network configurations, user connectivity, security, data and asset protection, problem solving, and troubleshooting.

Network problems and security issues can be resolved in one of two ways: preventing the situation before it happens through network planning and management or fixing the problem after it happens through troubleshooting techniques.

Troubleshooting techniques that are effective in solving problems in the enterprise network include the following:

- Implement a program for system upgrades and change control.
- Develop a baseline for the enterprise network.
- Use a systematic approach to isolate and correct network problems.
- Look at various alternatives and develop a hypothesis rather than getting tunnel vision.
- Change only one attribute at a time when troubleshooting and test each change thoroughly.
- Document the entire troubleshooting incident with the discoveries and conclusions.

Hardware and software solutions that can be utilized in the troubleshooting and problem-solving environment include protocol analyzers, monitors, sniffers, cable testers, specialty tools, and network management systems.

Computer and network incidents could involve the use of forensic techniques to recover and protect evidence in the event criminal activities have occurred or are suspected. Specialized data collection forms are used in this endeavor.

KEY TERMS

accounting management	investigation	Retina
baseline	IPCONFIG	SAINT
common management information protocol (CMIP)	keylogger	SATAN
	monitoring	security audit
computer security audit	network analyzer	security management
configuration management	network management	simple network management
data migration	network management system (NMS)	protocol (SNMP)
fault management	network monitoring	sniffer
forensic analysis	performance management	specific management functional
hearsay rule	PING	area (SMFA)
incident response	port scan	tracert
intrusion detection	protocol analyzer	WHOIS

SECURITY REVIEW QUESTIONS

1. A(n) _____ is a manual or systematic measurable technical assessment of a system or application.

2. _____ is a collection of activities that are required to plan, design, organize, control, maintain, and expand the communications network.

3. _____ consists of a cycle of data gathering and processing of evidence that has been gathered from some incident.

4. A(n) _____ displays and collects network activity by decoding the different protocols from devices on the network.

5. _____ processes and tactics must be developed for a successful response to some computer incident.

6. _____ concerns the ability to monitor and control access to network resources, including generating, distributing, and storing encryption keys.

7. Identify the five specific management functional areas (SMFAs).

8. _____ concerns the ability to detect, isolate, and correct abnormal conditions that occur in the network environment.

9. _____ concerns the ability to monitor and control access to network resources, including generating, distributing, and storing encryption keys.

10. A(n) _____ is a program and/or device that monitor data traveling over a network.

RESEARCH ACTIVITIES

1. Use the security audit in Appendix A to conduct an audit on some organization.

2. Develop a baseline for some organization or department.

3. Identify three network management systems, and develop a comparison of features and cost.

4. Identify a real forensic activity that addresses a network investigation.

5. Identify three intrusion detection systems, and provide a feature/cost comparison.

6. Identify five software products that accomplish network management. Provide an overview of each product.

7. Provide an overview of the five SMFAs. Provide examples.

8. Provide a functionality comparison for a sniffer, an analyzer, and a monitor.

9. Provide an overview of the NIST standards as they apply to network management and security.

10. Identify five entities that have experienced some network or computer disaster. Describe the corrective action taken.

PART FOUR

SECURITY RESOURCES, EDUCATION, AND STANDARDS

CHAPTER 12

Security Solutions for Digital Resources

🔒 CHAPTER CONTENTS

- Identify hardware and software security solutions.
- Understand the issues relating to the protection of digital resources.
- See why the procurement process and project management are important aspects of a security system implementation.
- Become familiar with the vendors and products that support computer security.
- Evaluate security solutions for various computer and network configurations.
- Look at the various security technologies that are available for digital resources.

INTRODUCTION

A number of system vendors such as IBM, Cisco, Sun Microsystems, Symantec, Network Associates, and Hewlett-Packard provide hardware and software solutions oriented toward an organization's security. Hardware, software, and management solutions addressing computer and network are presented in this chapter.

Managers and administrators must have an in-depth understanding of the issues that relate to security management of computer and network resources. Security solutions can be very expensive and time-consuming to implement and maintain. It is essential that all options and alternatives be fully investigated before attempting a security solution.

Security and quality control solutions can be developed and implemented in-house or provided by some external provider. Many organizations elect to outsource computer security systems. A cost/benefit analysis would be required before making such a critical decision.

Two very important aspects of procuring, installing, and implementing security systems are the procurement process and the project management process. Missing or omitting steps in these processes can be devastating to a successful implementation of a security system.

(*Note that software and hardware in this very volatile environment frequently change, and vendors provide different options for their products and services. Readers and developers should determine the most current details and specifications from reliable sources.*)

UNDERSTANDING THE ISSUES

When evaluating potential solutions to be implemented in an organization's computer and network, *ignorance is not bliss*. Security and network managers must possess a general understanding of the computer security requirements and the various product offerings. The SANS organization has published a list of questions that are relevant for identifying security solutions. These solutions could address such diverse issues such as hardware, software, networks, policy, procedures, management, and intrusions. These are available at the *SANS.org* Web site. A short list follows [SANS, 2008]:

- What is the best firewall?
- Explain the DMZ.
- What is a bastion host?
- What is a gateway architecture?
- How does a reverse proxy work?
- What are TCP wrappers?
- Explain IP spoofing.
- Explain fport.
- What does subseven mean?
- What is a war dialer?
- What is OS fingerprinting?
- What is password cracking?
- What is Snort?
- What is Netcat?
- What is Dsniff?
- What is Bluetooth?
- What is CIDR?
- What is a VLAN?
- What is MPLS?
- Explain social engineering.
- What is a security policy?
- Identify and understand security threats and vulnerabilities.
- Where can information on HIPAA and other security policies be found?

SECURITY SOLUTION CATEGORIES

An organization can either incorporate security guidance into its general project management processes or react to security failures. It is increasingly difficult to respond to new threats by simply adding new security controls. Security control is no longer centralized at the perimeter. Meeting security requirements now depends on the coordinated actions of multiple security devices, applications and supporting infrastructure, end-users, and system operations. Reengineering a system to incorporate security is a time-consuming and expensive alternative.

There are numerous categories of security solutions for addressing almost any issue occurring in an organization. A comprehensive list of these categories includes the following:

- Application security.
- Business continuity and disaster recovery.
- CLAS consultancy.
- Compliance.
- Computer forensics.
- Cryptography.
- Data protection.
- E-commerce security.
- Education and training.
- Governance.
- Incidence management.
- Information assurance.
- Information security management.
- Intrusion detection/intrusion prevention.
- ISO 17799.
- IT audit.
- IT security.
- Legal.
- Network security.
- Penetration testing.
- Risk analysis.
- Risk management.
- Security architecture.
- Security engineering.
- Security project management.
- Security sales, marketing, and business development.
- Senior security management.
- Wireless security.

COMPANIES PROVIDING SECURITY SOLUTIONS

With the rising number of people and hosts gaining access to the Internet, the basic integrity of the site must be maintained. Many of the security incidents that happen on the Internet could have been avoided by installing security patches that are available from vendors. It is important to get the recent patches and ensure that your systems are configured properly. With intruders and their underground networks having quick access to security vulnerabilities, it is important that administrators have security information available and not rely on just one organization.

There are numerous hardware, software, network, and management providers of security solutions. A perusal of the Web reveals many hits when searching for "security solutions." A short list follows:

- Cisco Systems, Inc.
- Computer Associates.
- Hewlett-Packard.
- IBM.
- Internet Security Systems.
- Intrusion.
- Lancope.
- NetIQ.
- Network Security Wizards.
- SUN.
- Symantec.
- Tripwire.

SECURITY SYSTEM PROCUREMENT

A number of discrete steps are required to initiate and complete a successful procurement of any system. This is especially true when procuring a computer and network security product. Steps for government purchasing can be located at *www.purchasing.tas.gov.au/buyingforgovernment/*. The major steps to accomplish the procurement tasks include:

- Identifying the need and planning the purchase.
- Developing the specification.
- Selecting the purchasing method.
- Purchasing documentation.
- Inviting, clarifying, and closing offers.
- Evaluating offers.
- Selecting the successful vendor.
- Negotiations.
- Contract management.

The next section identifies the various activities that should occur at each step of the process. Additionally, someone in the organization must take responsibility for managing this process. Of particular importance is the level of authority possessed by the project manager. Missing an activity or not properly managing the process can result in failure of the project. As a note, government procurement requirements are usually much more stringent than those in commercial organizations.

PROCUREMENT CHECKLIST FOR SECURITY SYSTEMS

There are a number of specific tasks for each step in the procurement process for security systems and components. This section provides a list of these functions for each major procurement task.

Identifying the need and planning the purchase

- Analyze need accurately.
- Use functional and performance requirements.
- Improve consultation with users.
- Obtain clear statement of work and definition of need.
- Obtain appropriate approvals before undertaking process.
- Improve forecasting, planning, and consultation with users.
- Improve communication with potential vendors.
- Implement best practice policies, guidelines, and practices.
- Maintain ethical environment.
- Put suitable controls and reviews in place.

Developing the specification

- Ensure specification is consistent with needs analysis.
- Be familiar with requirements.
- Improve market knowledge.
- Implement a control mechanism to review specification before release.
- Use a Request for Information to clarify requirements (be careful not to infringe intellectual property rights or copyright).

Selecting the purchasing method

- Seek industry participation.
- Clearly identify the evaluation criteria in Request for Proposals (RFPs).
- Provide staff with appropriate training and experience.

Purchasing documentation

- Use standard documentation.
- Select appropriate documentation for purchase type (i.e., goods, services, goods and services, or information technology related).
- Assess and allocate risks appropriately.
- Use commercially acceptable terms.
- Provide staff with appropriate vendor planning and procurement skills.
- Review vendor documents before issuing them, and ensure evaluation criteria contain the critical factors on which assessment of vendors will be based.

Inviting, clarifying, and closing offers

- Implement standardized procedures for responding to enquiries.
- Provide staff with appropriate vendor management training and experience.
- Respond in a timely manner to enquiries.
- Allow adequate time for vendors to respond.
- Answer queries in writing, and provide copies to all potential vendors.
- Ensure all potential vendors are provided with any addenda.
- Establish formal security procedures.
- Train staff in their obligations.
- Perform regular audits and reviews of security processes.
- Advise vendors of security measures.
- Use appropriate vendor advertisement strategy to increase competition.
- Provide potential vendors with advance notice of vendor requests.
- Review specifications or conditions.
- Seek feedback from known suppliers on their nonresponse.

Evaluating offers

- Provide staff with appropriate vendor assessment and evaluation training and experience.
- Maintain, audit, and review evaluation procedures.
- Ensure evaluation committee members declare any conflicts of interest.
- Maintain, audit, and review security procedures.
- Ensure evaluation committee members understand and sign confidentiality agreements.
- Develop functional and performance specifications.
- Ensure evaluation criteria are appropriate and measurable.

Selecting the successful vendor

- Provide staff with appropriate tender evaluation, financial, and technical skills training and commercial expertise.
- Reject unacceptable offers.
- Perform financial, technical, and company evaluations before awarding contract.
- Ensure that procurement review committee reviews vendor and selection process prior to awarding contract.
- Ensure users are involved in the evaluation/selection process.

Negotiations

- Provide staff with training in contract planning and management.
- Define terms carefully.
- Record each party's obligations.
- Clarify all ambiguities before signing the contract.

- Look at alternatives to share risk.
- Distinguish between essential and nonessential goals and requirements.
- Establish baseline before negotiations.
- Distinguish essential goals from others.
- Consider variations to contract.
- Negotiate commercial terms.
- Check final draft of contract with successful vendor.
- Keep records of all negotiations and agreements.

Contract management

- Agree on prices and the basis of prices.
- Agree on a formula for calculating variations.
- Seek legal redress if non-acceptance causes loss.
- Negotiate but retain integrity of the contract.
- Hold regular inspections/meetings, and ensure progress reports are timely.
- Confirm verbal acceptance of contract with written advice.
- Ensure approvals are received before allowing work to start.
- Ensure all contract amendments are issued in writing.
- Record all discussions and negotiations.
- Confirm instructions in writing.
- Ensure suitable clauses are included in the contract.
- Check that all obligations are covered in the contract.
- Agree on responsibilities.
- Implement appropriate safety standards and programs.
- Include appropriate packaging instructions in specification.
- Agree on insurance cover for supplier to provide.
- Accept delivery only after inspection.
- Know when title of goods is transferred to buyer.
- Follow and maintain fraud control procedures.

SECURITY SYSTEM PROJECT MANAGEMENT

Software errors can be introduced by miscommunications and misunderstandings during the planning, development, testing, and maintenance of the security system components. The likelihood of these situations increases as more system components have to satisfy security requirements. Project managers should consider the additional communications requirements, linkage among life cycle activities, and the potential usage environment as these items relate to security needs.

A major project management objective is to enhance an existing process by describing the security role for project checkpoints and deliverables, as well as discussing how security requirements affect project planning and monitoring. For organizations planning to make security a higher priority, project managers need to address how that change affects the following [Lipner, 2005]:

- Requirements and scope.
- The technical plan:
  - Project life cycle (deliverables and sequencing of deliverables).
  - Activities required to complete deliverables.
- Resources:
  - Skills needed.
  - Facilities, tools.
- Estimates:
  - Duration of resource requirements.
  - Other related estimates such as size and defects.
- Project and product risks.

Additional details and explanations are provided for each of these five major areas in the following sections.

Requirements and Scope

Security's impact on scope is influenced by the type and number of threats, by the sophistication and resources available to the attacker, and by the desired response to an attack. The scope is influenced by the desired response to attack. A passive response does not depend on the system having knowledge of an attack and is typically preventive. An active response is an action that takes place when a fault is detected. The level of assurance required affects all aspects of project management. In practice, the assurance level depends on the consequences of a security failure.

The Technical Plan

The nature of threats and their consequences affect both planning and resources. There should be a close tie between the outcome of risk analysis and requirements: risk analysis helps define the scope for security in terms of the threats to be considered, the response desired, and the assurance level required for that response. The factors involved with a risk assessment that is developed early in the development process are predominantly business rather than technical. Project management needs to ensure stakeholder participation in such activities.

Resources

The development environment requires a level of security commensurate with the planned security level of the product being produced. Appropriate controls and configuration management of the development artifacts are essential.

Security expertise on most projects is limited and may be an internal or a contracted service. The allocation of that resource is often difficult (even when security activity is limited to networks, authentication, and access control), but when security has to be incorporated into application development, that expertise is spread much thinner. An increase in the level of assurance can significantly affect the both the security and software engineering expertise required.

Estimates

An increase in the required assurance level can have a significant impact on costs and schedules, because such a change affects the development skills required, the tool support, development practices, and the procedures required to demonstrate that assurance. Cost-saving strategies such as reuse of existing components or general-purpose commercial components may not be applicable for medium- and high-assurance systems.

Risk analysis and mitigation have to be closely coupled with business risks and business operations. Hence, that connection must be maintained over the duration of the project. Software vulnerabilities may be intentionally inserted during in-house or contracted development. These vulnerabilities can be much more difficult to discover. Change and configuration management procedures provide some assurance for internal development. Some security risks are inherent in the operating environment or with the desired functionality and hence are unavoidable.

Project Management

Poor management of requirements scope is another frequent cause for project failure. Security mechanisms that mitigate a specific risk may create additional ones. Design decisions should involve a risk assessment to identify any new threats that require mediation, as well as the analysis of the operational costs after the system is deployed.

Generally, there are six project phases to a project life cycle. These include:

- *Planning*—requirements set forth.
- *Acquisition*—gather information on products and select a solution.
- *Pilot*—test the potential solution in a safe environment.
- *Deployment*—install agents and consoles in the production environment.
- *Operation*—monitor and respond to threats; ongoing operation.
- *Maintenance*—upgrades; signature updates.

FIGURE 12-1 shows in flowchart form the major steps involved in the project management process for a security system. (*Note that his process flow applies to the planning phase of the project life cycle.*)

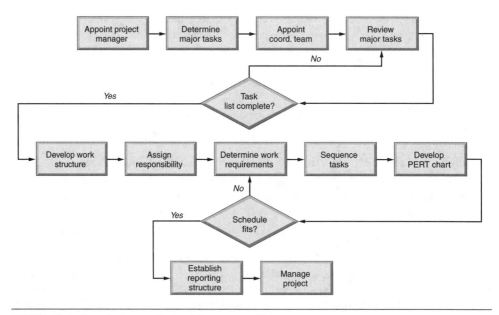

FIGURE 12-1 Security System Project Management Steps

SOFTWARE SECURITY SOLUTIONS

Searches for security software solutions result in numerous categories and features of products and services. A short list of these solutions includes the following:

- Anti-spam.
- Anti-virus.
- Audit trail.
- Best practices repository.
- Custom user interface.
- Customizable functionality.
- Customizable reporting.
- Data import/export.
- File access control.
- Financial data protection.
- Legacy system integration.
- Multiple standard compliance capabilities.
- Preventive maintenance scheduling.
- Real-time monitoring.
- Reporting.
- Security event log.

Research was conducted to identify those software solutions that addressed a wide range of security issues. Several software tools, some open source, are standard when installing and implementing security systems. These include Snort, honeyd, Nessus Vulnerability Scanner, and Samhain. A short description is included in this section. The next section summarizes a number of solutions that provide a wide variety of security applications. A more detailed description of these products and solutions can be found in Appendix F.

- **Snort®** is an open-source network intrusion prevention and detection system utilizing a rule-driven language that combines the benefits of signature-, protocol-, and anomaly-based inspection methods. Snort is the most widely deployed intrusion detection and prevention technology worldwide and has become the de facto standard for the industry.
- The **Nessus™ vulnerability scanner** is the world leader in active scanners, featuring high-speed discovery, configuration auditing, asset profiling, sensitive data discovery, and vulnerability analysis of a security posture. Nessus scanners can be distributed throughout an entire enterprise, inside DMZs, and across physically separate networks.
- **Honeyd** is a small daemon that creates virtual hosts on a network. The hosts can be configured to run arbitrary services, and their personality can be adapted so that they appear to be running certain operating systems. Honeyd improves cyber security by providing mechanisms for threat detection and assessment. It also deters adversaries by hiding real systems in the middle of virtual systems.
- **Samhain** is a multi-platform, open-source solution for centralized file integrity checking/host-based intrusion detection on UNIX, Linux, and Cygwin/Windows systems. It has been designed to monitor multiple hosts with potentially different operating systems from a central location, although it can also be used as stand-alone application on a single host.

SECURITY PRODUCTS AND VENDORS

Vendors have categorized security products according to function. The following section identifies the vendors and products, described in Appendix F, that address those particular solutions. These functions include:

- Network attacks protection.
- Internet security suite.
- Comprehensive security systems.
- Configuration audit and control systems.
- Data leak prevention or content monitoring and filtering.
- E-mail encryption.
- Database activity detection and monitoring.
- Unified network management.
- Network taps.

Various security functions are provided by a variety of products. Vendor offerings that provide for these functionalities are included in this section. Various Web sites provide a list of functions offered by the vendors in each category of security function. It should be noted that vendors come and go, vendors are purchased by other providers, product names change, and products are discontinued.

Network attacks protection

- Norton.
- Kaspersky.
- McAfee.
- BitDefender.

Comprehensive security systems

- StealthWatch.
- NetIQ.
- Novell.
- ZENworks.

Configuration audit and control systems

- Tripwire Enterprise.
- Intrusion.
- LogLogic.
- Check Point Software Technologies.
- Pointsec Protector.

Data leak prevention or content monitoring and filtering

- Sentry.
- Compliance Commander Sentry.

E-mail encryption

- Encrypted Email Server.
- Compliance Commander.

Database activity detection and monitoring

- Database Defender.
- Guardium's SQL Guard 6.0.

Intrusion detection and prevention systems (IDS/IPS)

- Juniper Networks.
- OSSEC.
- Prelude.
- NetworkICE.
- Preemptive Security.
- Trustwave.
- Cisco.
- SecureNet.
- Bro.
- Internet Security Systems (ISS).

Unified network management

- Provider.

Network taps

- Secure Tap.

QUALITY CONTROL ISSUES

The NSS Intrusion Prevention Group has conducted the first comprehensive IPS test of its kind. This exhaustive review will give readers a complete perspective of the capabilities, maturity, and suitability of the products tested for their particular needs.

As part of its extensive IPS test methodology the NSS Group subjects each product to a brutal battery of tests that verify the stability and performance of each IPS tested, determine the accuracy of its security coverage, and ensure that the device will not block legitimate traffic.

If a particular IPS has been designated as NSS approved, customers can be confident that the device will not significantly affect network/host performance, cause network/host crashes, or otherwise block legitimate traffic.

To assess the complex matrix of IPS performance and security requirements, the NSS Group has developed a specialized lab environment that is able to exercise every facet of an IPS product. The test suite contains more than 750 individual tests that evaluate IPS products in three main areas: performance and reliability, security accuracy, and usability. This thorough review should give readers a complete perspective of the capabilities, maturity, and suitability of the products tested for their particular needs.

SYSTEM EVALUATION CRITERIA

Various criteria are used to evaluate security solutions. These can include the following:

- Cost.
- Benefits.
- Installation and setup.
- Ease-of-use and user acceptability.
- Security features.
- Effectiveness.
- Configuration and change management.
- Policy control.
- Management and monitoring.
- System overhead.
- Scalability.
- Impact on other systems.
- Reporting.

After analyzing these criteria, it is useful and prudent to develop a cost/benefit analysis for comparison purposes. Cost is often not the most important criteria.

DEVELOP IN-HOUSE OR OUTSOURCE

Organizations can develop security solutions in-house or acquire them from external sources. There are a number of issues that play when making this decision of make-or-buy. **Outsourcing** is the purchasing of any product or service from another company. Organizations outsource products and services because they are unable or unwilling to produce themselves. Common areas for outsourcing have included maintaining computer centers and communication networks. Many smaller companies often do not possess the personnel or the expertise to develop a security system.

Firms that provide outsourcing state they can save the company between 10 and 40 percent over an in-house solution and provide a high-quality product. Talk is cheap, however the selling points are:

- *Staffing economies of scale*—highly skilled technical personnel.
- *Specialization*—this is a core competency of the provider.
- *Hardware economies of scale*—multiple customers can use one large computer.
- *Tax benefits*—outsourcing fees can be a deductible expense.

Outsourcing, however, can create problems and often does when the provider does not possess experience in the customer's business, there are contract problems, and project management has failed.

🔒 CHAPTER SUMMARY

Security and network administrators and managers must possess a general understanding of the computer security requirements and the various product and service offerings. Numerous organizations market products and services that respond to computer and networking security requirements. These solutions address such diverse issues such as hardware, software, networks, policy, procedures, management, and intrusions.

The options and categories of security solutions are enormous and varied. Application areas that involve security include business continuity, disaster recovery, intrusion detection and prevention, information assurance, network security, and numerous others.

Various criteria are used to evaluate security solutions. These can include costs/benefits, installation and setup, ease of use and user acceptability, management, monitoring, scalability, and impact on other systems.

Organizations can develop security solutions in-house or acquire them from external sources. There are a number of issues that play when making this decision of make-or-buy. Outsourcing can create problems and often does when the provider does not possess experience in the customer's business.

KEY TERMS

honeyd	outsourcing	Snort
Nessus vulnerability scanner	Samhain	

SECURITY REVIEW QUESTIONS

1. _____ is an open-source network intrusion prevention and detection system utilizing a rule-driven language that combines the benefits of signature-, protocol-, and anomaly-based inspection methods.
2. The _____ is the world leader in active scanners, featuring high-speed discovery, configuration auditing, asset profiling, sensitive data discovery, and vulnerability analysis of a security posture.
3. The _____ organization has published a list of questions that are relevant for identifying security solutions.
4. Identify the various criteria that are used to evaluate security solutions.
5. Identify the major steps to accomplish security procurement tasks.
6. Identify the six project phases for a project life cycle.
7. Project management for organizations planning to make security a higher priority includes _____.
8. _____ is the purchasing of any product or service from another company.
9. The advantages of outsourcing include _____.
10. The _____ has conducted the first comprehensive IPS test of its kind.

RESEARCH ACTIVITIES

1. Research the information presented at SANS.org/resources/popular. Provide an overview of the results of the search.
2. Select a security solution category, and identify software tools that are available to address the requirements.
3. Identify suppliers of software, network, and management security solutions. Describe the products and services offered.
4. Research a security technology expertise area. Provide an overview of the details obtained.
5. Identify companies that offer outsourcing for computer security requirements.
6. Develop a matrix of security product and services vendors. Indicate the functionality for each product.
7. Identify software products that can be utilized for security system project management and control. Provide a feature overview for each product.
8. Create a PowerPoint show that describes some software product listed in Appendix F.
9. Identify open-source software that can be used as security administration tools.
10. Answer five questions from the list the SANS organization has published that are relevant for identifying security solutions.

CHAPTER **13**

Standards, Specifications, and Protocols

🔒 CHAPTER CONTENTS

- Understand the role standards play in security issues.
- Identify those standards that address computer and network security.
- Become familiar with those protocols that support security operations.
- Look at the various security specifications.
- Identify those organizations that provide support for computer and network security initiatives.
- Become familiar with the laws and legal requirements that affect the security of computer operations.

INTRODUCTION

Standards are essential in creating and maintaining an open and competitive market for hardware and software providers and in guaranteeing national and international interoperability of data and telecommunications technology and processes. They provide guidelines to vendors, government entities, and other service providers to ensure the kind of interconnectivity necessary in today's marketplace.

Standards are developed by cooperation among standards creation committees, forums, and government regulatory agencies. Data and telecommunication standards in North America are usually published by ISO, IEEE, ITU-T, EIA, and ANSI.

This chapter is concerned with standards that have been developed and published for computer and networking products and services relating to security issues. These documents also provide specifications that can be utilized in the computer security environment.

Of particular importance are the data and communication protocols that are part of the framework and infrastructure in today's communication and e-commerce networks. Basic information concerning these protocols that involve computer security is described.

(Note that revisions, updates, and deletions are frequently applied to specifications and other technical documentation. Readers and researchers should obtain the most current details from reliable sources.)

STANDARDS

Standards are defined by the **International Organization for Standardization (ISO)** as documented agreements containing technical specifications or other precise criteria to be used consistently as rules, guidelines, or definitions of characteristics and to ensure that materials, products, and processes are standardized. Note that ISO is not an acronym; instead, the name derives from the Greek word *iso*, which means equal. Founded in 1946, ISO is an international organization composed of national standards bodies from more than 75 countries. For example, ANSI (American National Standards Institute) is a member of ISO. ISO has defined a number of important computer standards, the most significant of which is perhaps OSI (Open Systems Interconnection), a standardized architecture for designing networks.

Open Systems Interconnection

Open Systems Interconnection (OSI) is the internationally accepted framework of standards for communications between different systems made by different vendors. This seven-layer standard allows for an open systems environment so that any vendor's device can communicate with any other vendor's equipment. Many vendors manufacture their products to conform to layer 1 and layer 2 of the OSI model. The seven layers, depicted in **FIGURE 13-1**, from top to bottom are:

- Application.
- Presentation.
- Session.
- Transport.
- Network.
- Data Link.
- Physical.

A layer is a collection of related functions that provides services to the layer above it and receives service from the layer below it. For example, a layer that provides error-free communications across a network provides the path needed by applications above it, while it calls the next lower layer to send and receive packets that make up the contents of the path.

Even though newer IETF and IEEE protocols and indeed OSI protocol work subsequent to the publication of the original architectural standards that have largely superseded it, the OSI model is an excellent place to begin the study of network architecture. Not understanding that the pure seven-layer model is more historic than current, many beginners make the mistake of trying to fit every protocol they study into one of the seven basic layers. This is not always easy to do because many of the protocols in use on the Internet today were designed as part of the TCP/IP model and so may not fit cleanly into the OSI model [Merkow, 2006].

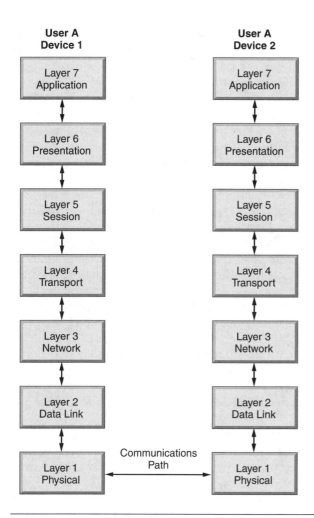

FIGURE 13-1 OSI Model

Standards Organizations

The **Internet Engineering Task Force (IETF)** develops and promotes Internet standards, cooperating closely with the W3C and ISO/IEC standard bodies and dealing in particular with standards of the TCP/IP and Internet protocol suite. It is an open, standards organization, with no formal membership or membership requirements. All participants and leaders are volunteers, although their work is usually funded by their employers or sponsors; for instance, the current chairperson is funded by *VeriSign* and the U.S. government's National Security Agency (NSA).

The **Institute of Electrical and Electronics Engineers (IEEE)** is an international non-profit, professional organization for the advancement of technology related to electricity. It has the most members of any technical professional organization in the world, with more than 360,000 members in approximately 175 countries.

The **World Wide Web Consortium (W3C)** is the main international standards organization for the World Wide Web. It is arranged as a consortium in which member organizations maintain full-time staff for the purpose of working together in the development of standards for the W3C. As of March 2007, the W3C had 441 members. It is always open for new organizations to join. W3C also engages in education and outreach, develops software, and serves as an open forum for discussion about the Web.

As the voice of the U.S. standards and conformity assessment system, the **American National Standards Institute (ANSI)** empowers its members and constituents to strengthen the U.S. marketplace position in the global economy while helping to ensure the safety and health of consumers and the protection of the environment. The Institute oversees the creation, promulgation, and use of thousands of norms and guidelines that directly affect businesses in nearly every sector: from acoustical devices to construction equipment, from dairy and livestock production to energy distribution, and on and on. The mission is to enhance both the global competitiveness of U.S. business and the U.S. quality of life by promoting and facilitating voluntary consensus standards and conformity assessment systems and safeguarding their integrity.

Founded in 1901, the **National Institute of Standards and Technology (NIST)** is a nonregulatory federal agency within the U.S. Department of Commerce. NIST's mission is to promote U.S. innovation and industrial competitiveness by advancing measurement science, standards, and technology in ways that enhance economic security and improve our quality of life.

The mission of the **International Telecommunications Union (ITU-T)** is to ensure the efficient and timely production of standards covering all fields of telecommunications on a worldwide basis, as well as defining tariff and accounting principles for international telecommunication services. The international standards that are produced by the ITU-T are referred to as "Recommendations," because they only become mandatory when adopted as part of a national law. The ITU-T is part of the ITU, which is a United Nations specialized agency, so its standards carry more formal international weight than those of most other standards development organizations that publish technical specifications of a similar form.

The **Internet Activities Board (IAB)** is the coordinating committee for Internet design, engineering, and management. The Internet is a collection of more than 2,000 packet-switched networks located principally in the United States, but also in many other parts of the world, all interlinked and operating using the protocols of the TCP/IP protocol suite. The IAB is an independent committee of researchers and professionals with a technical interest in the health and evolution of the Internet system. Membership changes with time to adjust to the current realities of the research interests of the participants, the needs of the Internet system, and the concerns of constituent members of the Internet.

Some additional organizations are listed here:

- The mission of the ICSA is to continually improve commercial computer security through certification of firewalls, anti-virus products, and Web sites. ICSA also shares and disseminates information concerning information security.
- SANS is the most trusted and by far the largest source for information security training, certification, and research in the world.
- The Internet Engineering Task Force (IETF) is the body that defines standard Internet operating protocols such as TCP/IP. This document defines a proposed data model for the Intrusion Detection Exchange Format (IDEF), which is the intended work product of the Intrusion Detection Exchange Format Working Group (IDWG).
- The Common Intrusion Detection Framework (CIDF) is an effort to develop protocols and application programming interfaces so that intrusion detection research projects can share information and resources and so that intrusion detection components can be reused in other systems.
- CVE® is international in scope and free for public use. CVE is a dictionary of publicly known information security vulnerabilities and exposures. CVE's common identifiers enable data exchange between security products and provide a baseline index point for evaluating coverage of tools and services.
- This worldwide benchmark of excellence validates that GIAC is a responsible, fair, and quality-oriented testing and certification-granting organization within the high-stakes testing and certification industry. By achieving this accreditation, GIAC demonstrates a commitment to process and procedures that adhere to an international standard of excellence.

ISO 17799

ISO 17799 provides information concerning compliance and implementing audit data and procedures, maintaining security awareness, and conducting post-mortem analysis for this standard. It is divided into 10 major sections:

- Business continuity planning
- System access control.
- System development and maintenance.
- Physical and environmental security.
- Compliance.
- Personnel security.
- Security organization.
- Computer and network management.
- Asset classification and control.
- Security policy.

In general use, ISO 17799 is a generic term, embracing both ISO 17799 and ISO 27001. The former of these two documents is a code of practice for information security management. The latter is a specification for information security management.

ISO/IEC 27002

ISO/IEC 27002 is part of a growing family of ISO/IEC ISMS standards; the ISO/IEC 27000 series is an information security standard published by the International Organization for Standardization (ISO) and the International Electro-technical Commission (IEC) and subsequently renumbered ISO/IEC 27002:2005 in July 2007. It is entitled "Information Technology—Security Techniques—Code of Practice for Information Security Management." The current standard is a revision of the version first published by ISO/IEC in 2000, which was a word-for-word copy of the British Standard (BS) 7799-1:1999.

ISO/IEC 27002 provides best practice recommendations on information security management for use by those who are responsible for initiating, implementing, or maintaining information security management systems (ISMSs). Information security is defined within the standard in the context of the C-I-A triad:

- The preservation of *confidentiality* (ensuring that information is accessible only to those authorized to have access).
- The preservation of *integrity* (safeguarding the accuracy and completeness of information and processing methods).
- The preservation of *availability* (ensuring that authorized users have access to information and associated assets when required).

Data Encryption Standard

The **Data Encryption Standard (DES)** is a widely used method of data encryption using a private (secret) key that was judged so difficult to break by the U.S. government that it was restricted for exportation to other countries. There are at least 72 quadrillion possible encryption keys that can be used. For each given message, the key is chosen at random from among this enormous number of keys. Like other private-key cryptographic methods, both the sender and the receiver must know and use the same private key.

DES applies a 56-bit key to each 64-bit block of data. The process can run in several modes and involves 16 rounds of operations. Although this is considered "strong" encryption, many companies use "triple DES," which applies three keys in succession. This is not to say that a DES-encrypted message cannot be "broken." Early in 1997, Rivest-Shamir-Adleman (RSA), owners of another encryption approach, offered a $10,000 reward for breaking a DES message. A cooperative effort on the Internet of more than 14,000 computer users trying out various keys finally deciphered the message, discovering the key after running through only 18 quadrillion of the 72 quadrillion possible keys! Few messages sent today with DES encryption are likely to be subject to this kind of code-breaking effort.

DES originated at IBM in 1977 and was adopted by the U.S. Department of Defense. Concerned that the encryption algorithm could be used by unfriendly governments, the U.S. government has prevented export of the encryption software. However, free versions of the software are widely available on bulletin board services and Web sites. Because there is some concern that the encryption algorithm will remain relatively unbreakable, NIST has indicated that DES will not be recertified as a standard, and submissions for its replacement are being accepted. The next standard will be known as the Advanced Encryption Standard (AES).

Triple DES (3DES) is a popular private-key encryption method, based on DES, the standard just described. Triple DES is a more secure version of the DES standard that encodes text three times, as opposed to just one.

Advanced Encryption Standard

The **Advanced Encryption Standard (AES)** is a cryptographic algorithm (symmetric block cipher) that supports three key sizes: 128, 192, and 256 bits. It has been analyzed extensively and is now used worldwide, as was the case with its predecessor, the *Data Encryption Standard* (DES). AES was announced by National Institute of Standards and Technology as U.S. FIPS PUB 197 (FIPS 197) on November 26, 2001, after a five-year standardization process. It became effective as a standard May 26, 2002. As of 2006, AES is one of the most popular algorithms used in symmetric key cryptography. It is available by choice in many different encryption packages. The cipher was developed by two Belgian cryptographers, Joan Daemen and Vincent Rijmen, and submitted to the AES selection process under the name "Rijndael."

Digital Signature Standard

The **Digital Signature Standard (DSS)** is a standard for digital signing, including the Digital Signing Algorithm, approved by the National Institute of Standards and Technology, defined in NIST FIPS PUB 186, "Digital Signature Standard," published May 1994 by the U.S. Department of Commerce.

A **digital signature** is an electronic identifier, created by computer, intended by the party using it to have the same force and effect as the use of a manual signature. It is a transformation of a message using an asymmetric cryptosystem such that a person having the initial message and the signer's public key can accurately determine:

- If the transformation was created using the private key that corresponds to the signer's public key.
- If the message has been altered since the transformation was made.

Payment Card Industry Standard

The **Payment Card Industry Data Security Standard (PCI DSS)** was developed by the major credit card companies as a guideline to help organizations that process card payments prevent credit card fraud, hacking, and various other security issues. A company processing, storing, or transmitting credit card numbers must be PCI DSS compliant or they risk losing the ability to process credit card payments. Merchants and service providers must validate compliance with an audit by a PCI DSS qualified security assessor (QSA) company.

In October 2007, Visa International announced new payment applications security mandates designed to help companies comply with PCI mandates. These mandates must be implemented by 2010 and call for new merchants that want to be authorized for payment card transactions to use only payment application best practice (PABP)–validated applications. These new mandates will help companies achieve PABP compliance, an implementation of PCI DSS in vendor software.

Request for Comments

In internetworking and computer network engineering, **Request for Comments (RFC)** documents are a series of memoranda encompassing new research, innovations, and methodologies applicable to Internet technologies. Through the Internet Society, engineers and computer scientists may publish discourse in the form of an RFC memorandum, either for peer review or simply to convey new concepts, information, or (occasionally) engineering humor. The Internet Engineering Task Force adopts some of the proposals published in RFCs as Internet standards.

RFC 2828 (Internet Security Glossary) contains 191 pages of definitions and 13 pages of references and provides abbreviations, explanations, and recommendations for use of information system security terminology. The intent is to improve the comprehensibility of writing that deals with Internet security, particularly Internet standards documents. Additional RFC information can be accessed through the RFC Index on the Web at *www.rfc-editor.org/cgi-bin/ rfcsearch.pl*. A search of this site using the word "security" produces more than 340 documents.

PROTOCOLS

Protocols are sets of rules governing the format of message exchange. They include an orderly sequence of steps that two or more parties take to accomplish some task. Anyone communicating over the enterprise network must utilize some protocol to successfully transmit data. It is essential that designers be aware of the protocol issues when designing a system and making a proposal in this environment. There are numerous protocols, including those for file transfers, data compression, error control, and modulation techniques.

The reason different networks are able to communicate over different interfaces, using different software, is the establishment of protocols. Protocols provide the rules for how communicating hardware and software components negotiate interfaces or talk to one another. Protocols may be proprietary or open, and they may be officially sanctioned by standards organizations or market driven. For every potential hardware-to-hardware and hardware-to-software interface, there is likely to be one or more possible protocols supported. The sum of all protocols used in a particular computer is sometimes referred to as that computer's protocol stack. Software specialists might wish to explore these protocols further.

Transmission Control Protocol/Internet Protocol

Transmission control protocol/Internet protocol (TCP/IP) is common shorthand referring to the suite of application and transport protocols running over IP. These include FTP, Telnet, SMTP, and UDP (a transport layer protocol). RFC 1213 describes the Management Information Base (MIB-II) for use with network management protocols in TCP/IP-based internets. The MIB-II groups included are:

- system.
- interfaces.
- at.
- ip.
- icmp.
- tcp.
- udp.
- egp.
- transmission.
- snmp.

The Internet protocol (IP) suite is the set of communications protocols that implement the protocol stack on which the Internet and most commercial networks run. It has also been referred to as the TCP/IP protocol suite, which is named after two of the most important protocols in it: the transmission control protocol (TCP) and the Internet protocol (IP), which were also the first two networking protocols defined. Today's IP networking represents a synthesis of two developments that began in the 1970s, namely LANs (local area networks) and the Internet, both of which have revolutionized computing.

The Internet protocol suite, like many protocol suites, can be viewed as a set of layers. Each layer solves a set of problems involving the transmission of data and provides a well-defined service to the upper layer protocols based on using services from some lower layers. Upper layers are logically closer to the user and deal with more abstract data, relying on lower layer protocols to translate data into forms that can eventually be physically transmitted.

User datagram protocol (UDP) is a connectionless communication transport method that offers a limited amount of service when messages are exchanged over the Internet protocol. It is an alternative to TCP. Unlike TCP, UDP does not acknowledge or guarantee delivery, nor does it provide sequencing of packets.

File transfer protocol (FTP) is a communication method for transferring data among computers on the Internet. FTP servers store files that can be accessed from other computers. FTP provides security services so only authorized access is allowed.

Trivial FTP (TFTP) is a simple form of the file transfer protocol. TFTP uses the user datagram protocol (UDP) and provides no security features. It is often used by servers to boot diskless workstations, X-terminals, and routers.

Common Management Information Protocol

Common management information protocol (CMIP) is a protocol used by an application process to exchange information and commands for the purpose of managing remote computer and communications resources.

CMIP was designed in competition with SNMP and has far more features than SNMP. For example, SNMP defines only "set" actions to alter the state of the managed device, while CMIP allows the definition of any type of action. CMIP was to be a key part of the telecommunications management network vision and was to enable cross-organizational as well as cross-vendor network management. On the Internet, however, most TCP/IP devices support SNMP and not CMIP. This is because of the complexity and resource requirements of CMIP agents and management systems. CMIP is supported mainly by telecommunication devices.

Simple Network Management Protocol

The **simple network management protocol (SNMP)** forms part of the Internet protocol suite as defined by the IETF. SNMP is used in network management systems to monitor network-attached devices for conditions that warrant administrative attention. It consists of a set of standards for network management, including an application layer protocol, a database schema, and a set of data objects.

SNMP exposes management data in the form of variables on the managed systems, which describe the system configuration. These variables can then be queried and sometimes set by managing applications.

RFC 1157 describes the specifications for SNMP. An important element of SNMP is the "trap." The trap protocol data unit (PDU) is generated by a protocol entity only at the request of the SNMP application entity. The means by which an SNMP application entity selects the destination addresses of the SNMP application entities is implementation-specific. Upon receipt of the Trap-PDU, the receiving protocol entity presents its contents to its SNMP application entity. Interpretations of the value of the generic trap field are:

- coldStart (0).
- warmStart (1).
- linkDown (2).
- linkUp (3).
- authenticationFailure (4).
- egpNeighborLoss (5).
- enterpriseSpecific (6).

IP Security

IP Security (IPsec) is a set of protocols developed by the IETF to support secure exchange of packets at the IP layer. IPsec has been deployed widely to implement virtual private networks (VPNs). IPsec supports two encryption modes: Transport and Tunnel. Transport mode encrypts only the data portion (*payload*) of each packet, but leaves the header untouched. The more secure Tunnel mode encrypts both the header and the payload. On the receiving side, an IPSec-compliant device decrypts each packet.

For IPsec to work, the sending and receiving devices must share a public key. This is accomplished through a protocol known as *Internet security association and key management protocol/Oakley (ISAKMP/Oakley)*, which allows the receiver to obtain a public key and authenticate the sender using digital certificates.

Internet protocol version 4 (IPv4) is the current generation of IP, in which an IP address has two parts: The first is the network ID and the second is the host ID. Under IPv4, there are five classes (Class A through Class E), which differ in how many networks and hosts are supported. It is the most widely used version of Internet protocol today, using a system of unique 32-bit identifiers to address data to computers (or hosts) on the Internet.

Internet protocol version 6 (IPv6) is the replacement for the aging IPv4, which was released in the early 1980s. IPv6 will increase the number of available Internet addresses (from 32 to 128 bits), resolving a problem associated with the growing number of computers attached to the Internet. (See Appendix E.)

Simple Mail Transfer Protocol

Simple mail transfer protocol (SMTP) is a TCP/IP protocol used in sending and receiving e-mail—primarily between mail servers and from the e-mail client to the mail server. Because of SMTP's limited ability to manage e-mail queues, the e-mail client uses other e-mail protocols, such as post office protocol (POP), to retrieve mail.

Hypertext Transfer Protocol

Hypertext transfer protocol (HTTP) is the set of rules for exchanging files (text, graphic images, sound, video, and other multimedia files) on the World Wide Web. It is a relative to the TCP/IP suite of protocols, which are the basis for information exchange on the Internet. As soon as a Web user opens his or her Web browser, the user is indirectly making use of HTTP.

HTTP concepts include the idea that files can contain references to other files, whose selection can elicit additional transfer requests. Any Web server machine contains, in addition to the Web page files it can serve, an HTTP daemon, a program that is designed to wait for HTTP requests and handle them when they arrive. The browser is an HTTP client, sending requests to server machines. When the browser user enters file requests by either "opening" a Web file (typing in a uniform resource locator, or URL) or clicking on a hypertext link, the browser builds an HTTP request and sends it to the Internet Protocol address (IP address) indicated by the URL. The HTTP daemon in the destination server machine receives the request and sends back the requested file or files associated with the request. A Web page often consists of more than one file.

Hypertext Transfer Protocol Over Secure Socket Layer

HTTPS (hypertext transfer protocol over Secure Socket Layer) is a Web protocol developed by Netscape and built into its browser that encrypts and decrypts user page requests as well as the pages that are returned by the Web server. HTTPS is really just the use of Netscape's Secure Socket Layer (SSL) as a sub-layer under its regular HTTP application layering. (HTTPS uses port 443 instead of HTTP port 80 in its interactions with the lower layer, TCP/IP.) SSL uses a 40-bit key size for the RC4 stream encryption algorithm, which is considered an adequate degree of encryption for commercial exchange.

HTTPS and SSL support the use of X.509 digital certificates from the server so that, if necessary, a user can authenticate the sender. SSL is an open, nonproprietary protocol that Netscape has proposed as a standard to the World Wide Web Consortium (W3C). HTTPS is not to be confused with S-HTTP, a security-enhanced version of HTTP developed and proposed as a standard by EIT.

Hypertext markup language (HTML) is a markup language designed for the creation of Web pages with hypertext and other information to be displayed in a web. HTML can be created directly with text editors or Web publishing programs, such as DreamWeaver, or it can be the output of other programs that make dynamic Web pages on the fly.

Secure Hypertext Transfer Protocol

Secure Hypertext Transfer Protocol (S-HTTP) is an extension to the HTTP protocol to support sending data securely over the World Wide Web. Not all Web browsers and servers support S-HTTP. Another technology for transmitting secure communications over the World Wide Web—*Secure Sockets Layer (SSL)*—is more prevalent. However, SSL and S-HTTP have very different designs and goals, so it is possible to use the two protocols together. Whereas SSL is designed to establish a secure connection between two computers, S-HTTP is designed to send individual messages securely. Both protocols have been submitted to the Internet Engineering Task Force for approval as a standard. S-HTTP was developed by Enterprise Integration Technologies (EIT).

Secure Socket Layer

The **Secure Socket Layer (SSL)** is a commonly used protocol for managing the security of a message transmission on the Internet. SSL enables client/server applications to communicate in a way that is designed to prevent eavesdropping, tampering, and message forgery. SSL was developed by Netscape Communications Corp. and RSA Data Security, Inc.

SSL uses a cryptographic system that uses two keys to encrypt data—a public key known to everyone and a private or secret key known only to the recipient of the message. Both Netscape Navigator and Internet Explorer support SSL; and many Web sites use the protocol to obtain confidential user information, such as credit card numbers. By convention, URLs that require an SSL connection start with *https:* instead of *http:*.

SSL has recently been succeeded by Transport Layer Security (TLS), which is based on SSL. SSL uses a program layer located between the Internet's hypertext transfer protocol (HTTP) and transport control protocol (TCP) layers. TLS is a protocol that ensures privacy between communicating applications and their users on the Internet. When a server and client communicate, TLS ensures that no third party may eavesdrop or tamper with any message.

SPECIFICATIONS

Specifications are engineering requirements for judging the acceptability of a part characteristic. For the production part approval process, every feature of the product as identified by engineering specifications must be measured. Actual measurement and test results are required.

Security specifications describe requirements of message integrity, message confidentiality, and single message authentication. These mechanisms can be used to accommodate a wide variety of security models and encryption technologies. The security specification provides a set of mechanisms to help developers ensure secure message exchanges. Specifically, basic mechanisms can be combined in various ways to accommodate building a wide variety of security models using a variety of cryptographic and other security technologies.

International Data Encryption Algorithm

The **International Data Encryption Algorithm (IDEA)** is a symmetric key block cipher algorithm based on a 128-bit key, developed by Xuejia Lai and James Massey in 1991. It is covered by patents that will expire in 2010–2011; as a result, it is not as commonly used in conjunction with open-source servers like Apache. It was introduced in 1992 as a potential alternative to DES and is regarded as very secure. IDEA is the data encryption algorithm used in PGP.

Rivest, Shamir, and Adleman Algorithm

Rivest, Shamir, and Adleman (RSA) is the best-known public-key algorithm, named after its inventors: Rivest, Shamir, and Adleman. RSA uses public and private keys that are functions of a pair of large prime numbers. The algorithm is best known for its application in PGP. Its security depends on the difficulty of factoring large integers. It is patented in the United States only.

Message Digest Algorithm 5

Message Digest Algorithm 5 (MD5) is one of the two most popular non-keyed message digest programs. It makes a 128-bit digest, which means a birthday attack against its strong collision resistance using $128 \div 2 = 64$ bits makes it vulnerable. In addition, MD5 collisions have been found for small messages. MD5 is a standard algorithm that takes as input a message of arbitrary length and produces as output a 128-bit fingerprint or message digest of the input. Any modifications made to the message in transit can then be detected by recalculating the digest. This secure hash—or message digest—algorithm was developed by Ron Rivest.

Secure Hash Algorithm

The **Secure Hash Algorithm (SHA)** is defined in FIPS PUB 180–1. It produces a 20-byte output. Note that all references to SHA actually use the modified SHA-1 algorithm. It is a one-way hash or message digest function developed by NIST. The current version is called SHA2.

Cyclic Redundancy Check

A **cyclic redundancy check (CRC)** is used to detect errors in the transmission of data across the bus. The CRC is transmitted along with the data packets for comparison with a CRC calculated by the receiving device. The CRC is a method of error detection and correction that is applied to a certain field of data. CRC is an efficient method of error detection because the odds of erroneously detecting a correct payload are low.

Secure Electronic Transaction

Secure electronic transaction (SET) is a system for encrypting e-commerce transactions, such as online credit card purchases. Developed by Visa, MasterCard, Microsoft, and several major banks, SET combines 1,024-bit encryption with digital certificates to ensure security. SET is a system for ensuring the security of financial transactions on the Internet. With SET, a user is given an *electronic wallet* (digital certificate), and a transaction is conducted and verified using a combination of digital certificates and digital signatures among the purchaser, a merchant, and the purchaser's bank in a way that ensures privacy and confidentiality. SET makes use of Netscape's Secure Sockets Layer (SSL), Microsoft's Secure Transaction Technology (STT), and Terisa System's secure hypertext transfer protocol (S-HTTP). SET uses some but not all aspects of a public key infrastructure.

SOCKS

SOCKS is a proxy protocol that provides a secure channel between two TCP/IP systems. This is typically used where a Web client on an internal corporate network wants to access an outside Web server located on the Internet, another company's network, or on another part of an intranet. SOCKS provides firewall services, as well as auditing, fault tolerance, management, and other features. This allows an internal corporate network to be connected to the Internet and provides a safe method for internal users to access servers on the Internet.

Public-Key Infrastructure

Public-key infrastructure (PKI) is the combination of software, encryption technologies, and services designed to protect the security of communications and business transactions on the Internet. The infrastructure used to create a secure chain of trust for Internet-based communications. A PKI solution consists of a security policy, a certificate authority (CA), a registration authority (RA), a certificate distribution system, and PKI-enabled applications.

Pretty Good Privacy

Pretty Good Privacy (PGP) is a public–private key cryptography system that allows users to more easily integrate the use of encryption in their daily tasks, such as electronic mail protection and authentication, and protect files stored on a computer. This program, developed by Phil Zimmerman, uses cryptography to protect files and electronic mail from being read by others. PGP also includes a feature that allows users to digitally "sign" a document or message in order to provide non-forgeable proof of authorship.

Authentication is via a digital signature (RFC 4880). The digital signature uses a hash code or message digest algorithm and a public-key signature algorithm. The sequence is as follows:

1. The sender creates a message.
2. The sending software generates a hash code of the message.
3. The sending software generates a signature from the hash code using the sender's private key.
4. The binary signature is attached to the message.
5. The receiving software keeps a copy of the message signature.
6. The receiving software generates a new hash code for the received message and verifies it using the message's signature. If the verification is successful, the message is accepted as authentic.

Rainbow Series

The **Rainbow Series** is a series of computer security standards published by the U.S. government in the 1980s and 1990s. They were originally published by the U.S. Department of Defense, Computer Security. These standards describe a process of evaluation for trusted systems. In some cases, U.S. government entities as well as private firms would require formal validation of computer technology using this process as part of their procurement criteria. Many of these standards have influenced, and have been superseded by, the **Common Criteria**. The books have nicknames based on the color of their covers. For example, the Trusted Computer System Evaluation Criteria was referred to as "the Orange Book."

Trusted Computer System Evaluation Criteria/Orange Book

The U.S. National Security Agency has outlined the requirements for secure products in a document entitled **Trusted Computer System Evaluation Criteria (TCSEC)**. TCSEC is commonly called the **Orange Book**. This standard defines access control methods for computer systems that computer vendors can follow to comply with Department of Defense (DOD) security standards. TCSEC is a collection of criteria used to grade or rate the security offered by computer systems. The documents are printed with different-colored folders, thus the name Rainbow Series.

The Orange Book

The Orange Book was the first guideline for evaluating security products for operating systems. Security evaluation examines the security-relevant part of a system. The initial efforts were concentrated in the national security sector. The purpose of the Orange Book was to provide:

- A basis for specifying security requirements when acquiring a computer system.
- A yardstick for users to assess the degree of trust that can be placed in a computer security system.
- Guidance for manufacturers of computer security systems.

The evaluation classes of the Orange Book are designed to address typical patterns of security requirements. These security feature and assurance requirement categories include the following classes:

- *Security policy*—mandatory and discretionary access control policies expressed in terms of subjects and objects.
- *Accountability*—audit logs of security relevant events maintained.
- *Assurance*—(1) operational: security architecture; and (2) life cycle: design methodology, testing, and configuration management.
- *Marking of objects*—labels specify the sensitivity of objects.
- *Identification of subjects*—individual subjects identified and authenticated.
- *Documentation*—guidance to install and use security features; test and design instructions.
- *Continuous protection*—security mechanisms made tamper-proof.

Trusted Network Interpretation/Red Book

Secure networking is defined in the **Red Book** or **Trusted Network Interpretation (TNI)**. The Red Book is part of the Rainbow Series of documents published by the National Computer Security Center (NCSC) that describe the requirements in the TCSEC. It describes TCSEC in terms of computer networks. It also attempts to address network security with the concepts and terminology introduced in the Orange Book. The Red Book may be viewed as a link between the Orange Book and the new criteria that have been proposed in later years. The Red Book differentiates between independent and centralized network structures.

The **Bell-LaPadula model** is a formal description of the allowable paths of information flow in a secure system. The goal of the model is to identify allowable communication where it is important to maintain secrecy. The model has been used to define the security requirements for systems concurrently handling data at different sensitivity levels. The model is a formalization of the military security policy. Access permissions are defined both through an access control matrix and through security levels [Gollmann, 2006]. Security policies prevent information flowing downward from a high-security level to a low-security level.

ITU Standards

Communication standards have been developed and published by the International Telecommunications Union (ITU). Of particular interest are X.25, X.75, and X.509.

X.25 is a network (layer 3), packet-based protocol typically run over a LAPB (link access procedure balanced) layer 2 protocol. It is generally a wide area protocol. The protocol has a large amount of built-in resilience and, as such, can guarantee delivery and integrity of data from one node to another.

X.75 is an ITU standard specifying the interface between data communication equipment (DCE) units in a network. It describes the interconnection of two X.25 networks.

X.509 is a specification for digital certificates published by the ITU-T (International Telecommunications Union—Telecommunication). X.509 (version 1) was first issued in 1988 as a part of the *ITU* X.500 Directory Services standard. When X.509 was revised in 1993, two more fields were added, resulting in the version 2 format. These two additional fields support directory access control. X.509 version 3 defines the format for certificate extensions used to store additional information regarding the certificate holder and to define certificate usage. Collectively, the term *X.509* refers to the latest published version, unless the version number is stated.

X.509 is published as ITU recommendation ITU-T X.509 (formerly CCITT X.509) and ISO/IEC/ITU 9594–8, which defines a standard certificate format for public-key certificates and certification validation. With minor differences in dates and titles, these publications provide identical text in the defining of public-key and attribute certificates.

Physical Interface Standards

A number of standards address the issues of device interfaces for media, hardware, and communication. These include STP and UTP cabling and computer storage-device interfaces such as SCSI, IDE, and EIDE.

Unshielded twisted pair (UTP) cable is installed for normal telephone use, to CAT5 and above, for connecting computer devices in a LAN. The cable consists of two or more insulated conductors in which each pair of conductors are twisted around each other. There is no external protection, and noise resistance comes solely from the twists.

Shielded twisted pair (STP) cable consists of telephone wire pairs that are wrapped in a metal sheath to eliminate external interference. Compare with UTP that is not shielded.

Small computer system interface (SCSI) is a standard interface for connecting a wide variety of devices to a computer. Although the most popular SCSI devices are disk drives, SCSI tape drives and scanners are also common.

Enhanced IDE (EIDE) is a newer version of the IDE mass storage device interface standard developed by Western Digital Corporation. It supports data rates of between 4 and 16.6 Mbps, about three to four times faster than the old IDE standard.

Integrated drive electronics (IDE) is a hard drive connection type. It is an advanced technology attachment (ATA) specification (the terms are often used interchangeable). This is the most common disk interface for hard drives, CD-ROM drives, and so forth. It is easy to use, but also the most limited.

LAWS AND REGULATIONS

Federal Rules of Civil Procedure

The **Federal Rules of Civil Procedure (FRCP)** are rules governing civil procedure in U.S. district (federal) courts—that is, court procedures for civil suits. The FRCP are promulgated by the U.S. Supreme Court pursuant to the Rules Enabling Act, and then approved by the U.S. Congress. The Court's modifications to the rules are usually based on recommendations from the Judicial Conference of the United States, the federal judiciary's internal policy-making body. Although federal courts are required to apply the substantive law of the states as rules of decision in cases where state law is in question, the federal courts almost always use the FRCP as their rules of procedure.

FRCP rules require that companies be able to identify relevant electronic evidence in a timely and complete way. Exceptions could be granted for data that was not reasonably accessible or not kept as a matter of routine operations.

Security Reform Act

The Government Information Security Reform Act, also called the **Security Act**, was passed in 2000 as part of the fiscal year 2001 Defense Authorization Act. The Security Act focuses on program management, implementation, and evaluation aspects of the security of unclassified and national security systems. It codifies existing Office of Management and Budget (OMB) security policies and reiterates security responsibilities outlined in the Computer Security Act of 1987.

The purpose of the Security Act is to improve program management and evaluation of agency security efforts. The major elements are as follows:

- Provides a comprehensive framework for establishing and ensuring effective controls over federal information technology (IT) resources.
- Requires interoperability between federal systems in a cost-effective manner, and provides for the development and maintenance of controls required to protect federal information systems.
- Provides a mechanism for improved oversight of federal agency information security programs.

The major requirements of the act are as follows:

- Annual agency program reviews are required.
- Annual inspector general of independent party evaluations are required.
- Annual OMB report to Congress is required.
- Agencies must incorporate security into their information systems.
- Security assessments of systems must be performed on systems used by outside contractors.
- Reports by agencies must include implementation plans, budgets, staffing, and training resources for security programs.

In addition to those requirements, the Security Act directs agencies to:

- Identify, use, and share best practices.
- Develop agency-wide information security plans.
- Incorporate information security principles and practices through the life cycles of the agency's information systems.
- Ensure that the agency's information security plan is practiced throughout all life cycles of the agency's information systems.

The Security Act pertains to existing systems as well as contractor systems. Once these security principles are established for all information systems, taking steps to ensure the security plan and procedures are practiced by all users will further safeguard security. Analysts advise that personnel are one key to ensuring security practices become effective. Additional reasons information systems are breached include unsafe configurations, failure to fix vulnerabilities, and errors in system settings.

Server-Gated Cryptography

Server-gated cryptography (SGC) was created in response to U.S. federal legislation on the export of strong cryptography in the 1990s. The legislation had limited encryption to weak algorithms and shorter key lengths if used in software outside of the United States. As the legislation included an exception for financial transactions, SGC was created as an extension to SSL, with SGC certificates only issued to financial organizations. When an SSL handshake takes place, the software (e.g., a Web browser) would list the ciphers that it supports. Although a weaker exported browser would only include weaker ciphers in its SSL handshake, the browser also contained stronger cryptography algorithms. To comply with the legislation, the browser would only renegotiate the handshake to use the stronger ciphers if the browser detected that the server had a SGC certificate. This legislation has now been revoked, and SGC certificates can now be issued to any organization. However, there are still large numbers of older browsers in use, especially outside the United States, which will only use weaker encryption unless connecting to a server that is SGC enabled.

Sarbanes-Oxley Regulation

In response to a series of corporate scandals, Congressman Michael Oxley and Senator Paul Sarbanes sponsored the **Sarbanes-Oxley (SOX) Act** of 2002. It was conceived as an investor protection law, with wide-ranging legislation affecting U.S. public companies in many ways. Supporters of these reforms applaud SOX as necessary and useful, while critics have consistently voiced concerns over cost and resource requirements of compliance [Dhillon, 2007].

As companies work on complying with Section 404 of the Sarbanes-Oxley Act—which requires officers of a public company to establish, monitor, and report on the effectiveness of the controls that ensure the integrity and accuracy of financial data—the challenge they face is not what IT controls to enforce and monitor. Instead, they deal with:

- Identifying the scope of the network that is affected by this regulation.
- Recognizing and standardizing a set of controls that need to be applied uniformly across all affected IT systems.
- Managing the volume of information that is required to demonstrate that compliance requirements have been met across the entire organization, in a changing threat environment.

HIPAA Privacy Regulation

The **Health Insurance Portability and Accountability Act (HIPAA)** Privacy Rule covers "protected health information" (PHI) and limits its scope only to PHI that is in electronic form. However, note that this refinement does not eliminate the requirement for security on non-electronic PHI; the HIPAA Privacy Rule (164.530©) still requires appropriate security for all PHI, regardless of its format.

Section 164.316 requires covered entities to implement reasonable and appropriate policies and procedures to comply with the standards, implementation specifications, or other requirements of the Security Rule. A covered entity may change its policies and procedures at any time. The section also requires covered entities to maintain the policies and procedures and any other required action, activity, or assessment in written form (which may be electronic). Three required implementation specifications complete this standard, requiring that the covered entity must [Strom, 2007, p. 34; Roiter, 2007, p. 60]:

- Maintain the documentation for six years from the date of its creation or the date when it last was in effect, whichever is later.
- Make the documentation available to those persons responsible for implementing the procedures to which the documentation pertains.
- Review documentation periodically, and update as needed, in response to environmental or operational changes affecting the security of the electronic protected health information.

FFIEC Guideline

The **Federal Financial Institutions Examination Council (FFIEC)** guideline regulates the financial industry and contains mandates for protecting online banking transactions. These guidelines are distributed by the Office of the Comptroller of the Currency (OCC), which regulates banks and reviews IT security controls, among its other oversight functions.

🔒 CHAPTER SUMMARY

Standards are defined by a number of organizations as documented agreements containing technical specifications or other precise criteria to be used consistently as rules, guidelines, or definitions of characteristics; standards are also used to ensure that materials, products, and processes are consistent and standardized.

Protocols are sets of rules governing the format of message exchange. They include an orderly sequence of steps that two or more parties take to accomplish some task. The reason different networks are able to communicate over different interfaces, using different software, is the establishment of protocols. Protocols provide the rules for how communicating hardware and software components negotiate interfaces or talk to one another.

Specifications are engineering requirements for judging the acceptability of a part characteristic. For the production part approval process, every feature of the product as identified by engineering specifications must be measured. Actual measurement and test results are required. Security specifications describe requirements of message integrity, message confidentiality, and single message authentication.

 KEY TERMS

Advanced Encryption Standard (AES)

American National Standards Institute (ANSI)

Bell-LaPadula model

Common Criteria

common management information protocol (CMIP)

cyclic redundancy check (CRC)

data communication equipment (DCE)

Data Encryption Standard (DES)

digital signature

Digital Signature Standard (DSS)

enhanced integrated drive electronics (EIDE)

Federal Financial Institutions Examination Council (FFIEC)

Federal Rules of Civil Procedure (FRCP)

file transfer protocol (FTP)

Health Insurance Portability and Accountability Act (HIPAA)

HTTP over Secure Socket Layer (HTTPS)

hypertext markup language (HTML)

hypertext transfer protocol (HTTP)

Institute of Electrical and Electronics Engineers (IEEE)

integrated drive electronics (IDE)

International Data Encryption Algorithm (IDEA)

International Organization for Standardization (ISO)

Internet Activities Board (IAB)

Internet Engineering Task Force (IETF)

IP Security (IPsec)

IPv4

IPv6

ISO 17799

ISO/IEC 27002

Message Digest Algorithm 5 (MD5)

National Institute of Standards and Technology (NIST)

Open Systems Interconnection (OSI)

Orange Book

Payment Card Industry Data Security Standard (PCI DSS)

Pretty Good Privacy (PGP)

protocol

public key infrastructure (PKI)

Rainbow Series

Red Book

Request for Comments (RFC)

Rivest, Shamir, and Adleman (algorithm) (RSA)

Sarbanes-Oxley Act (SOX)

secure electronic transaction (SET)

Secure Hash Algorithm (SHA)

secure hypertext transfer protocol (S-HTTP)

Secure Socket Layer (SSL)

Security Act

security specification

server-gated cryptography (SGC)

shielded twisted pair (STP)

simple network management protocol (SNMP)

small computer system interface (SCSI)

SOCKS

specification

standards

transmission control program/ Internet protocol (TCP/IP)

triple DES (3DES)

trivial FTP (TFTP)

Trusted Computer System Evaluation Criteria (TCSEC)

Trusted Network Interpretation (TNI)

unshielded twisted pair (UTP)

user datagram protocol (UDP)

World Wide Web Consortium (W3C)

X.25

X.509

X.75

SECURITY REVIEW QUESTIONS

1. _____ are defined as documented agreements containing technical specifications or other precise criteria to be used consistently as rules, guidelines, or definitions of characteristics.

2. _____ is the internationally accepted framework of standards for communications between different systems made by different vendors.

3. The _____ empowers its members and constituents to strengthen the U.S. marketplace position in the global economy while helping to ensure the safety and health of consumers and the protection of the environment.

4. _____ provides best practice recommendations on information security management for use by those who are responsible for initiating, implementing, or maintaining information security management systems.

5. The _____ was developed by the major credit card companies as a guideline to help organizations that process card payments to prevent credit card fraud, hacking, and various other security issues.

6. A(n) _____ is an electronic identifier, created by computer, intended by the party using it to have the same force and effect as the use of a manual signature.

7. _____ is a proxy protocol that provides a secure channel between two TCP/IP systems.

8. _____ is the combination of software, encryption technologies, and services designed to protect the security of communications and business transactions on the Internet.

9. _____ is a specification for digital certificates published by the ITU-T.

10. The _____ focuses on program management, implementation, and evaluation aspects of the security of unclassified and national security systems.

RESEARCH ACTIVITIES

1. Provide an overview of the ISO, IEEE, ITU-T, EIA, and ANSI standards.
2. Provide an overview of the ISO/IEC 27002 and ISO 17799 standards.
3. Describe the security provisions for each layer of the OSI model.
4. Provide a list of the security initiatives available from the NIST Web site.
5. Develop an overview of the various data encryption standards.
6. Access the RFC 2828 security glossary, and produce a subset that addresses some security subject.
7. Research RFC 1213, and provide a description of the MIB-II groups.
8. Research RFC 1157, and describe the Trap-PDU.
9. Provide an overview of IP Security.
10. Provide a comparison of S-HTTP and HTTPS protocols.
11. Provide an overview of SET.
12. Describe how PGP works.
13. What is the importance of the X.509 specification?

CHAPTER 14

Training, Certifications, and Careers

🔒 **CHAPTER CONTENTS**

- Identify those certifications that apply to computer security.
- Become familiar with the various offerings of computer and network security training alternatives.
- Identify those providers and organizations that offer security training and certifications.
- Look at the career options and opportunities that exist in computer security.
- See how to prepare for a career in computer security.

INTRODUCTION

Computer and information security professionals are afforded a great deal of responsibility and trust in protecting the confidentiality, integrity, and availability of an organization's digital resources. Computer security professionals must hold themselves and the digital discipline to the highest standards of ethical and professional conduct.

The scope and responsibilities of computer security professionals are diverse. The services provided by these security professionals are critical to the success of an organization and to the overall security posture of the computer technology community. Such responsibilities place a significant expectation on certified professionals to uphold a standard of ethics to guide the application and practice of the computer security discipline.

Security is essential to every business and organization. Data theft, loss of productivity, and decreased profits are unfortunately commonplace due to security breaches. Information technology (IT) security professionals must be specifically trained to think proactively. Security certifications provide a solid knowledge of both defensive computer and network security systems and the newer trusted needs of security. Historically, certification has become the foundation for verification of an employee's skill.

The demand for IT professionals with the necessary skills in the fast-changing world of digital security has been hard to fulfill. Today's complex electronic world requires IT professionals with security skills above the standard. Certification programs assure employers that security candidates have undergone extensive training and have passed the difficult and detailed examinations.

(Note that vendors leave and enter the market on a continuous basis; therefore, the various training and certifications are subject to change, usually based on market and technology conditions. Readers are encouraged to obtain the latest details from reliable sources.)

SECURITY CERTIFICATIONS

A **certificate** is a document issued to a person completing a course of study not leading to a diploma and may be required for an individual to practice in a particular profession or job. The official **certification** is presented by some organization that is empowered to state that an individual has completed some course of training and testing requirements. Unfortunately, there are "bad" security professionals with certifications and many excellent security professionals without certifications. While certifications are not perfect, they are a standardized method for a security professional to learn security techniques required and for a potential employer to assess whether a job candidate has the security expertise needed.

Some computer security expertise cannot be found in a certification. It is a combination of an innate feel for security, extensive knowledge of the academic security literature, extensive experience in existing security systems, and practice. Computer security has become standardized, and organizations need a practitioner, not a researcher. This is good because there is so much demand for these practitioners that there are not enough researchers to go around.

Certification programs are good at churning out practitioners, and over the years certification programs have gotten better because they really do teach the knowledge security practitioners need. An administrator might not want a graduate designing a security protocol or evaluating a cryptosystem, but certifications are sufficient for any of the handful of computer security jobs a large organization needs. Certification courses may be the most cost-effective way to give employees the skills needed to perform ever-more-complex security jobs.

Just because someone has a particular certification does not mean this individual has the security expertise required (false positives). And just because someone doesn't have a security certification doesn't mean this individual doesn't have the required security expertise (false negatives). Certifications are used for the same reasons an administrator profiles: often administrators don't have the time, patience, or ability to test for employee search criteria.

Profiling based on security certifications is the easiest way for an organization to make a good hiring decision, and the easiest way for an organization to train its existing employees [Schneier, 2007].

Certification Programs

Today, the **Certified Information Systems Security Professional (CISSP)**, the SANS Institute's **Global Information Assurance Certification (GIAC)**, and the **Certified Protection Professional (CPP)** are probably the best known and most widely followed IT security certifications/programs. The number of certified individuals in these programs varies from 7,000 to more than 48,000. Broader programs such as the **Certified Information Systems Auditor (CISA)** or the **Certified Fraud Examiner (CFE)** have populations as large as 70,000 or more.

CompTIA (Computing Technology Industry Association) and its **Security+** have changed the entry-level security certification landscape, and continue to attract strong interest and participation. The number of Security+ certifications exceeds 32,000 individuals. Microsoft, Symantec, and IBM have incorporated Security+ certification into some of their own certification programs. Security+ can also substitute for one year of job experience for the **Certified Information Security Manager (CISM)** certification. Security+ remains the leading choice as the best recognized and arguably the best entry-level information security certification currently available.

Entry-level credentials with the most content are CompTIA Security+, SANS **GSEC (GIAC Security Essentials Certification)**, and the ISC²'s **Systems Security Certified Practitioner (SSCP)**. The CISSP and the SANS GIAC intermediate and senior credentials continue to be the best bets for those seeking more senior security credentials, with the **Certified Ethical Hacker (CEH)** for those interested in current system penetration techniques and counter-hacks. The Certified Protection Professional (CPP), **Professional Certified Investigator (PCI)**, **Physical Security Professional (PSP)**, and the various CISSP concentrations are restricted to the most senior members of the security community—simply because they require five to nine years of work experience in the security field for candidates to qualify for the exam.

Security professionals recommend the following "security certification ladder"; individuals can start—depending on current knowledge, skills, and experience—and continue from there:

- Start with the **Brainbench** Internet and Network Security exams, or perhaps the Brainbench Information Technology Security Fundamentals exam. These exams are inexpensive, provide good basic coverage of their subjects, and will get students motivated to make progress. This should take two to four months to complete.
- Next, attempt the Certified Internet Webmaster Security Professional (CIW-SP) exam. Combined with a completed CIW Certification Agreement and MCSE (or similar credential), passing this exam qualifies as a CIW Security Analyst and may enhance the "merit badge count." This is a good entry-level exam on basic Internet, network, and systems security. This will take another two to four months to complete.
- After that, a broader, more formal, but still entry-level security certification is needed. This could be any of the credentials presented in this chapter, which will provide individuals with an excellent and thorough background in computer security theory, operations, practices, and policies.

For additional information on these certifications and more, visit the *SearchSecurity.com* Guide to InfoSec Certifications, or send inquiries to etittel@techtarget.com.

TRAINING

One of the main ways of validating skills as a computer security professional is through certification by some **training** and testing program. Security training is usually provided by some vocational or technical school or training contractor. Testing is usually required to ensure the candidates have successfully completed the course of study. Nothing can replace hands-on experience for getting the knowledge needed, but when preparing for the actual certification exam, reference books are invaluable for self-tests and cramming.

The overall count of vendor-neutral certifications is approaching 100, while the count of vendor-specific certifications jumps to more than 50. It is easy to decide which vendor-neutral certifications to pursue—either earn those that apply to one a current employer or customer requires or attempt those that a potential employer or customer would accept. Deciding what to pursue on the vendor-neutral side involves understanding where they fit in the overall scheme of coverage, but also requires comparing similar programs to decide which ones to pursue.

With almost 100 vendor-neutral certifications comprising the security certification landscape, there is obviously no shortage of options for would-be computer security experts to choose. The question is, how does a candidate know which certification is right? A brief analysis of the landscape and a suggested educational path candidates can choose at any point of a career is available at *techtarget.com*.

Centers of Excellence

A **Center of Excellence (CoE)** is a formalized, documented relationship among a vendor, the educational institution, and a third party. All parties involved in the CoE may bring to the partnership a special expertise of strategic importance to the technology vendor. Typically, the relationship could span anywhere from one to three years in length, and will vary according to the nature of the goals and objectives of the vendor and the educational institution.

A CoE could represent either a physical place on a campus of an educational institution or a virtual space on the Internet. It may provide a unique opportunity to showcase a vendor's technology in use, demonstrating how such technology can improve learning in the classroom and/or the administrative functions of an institution.

For the educational institution, a commitment to a vendor's training program distinguishes it as being advanced in its use of information technology. It further provides the institution with expanded opportunities for partnership with both the vendor group and the third party. This might include, but is not limited to, senior-level relationships, recruiting opportunities, joint event participation, and so forth. A CoE may experience increased leverage with funding agencies because business and education partnerships are increasingly becoming prerequisites for grant funding.

NIST 800 Series Publications

National Institute of Standards and Technology (NIST) 800 Series publications evolved as a result of exhaustive research into workable and cost-effective methods for optimizing the security of information technology systems and networks in a proactive manner. The publications cover all NIST-recommended procedures and criteria for assessing and documenting threats and vulnerabilities and for implementing security measures to minimize the risk of adverse events. The publications can be useful as guidelines for enforcement of security rules and as legal references in case of litigation involving security issues.

The U.S. Office of Personnel Management (OPM) regulations require federal agencies to provide training as set forth in NIST guidelines. It requires training for current employees; for new employees within 60 days of hire; whenever there is a significant change in the agency's IT security environment or procedures or when an employee enters a new position that deals with sensitive information; and periodically as refresher training, based on the sensitivity of the information the employee handles. In addition, it requires that prior to being granted access to IT applications and systems, all individuals must receive specialized training focusing on their IT security responsibilities and established system rules.

Security awareness and training is set forth in Administrative Safeguards Section 164.308 in the Health and Human Services (HHS) Final HIPAA Security Rules. Four implementation specifications include:

- Establish a security awareness program.
- Provide training in malicious software.
- Provide training on login monitoring procedures.
- Provide training on password management.

Public Law 100-235, "The Computer Security Act of 1987," mandated NIST and OPM to create guidelines on computer security awareness and training based on functional organizational roles. Guidelines were produced in the form of NIST Special Publication 800-16, "Information Technology Security Training Requirements: A Role- and Performance-Based Model." The learning continuum modeled in this guideline provides the relationship between awareness, training, and education. The publication also contains a methodology that can be used to develop training courses for a number of audiences that may be deemed to have significant information security responsibilities. In October 2003, NIST also published Special Publication 800-50, "Building an Information Technology Security Awareness and Training Program." The four areas addressed are:

- *Awareness*—to focus attention on security.
- *Training*—to produce relevant and needed security skills and competency.
- *Education*—to integrate all (security skills and competencies) into a common body of knowledge, adding a multidisciplinary study of concepts, issues, and principles.
- *Professional development (organizations and certifications)*—implies a guarantee as meeting a standard by applying evaluation or measurement criteria.

NSA National Centers of Academic Excellence

The National Centers of Academic Excellence in Information Assurance Education (CAEIAE) and the CAE-Research (CAE-R) are outreach programs designed and operated initially by the **National Security Agency (NSA)**. The NSA and the Department of Homeland Security (DHS), in support of the President's National Strategy to Secure Cyberspace, February 2003, jointly sponsor the program. The goal of the program is to reduce vulnerability in our national information infrastructure by promoting higher education in information assurance (IA), and producing a growing number of professionals with IA expertise in various disciplines. Additional details are located at the NSA Web site (*nsa.gov/ia/academia/caeiae.cfm*).

Under the CAEIAE program, four-year colleges and graduate-level universities are eligible to apply to be designated as a National Center of Academic Excellence in IA Education. Each institution applicant must pass a rigorous review demonstrating its commitment to academic excellence in IA education.

SECURITY ORGANIZATIONS

Organizations that play a major part in the training and certification process for computer and network offering and programs include SANS, Computer Security Institute, and InfoSec Institute. Many other providers also offer these services and products and are listed and described in subsequent sections of this chapter.

SANS

SysAdmin, Audit, Network, Security (SANS) is the most trusted and the largest source for information security training and certification in the world. It also develops, maintains, and makes available (at no cost) the largest collection of research documents about various aspects of information security, and it operates the Internet's early warning system—Internet Storm Center. The SANS Institute was established in 1989 as a cooperative research and education organization. Its programs now reach more than 165,000 security professionals around the world. A range of individuals—from auditors and network administrators to chief information security officers—are sharing the lessons learned and are jointly finding solutions to the challenges faced. At the heart of SANS are the many security practitioners in varied global organizations from corporations to universities working together to help the entire information security community.

Many of the valuable SANS resources are free to all who ask. They include the very popular Internet Storm Center, the weekly news digest (NewsBites), the weekly Consensus Security Alert (@RISK), flash security alerts, and more than 1,200 award-winning, original research papers.

SANS Computer and Information Security Training

SANS provides intensive immersion training designed to help individuals master the practical steps necessary for defending systems and networks against the most dangerous threats, which are the ones being actively exploited. The courses are full of important and immediately useful techniques that can be implemented quickly. These courses were developed through a consensus process involving hundreds of administrators, security managers, and information security professionals. They address both security fundamentals and awareness, and the in-depth technical aspects of the most crucial areas of IT security.

SANS training can be taken in a classroom setting from SANS-certified instructors, self-paced over the Internet, or in mentored settings in cities around the world. Each year, SANS programs educate more than 12,000 people in the United States and internationally. To find the best teachers in each topic in the world, SANS runs a continuous competition for instructors. Last year more than 90 people tried out for the SANS faculty, but only five new people were selected.

SANS also offers a Volunteer Program through which, in return for acting as an important extension of SANS's conference staff, volunteers may attend classes at a greatly reduced rate. Volunteers are most definitely expected to pull their weight, but the educational rewards for their doing so are substantial.

Computer Security Institute

The **Computer Security Institute (CSI)** serves the needs of information security professionals through membership, educational events, security surveys, and awareness tools. Joining CSI provides individuals with high-quality CSI publications, discounts on CSI conferences, access to online archives, career development, and networking opportunities.

CSI holds two conferences annually: CSI NetSec in June and the Annual Computer Security Conference and Exhibition in the fall. These conferences are targeted both to those entering the field and to experienced practitioners; it draw attendees from around the world.

CSI publishes the annual CSI/FBI Computer Crime & Security Survey, which attracts widespread media attention, and holds an annual Security Survey Road Show in various cities. CSI Awareness offers products and training to help improve awareness that includes a frontline end-user awareness newsletter, World Security Challenge Web-based awareness training, and awareness peer groups.

InfoSec Institute

InfoSec Institute was founded in 1998 by a group of information security instructors who desired to build a business by offering the best possible training experience for students. By providing the best possible hands-on training that was most practical for today's demanding workplace requirements, businesses can grow by leaps and bounds. This original assumption proved true as InfoSec Institute has trained more than 10,000 individuals on everything from industry standard certifications such as the CISSP to highly technical customized Windows Kernel Reverse Engineering courses.

Unlike other training companies that have been founded by nontechnical business persons, InfoSec Institute understands the needs of today's IT professionals and is positioned to offer world-class training. A wide range of security specific classes and boot camps help a diverse group of customers get the training they deserve. Customers include many government and commercial organizations. Course categories and boot camps include the following:

Ethical Hacking	Intrusion Prevention	Data Recovery Training
Hacker Training Online	Computer Forensics	Security Architecture Design
Advanced Ethical	Training	Application Security
Hacking	Computer Forensics Online	CADA Security
Penetration Testing—	Advanced Computer	Reverse Engineering
10 Day	Forensics	Training

Information Security Training	VOIP Security Course	CISA Boot Camp
Linux Security Training	Wireless Security Training	CISM Boot Camp
Windows Security Training	CEH Boot Camp	ECSA/LPT Boot Camp
	CISSP Boot Camp	Security+ Boot Camp

CERTIFICATES

Numerous organizations provide certificates oriented toward computer and network security. The following section provides an overview of these along with sample programs and/or course offerings and education schedules and timelines.

Trustwave Certificate

SSL certificates are used by thousands of organizations worldwide to secure critical business information across numerous communication protocols including: Intranet, e-mail, e-commerce Web sites, Web portals, and control panel servers.

Organizations seeking the highest level of security for all of their online communication and transactional needs rely on SSL certificates. For e-commerce merchants, compliance with the PCI DSS makes SSL certificates a requirement for doing business. The SSL certificate includes the Trusted Commerce℠ seal to showcase efforts to prevent fraud.

Trustwave SSL certificates are trusted by 99 percent of the browsers. The **Trustwave** seal indicates that any credit card data transmitted and/or processed through a business is done so in accordance with the Payment Card Industry Data Security Standard (PCI DSS) and best practices. The PCI collectively describes the debit, credit, prepaid, e-purse, ATM, and point-of-sale (POS) cards and associated businesses.

CAP

Organizations are compelled to hire qualified personnel to assess and manage the risks of security threats to information systems. In recognition of this critical need within the information assurance field, the U.S. Department of State's Office of Information Assurance and ISC^2, the gold standard in global information security, have collaborated to develop a credential for the **Certification and Accreditation Professional (CAP^{CM})**.

The CAP credential is an objective measure of the knowledge, skills, and abilities required for personnel involved in the process of certifying and accrediting the security of information systems. Specifically, the credential applies to professionals responsible for formalizing processes used to assess risk and establish security requirements, as well as ensuring that information systems possess security commensurate with the level of exposure to potential risk.

ISC^2

ISC^2 provides for global recognition of information security practitioners. These certifications include the SSCP and the CISSP.

The Systems Security Certified Practitioner (SSCP®) credential offers information security tacticians, with implementation orientations, the opportunity to demonstrate their level of competence with the seven domains of the compendium of best practices for information security, the ISC² SSCP Common Body of Knowledge (CBK®).

The SSCP credential is ideal for those working toward or who have already attained positions as senior network security engineers, senior security systems analysts, or senior security administrators.

As an SSCP, individuals gain access to ISC² services and programs that support and enhance growth throughout the information security career. These services and programs include:

- Ongoing education.
- Peer networking.
- Forums.
- Events.
- Job postings.
- Industry communications.
- Concentrations for proven subject matter expertise.
- Speaking and volunteer opportunities.

As the first ANSI ISO accredited credential in the field of information security, the Certified Information Systems Security Professional (CISSP®) certification provides information security professionals with not only an objective measure of competence but a globally recognized standard of achievement. The CISSP credential demonstrates competence in the 10 domains of the ISC² CISSP® CBK®.

The CISSP credential is ideal for mid- and senior-level managers who are working toward or have already attained positions as chief information security officers (CISOs), chief security officers (CSOs), or senior security engineers.

As a CISSP, individuals gain access to ISC² services and programs which support and enhance growth throughout the information security career. These services and programs include the same benefits as the SSCP.

CompTIA Security+™ Certifications

CompTIA vendor-neutral certifications are credentials achieved through a testing process, to validate knowledge within a specific IT support function. All CompTIA exams are developed by subject matter experts, and the certifications are recognized throughout the industry as the standard for proving foundation-level skill sets. Certified professionals report that they have more confidence on the job, see an improvement in the quality of their work, and have a higher demand for their services.

Large or small, every organization faces the risk of a network security breach. Almost daily, headlines announce a threatening new virus, worm, or hacker technique. Certifying employees with CompTIA Security+ eliminates the number-one cause of security breaches: human error. Certified professionals demonstrate a foundational knowledge of information security and have the skills to keep the business safe.

CompTIA Security+

CompTIA's Security+ certification has become the entry-level information security certification of choice for IT professionals seeking to pursue further work and knowledge in this area. It is our first choice and leading recommendation at this level.

Key benefits of having CompTIA Security+ certified employees include:

- Improved ability to prevent an attack.
- Creation of best practices and uniform security processes.
- Reduced risk of a network security breach.
- Established credibility as a secure company.

SANS

Certifications are offered in conjunction with many full five- or six-day SANS training courses. Candidates are given four months to complete the exam for Silver certification. The exam is taken in a proctored environment through the candidate's portal account. Full certifications must be renewed periodically, ensuring that certified individuals remain up-to-date on the latest threats, technology, and best practices to meet today's security challenges. The Software Security Certifications are currently offered only through proctored exams given at specific locations.

Each Global Information Assurance Certification (GIAC) certification is designed to stand on its own and represents a certified individual's mastery of a particular set of knowledge and skills. There is no particular order in which GIAC certifications must be earned, although candidates should master fundamentals before moving on to more advanced topics. There are now two types of certification: Silver and Gold. The requirements for Silver certification are the completion of one exam administered in a proctored environment. For detailed information regarding the GIAC Proctor Program, please see *http://www.giac.org/proctor/*. Certificates require a single online exam. After earning Silver certification, a candidate can apply for Gold certification, which requires a technical paper. Further details can be seen at *http://www.giac.org/gold/*. The technical paper demonstrates real-world, hands-on mastery of security skills. Passing technical papers will be posted to the GIAC List of Certified Professionals (*http://www.giac.org/certified_professionals/*) pages and to the SANS Information Security Reading Room (*http://www.sans.org/rr*) to share candidates' knowledge and research and to further educate the security community.

Candidates may wish to earn a single certification that is most suited to individual needs and/or job responsibilities. GIAC currently offers various level 3 through level 6 individual security administration certifications. Example courses include Information Security Fundamentals and Security Essentials Certification.

Cisco

The **Cisco Certified Network Associate (CCNA)** course is offered by CCBOOTCAMP, sponsored by a Cisco Learning Solutions Partner®, and is designed specifically to prepare students for the CCNA Exam. The CCNA certification validates the ability to install, configure, operate, and troubleshoot medium-size routed and switched networks, including implementation and verification of connections to remote sites in a WAN. This new curriculum includes basic mitigation of security threats, introduction to wireless networking concepts and terminology, and performance-based skills. This new curriculum also includes the use of these protocols: IP, enhanced interior gateway routing protocol (EIGRP), serial line interface protocol frame relay, routing information protocol version 2 (RIPv2), VLANs, Ethernet, and access control lists (ACLs).

The **Cisco Certified Security Professional (CCSP)** certification validates advanced knowledge and skills required to secure Cisco networks. With a CCSP, a network professional demonstrates the skills required to secure and manage network infrastructures to protect productivity and reduce costs. The CCSP curriculum emphasizes secure VPN management, Cisco adaptive security device manager (ASDM), PIX firewall, adaptive security appliance (ASA), intrusion prevention systems (IPS), Cisco security agent (CSA), and techniques to combine these technologies in a single, integrated network security solution.

New Horizons Information Security

A recent study by the CompTIA cited human error as the most common cause of information security breaches, with 80 percent of respondents citing a potential lack of security knowledge, training, or failure to follow security procedures.

In today's information-driven economy, keeping a company's vital data secure is the responsibility of every employee in the company. **New Horizons Information Security** courses can significantly reduce the odds of a business experiencing a serious information security breach and can also help minimize negative impact should a breach occur. Specific training includes:

- Security Awareness Concepts and Practices.
- Security+ Certification.
- Security Certified Network Professional Certification.
- Security Certified Network Architect SCNA.
- Certified Ethical Hacker.
- New Horizons Training for Certified Information Systems Security Professional Certification.
- Microsoft Certified Systems Administrator on Windows Server 2003.
- Microsoft Certified Systems Engineer on Windows Server 2003: Security Specialization.

ITT Technical Institute

The **ITT Technical Institute** offers online programs in information systems security. These programs are offered online to allow students the flexibility to participate when it is convenient to them. Employees with knowledge of information systems security are now considered to be an important part of many information technology infrastructure teams. Rather than teach only the business or strategic planning side of information systems security, ITT Tech's program covers both management and technical aspects of this field. These are the kinds of skills that can be valuable in today's digital marketplace.

An online education can offer opportunities for students to pursue their educational objectives when attending school in a traditional classroom is just not practical. With ITT Tech's online education, a quality technical education is now available when and where it is convenient for the student.

Technology at ITT Tech will have a credential that can help students pursue career opportunities in a variety of entry-level positions involving information systems security, some of which may include security professionals as part of software development and information technology infrastructure teams; security technicians working with Internet service providers, application service providers, and systems integrators; and security auditors.

Security University

Security University provides the highest level of qualified information security professional training and information assurance classes in the industry. Its mission is to show companies how to protect electronic assets. SU "helps raise the level of computer security and information assurance in your company" by providing hands-on computer security training for executives, network professionals, system administrators, security administrators, consultants, and staff. Security University is the leading provider of hands-on computer security and information assurance training and certifications for IT professionals in the world.

Since 1999, Security University has been the first and only computer security training company to provide IT professionals with a complete hands-on computer security curriculum for the creation of secure infrastructures. In 2007, it became the first to provide Qualified Information Security Professional (QISP) training, education, and testing.

Each SU class provides escalating security workshops and hands-on technical labs that teach how to plan, implement, build, and maintain security and compliance to reduce risk. For additional information, visit *http://www.securityuniversity.net/*.

Qualified Information Security Professional (QISP) and Qualified Information Assurance Professional (QIAP) classes are for IT security professionals, system administrators, security auditors, network auditors, CISOs, and all IT personnel who are looking to build tactical security skills and improve their career and income.

After completing the designated QISP, QIAP, and QSSEP classes, the network security professional will have gained a qualified computer security skill set necessary to protect electronic assets and the critical paths to that information from attack. They are trained to defend networks and critical assets by detecting, reacting, and responding to malicious insider and external activity in any network from both the technical and management perspective.

Security University's certification requires some of the best, most intense, hands-on information security training around. Highly popular with government and industry security heavies' executives, this program is expensive, demanding, and time-consuming—but worth the intensive investment it requires to complete.

COMPUTER SECURITY CAREERS

Occupational Outlook

In some organizations, computer security specialists may plan, coordinate, and implement the organization's information security. These workers may be called upon to educate users about computer security, install security software, monitor the network for security breaches, respond to cyber attacks, and, in some cases, gather data and evidence to be used in prosecuting cyber crime. The responsibilities of computer security specialists have increased in recent years because there has been a large increase in the number of cyber attacks on data and networks. This and other growing specialty occupations reflect an increasing emphasis on client/server applications, the expansion of Internet and intranet applications, and the demand for more end-user support.

Security-Related Career Titles

Security careers are where an individual finds them. Often a job title or job description may not mention the security requirement, but it exists in the actual job. Many network and system administration jobs have a computer security element. Specific requirements could include information technology (IT) information security, IT risk, IT audit, and business continuity/disaster recovery training, certifications, or experience. A short list of some job titles that could contain a computer security element follows:

Internet Security Specialist	Professional Services Director	Software Compliance Manager
Computer Forensics	Sales Engineering Director	Information Security Policy and Risk Analyst
Information Security Engineer	Senior Penetration Tester	Security Systems Administrator
Managing Principal Consultant	Senior Project Manager Technical Sales	Security Consultant/ Team Leader
Network Security Architect	Head of IT Security EMEA	Security Architect
Security Architect—IBM Mainframe	Head of Corporate Compliance EMEA	
Security Consultant		

CAREER AND CERTIFICATION TIPS

A document developed by Ed Tittel and Kim Lindros charts a path through the security certification landscape; this document is a great start in the pursuit of a security career.

Navigating the security certification landscape can be a difficult task. Simply identifying the vast array of offerings can be time-consuming and overwhelming. A semiannual vendor-neutral certification update outlines the many certifications available and offers a plan for moving up the security certification ladder. Many academic institutions now offer various certificates in information security, computer forensics, and other specialties, so only formal InfoSec Institute certification programs are listed. A brief explanation and a pointer to more information follow in this section. The providers and organizations are listed in alphabetical order. Interested candidates are encouraged to visit the source of the information.

American Society for Industrial Security

Certified Protection Professional (CPP)

The CPP demonstrates a thorough understanding of physical, human, and information security principles and practices. The most senior and prestigious IT security professional certification covered in this discussion, the CPP requires extensive on-the-job experience (nine years, or seven years with a college degree), as well as a profound knowledge of technical and procedural security topics and technologies. Only those who have worked with and around security for some time are able to qualify for this credential.

ASIS International

Professional Certified Investigator (PCI)

This is a high-level certification from the American Society for Industrial Security for those who specialize in investigating potential cybercrimes. ASIS is also home to the CPP and PSP certifications. Thus, in addition to technical skills, this certification concentrates on testing individuals' knowledge of legal and evidentiary matters required to present investigations in a court of law, including case management, evidence collection, and case presentation. This certification requires seven to nine years of investigation experience, with at least three years in case management (a bachelor's degree or higher counts for up to two years of such experience) and a clean legal record for candidates.

Physical Security Professional (PSP)

Another high-level security certification from ASIS, this program focuses on matters relevant to maintaining security and integrity of the premises and access controls over the devices and components of an IT infrastructure. Key topics covered include physical security assessment and selection and implementation of appropriate integrated physical security measures. Requirements include five years of experience in physical security, a high school diploma (or GED), and a clean criminal record.

Association of Certified Fraud Examiners

Certified Fraud Examiner (CFE)

The CFE demonstrates ability to detect financial fraud and other white-collar crimes. This certification is of primary interest to full-time security professionals in law or law enforcement or those who work in organizations (such as banking, securities trading, or classified operations) with legal mandates to audit for possible fraudulent or illegal transactions and activities.

Brainbench

Brainbench HIPAA (Security)

The Brainbench HIPAA (Security) certification deals with topics and requirements that drive the Health Insurance Portability and Accountability Act of 1996 (HIPAA) and help IT professionals understand and implement related information handling and processing requirements.

Brainbench Information Technology Security Fundamentals

This Brainbench certification tests basic knowledge of information security concepts, skills, and best practices. Topics covered include:

- Attack recognition, prevention, and response.
- Content security.
- Database infrastructure protection.
- General concepts.
- Network infrastructure protection.
- Perimeter and Internet security.
- Security management systems and security technologies.

Brainbench Internet Security (BIS)

The BIS seeks to identify individuals with a good working knowledge of Internet security practices, principles, and technologies. It is aimed at full-time network or system administrators who must manage systems with Internet connections or access.

Brainbench Network Security (BNS)

The BNS seeks to identify individuals with a good working knowledge of network security practices, principles, and technologies. This certification is aimed at full-time network administrators who must deal with external threats through boundary devices like routers, firewalls, or intrusion detection systems, as well as more typical internal threats.

CERT®

The CERT®-certified Computer Security Incident Handler (CSIH) program has been created for incident-handling professionals, computer security incident response team (CSIRT) technical staff, systems and network administrators with incident-handling experience, incident-handling trainers and educators, and individuals with some technical training who want to enter the incident-handling field. It is recommended for those computer security professionals with three or more years of experience in incident-handling and/or equivalent security-related experience. The specific requirements are available at *www.cert.org/certification/*.

General requirements for earning the certification include:

- Formal security training classes.
- Experience in incident handling in a technical and/or management role.
- Detailed résumé listing experience and work experience in the incident management field.
- Completed Certification Recommendation Form signed by current manager.
- Certification examination fee and a nonrefundable processing fee.
- Successful completion of the application review by the SEI.
- Passing the certification examination.

CompTIA

Security+

Security+ is an entry-level security certification that focuses on important security fundamentals related to security concepts and theory, as well as best operational practices. In addition to functioning as a stand-alone exam for CompTIA, Microsoft accepts the Security+ as an alternative to one of the specialization exams for the Microsoft Certified Systems Administrator (MCSA) and Microsoft Certified Systems Engineer (MCSE) messaging and security specializations.

Cyber Enforcement Resources, Inc.

CERI Advanced Computer Forensic Examination (CERI-ACFE)

The CERI-ACFE seeks to identify law enforcement officials with advanced computer crime investigation experience and training. Basic requirements include two years of computer investigation/debugging, two years of Microsoft platform analysis, two years of non-Microsoft platform analysis, 80 hours of approved training, a written exam, and successful completion of hands-on exercises.

CERI Advanced Computer System Security (ACSS)

The CERI-ACSS seeks to identify law enforcement officials with advanced computer crime investigation experience and training. Basic requirements include two years of computer investigation/debugging, three years of Microsoft platform analysis, one year of non-Microsoft platform analysis, 40 hours of approved training, a written exam, and successful completion of hands-on exercises.

CERI Computer Forensic Examination (CFE)

The CERI-CFE seeks to identify law enforcement officials with basic computer crime investigation experience and training. Basic requirements include two years of computer investigation/debugging, one year of Microsoft platform analysis, six months of non-Microsoft platform analysis, 40 hours of approved training, a written exam, and successful completion of hands-on exercises.

CyberSecurity Institute

CyberSecurity Forensic Analyst (CSFA)

The CSFA aims to identify individuals who are interested in information technology security issues, especially at the hardware level. Prerequisites include at least one certification in computer and software support, networking, or security (such as CompTIA's A+, Microsoft's MCSA or MCSE, or Cisco's CCNA); successful completion of an introductory and an advanced computer forensics course offered through the CyberSecurity Institute; and no criminal record.

eBusiness Process Solutions
Certified Cyber-Crime (C3C) Expert

The C3C Expert identifies computer forensics investigators, information technology and security personnel, law enforcement officials, lawyers, and others with the knowledge and tools to effectively collect, handle, process, and preserve computer forensic evidence. The certification requires successful completion of the Computer Forensic and Cyber Investigation course and a practical and written exam.

EC-Council
Certified Ethical Hacker (CEH)

The CEH identifies security professionals capable of finding and detecting weaknesses and vulnerabilities in computer systems and networks by using the same tools and applying the same knowledge as a malicious hacker. Candidates must pass a single exam and prove knowledge of tools used both by hackers and security professionals.

Computer Hacking Forensic Investigator (CHFI)

The CHFI is geared toward personnel working in the areas of law enforcement, defense, military, information technology, law, banking, and insurance, among others. To obtain CHFI certification, a candidate needs to successfully complete one exam.

Espionage Research Institute
Certified Counterespionage and Information Security Manager (CCISM)

The purpose of CCISM is to prepare individuals to study potential sources of threat, defeat attacks, and manage information security at an organizational level. This is a management-level certification, where CCISMs generally manage, work with, or consult IT organizations, technical specialists, and other IT security professionals.

Field Certified Professional Association
Field Certified Security Specialist (FCSS)

FCSS certification permits individuals to specialize in Cisco, Check Point, or cross-platform topics. This is why it is listed in both the vendor-specific (although the parent organization points out that these certifications are "vendor-independent") and vendor-neutral surveys. Candidates must pass a hands-on, performance-based test to obtain FCSS certification.

Global Information Assurance Certification
Global Information Assurance Certification (GIAC)

GIAC certification demonstrates knowledge of and the ability to manage and protect important information systems and networks. The SANS organization is well known for its timely, focused, and useful security information and certification programs. A shining star on this landscape, the GIAC is aimed at serious, full-time security professionals responsible for designing, implementing, and maintaining a state-of-the-art security infrastructure that may include incident handling and emergency response team management. Certifications available include the following:

Entry-level/basic prerequisite:
- GIAC Information Security Fundamentals (GISF).
- GIAC Security Essentials Certification (GSEC).

Mid-level specializations:
- GIAC Certified Firewall Analyst (GCFW).
- GIAC Certified Intrusion Analyst (GCIA).
- GIAC Certified Incident Handler (GCIH).
- GIAC Certified Windows Security Administrator (GCWN).
- GIAC Certified UNIX Security Administrator (GCUX).
- GIAC Certified Forensic Analyst (GCFA).
- GIAC IT Security Audit Essentials (GSAE).
- GIAC Systems and Network Auditor (GSNA).
- GIAC Certified Security Consultant (GCSC).

Senior-level (all specializations, plus additional exams and work):
- GIAC Security Engineer (GSE) track.

Role-oriented credentials:
- GIAC HIPAA Security Certificate (GHSC).
- GIAC Certified ISO 17799 Specialist (G7799).
- GIAC Certified Security Leadership Certificate (GSLC).
- GIAC Solaris Gold Standard Certificate (GGSC-0200)
- GIAC Systems and Network Auditor (GSNA).
- GIAC Windows 2000 Gold Standard Certificate (GGSC-0100).

High-Tech Crime Network Certifications
Certified Computer Crime Investigator—Basic and Advanced (CCCI)

The CCCI is one of two computer forensic certifications aimed at law enforcement and private IT professionals seeking to specialize in the investigative side of the field. Basic requirements include two years of experience (or a college degree, plus one year of experience), 18 months of investigations experience, 40 hours of computer crimes training, and documented experience from at least 10 cases investigated. Advanced requirements bump experience to three years, four years of investigations, 80 hours of training, and involvement as a lead investigator in 20 cases with involvement in more than 60 cases overall.

Certified Computer Forensic Technician—Basic and Advanced (CCFT)

The CCFT is one of two computer forensic certifications aimed at law enforcement and private IT professionals seeking to specialize in the investigative side of the field. Basic requirements include three years of experience (or a college degree, plus one year of experience), 18 months of forensics experience, 40 hours of computer forensics training, and documented experience from at least 10 cases investigated. Advanced requirements include three years of experience (or a college degree, plus two years of experience), four years of investigations, 80 hours of training, and involvement as a lead investigator in 20 cases with involvement in more than 60 cases overall.

Information Systems Audit and Control Association

Certified Information Systems Auditor (CISA)

The CISA demonstrates knowledge of IS auditing for control and security purposes. This certification is of primary interest to IT security professionals responsible for auditing IT systems, practices, and procedures to make sure organizational security policies meet governmental and regulatory requirements, conform to best security practices and principles, and meet or exceed requirements stated in an organization's security policy.

Certified Information Security Manager (CISM)

The CISM demonstrates knowledge of information security for IT professionals responsible for handling security matters, issues, and technologies. This certification is of primary interest to IT professionals responsible for managing IT systems, networks, policies, practices, and procedures to make sure organizational security policies meet governmental and regulatory requirements, conform to best security practices and principles, and meet or exceed requirements stated in an organization's security policy.

Institute of Internal Auditors

Certification in Control Self-Assessment (CCSA)

The CCSA demonstrates knowledge of internal control self-assessment procedures, primarily aimed at financial and records controls. This certification is of primary interest to those professionals who must evaluate IT infrastructures for possible threats to financial integrity, legal requirements for confidentiality, and regulatory requirements for privacy.

Certified Internal Auditor (CIA)

The CIA demonstrates knowledge of professional financial auditing practices. The certification is of primary interest to financial professionals responsible for auditing IT practices and procedures, as well as standard accounting practices and procedures to ensure the integrity and correctness of financial records, transaction logs, and other records relevant to commercial activities.

International Association of Computer Investigative Specialists

Certified Electronic Evidence Collection Specialist (CEECS)

The CEECS identifies individuals who successfully complete the CEECS certification course. No prerequisites are required to attend the course, which covers the basics of evidence collection in addition to highly technical terminology, theories, and techniques.

Certified Forensic Computer Examiner (CFCE)

One of a growing number of law enforcement–related forensic IT credentials; the International Association of Computer Investigative Specialists (IACIS) offers the CFCE credential to law enforcement and private industry personnel alike. Candidates must have broad knowledge, training, or experience in computer forensics, including forensic procedures and standards, as well as ethical, legal, and privacy issues. Certification includes both hands-on performance-based testing and a written exam.

International Information Systems Forensics Association

Certified Information Forensics Investigator (CIFI)

Obtaining CIFI certification requires adherence to a code of ethics, successful completion of a rigorous exam, and fulfillment of specific experience requirements. Aimed at full-time professional practitioners, this certification is vendor-neutral and devoid of sponsored training requirements or the use or purchase of specific products.

International Webmasters' Association (IWA)

Certified Web Professional (CWP) Security Specialist

Obtaining this certification requires passing the Certified Internet Webmaster Security Professional (CIW-SP) exam and meeting additional work experience requirements. Please see the CIW-SP listing for more information.

ISC²

Information Systems Security Architecture Professional (ISSAP)

The ISSAP permits CISSPs to concentrate further in information security architecture and stresses the following elements of the Common Body of Knowledge (CBK):

- Access control systems and methodologies.
- Telecommunications and network security.
- Cryptography.
- Requirements analysis and security standards, guidelines, and criteria.
- Technology-related business continuity and disaster recovery planning (BCP and DRP).

Information Systems Security Engineering Professional (ISSEP)

The ISSEP permits CISSPs who work in areas related to national security to concentrate further in security engineering, in cooperation with the NSA. The ISSEP stresses the following elements of the CBK:

- Systems security engineering.
- Certification and accreditation.
- Technical management.

It also adds profound coverage of U.S. government information assurance regulations.

Information Systems Security Management Professional (ISSMP)

The ISSMP permits CISSPs to concentrate further in security management areas and stresses the following elements of the CBK:

- Enterprise security management practices.
- Enterprise-wide system development security.
- Overseeing compliance of operations security.
- Understanding BCP, DRP, and continuity of operations planning (COOP).
- Law, investigations, forensics, and ethics.

Systems Security Certified Practitioner (SSCP)

The entry-level precursor to the ISC²'s CISSP covered previously in this survey, the SSCP exam covers 7 of the 10 domains in the CISSP CBK. The exam focuses more on operational and administrative issues relevant to information security and less on information policy design, risk assessment details, and other business analysis skills that are more germane to a senior IT security professional (and less so to a day-to-day security administrator, which is where the SSCP is really focused).

Certified Information Systems Security Professional (CISSP)

The CISSP demonstrates knowledge of network and system security principles, safeguards, and practices. CISSP certification is of primary interest to full-time IT security professionals who work in internal security positions or who consult with third parties on security matters. CISSPs are capable of analyzing security requirements, auditing security practices and procedures, designing and implementing security policies, and managing and maintaining an ongoing and effective security infrastructure. CISSP candidates must have four years of experience (or a college degree plus three years of experience).

The CISSP is arguably the best-known senior-level security certification in North America. It shows up most often in top 10 certification wish and want lists, and it remains the most often requested certification by name in job postings and classified ads. Those who are interested in extending their CISSP credentials should also look into its three add-on credentials. Although one of them applies only to those working in national security–related positions, the other two deal with policy and practice matters and are of definite value and interest to security practitioners outside the national defense infrastructure.

Key Computer Service

Certified Computer Examiner (CCE)

The CCE, offered by the Southeast Cybercrime Institute at Kennesaw State University in partnership with Key Computer Service, seeks to identify individuals with appropriate computer forensics training or experience, which includes evidence gathering, handling, and storage, and no criminal record. In addition, candidates must pass an online examination and successfully perform a hands-on examination on three test media.

Learning Tree International

Network Security Certified Professional (NSCP)

The NSCP demonstrates the ability to design and implement organizational security strategies and secure the network perimeter and component systems. It is an intermediate-level IT security certification aimed at network or systems administrators with heavy security responsibilities or those who work full-time on IT security matters.

Prosoft Training, Inc.

CIW Security Analyst

Individuals who take and pass the Certified Internet Webmaster Security Professional (CIW-SP) exam, and who hold one of the following certifications, qualify as a CIW Security Analyst (CIW-SA):

- Microsoft Certified Systems Administrator (MCSA).
- Microsoft Certified Systems Engineer (MCSE) 4.
- Microsoft Certified Systems Engineer (MCSE) 2000.
- Certified Novell Engineer (CNE) 4.
- Certified Novell Engineer (CNE) 5.
- Cisco Certified Network Associate (CCNA).
- Cisco Certified Network Professional (CCNP).
- Cisco Certified Internetwork Expert (CCIE).
- Linux Professional Institute (LPI) Level 2.

Individuals who hold this credential can carry out security policy; identify and handle security threats; and apply countermeasures using firewalls, intrusion detection, and related systems. The program's Web focus also includes coverage of online payments, transaction processing, and related security matters.

Certified Internet Webmaster Security Professional (CIW-SP)

The CIW-SP demonstrates knowledge of Web- and e-commerce–related security principles and practices. It is of primary interest to Web administrators who must implement and manage a secure and working Web presence that may also include e-commerce capabilities.

SANS
SANS GIAC Security Essentials Certification (GSEC)

The SANS Institute is an ongoing and well-recognized powerhouse in the security industry. Likewise, its certifications continue to accrue visibility and acceptance. The GSEC opens the door to other certifications in the SANS GIAC program.

Those who gain GSEC will be ready to tackle a premium or senior-level security certification. Most such certifications require three or more years of relevant, on-the-job experience. Many require submitting papers or research results in addition to passing exams; some also require taking specific classes. Of these, three are particularly worthy of mention and pick up where the previous three leave off.

SANS GIAC Security Specialist Certifications

The SANS Institute offers numerous topical specializations that extend on the GSEC including firewalls, incident handling, intrusion analysis, Windows and Unix administration, information security officer, and systems and network auditor certifications. This is a topical, timely, and highly technical program based on outstanding training online or at SANS conferences. For those willing to acquire three of these individual credentials and sit for two lengthy exams, moving on to the GIAC Security Engineer (GSE) certification probably makes sense.

Security Certified Program
Security Certified Network Architect (SCNA)

This is a mid- to senior-level security certification that focuses on concepts, planning, and implementation of private-key infrastructure and biometric authentication and identification systems. Individuals who attain this certification will be able to implement either or both of these technologies within organizations or as consultants to such organizations.

Security Certified Network Professional (SCNP)

This is an entry- to mid-level security certification that focuses on two primary topics: firewalls and intrusion detection. Related curriculum and exams cover network security fundamentals and network defense and countermeasures. Individuals who attain this certification will be able to work as full-time IT security professionals with an operations focus.

Security University
Advanced Information Security (AIS)

Offered by a premier training organization, Security University's AIS program combines coverage of key information security topics, tools, and technologies with perhaps the best overall hands-on, lab-oriented learning and testing program around. To obtain AIS certification, security professionals must complete eight courses, including six tools-oriented classes on topics such as:

- Network penetration testing.
- Firewalls and VPNs.

- Virus analysis.
- Patch management and incident response.
- PKI.
- Intrusion detection and computer forensics.

Two management classes on network security policy and architecture security are also required. Students must take and pass a demanding exam.

TruSecure ICSA Practitioner Certification
TruSecure ICSA Certified Security Associate (TICSA)

TICSA demonstrates basic familiarity with vendor-neutral system and network security principles, practices, and technologies. It is an entry-level security certification for network or system administrations and for those interested in climbing the first rung in a security certification ladder suitable for full-time IT security work.

TOP 10 BENEFITS OF A SECURITY CERTIFICATION

The following list of the top 10 benefits of obtaining a security certification have been developed by unknown persons. Individuals may rank-order these differently!

1. Programmers, network engineers, site administrators, and analysts will benefit from the right certification.
2. It is a concrete way to defy hackers (or become one!).
3. Owners get to use words like *anarchy, anonymity, cracking, cryptography,* and *hacking* in everyday work.
4. It is a great add-on to current certifications.
5. Owners can become self-styled gurus while the issues are still very hot.
6. The certification paths are relatively inexpensive and reap bigger benefits than, say, an MCSE.
7. New security certifications are being developed at a rapid rate to meet the specific needs of many companies.
8. Security certifications are in demand.
9. Getting a security certification is also a great way to break into the IT industry.
10. The salary is good and seems unaffected by any downturn in the IT industry.

CHAPTER SUMMARY

The scope and responsibilities of computer and network security professionals are diverse. The services provided by these security professionals are critical to the success of the computer technology and systems being utilized in most public and private organizations.

Certifications can be provided by either a vendor-neutral or vendor-specific company. Individuals must decide which vendor-neutral certifications to pursue—either earn those that apply to the current employer or customer requirements or attempt those that a potential employer or customer would accept. It is essential to understand where these providers fit in the overall scheme of security topic coverage.

Security certifications provide a solid knowledge of both defensive computer and network security systems and the newer trusted needs of security. Training programs are required that address these security certification requirements. Numerous organizations and providers offer programs and courses that address these educational and certification requirements.

KEY TERMS

Brainbench	Cisco	Physical Security Professional (PSP)
Center of Excellence (CoE)	Cisco Certified Network Associate (CCNA)	Professional Certified Investigator (PSI)
certificate	Cisco Certified Security Professional (CCSP)	SANS (SysAdmin, Audit, Network, Security)
certification	CompTIA	Security University
Certification and Accreditation Professional (CAP)	Computer Security Institute (CSI)	Security+
Certified Ethical Hacker (CEH)	GIAC Security Essentials Certification (GSEC)	SSL certificate
Certified Fraud Examiner (CFE)	Global Information Assurance Certification (GIAC)	Systems Security Certified Practitioner (SSCP)
Certified Information Security Manager (CISM)	InfoSec Institute	training
Certified Information Systems Auditor (CISA)	ISC²	Trustwave
Certified Information Systems Security Professional (CISSP)	ITT Technical Institute	
Certified Protection Professional (CPP)	National Security Agency (NSA)	
	New Horizons Information Security	

SECURITY REVIEW QUESTIONS

1. A(n) _____ is a document issued to a person completing a course of study not leading to a diploma and may be required for an individual to practice in a particular profession or job.
2. Identify the three best-known and most widely followed IT security certifications/programs.
3. The _____ mandated NIST and OPM to create guidelines on computer security awareness and training based on functional organizational roles.
4. Special Publication 800–50, "Building an Information Technology Security Awareness and Training Program," addresses which areas?
5. HHS Final HIPAA Security Rules include which four specifications?
6. _____ is the most trusted and the largest source for information security training and certification in the world.
7. _____ level security certification offered by CompTIA focuses on important security fundamentals related to security concepts and theory, as well as best operational practices.
8. The _____ demonstrates knowledge of network and system security principles, safeguards, and practices. It is arguably the best-known senior-level security certification in North America.
9. Provide a list of activities that performed by computer security specialists.
10. Identify specific requirements for security system employment opportunities.

RESEARCH ACTIVITIES

1. Develop a list of security-related job titles, and provide a brief description of each.
2. Create a report of security certifications that includes training requirements.
3. Use various sources to develop a list of training and certification organizations. Describe the products being delivered.
4. Create a report that depicts current security-related jobs along with the salary range.
5. Use current magazines, newspapers, the Web, and so forth, to identify individuals who currently hold security positions.
6. Arrange for a "headhunter" to give a presentation on the current state of the security job and career market.
7. Rank-order the top 10 benefits of a security certification, and provide the logic.
8. Identify those academic institutions that are Centers of Excellence.
9. Provide a list and summary of the various training sections of NIST 800.
10. Describe the requirements necessary for an institution to be certified as a NSA Center of Excellence.

APPENDICES

Computer and Information Systems Security Review

This security review provides an audit device for determining the level of security in an IS/IT organization. Elements and components that could affect the security and integrity of the organization are listed. For each component, enter a check mark for compliance or leave it blank for noncompliance. Additional elements can be added to the miscellaneous section of the form.

- Policies and procedures.
- Training.
- Personnel.
- Data integrity and security.
- Computer and network access.
- Building equipment rooms, raised floors, and closets.
- Computer and networking equipment.
- Wiring and cabling plant.
- Trouble reporting and maintenance.
- System administration.
- Operational performance.
- Contingency planning and disaster recovery.
- Intrusion detection and prevention.
- Identity theft and fraud prevention.
- Voice systems.

COMPUTER SYSTEM SECURITY REVIEW

Check each box for compliance.

Policies and Procedures

☐ Documented security policy.
☐ Enforced security policy and procedures.
☐ Documentation sufficient for system restoration.
☐ Documentation sufficient for data and database restoration.
☐ Paperwork and sensitive documents shredded or destroyed.
☐ Scheduled changing of passwords.
☐ Background checks for sensitive area and document access.
☐ Audits conducted for compliance.
☐ Maintained current CERT publications.
☐ Distribution of current CERT alerts.
☐ _____
☐ _____

Training

☐ Security awareness for new employees.
☐ Annual security training for all personnel.
☐ Users educated on consequences of fraud and negligence.
☐ Users educated on dial-up issues.
☐ Users trained on client/server security issues.
☐ Train system administrator on security tools.
☐ _____
☐ _____

Personnel

☐ Incidents of personal use of telecommunications documented.
☐ User passwords changed on a regular basis.
☐ Passwords changed when employees are no longer employed by the organization.
☐ Unused e-mail boxes deactivated.
☐ Audits on system administrators.
☐ Multiple system administrators.
☐ Background checks for sensitive positions.
☐ _____
☐ _____

Data Integrity and Security

- ☐ Media security methods and procedures in force.
- ☐ Off-site backup database maintained.
- ☐ Virus checking software in place and up-to-date.
- ☐ Password protection enabled.
- ☐ Reviews of accounting and log information conducted.
- ☐ Restriction of uploads to databases and hard drives.
- ☐ Maintaining authorized file permissions database.
- ☐ Protection of centralized database servers.
- ☐ Regular backups of system and application software.
- ☐ _____
- ☐ _____

Computer and Network Access

- ☐ Equipment and cable secure from monitoring and tapping.
- ☐ Access control on all sensitive areas.
- ☐ Terminal passwords guarded.
- ☐ Different security levels for sensitive systems and databases in place.
- ☐ Protection of dial-up ports.
- ☐ Firewall protection with access control lists.
- ☐ Router and gateway optioning in-band or out-of-band.
- ☐ Enforcement of idle time-outs for dial-up connections.
- ☐ _____
- ☐ _____

Building Equipment Rooms, Raised Floors, and Closets

- ☐ Humidity and temperature controls monitored.
- ☐ Perimeter and access control procedures.
- ☐ Equipment cabinets and rooms locked.
- ☐ Building and equipment free of fire hazards.
- ☐ Equipment room free of flammable materials.
- ☐ No water pipes in electronic areas.
- ☐ Equipment rooms properly ventilated.
- ☐ Backup air conditioning.
- ☐ Entrance access secured.
- ☐ _____
- ☐ _____

Computer and Networking Equipment

☐ Facility earthquake proofed.
☐ Fire suppression system operational.
☐ Backup power, UPS tested routinely.
☐ Power spike and surge suppression active.
☐ Fire extinguishers full.
☐ Smoke and fire detectors operational.
☐ Redundant device configuration.
☐ _____
☐ _____

Wiring and Cable Plant

☐ Wiring closets secure.
☐ Entrance cable protected from damage.
☐ Duplicate facilities.
☐ Records of all wiring and cable plant.
☐ Wiring diagrams and cable assignments.
☐ Cables labeled or tagged.
☐ Provide covers for all copper cable.
☐ Uses a cable scanner to detect faults.
☐ _____
☐ _____

Trouble Reporting and Maintenance

☐ Detection alarms operational.
☐ Management review of trouble reports and alarm reports.
☐ Database record of trouble reports and maintenance.
☐ Formal trouble report process.
☐ MTTR and MTBF documents for all devices.
☐ _____
☐ _____

System Administration

- ☐ Equipment inventory.
- ☐ System baseline.
- ☐ Scheduled audits.
- ☐ Scheduled system upgrades.
- ☐ Protect configuration files.
- ☐ Maintain full backup image.
- ☐ _____
- ☐ _____

Operational Performance

- ☐ Call accounting equipment secured.
- ☐ Trouble reports documented and retained.
- ☐ Monitor network for illegal traffic.
- ☐ _____
- ☐ _____

Contingency Planning and Disaster Recovery

- ☐ Fire prevention system.
- ☐ Backup power systems.
- ☐ Off-site backup systems.
- ☐ Servers and databases backed up regularly.
- ☐ Critical services redundant.
- ☐ Backup circuits.
- ☐ Power-fail transfer for PBX.
- ☐ Test of disaster recovery procedures.
- ☐ _____
- ☐ _____

Intrusion Detection and Prevention

- ☐ Baseline.
- ☐ Audits.
- ☐ Upgrades.
- ☐ Procedures.
- ☐ Tests.
- ☐ Documentation.
- ☐ Training/education.
- ☐ Security.
- ☐ _____
- ☐ _____

Identity Theft and Fraud Prevention

- ☐ Trouble reports analyzed.
- ☐ Unusual trouble patterns identified and investigated.
- ☐ Evidence of repeated troubles and incidents documented.
- ☐ Remote access DISA deactivated.
- ☐ Consoles secure.
- ☐ Calls blocked to high-fraud areas.
- ☐ International calls blocked.
- ☐ Barriers in place to counter toll fraud.
- ☐ Voicemail secure.
- ☐ Wireless security.
- ☐ _____
- ☐ _____

Voice Systems

- ☐ Remote access (DISA) disabled or controlled.
- ☐ Password for system administration console secure.
- ☐ International calls to unneeded countries blocked.
- ☐ Barriers to toll fraud in place.
- ☐ Paperwork such as bills and company directories shredded.
- ☐ Voicemail programmed to prohibit dialing to unassigned extensions.
- ☐ _____
- ☐ _____

Miscellaneous

- [ ] _____
- [ ] _____
- [ ] _____
- [ ] _____
- [ ] _____
- [ ] _____
- [ ] _____
- [ ] _____

Information Security (InfoSec) Acceptable Use Policy

1.0 OVERVIEW

InfoSec's intentions for publishing an Acceptable Use Policy are not to impose restrictions that are contrary to **Company Name**'s established culture of openness, trust, and integrity. InfoSec is committed to protecting **Company Name**'s employees, partners, and the company from illegal or damaging actions by individuals, either knowingly or unknowingly.

Internet/Intranet/Extranet-related systems, including but not limited to computer equipment, software, operating systems, storage media, network accounts providing electronic mail, WWW browsing, and FTP, are the property of **Company Name**. These systems are to be used for business purposes in serving the interests of the company, and of our clients and customers in the course of normal operations. Please review Human Resources policies for further details.

Effective security is a team effort involving the participation and support of every **Company Name** employee and affiliate who deals with information and/or information systems. It is the responsibility of every computer user to know these guidelines and to conduct their activities accordingly.

2.0 PURPOSE

The purpose of this policy is to outline the acceptable use of computer equipment at **Company Name**. These rules are in place to protect the employee and **Company Name**. Inappropriate use exposes **Company Name** to risks including virus attacks, compromise of network systems and services, and legal issues.

3.0 SCOPE

This policy applies to employees, contractors, consultants, temporaries, and other workers at **Company Name**, including all personnel affiliated with third parties. This policy applies to all equipment that is owned or leased by **Company Name**.

4.0 POLICY

4.1 General Use and Ownership

1. While **Company Name**'s network administration desires to provide a reasonable level of privacy, users should be aware that the data they create on the corporate systems remains the property of **Company Name**. Because of the need to protect **Company Name**'s network, management cannot guarantee the confidentiality of information stored on any network device belonging to **Company Name**.

2. Employees are responsible for exercising good judgment regarding the reasonableness of personal use. Individual departments are responsible for creating guidelines concerning personal use of Internet/Intranet/Extranet systems. In the absence of such policies, employees should be guided by departmental policies on personal use, and if there is any uncertainty, employees should consult their supervisor or manager.

3. InfoSec recommends that any information that users consider sensitive or vulnerable be encrypted. For guidelines on information classification, see InfoSec's Information Sensitivity Policy. For guidelines on encrypting e-mail and documents, go to InfoSec's Awareness Initiative.

4. For security and network maintenance purposes, authorized individuals within **Company Name** may monitor equipment, systems, and network traffic at any time, per InfoSec's Audit Policy.

5. **Company Name** reserves the right to audit networks and systems on a periodic basis to ensure compliance with this policy.

4.2 Security and Proprietary Information

1. The user interface for information contained on Internet/Intranet/Extranet-related systems should be classified as either confidential or not confidential, as defined by corporate confidentiality guidelines, details of which can be found in Human Resources policies. Examples of confidential information include, but are not limited to, company private information, corporate strategies, competitor-sensitive information, trade secrets, specifications, customer lists, and research data. Employees should take all necessary steps to prevent unauthorized access to this information.

2. Keep passwords secure, and do not share accounts. Authorized users are responsible for the security of their passwords and accounts. System-level passwords should be changed quarterly; user-level passwords should be changed every six months.

3. All PCs, laptops, and workstations should be secured with a password-protected screensaver with the automatic activation feature set at 10 minutes or less, or by logging off (control-alt-delete for Win2K users) when the host will be unattended.

4. Use encryption of information in compliance with InfoSec's Acceptable Encryption Use policy.

5. Because information contained on portable computers is especially vulnerable, special care should be exercised. Protect laptops in accordance with the "Laptop Security Tips."

6. Postings by employees from a **Company Name** e-mail address to newsgroups should contain a disclaimer stating that the opinions expressed are strictly their own and not necessarily those of **Company Name**, unless posting is in the course of business duties.
7. All hosts used by the employee that are connected to the **Company Name** Internet/Intranet/Extranet, whether owned by the employee or **Company Name**, shall be continually executing approved virus-scanning software with a current virus database unless overridden by departmental or group policy.
8. Employees must use extreme caution when opening e-mail attachments received from unknown senders, which may contain viruses, e-mail bombs, or Trojan horse code.

4.3 Unacceptable Use

The following activities are, in general, prohibited. Employees may be exempted from these restrictions during the course of their legitimate job responsibilities (e.g., systems administration staff may have a need to disable the network access of a host if that host is disrupting production services).

Under no circumstances is an employee of **Company Name** authorized to engage in any activity that is illegal under local, state, federal, or international law while utilizing **Company Name**-owned resources.

The following lists are by no means exhaustive, but attempt to provide a framework for activities that fall into the category of unacceptable use.

System and Network Activities

The following activities are strictly prohibited, with no exceptions:

1. Violations of the rights of any person or company protected by copyright, trade secret, patent or other intellectual property, or similar laws or regulations, including, but not limited to, the installation or distribution of "pirated" or other software products that are not appropriately licensed for use by **Company Name**.
2. Unauthorized copying of copyrighted material including, but not limited to, digitization and distribution of photographs from magazines, books, or other copyrighted sources; copyrighted music; and the installation of any copyrighted software for which **Company Name** or the end user does not have an active license is strictly prohibited.
3. Exporting software, technical information, encryption software, or technology, in violation of international or regional export control laws, is illegal. The appropriate management should be consulted prior to export of any material that is in question.
4. Introduction of malicious programs into the network or server (e.g., viruses, worms, Trojan horses, e-mail bombs, etc.).
5. Revealing your account password to others or allowing use of your account by others. This includes family and other household members when work is being done at home.
6. Using a **Company Name** computing asset to actively engage in procuring or transmitting material that is in violation of sexual harassment or hostile workplace laws in the user's local jurisdiction.

7. Making fraudulent offers of products, items, or services originating from any **Company Name** account.

8. Making statements about warranty, expressly or implied, unless it is a part of normal job duties.

9. Effecting security breaches or disruptions of network communication. Security breaches include, but are not limited to, accessing data of which the employee is not an intended recipient or logging into a server or account that the employee is not expressly authorized to access, unless these duties are within the scope of regular duties. For purposes of this section, "disruption" includes, but is not limited to, network sniffing, pinged floods, packet spoofing, denial of service, and forged routing information for malicious purposes.

10. Port scanning or security scanning is expressly prohibited unless prior notification to InfoSec is made.

11. Executing any form of network monitoring that will intercept data not intended for the employee's host, unless this activity is a part of the employee's normal job/duty.

12. Circumventing user authentication or security of any host, network, or account.

13. Interfering with or denying service to any user other than the employee's host (e.g., denial of service attack).

14. Using any program/script/command, or sending messages of any kind, with the intent to interfere with, or disable, a user's terminal session, via any means, locally or via the Internet/Intranet/Extranet.

15. Providing information about, or lists of, **Company Name** employees to parties outside **Company Name**.

E-Mail and Communications Activities

1. Sending unsolicited e-mail messages, including the sending of "junk mail" or other advertising material to individuals who did not specifically request such material (e-mail spam).

2. Any form of harassment via e-mail, telephone, or paging, whether through language, frequency, or size of messages.

3. Unauthorized use, or forging, of e-mail header information.

4. Solicitation of e-mail for any other e-mail address, other than that of the poster's account, with the intent to harass or to collect replies.

5. Creating or forwarding "chain letters," "Ponzi," or other "pyramid" schemes of any type.

6. Use of unsolicited e-mail originating from within **Company Name**'s networks of other Internet/Intranet/Extranet service providers on behalf of, or to advertise, any service hosted by **Company Name** or connected via **Company Name**'s network.

7. Posting the same or similar non-business-related messages to large numbers of Usenet newsgroups (newsgroup spam).

4.4 Blogging

1. Blogging by employees, whether using **Company Name**'s property and systems or personal computer systems, is also subject to the terms and restrictions set forth in this Policy. Limited and occasional use of **Company Name**'s systems to engage in blogging is acceptable, provided that it is done in a professional and responsible manner, does not otherwise violate **Company Name**'s policy, is not detrimental to **Company Name**'s best interests, and does not interfere with an employee's regular work duties. Blogging from **Company Name**'s systems is also subject to monitoring.

2. **Company Name**'s Confidential Information policy also applies to blogging. As such, employees are prohibited from revealing any **Company Name** confidential or proprietary information, trade secrets, or any other material covered by **Company Name**'s Confidential Information policy when engaged in blogging.

3. Employees shall not engage in any blogging that may harm or tarnish the image, reputation, and/or goodwill of **Company Name** and/or any of its employees. Employees are also prohibited from making any discriminatory, disparaging, defamatory, or harassing comments when blogging or otherwise engaging in any conduct prohibited by **Company Name**'s Nondiscrimination and Anti-Harassment policy.

4. Employees may also not attribute personal statements, opinions, or beliefs to **Company Name** when engaged in blogging. If an employee is expressing his or her beliefs and/or opinions in blogs, the employee may not, expressly or implicitly, represent him- or herself as an employee or representative of **Company Name**. Employees assume any and all risk associated with blogging.

5. Apart from following all laws pertaining to the handling and disclosure of copyrighted or export controlled materials, **Company Name**'s trademarks, logos, and any other **Company Name** intellectual property may also not be used in connection with any blogging activity

5.0 ENFORCEMENT

Any employee found to have violated this policy may be subject to disciplinary action, up to and including termination of employment.

6.0 DEFINITIONS

Term Definition

Blogging　　Writing a blog. A blog (short for weblog) is a personal online journal that is frequently updated and intended for general public consumption.

Spam　　Unauthorized and/or unsolicited electronic mass mailings.

7.0 REVISION HISTORY

This template is available from the SANS Institute.

Answers to Chapter Security Review Questions

CHAPTER 1

1. Value of the resource, the portability and size of the resource, and personal contact required.

2. Composite of availability, performance, and security.

3. The Internet (capital I) is a self-regulated network of computer networks, and an internet (small i) is a government, education, or corporate internal network.

4. Cybercrime encompasses any criminal act dealing with computers and networks (sometimes called hacking or cracking). Additionally, cybercrime includes traditional crimes that are now being conducted through the Internet and the Web. For example, telemarketing and Internet fraud, identity theft, sex crimes, and credit card account thefts are considered to be cybercrimes when the illegal activities are committed through the use of a computer and the Internet.

5. Cyber-terrorism includes attacks that result in violence against infrastructure, persons, and property and often lead to death or bodily injury, explosions, plane crashes, water contamination, or severe economic damage.

6. Steganography or Stego is the art and science of hiding information by embedding messages within other, seemingly harmless, messages. Steganography works by replacing bits of useless or unused data in regular computer files (such as graphics, sound, text, HTML, or even floppy disks) with bits of different, invisible information.

7. User passwords to biometrics, and from firewalls to intrusion detection technologies.

8. Virus, e-mail virus, worm, Trojan.

9. Availability, integrity, and confidentiality.

10. Predation, pornography, violence, fraud, identity theft, and obscenity.

CHAPTER 2

1. Virus/Trojan/worm, predator, device failure, internal hacker, equipment theft, external hacker, natural disaster, industrial espionage, terrorist.

2. Computers, servers, PCs, administrative workstations, laptops, PDAs; communication circuits (DSL and cable); cell phones, BlackBerrys, iPhones; network devices such as

routers, gateways, switches; local area network devices such as hubs, repeaters, bridges; communication devices such as modems, data service units (DSUs), splitters; front-end processors, communication controllers, multiplexers; network and operating system software; application software; power and air conditioning systems.

3. Ensure that employees are educated on the basics of a secure environment. Develop a security policy and computer-use policy. Enforce a strict policy for internal and external technical support procedures. Require some sort of user, contractor, or customer ID. Limit data leakage by restricting the detail of information published in directories, Yellow Pages, Web sites, and public databases. Be especially careful about using remote access. Validate the destination. Learn the techniques for sending and receiving secure e-mail. Remove the opportunity of "dumpster diving" in corporate and personal trash.

4. Phishing is a type of fraud whereby a criminal attempts to trick their victim into accepting a false identity presented by the criminal. Spear phishing is an e-mail spoofing fraud attempt that targets a specific organization, seeking unauthorized access to confidential data.

5. Create an education program oriented towards virus protection. Post regular bulletins about virus problems. Never transfer files from an unknown or untrusted source unless the computer has an anti-virus scan utility installed. Test new programs or open documents on a "quarantine computer" before introducing them to the production environment. Secure computers to prevent malicious people from infecting systems or installing Trojan horse programs. Use an operating system that uses a secure logon and authentication process.

6. A Trojan is a type of computer program that performs an ostensibly useful function, but contains a hidden function that compromises the host system's security.

   A worm is a single destructive program on a single system often planted by someone who has direct access to the system. A worm has the ability to copy itself from machine to machine. A virus is a computer program that infects other programs via replication. It clones itself from disk to disk or from one system to the next over computer networks.

7. A brute force attack is a cracker term for trying different passwords until it is successful. A dictionary attack is a simple cracker program that takes all the words from a dictionary file and attempts to gain entry by entering each one as a password. A masquerade attack usually includes one of the other forms of active attack, such as address spoofing or replaying. Eavesdropping or snarfing is when a host sets its network interface on promiscuous mode and copies packets that pass by for later analysis. Spoofing is a type of attack in which one computer disguises itself as another in order to gain access to a system. Hijacking is a type of network security attack in which the attacker takes control of a session between two entities and masquerades as one of them. In session hijacking, instead of attempting to initiate a session via spoofing, the attacker attempts to take over an existing connection between two network computers. Replay involves the passive capture of a data unit and its subsequent retransmission to produce an unauthorized effect. In man-in-the-middle type of attack, an attacker gets between two parties and intercepts messages before transferring them on to their intended destination.

8. Spam is flooding the Internet with many copies of the same message, in an attempt to force the message on people who would not otherwise choose to receive it. A hoax is some act intended to deceive or trick. Spyware is any software that covertly gathers user information through the user's Internet connection without the user's knowledge, usually for advertising purposes. A cookie is a message given to a Web browser by a Web server.

9. Hackers, crackers, white hats, black hats, script kiddies.

10. Software tools included viruses, Trojans, and worms (botnets). Additional tools and techniques could include sniffers, Rootkits, cookies, war dialers, hijackers, keyloggers, and scanners.

CHAPTER 3

1. Dumpster diving, mail theft, and lost/stolen wallets.

2. Equifax, Experian, TransUnion.

3. By overhearing conversations made on cell phones, from faxes and e-mails, by hacking into computers, from telephone and e-mail scams, from careless online shopping and banking.

4. Free prizes, pyramid schemes and chain letters, work at home, charities, job advertisements, free credit reports, credit information requests, check cashing, questionnaires.

5. Only provide credit card or bank account numbers when actually paying for a purchase. Beware of imposters. Keep personal mail safe. Memorize computer passwords and PIN numbers. Practice safe Internet usage.

6. Resist pressure for a quick answer. Be cautious about unsolicited e-mails. Beware of imposters. Guard personal information. Beware of "dangerous downloads."

7. Address, telephone number, parents' first and last name, parents' work phone numbers and schedule, parents' employer names, names of relatives, credit card and debit card numbers, Social Security numbers, family member birth dates.

8. Children can unwittingly assist scammers and thieves in providing confidential information that can result in property crimes against the family unit.

9. Use a secure browser. Shop with known companies. Keep passwords private. Pay by credit or charge card. Keep a record.

10. HIPAA, Sarbox or SOX, GLBA, COPPA.

CHAPTER 4

1. It has been estimated that 99 percent of laptops stolen are not recovered! Many laptops are stolen from unlocked vehicles, office areas, coffeehouses, or airport work areas.

2. Students must record the make, model, and serial number of computer and electronic devices. Keep laptops and other electronics away from accessible windows where a thief can quickly break the window, reach in, and remove the machine. The doors to labs, office spaces, and residence halls should be secured whenever laptops are left unattended.

3. Keep the password secret. Choose a password that is different from a user name or an account name. Use an invalid word—not one that can be found in the dictionary. Change the password when required. Do pick a mixture of letters, special characters, and at least one number. Don't pick a word that is currently newsworthy. Don't pick a password that is similar to previous passwords.

4. Detailed information on make, model, and serial number and any other distinctive markings. This information is stored on a central law enforcement database. Take photographs of all computer devices, and maintain an inventory database.

5. Keep portable equipment, such as laptop computers, out of sight in locked desks, cabinets, rooms, automobiles, and so on, when not in use. Clearly and permanently mark computer devices with identification to deter theft and improve chances of recovery if stolen. Take photographs of any computer device to assist with potential insurance claims. Make a concerted effort to keep track of flash drives and other storage media.

6. One of the most common causes of water damage is from overhead sprinkler systems within the facility and runoff from other floors. Another common hazard is from ruptured pipes that can flood equipment rooms.

7. Natural events, human vandals, power loss, fire, water, heat and humidity levels.

8. Common areas of security issues for media access include cable trays in the crawl space under raised floors, wall-mounted wiring access, and overhead cable and wire trays.

9. How is the terminal/computer user identified? Is this user authorized to access the computer? What operations can this user execute? Are the communication lines being monitored or sniffed?

10. Awareness and security training.

CHAPTER 5

1. These include modems, data service units (DSUs), splitters, wireless interface cards, and network terminations.

2. Customer service, distance learning, electronic commerce, Internet access, telemarketing, Web design, Web hosting.

3. The idea of the VPN is to give the user and organization the same capabilities at much lower cost by using the shared public infrastructure rather than a private one.

4. Several areas of security that are implemented in VPNs include authentication, encryption, integrity, nonrepudiation, and content filtering.

5. An intranet is an internal network that implements Internet and Web technologies. Contrast this with an extranet, which is an intranet extended outside the organization to a business partner, with transmissions moving over the Internet or across private facilities.

6. There are various threats that can affect the network, hardware, and software components. Each has different identities and repercussions.

7. These tools include the FTP, Anonymous FTP, Telnet, Gopher, Veronica, Archie, and Wide Area Information Servers (WAIS).

8. IP addresses reachable by the Internet; TCP and UDP services running on which systems; system architecture; access control mechanisms; intrusion detection systems; routing tables and access control lists; network management information; demographics; organization structure; personnel lists; contact lists with telephone numbers; network equipment type, model, and configurations.

9. *Access control*—prevention of unauthorized use of a resource.
Authentication—assurance that traffic is sent by legitimate users.
Confidentiality—assurance that a user's traffic is not examined by unauthorized users.
Integrity—assurance that received traffic has not be modified after the initial transmission.
Nonrepudiation—inability to disavow a transaction.

10. Which Internet services does the organization plan to use? Which departments within the organization will be part of this network? Will access to network services be accessible remotely or locally? What security methods will be required and supported? What are the risks for providing distributed access? What is the cost to provide secure distributed access? How will security impact usability? What will be the availability of the network resources? What are the backup capabilities of the network? Will users and employees require any training to use the system?

CHAPTER 6

1. A **local area network (LAN)** consists of a group of data devices, such as computers, servers, printers, and scanners that are linked with each other within a limited area such as on the same floor or building.

2. Star.

3. A VLAN can prevent hosts on virtual segments from reaching one another and can provide isolation from errant broadcasts as well as introducing additional security behind these virtual segments.

4. A **wireless LAN** or **WLAN** transmits and receives data over the air, combining data connectivity with user mobility.

5. An **access point** broadcasts messages in wireless format, which must be directed to wireless users, and relays messages sent by wireless users directed to resources or users on the wired side of its connection.

6. **Filters**, also called **access lists**, blocks users who are not authorized to access segments of the network and allows access only to authorized users.

7. A **firewall** is a combination of hardware and software that limits the exposure of a computer or group of computers to an attack from an outside source by controlling the flow of incoming and outgoing network traffic.

8. **Packet filtering** limits communications based on the type of traffic, source and destination IP addresses, ports, and other information.

9. The **demilitarized zone** or **DMZ** sits between the Internet and the internal network's security shield and contains a combination of firewalls and bastion hosts.

10. Biometric methods discussed include finger scanning; finger and hand geometry; iris, retina, and palm imaging; face and voice recognition; and signature verification.

CHAPTER 7

1. A **directory** is a structure containing one or more files and a description of these files.
2. **Redundant array of inexpensive disks (RAID)** devices are used to improve performance and automatically recover from a system failure. They can maintain backup files and protect data by continuously writing two copies of the data to a different hard drive.
3. A **client/server** is a computer located on a local area network that splits the workload between itself and desktop computers.
4. A **database management system (DBMS)** is a software program that operates on a mainframe system or database server to manage data, accept queries from users, and respond to those queries.
5. The **inference problem** involves a malicious attacker combining information that is available from a database, where individual data elements, viewed separately, reveal confidential information when viewed collectively.
6. The database disclosure problem called **aggregation** occurs when pieces of information, which are not sensitive in isolation, become sensitive when viewed as a whole.
7. **Polyinstantiation** means there are several views of a database object existing so that a user's view of the database is determined by that user's security attributes.
8. Identify the typical access rights or permissions, no permission, write-only, write/execute, read-only, read/execute, read/write, read/write/execute.
9. **Computer-telephony integration (CTI)** is utilized with the PBX, ACD, and computer system to provide a link for passing information to a database system.
10. Uninterruptible power supply (UPS).

CHAPTER 8

1. **Business-to-business (B2B)** is defined as e-commerce where both the buyers and sellers are organizations, whereas **business-to-consumer (B2C)** is a business selling online to individual consumers. Another type of transaction is **consumer-to-consumer (C2C)**, with individuals buying and selling over the Internet.
2. **Secure electronic transaction (SET)** is an open specification for handling credit card transactions over a network, with emphasis on the Web and Internet.
3. A **certificate** is a unique collection of information, transformed into un-forgeable form, used for authentication of users.
4. Secure electronic transaction (SET) is an open specification for handling credit card transactions over a network, with emphasis on the Web and Internet.
5. **Encryption** is the conversion of plain text or data into unintelligible form by means of a reversible translation, based on some algorithm or translation table.
6. A **smart card** is about the size of a credit card and contains a microprocessor for performing a number of functions.

7. The **Payment Card Industry (PCI)** data security standard was developed by the major credit card companies as a guideline to help organizations processing card payments prevent credit card fraud, hacking, and other security issues.

8. An **access point (AP)** or **service access point (SAP)** is a hardware device or a computer's software that acts as a communication point for users of a wireless device to connect to a wired LAN.

9. **War-driving** is a term used to describe the act of driving around in a vehicle with a laptop computer, an antenna, and an IEEE 802.11 wireless LAN adapter to exploit existing wireless networks.

10. **IPSec** provides the capability to secure communications across a LAN, private and public WANs, and the Internet.

CHAPTER 9

1. **Availability** means the network resources are accessible to authorized users; however, they may also be available to illegitimate users.

2. Controlled concurrency, fair allocation, fault tolerance, timely response, usability.

3. **Confidentiality** describes security and secrecy, meaning only authorized people can see protected data or resources.

4. **Triple-A** techniques include authentication, authorization, and accounting.

5. Biometric techniques, certificates, challenge-response handshakes, kerberos authentication, one-time passwords, passwords and PINs, RADIUS, security tokens.

6. A **demarcation** is the physical point where a regulated service or network cabling is provided to the user.

7. A **baseline** defines a point of reference against which to measure network performance and behavior when problems occur.

8. **Data migration** is an archiving process that moves stagnant files to a secondary storage system, such as optical disk, zip disks, or streaming tapes.

9. **Risk analysis** is the process of understanding how the loss of an asset will affect an organization.

10. **Prototyping** involves developing a scenario concerning a security violation and determining the effect on the organization.

CHAPTER 10

1. **Intrusion detection** is the art of detecting and responding to situations involving computer, database, and network misuse.

2. An **intrusion detection system (IDS)** generally detects unwanted manipulations of computer systems, mainly through the Internet; however, it also functions in a corporate internetwork environment.

3. Event log analysis for insider threat detection; network traffic analysis for perimeter threat detection; file and database integrity checking; security configuration management.

4. A **network-based intrusion detection system (NIDS)** is an intrusion detection system that contains capabilities to detect malicious activity such as denial of service attacks, port scans.

5. A **host-based intrusion detection system (HIDS)** is an intrusion detection system that monitors and analyzes the internals of a computing system rather than on its external interfaces of the NIDS.

6. **Network behavior analysis (NBA)** is a method of enhancing the security of a proprietary network by monitoring traffic and noting unusual actions or departures from normal (behavior) operation.

7. An **anomaly-based intrusion detection system** is based on heuristics or rules, rather than patterns or signatures.

8. **Intrusion prevention** is a preemptive approach to network security used to identify potential threats and respond to them swiftly.

9. An **intrusion prevention system** is a computer security device that monitors network and/or system activities for malicious or unwanted behavior and can react, in real-time, to block or prevent those activities.

10. **Deep packet inspection (DPI)** is a form of computer network packet filtering that examines a packet as it passes an inspection point, searching for non-protocol compliance, viruses, spam, intrusions, or predefined criteria to decide if the packet can pass.

CHAPTER 11

1. A **computer security audit** is a manual or systematic measurable technical assessment of a system or application.

2. **Network management** is a collection of activities that are required to plan, design, organize, control, maintain, and expand the communications network.

3. **Forensic analysis** consists of a cycle of data gathering and processing of evidence that has been gathered from some incident.

4. A **protocol analyzer** displays and collects network activity by decoding the different protocols from devices on the network.

5. **Incident response** processes and tactics must be developed for a successful response to some computer incident.

6. **Security management** concerns the ability to monitor and control access to network resources, including generating, distributing, and storing encryption keys.

7. Accounting management, configuration management, fault management, performance management, security management.

8. **Intrusion detection** concerns the ability to detect, isolate, and correct abnormal conditions that occur in the network environment.

9. **Sniffer** concerns the ability to monitor and control access to network resources, including generating, distributing, and storing encryption keys.

10. A **network analyzer** is a program and/or device that monitor data traveling over a network.

CHAPTER 12

1. **Snort®** is an open-source network intrusion prevention and detection system utilizing a rule-driven language, which combines the benefits of signature-, protocol-, and anomaly-based inspection methods.

2. The **Nessus™ vulnerability scanner** is the world-leader in active scanners, featuring high-speed discovery, configuration auditing, asset profiling, sensitive data discovery, and vulnerability analysis of a security posture.

3. The **SANS** organization has published a list of questions that are relevant for identifying security solutions.

4. Cost, benefits, installation and setup, ease of use and user acceptability, security features, effectiveness, configuration and change management, policy control, management and monitoring, system overhead, scalability, impact on other systems, reporting.

5. Identifying the need and planning the purchase. Developing the specification. Selecting the purchasing method. Purchasing documentation. Inviting, clarifying, and closing offers. Evaluating offers. Selecting the successful vendor. Negotiations. Contract management.

6. Requirements and scope, the technical plan, resources, estimates, products, and project risks.

7. Planning, acquisition, pilot, deployment, operation, maintenance.

8. **Outsourcing** is the purchasing of any product or service from another company.

9. Staffing economies of scale; specialization; hardware economies of scale; tax benefits.

10. NSS Intrusion Prevention Group.

CHAPTER 13

1. **Standards** are defined as documented agreements containing technical specifications or other precise criteria to be used consistently as rules, guidelines, or definitions of characteristics.

2. **Open Systems Interconnection (OSI)** is the internationally accepted framework of standards for communications between different systems made by different vendors.

3. The **American National Standards Institute (ANSI)** empowers its members and constituents to strengthen the U.S. marketplace position in the global economy while helping to ensure the safety and health of consumers and the protection of the environment.

4. **ISO/IEC 27002** provides best practice recommendations on information security management for use by those who are responsible for initiating, implementing, or maintaining information security management systems.

5. The **Payment Card Industry Data Security Standard (PCI DSS)** was developed by the major credit card companies as a guideline to help organizations that process card payments prevent credit card fraud, hacking, and various other security issues.

6. A **digital signature** is an electronic identifier, created by computer, intended by the party using it to have the same force and effect as the use of a manual signature.

7. **SOCKS** is a proxy protocol that provides a secure channel between two TCP/IP systems.

8. **Public-key infrastructure (PKI)** is the combination of software, encryption technologies, and services designed to protect the security of communications and business transactions on the Internet.

9. **X.509** is a specification for digital certificates published by the ITU-T.

10. The **Security Act** focuses on program management, implementation, and evaluation aspects of the security of unclassified and national security systems.

CHAPTER 14

1. A **certificate** is a document issued to a person completing a course of study not leading to a diploma and may be required for an individual to practice in a particular profession or job.

2. Certified Information Systems Security Professional (CISSP), the SANS Institute's Global Information Assurance Certification (GIAC), and the Certified Protection Professional (CPP).

3. The **Computer Security Act of 1987** mandated NIST and OPM to create guidelines on computer security awareness and training based on functional organizational roles.

4. Awareness, training, education, professional development.

5. Establish a security awareness program; providing training in malicious software; provide training on login monitoring procedures; provide training on password management.

6. **SysAdmin, Audit, Network, Security (SANS)** is the most trusted and the largest source for information security training and certification in the world.

7. **Security+** level security certification offered by CompTIA focuses on important security fundamentals related to security concepts and theory, as well as best operational practices.

8. The **CISSP** demonstrates knowledge of network and system security principles, safeguards, and practices. It is arguably the best-known senior-level security certification in North America.

9. Computer security specialists may plan, coordinate, and implement the organization's information security.

10. Information technology (IT) information security, IT risk, IT audit, and business continuity/disaster recovery training, certifications, or experience.

Computer Security Acronyms

3DES	triple data encryption standard
ACD	automatic call distributor
AES	Advanced Encryption Standard
ANSI	American National Standards Institute
AP	access point
API	application programming interface
B2B	business to business
B2C	business to consumer
BBB	Better Business Bureau
BCP	business continuity planning
C2C	consumer to consumer
CA	certificate authority
CAP	Certification and Accreditation Professional
CAUCE	Coalition Against Unsolicited Commercial Email
CCC	CERT Coordination Center
CCNA	Cisco Certified Network Associate
CERT	Computer Emergency Response Team
CFE	Certified Fraud Examiner
CISA	Certified Information Systems Auditor
CISM	Certified Information Security Manager
CISSP	Certified Information System Security Professional
CMIP	common management information protocol
COPPA	Children's Online Privacy Protection
CRC	cyclic redundancy check
CSI	Computer Security Institute
CTI	Computer Telephony Integration
DBMS	database management system

DDoS	distributed denial of service
DES	Data Encryption Standard
DMZ	demilitarized zone
DoS	denial of service
DPI	deep packet inspection
DRP	disaster recovery plan
DSL	digital subscriber line
DSS	Digital Signature Standard
DSU	data service unit
EDI	Electronic Data Interchange
EIDE	Enhanced IDE
FACTA	Fair and Accurate Credit Transactions Act
FAR	false acceptance rate
FBI	Federal Bureau of Investigation
FDIC	Federal Deposit Insurance Corporation
FEP	front-end processor
FRCP	Federal Rules of Civil Procedure
FRR	false rejection rate
FTC	Federal Trade Commission
FTP	file transfer protocol
GIAC	Global Information Assurance Certification
GLBA	Gramm-Leach-Bliley Act
HIDS	host-based intrusion detection system
HIPAA	Health Insurance Portability and Accountability Act
HIPS	host-based intrusion prevention system
HTTP	hypertext transfer protocol
HTTPS	HTTP over Secure Socket Layer
HTML	hypertext markup language
IAB	Internet Activities Board
IDEA	International Data Encryption Algorithm
IDPS	intrusion detection and prevention
IDS	intrusion detection system
IEEE	Institute of Electrical and Electronics Engineers
IETF	Internet Engineering Task Force
InfoSec	information security
IPS	intrusion prevention system
IPSec	IP Security

IPv4	Internet protocol version 4
IPv6	Internet protocol version 6
IRS	Internal Revenue Service
ISC²	International Information System Security Certification Consortium
ISO	International Organization for Standardization
ISP	Internet service provider
ISS	Internet security systems
ITRC	Identity Theft Resource Center
IVR	interactive voice response
LAN	local area network
MAN	metropolitan area network
MD5	Message Digest 5
modem	modulator demodulator
NFIC	National Fraud Information Center
NIDS	network intrusion detection system
NIPS	network intrusion prevention system
NIST	National Institute of Standards and Technology
NMS	network management system
OS	operating system
OSI	open system interconnection
PBX	private branch exchange
PCI	Payment Card Industry
PGP	Pretty Good Privacy
PKI	public-key infrastructure
RAID	redundant array of inexpensive disks
RFC	Request for Comments
RSA	Rivest, Shamir, and Adleman (algorithm)
SAN	storage area network
SANCP	Security Analyst Network Connection Profiler
SANS	SysAdmin, Audit, Network, Security
SAP	service access point
SCSI	small computer system interface
SET	Secure electronic transaction
SGC	server-gated cryptography
SHA	Secure Hash Algorithm
S-HTTP	secure HTTP
SLA	service level agreement

SMFA	specific management functional area
SNMP	simple network management protocol
SOX	Sarbanes-Oxley Act of 2002 (also **Sarbox**)
SSA	Social Security Administration
SSCP	Systems Security Certified Practitioner
SSL	Secure Socket Layer
SSO	single system sign-on
STP	shielded twisted cable
TCP/IP	Transmission Control Protocol/Internet Protocol
TCSEC	Trusted Computer System Evaluation Criteria
TFTP	Trivial File Transfer Protocol
TNI	Trusted Network Interpretation
UDP	User Datagram Protocol
UPS	uninterruptible power supply
UTP	unshielded twisted cable
VLAN	virtual local area network
VOIP	Voice over Internet Protocol
VPN	virtual private network
WAN	wide area network
WLAN	wireless local area network
WNIC	wireless network interface card
W3C	World Wide Web Consortium
WWW	World Wide Web

APPENDIX E

Internet Protocol Addresses

An **Internet protocol (IP) address** is a unique address that certain electronic devices currently use in order to identify and communicate with each other on a computer network utilizing the IP standard computer address. Any participating network device—including routers, switches, computers, infrastructure servers, printers, Internet fax machines, and some telephones—can have its own address that is unique within the scope of the specific network. Some IP addresses are intended to be unique within the scope of the global Internet, while others need to be unique only within the scope of an enterprise.

The IP address acts as a locator for one IP device to find and interact with another. It is not intended, however, to act as an identifier that always uniquely identifies a particular device. In current practice, an IP address is less likely to be an identifier, due to technologies such as dynamic assignment and network address translation.

IP addresses are managed and created by the **Internet Assigned Numbers Authority (IANA)**. The IANA generally allocates super-blocks to regional Internet registries, who in turn allocate smaller blocks to Internet service providers and enterprises.

Internet Protocol version 4 (IPv4) is the fourth iteration of the Internet Protocol, and it is the first version of the protocol to be widely deployed. IPv4 is the dominant network layer protocol on the Internet and, apart from IPv6, it is the only standard internetwork-layer protocol used on the Internet. It is described in IETF RFC 791. The U.S. Department of Defense also standardized it as MIL-STD-1777.

IPv4 is a data-oriented protocol to be used on a packet switched internetwork. It is a best-effort protocol in that it does not guarantee delivery. It does not make any guarantees on the correctness of the data and may result in duplicated packets and/or packets out of order. These aspects are addressed by an upper-layer protocol, such as TCP or UDP.

Internet Protocol version 6 (IPv6) is a network layer for packet-switched *internetworks*. It is designated as the successor of IPv4, the current version of the Internet Protocol, for general use on the Internet.

The main change brought by IPv6 is a much larger address space that allows greater flexibility in assigning addresses. It was not the intention of IPv6 designers, however, to give permanent unique addresses to every individual and every computer. Rather, the extended address length eliminates the need to use network address translation to avoid address exhaustion; it also simplifies aspects of address assignment and renumbering when changing providers.

IPV4 ADDRESSING NOTATION

An IPv4 address consists of four bytes (32 bits). These bytes are also known as octets.

For readability purposes, humans typically work with IP addresses in **dotted decimal notation**. This notation places periods between each of the four numbers (octets) that comprise an IP address.

For example, an IP address computers see as

`00001010  00000000  00000000  00000001`

is written in dotted decimal as 10.0.0.1.

Because each byte contains eight bits, each octet in an IP address ranges in value from a minimum of 0 to a maximum of 255. Therefore, the full range of IP addresses is from 0.0.0.0 through 255.255.255.255. That represents a total of 4,294,967,296 possible IP addresses.

IPV6 ADDRESSING NOTATION

IP addresses change significantly with IPv6. IPv6 addresses are 16 bytes (128 bits) long rather than 4 bytes (32 bits). This larger size means that IPv6 supports more than 300,000,000,000,000,000,000,000,000,000,000,000,000 possible addresses! In the coming years, as an increasing number of cell phones, PDAs, and other consumer electronics expand their networking capability, the smaller IPv4 address space will likely run out and IPv6 addresses will become necessary.

IPv6 addresses are generally written in the following form:

hhhh:hhhh:hhhh:hhhh:hhhh:hhhh:hhhh:hhhh

In this full notation, pairs of IPv6 bytes are separated by a colon, and each byte in turn is represented as a pair of hexadecimal numbers, like in the following example:

E3D7:0000:0000:0000:51F4:9BC8:C0A8:6420

Security Applications and Solutions

This appendix includes information concerning a number of software tools that can be implemented to provide security for both individual and organizational applications. Several software tools, some open source, are standard when installing and implementing security systems. These include Snort, honeyd, Nessus Vulnerability Scanner, and Samhain.

Snort

Snort® is an open-source network intrusion prevention and detection system utilizing a rule-driven language, which combines the benefits of signature-, protocol-, and anomaly-based inspection methods. With millions of downloads to date, Snort is the most widely deployed intrusion detection and prevention technology worldwide and has become the de facto standard for the industry.

Barnyard and SANCP are utilized to enhance the functionality of Snort. Barnyard is a tool built specifically to read Snort's unified output and send it to the database. The Security Analyst Network Connection Profiler works in parallel with Snort to collect all network traffic on the listening interface [McRee, 2007].

Nessus

The **Nessus**™ **vulnerability scanner** is the world leader in active scanners, featuring high-speed discovery, configuration auditing, asset profiling, sensitive data discovery, and vulnerability analysis of a security posture. Nessus scanners can be distributed throughout an entire enterprise, inside DMZs, and across physically separate networks.

The Nessus Project was started by Renaud Deraison in 1998 to provide to the Internet community with a free, powerful, up-to-date, and easy to use remote security scanner. Nessus is currently rated among the top products of its type throughout the security industry and is endorsed by professional information security organizations such as the SANS Institute.

Honeyd

Honeyd is a small daemon that creates virtual hosts on a network. The hosts can be configured to run arbitrary services, and their personality can be adapted so that they appear to be running certain operating systems. Honeyd enables a single host to claim multiple addresses (tested up to 65536) on a LAN for network simulation. Honeyd improves cyber security by providing mechanisms for threat detection and assessment. It also deters adversaries by hiding real systems in the middle of virtual systems. Honeyd is open-source software released under GNU General Public License.

Samhain

Samhain is a multiplatform, open-source solution for centralized file integrity checking/host-based intrusion detection on POSIX systems (Unix, Linux, Cygwin/Windows). It has been designed to monitor multiple hosts with potentially different operating systems from a central location, although it can also be used as standalone application on a single host.

This appendix groups software security applications and solutions into various categories, including:

- Network Attacks Protection.
- Comprehensive Security Systems.
- Configuration Audit and Control Systems.
- Data Leak Prevention or Content Monitoring and Filtering.
- E-Mail Encryption.
- Database Activity Detection and Monitoring
- Intrusion Detection and Prevention Systems (IDS/IPS) Systems
- Unified Network Management.
- Network Taps.

NETWORK ATTACKS PROTECTION

Numerous vendors provide solutions that address network issues such as viruses, Trojans, worms, adware, and spyware. One such vendor is Symantec.

Symantec

Symantec offers a plethora of software solutions including those in the following categories:

- All-in-one security.
- PC security.
- Online transaction security.
- PC tune-up.
- Backup and restore.
- Macintosh.

Various products provide the following functions:

- Security, backup, and tune-up service.
- Products that meet online security and personal firewall needs.
- Computer protection from malicious software and identity theft.
- Solutions to prevent and resolve computer problems.
- Backup and recovery tools to safeguard user data.
- Security tools to protect the Macintosh.
- Security for mobile devices and remote platforms.

Internet Security Suite

Numerous vendors offer products that address network and computer security deficiencies. A good place to start a comparison of products is *http://internet-security-suite-review.* *toptenreviews.com/.* As an example, Computer Associates (CA) Internet Security Suite includes these products:

- CA Anti-Virus 2008.
- CA Personal Firewall 2008.
- CA Anti-Spyware 2008.
- CA Anti-Spam 2008.

COMPREHENSIVE SECURITY SYSTEMS

A comprehensive security system provides a wide range of features and benefits.

StealthWatch

Lancope's **StealthWatch** delivers best-of-breed, flow-based, enterprise solutions that optimize security and network operations to save limited resources by:

- Streamlining the network optimization and security into one process.
- Reducing the time and resources allocated to network optimization and network security.
- Eliminating the cost and complexity associated with non-integrated point solutions.

The StealthWatch system is aimed at both network and security administrators—with an integrated platform that leverages network intelligence for both parties. Leveraging Net-Flow, sFlow, and packet capture, StealthWatch unifies and optimizes behavior-based anomaly detection and network operations to protect critical information assets and ensure network performance by preventing costly downtime, repair, and loss of reputation.

NetIQ

NetIQ offers a comprehensive and unique approach to security information and event management (SIEM) that includes change and threat detection, user and access control monitoring, real-time security event management, and enterprise log management as a single solution. By providing these powerful features together, NetIQ enables users to:

- Satisfy log management requirements quickly through a start fast and simple approach.
- Implement change detection and access monitoring quickly, without requiring third-party product integration.
- Enable and leverage real-time event management, including correlation, as an organization is ready.
- Address changing threat vectors by focusing SIEM protection on host platforms.

NetIQ provides SIEM protection for Windows, UNIX, Linux, and iSeries host platforms; network and security devices such as routers, switches, and firewalls; and applications such as Web servers and databases. Custom integration is also supported.

Novell

Novell's **ZENworks** Endpoint Security Management is a comprehensive endpoint security management solution that provides organizations with the ability to control applications, protocols, and removable storage devices. It delivers encryption to files and folders and network access control to ensure protection levels are current.

ZENworks allows companies to establish and enforce security policies down to the endpoints, protecting corporate resources without affecting the productivity of users. It automates corporate security policy enforcement, providing control over data and endpoint access for organizations, while enabling removable drives to be used safely and ensuring wireless security.

The solution offers a personal firewall and includes Location-Aware Enforcement, which automatically adjusts security controls and protections, based on the location of the user, preventing unauthorized access.

CONFIGURATION AUDIT AND CONTROL SYSTEMS

Tripwire Enterprise

Tripwire is the first configuration audit and control solution to combine change auditing with configuration assessment to enable users to achieve continuous operational, regulatory, and security compliance while reducing costs and improving efficiencies.

Tripwire Enterprise is the recognized leader of configuration audit and control solutions that ensures continuous operational, regulatory, and security compliance across the data center. Tripwire Enterprise 7 helps nearly 5,700 customers worldwide achieve and maintain a known, trusted, and compliant state. By proactively assessing configuration settings against internal policies and external industry benchmarks, Tripwire Enterprise generates an enterprise-wide risk profile to identify and remediate weak links. Once a known and trusted state is achieved, Tripwire Enterprise detects change in real time across the IT infrastructure to help maintain the known good state.

Tripwire supports a broad range of devices including servers, databases, network devices, virtual environments, desktops, directory servers, and more. Tripwire Enterprise also delivers actionable information through reporting, reconciliation, and remediation capabilities. As the trusted leader in configuration audit and control, Tripwire Enterprise delivers continuous compliance throughout the data center to reduce risks, increase operational efficiencies, enforce internal and external policies, automate compliance, and deliver better service to the business. Major features in Tripwire Enterprise include:

- Centralized management console with Web interface.
- Centralized database that stores historical changes.
- Configurable reports and dashboards.
- Customizable roles and permissions to ensure a secure audit trail.
- Easy-to-use graphical user interface.
- Integration with change management systems, providing automated change reconciliation.
- Policy compliance configuration assessment.
- Real-time, tunable change detection.

Intrusion

Intrusion has a long track record of delivering proven, robust security solutions to high-profile customers, including Fortune 500 financial services companies, as well as the U.S. government. **Compliance Commander** is the only unified solution that protects all ports, protocols, and applications—known and unknown—against confidential data leakage, including:

- E-mail/SMTP.
- HTTP (includes Web mail).
- Instant messaging.
- FTP.
- Peer-to-peer (P2P).
- Telnet.
- Proprietary applications.
- All other ports and protocols, known or unknown.

All file attachments, including Microsoft Office and all other document types (.doc, .ppt, .xls, .pdf, .txt, etc.), are also protected.

LogLogic

The **LogLogic LX** family is the first log management and intelligence solution directly targeted at meeting the compliance and risk mitigation requirements of the most demanding enterprises. With all log data available for queries and reports, users can pinpoint the locations of threats or other network problems, creating graphical or text-based reports for management, audits, network planning, and policy validation.

LogLogic offers enterprise-class appliances for analyzing and archiving log data that enables organizations to achieve compliance, while offering decision support and improved availability. LogLogic LX provides logging for regulations such as SOX, HIPAA, and PCI.

Check Point Software Technologies

Pointsec Protector from Check Point addresses the internal threat from unauthorized copying of enterprise data to personal storage devices through a combination of port management, content filtering, centralized auditing and management of storage devices, and optional media encryption. It plugs these potential leak points and provides a comprehensive audit-reporting capability of how data files move on and off these devices, giving enterprises complete control of their security policies.

It addresses the growing problem of unsecured ports and endpoint devices while transparently delivering encryption, filtering content, enforcing policies, and maintaining an audit trail. Protector can both track the use of ports on devices attached to the company's network and encrypt key data.

DATA LEAK PREVENTION OR CONTENT MONITORING AND FILTERING

Sentry

Compliance Commander Sentry offers industry-leading data leak prevention for the financial services and health care sectors. Organizations that handle confidential customer data are under strict regulations and guidelines for the protection of personally identifiable information (PII) that typically include:

- Names.
- Addresses.
- Dates of birth.
- Social Security numbers.
- Accounts.
- Credit card numbers.
- Any other database information.

Sentry is a gateway appliance that uses exact data-matching and Dynamic Application Detection™ technology for complete protection against any PII from leaking outside an organization across all ports, protocols, and applications.

E-MAIL ENCRYPTION

Encrypted E-Mail Server

Compliance Commander offers an integrated e-mail encryption solution that works seamlessly with Sentry, our data leak prevention appliance. The **Encrypted E-mail Server** automatically encrypts any outbound e-mails that contain sensitive information. The process is simple and is completely transparent to all corporate users. All that is needed for external e-mail recipients, such as customers or third-party businesses, is a standard Web browser to pick up any e-mails and file attachments. The Encrypted E-mail Server offers the lowest cost of ownership in the industry for e-mail encryption.

DATABASE ACTIVITY DETECTION AND MONITORING

Database Defender

Databases and file servers are among the highest value IT assets an organization has. Consequently, many network attacks will target these assets, often through inside channels that are difficult to protect against with existing security infrastructure. The most effective approach is to place protection as close as possible to databases and file servers. **Database Defender** follows this strategy, and it offers robust, independent database security with zero impact on performance. Its **AccuParse Logic**™ provides automatic analysis and identifies suspicious database activity. North America's leading credit card processing company trusts Database Defender to protect its database assets.

Guardium

Guardium's SQL Guard 6.0 functions include monitoring and managing connects to and from a wide variety of enterprise database products. SQL Guard ensures a system of checks and balances between the security and database engineering teams.

INTRUSION DETECTION AND PREVENTION SYSTEMS (IDS/IPS) SYSTEMS

Intrusion detection and prevention systems were discussed in Chapter 10. Systems solutions can be provided for both host IDS and network IDS.

Juniper Networks

The **Juniper Networks** intrusion detection and prevention products (Juniper Networks IDP) provide comprehensive and easy-to-use protection against current and emerging threats at both the application and network layers. Using industry-recognized stateful detection and prevention techniques, Juniper Networks IDP provides zero-day protection against worms, Trojans, spyware, keyloggers, and other malware. The Juniper Networks IDP can be quickly and confidently deployed in-line to effectively identify and stop network- and application-level attacks before they inflict any damage, minimizing the time and costs associated with intrusions.

Juniper Networks IDP not only helps protect networks against attacks, it also provides information on rogue servers and applications that may have been unknowingly added to the network. This intrusion prevention and detection solution gives administrators visibility into specific applications and assets that are present and/or being used on the network and how, when, and by whom they are being used. Administrators can have the Juniper intrusion prevention and detection solution enforce application usage policies or simply check to see if the current use of the network and resources meets the desired application policies. A centralized, rule-based management approach offers granular control over the system's behavior with easy access to extensive auditing and logging, and fully customizable reporting.

OSSEC

OSSEC is an open-source, scalable, multi-platform, host-based IDS. It runs on most operating systems, including Linux, OpenBSD, FreeBSD, MacOS, Solaris, and Windows. It has a powerful correlation and analysis engine, integrating:

- Log analysis.
- File integrity checking.
- Windows registry monitoring.
- Centralized policy enforcement.
- Rootkit detection.
- Real-time alerting.
- Active response.

Prelude

Prelude is a hybrid IDS framework; that is, it is a product that enables all available security applications, either open source or proprietary, to report to a centralized system. To achieve this task, Prelude relies on the IDMEF (Intrusion Detection Message Exchange Format) IETF standard, which enables different kinds of sensors to generate events using a unified language. Prelude benefits from its ability to find traces of malicious activity from different sensors (Snort, honeyd, Nessus Vulnerability Scanner, Samhain, more than 30 types of systems logs, and many others) in order to better verify an attack and in the end to perform automatic correlation between the various events.

Prelude is committed to providing a hybrid IDS that offers the ability to unify currently available tools into one, powerful, and distributed application.

NetworkICE

The first commercial/retail IPS was the BlackICE product from NetworkICE Corporation. It debuted in 1998 with a business and personal version of the product. It provided host and in-line network IPS capabilities using protocol analysis as its core detection technique. The first products were:

- BlackICE Desktop—a host-based IPS for end-user systems.
- BlackICE Guard—an in-line network IPS.
- BlackICE Sentry—a passive, IDS solution.

Enterprise users managed BlackICE agents from the ICEcap Management Console. The BlackICE product included a firewall that could respond, in real time, to intrusions and block attackers. NetworkICE was purchased in June 2000 by Internet Security Systems (ISS), which was in turn purchased by IBM in 2006. The BlackICE engine is still used in most ISS products, including IBM's Proventia line of products.

Intrusion prevention systems may also serve secondarily at the host level to deny potentially malicious activity. There are advantages and disadvantages to host-based IPS compared with network-based IPS. In many cases, the technologies are thought to be complementary.

Internet Security Systems

Conventional security methods respond to attacks only after they occur. **Preemptive security** from Internet Security Systems (ISS) stops Internet threats before they affect a network. Internet-driven organizations cannot afford reactive security techniques. Preemptive security is the only way to keep security- and cost-conscious organizations ahead of the threat. The ISS protection platform is the new standard against which Internet security solutions are measured. It defines several rules for effective security:

- Preemption beats reaction. With sophisticated new Internet threats, business losses are measured in seconds. No reaction can be fast enough.
- The Internet security challenge is not about networks or hardware. It is about the software vulnerabilities in these systems. Vulnerability-based security defines the performance standard and preemptive approach.
- To be effective, security must stay ahead of the threat. Preemptive security applies ever-evolving intelligence and techniques developed from innovative research methods.
- Online risk can be managed with confidence. With preemptive security in place, online risk is no longer a function of doing business.

Preemption lowers security costs by making security less work. By automatically stopping threats before they affect a business, preemptive security can dramatically reduce workloads and expenses. With preemptive security delivered within an integrated platform, organizations can have comprehensive protection that is not only more effective, but can also scale, be centrally managed, and actually be guaranteed to prevent business losses.

Trustwave

Trustwave's consultants have experience working with numerous security technologies. From firewall to the latest encryption solutions, Trustwave can procure and deploy any technology as part of a solution. In addition, Trustwave is a trusted partner of Cisco Systems and has extensive experience implementing the Cisco Security Agent (CSA) Intrusion Protection System.

The security technology expertise includes:

- Application security.
- Authentication.
- Anti-virus and anti-spam.
- Content filtering and caching.
- Encryption.
- Firewall/virtual private network (VPN).
- Intrusion prevention.
- Intrusion detection (network and host-based).
- High availability/load balancing
- Physical security.
- Secure Socket Layer (SSL).
- Security management.
- Quality of service/traffic shaping.
- Wireless security.

Cisco

Cisco provides numerous solutions for network intrusion prevention and device management. These include the following categories of solutions:

- IPS appliances.
- IPS management.
- Integrated router security.
- Security management.
- Management applications.
- Security information management.

SecureNet

The **SecureNet** system provides critical deep-packet analysis and application awareness and can be deployed passively for intrusion detection, or actively for intrusion prevention. In both deployment scenarios, SecureNet gives the user unsurpassed intelligence about the traffic on the network and provides effective tools for shutting down vulnerabilities before attackers can compromise the network.

Beyond firewalls, making the network secure requires visibility into the nature and characteristics of network traffic for identifying and controlling threats from unauthorized users, backdoor attackers, and worms and other network malware. The Intrusion SecureNet System provides critical deep-packet analysis and application awareness and can be deployed passively for intrusion detection or actively for intrusion prevention. In both deployment scenarios, the SecureNet System provides unsurpassed intelligence about the traffic on the network and removes all of the guess work involved with establishing perimeter defenses.

The SecureNet System can be deployed with the broadest range of network configurations. Passive intrusion detection deployments are possible without costly switch and router resources or reconfiguration and without creating a failure point in the network. Intrusion prevention deployments can be configured to block or pass network traffic on failure, with the option for hot-standby and high availability.

When used for detection, prevention, or both, the Intrusion SecureNet technology is peerless in accurately detecting attacks and proactively reporting indicators of future information loss or service interruption. By using pattern matching for performance and protocol decoding for detecting intentional evasion, polymorphic attacks, as well as protocol and network anomalies, the SecureNet System is ideal for protecting critical networks and valuable information assets. The SecureNet family uses a hybrid detection model allowing quick and easy updating of network signatures. It also has a scripting language and graphical interface for tuning, tweaking, and creating highly accurate and very specific protocol decode detection signatures.

Software and hardware appliance options include the following:

- Available for 10, 100, 250, and 1.000 Mbit per second networks.
- Industry-leading price/performance metrics.
- Tweak, tune, and create pattern-matching and protocol-decode signatures.
- Highly scalable and flexible management with provider interface.

Bro

Bro is an open-source, Unix-based network intrusion detection system (NIDS) that passively monitors network traffic and looks for suspicious activity. Bro detects intrusions by first parsing network traffic to extract its application-level semantics and then executing event-oriented analyzers that compare the activity with patterns deemed troublesome. Its analysis includes:

- Detection of specific attacks.
- Those attacks defined by signatures.
- Those attacks defined in terms of events.
- Unusual activities of certain hosts connecting to certain services.
- Patterns of failed connection attempts.

Bro uses a specialized policy language that allows a site to tailor Bro's operation, both as site policies evolve and as new attacks are discovered. If Bro detects something of interest, it can be instructed to either generate a log entry, alert the operator in real time, or execute an operating system command (e.g., to terminate a connection or block a malicious host on the fly). In addition, Bro's detailed log files can be particularly useful for forensics.

Bro targets high-speed, high-volume intrusion detection. By leveraging packet-filtering techniques, Bro is able to achieve the necessary performance while running on commercially available PC hardware, and thus can serve as a cost-effective means of monitoring a site's Internet connection.

Bro is intended for use by sites requiring flexible, highly customizable intrusion detection. It is important to understand that Bro has been developed primarily as a research platform for intrusion detection and traffic analysis. It is not intended for someone seeking an "out of the box" solution. Bro is designed for use by Unix experts who place a premium on the ability to extend an intrusion detection system with new functionality as needed, which can greatly aid with tracking evolving attacker techniques as well as inevitable changes to a site's environment and security policy requirements.

Because Bro is open source and runs on commodity PC hardware, it provides a low-cost means to experiment with alternative techniques. Some sites may wish to run a commercial IDS as a front line of defense, and then also run Bro as a way to:

- Verify the results of the commercial IDS / defense-in-depth.
- Attain richer forensics capabilities.
- Provide policy-checking capabilities not facilitated by the commercial IDS.
- Experiment with new approaches and incorporate leading-edge research.

Internet Security Systems (ISS)

IBM Internet Security Systems (ISS) delivers preemptive security solutions that stop threats before they affect a business. IBM ISS products secure the IT infrastructure, ensuring business continuity and enabling cost-effective processes while supporting compliance and risk management requirements. IBM ISS offers fully integrated solutions for desktops, laptops, servers, networks, and remote locations.

UNIFIED NETWORK MANAGEMENT
Provider

The **Provider** management application enables an organization to manage its suite of Intrusion security products from one easy interface. It seamlessly unifies management and reporting of these products so users can recognize one of the lowest total costs of ownership (TCO) in the industry. Provider has a wealth of features that bring powerful tools for managing the remediation process of security issues. It is also tremendously flexible and scalable so that it can meet any organization's requirements, regardless of network topology or organizational hierarchy.

NETWORK TAPS
Secure Tap

The Intrusion line of network taps enable easy, fast, and robust deployment of any of Intrusion's network security appliances. Each Secure Tap quickly connects into any network, at any location, so that traffic can be monitored. Because Secure Taps are invisible—they do not have MAC or IP addresses—they are invulnerable to attack and they are inherently nondisruptive. They also utilize "fail-to-pass" architectures so that no interruptions will occur should they fail, or if a power supply fails. Using a Secure Tap is the method for deploying network appliances.

Glossary

A

Access lists. Filters that are usually enabled in a firewall, router, or gateway that allow or disallow network traffic.

Access point (AP). A transceiver or radio component in a wireless LAN that acts as the transfer point between wired and wireless signal, and vice versa. The access point (AP) is connected to antennas as well as to the wired LAN system.

Access rights. File access rights such as read, write, execute, delete, and modify.

Accounting. A service that keeps track of the users who access network resources.

Accounting management. Concerns the ability to identify costs and establish charges related to network resources.

Active attack. Involves some modification of the data stream or the creation of a false data stream.

Advanced Encryption Standard (AES). A cryptographic algorithm (symmetric block cipher) that supports three key sizes: 128, 192, and 256 bits. AES is the standard name for the Rijndael algorithm that was approved by NIST to succeed the Data Encryption Standard (DES).

Adware. Allows units to spy on purchasing activity of the users. See also **malware**.

Aggregation. The act of obtaining information of a higher sensitivity by combining information from lower levels of sensitivity.

Application programming interface (API). Provides a set of standard command supported by both application programs and the operating systems with which they interact.

Asymmetric encryption. A form of cryptosystem in which encryption and decryption are performed using two different keys. One key is called the public key and the other is a private key.

Attack. Involves the exploitation of the vulnerabilities of a computer system or network, which can result in a threat against the resource.

Auditing. Involves the process of collecting and monitoring all aspects of the computer network to identify potential holes and flaws in the systems.

Authentication. The process whereby a user proves they are who they claim to be.

Authorization. Refers to securing the network by specifying which area of the network—whether an application, a device, or a system—a user is allowed to access.

Automatic call distributor (ACD). Specialized telephone system used for processing many calls, such as airline reservations.

Availability. Network resources are accessible to authorized parties. This also means that they are also available to illegitimate users.

B

Backdoor. Software tools that allow an intruder to access a computer using an alternate entry method.

Backup. A copy of online storage that provides fault protection.

Baseline. Defines a point of reference against which to measure network performance and behavior when problems occur.

Bastion host. Hosts that can limit the nature of network traffic and force both incoming and outgoing traffic through special computer systems of the screen.

Bell-LaPadula model. A formal description of the allowable paths of information flow in a secure system.

Biometrics. The process of using hard-to-forge physical characteristics of individuals—such as fingerprints, voiceprints, and retinal patterns—to authenticate users.

Black hat. A hacker who has private software that exploits security vulnerabilities.

Botnet. Jargon term for a collection of software robots, or bots, that run autonomously.

Browsing. The process of unauthorized users searching through files or storage directories for data and information that they are not privileged to read.

Brute force attack. A cracker term for hurling passwords at a system until it cracks.

Business continuity planning (BCP). Plans created to prevent interruptions to normal business activity.

Business-to-business (B2B). Defined as e-commerce where both the buyers and sellers are organizations.

Business-to-consumer (B2C). Defined as a business selling online to individual consumers.

C

CERT Coordination Center (CCC) is responsible for studying Internet security and responding to security incidents reported to it.

Certificate. A unique collection of information, transformed into un-forgeable form, used for authentication of users.

Certificate Authority (CA). A trusted organization that verifies the credentials of people and puts a stamp of approval on these credentials.

Check verification. Companies perform checks on the validity of a check.

Client/server. A computer located on a LAN that splits the workload between itself and desktop computers.

Coalition Against Unsolicited Commercial Email (CAUCE). A nonprofit advocacy group that works to reduce the amount of unsolicited commercial e-mail, or spam, via legislation.

Computer Emergency Response Team (CERT). An organization with teams around the world that recognizes and responds to computer attacks.

Common Management Information Protocol (CMIP). Network management protocol.

Compression. The process of encoding information using fewer bits than an unencoded representation.

Computer telephony integration (CTI). A PBX provides call information to a computer and accepts call-handing instruction from a computer.

Confidentiality. Means that only authorized people can see protected data or resources.

Configuration management. Ability to identify the various components for processing changes, deletions, and additions to the configuration.

Consumer-to-consumer (C2C). Concerned with individuals buying and selling over the Internet.

Content filtering. The blocking, or "filtering," of undesirable Internet content. Businesses can block content based on traffic type.

Content management. Security involves the protection of data and database resources, and also the contents of these assets.

Contingency. Described as an event that might occur; however, it is not intended nor planned.

Cookie. A message given to a Web browser by a Web server.

Copyright. A form of protection provided by the laws of the United States to the authors of "original works of authorship," including literary, dramatic, musical, artistic, and certain other intellectual works.

Covert channel. A hidden unauthorized network connection to communicate unauthorized information.

Cracker. Individual who attempts to access computer facilities illegally. Cracking is a serious crime that has caused millions of dollars in damage.

Cryptanalysis. The study of a cryptographic system for the purpose of finding weaknesses in the system and breaking the code used to encrypt the data without knowing the code's key.

Cryptography. The art of protecting information by transforming (encrypting) it into an unreadable format, called cipher text.

Cryptology. The study of secure communications, which includes both cryptography and cryptanalysis.

Cyber. A prefix used to describe new things that are being made possible by the spread of computers.

Cybercrime. Encompasses any criminal act dealing with computers and networks (sometimes called hacking).

Cyber-terrorism. The convergence of terrorism and cyberspace. It is usually understood to mean unlawful attacks and threats against computers, networks, and databases.

Cyberspace. Defined as the global network of interconnected computers and communication systems.

D

Data. Any material represented in a formalized manner so that it can be stored, manipulated, and transmitted by machine; in contrast, *information* is the meaning assigned to data by people.

Database. A collection of files serving as a data resource for computer-based information systems.

Database management system (DBMS). A software program that manages and provides access to a database.

Data Encryption Standard (DES). Encryption method.

Data migration. Archiving process that moves stagnant files to a secondary storage location.

Decryption. The reverse process of encryption.

Demarcation point. Location of network connectivity to an organization's resources. This can include wiring closets for telephone and LAN access.

Demilitarized zone (DMZ). An external private network that contains Web servers and mail servers. This buffer zone is the location of systems that are accessible by untrusted users.

Denial of service (DoS). Defined as an attack that attempts to deny enterprise network resources to legitimate users.

Dictionary attack. A simple cracker program that takes all the words from a dictionary file and attempts to gain entry by entering each one as a password.

Differential backup. Copies the elements that were created or changed since the last normal or incremental process was backed up.

Digital certificate. A password-protected file that contains identification about its holder.

Digital envelope. A message that is encrypted using private-key cryptography, but that also contains the encrypted secret key.

Directory. A structure containing one or more files and description of those files.

Disaster recovery plan (DRP). A comprehensive statement of consistent actions to be taken before, during, and after a disruptive even that causes a significant loss of information systems resources.

Disclosure. Dissemination of information to someone other than the intended individual, sometimes called a "leak."

Disclosure threat. A compromise that occurs whenever some confidential information is leaked.

Distributed denial of service (DDoS). Involves flooding one or more target computers with false or spurious requests, which overloads the computer, denying service to legitimate users.

Domain name system (DNS). Uniquely identifies all hosts connected to the Internet by name. The server is used on the Internet and some private networks.

Dual-homed gateway. An applications layer firewall that checks all traffic using a bastion host between the network and the Internet.

Dynamic host configuration protocol (DHCP). A protocol for assigning dynamic IP addresses to devices on a network. In some systems, the device's IP address can even change while it is still connected.

E

Eavesdropping. Occurs when a host sets its network interface on promiscuous mode and copies packets that pass by for later analysis. Also called "snarfing."

E-business. Includes customer service and support and other business activities.

E-mail virus. Virus that moves around in e-mail messages; it usually replicates itself by automatically mailing itself to dozens of people in the victim's e-mail address book.

Electronic commerce (e-commerce). The exchange of products, services, information, or money with the support of computers and networks.

Electronic data interchange (EDI). A process whereby standardized forms of e-commerce documents are transferred between diverse and remotely located computer systems.

Electronic serial number (ESN). The unique identification number embedded in a wireless phone by the manufacturer. Each time a call is placed, the ESN is automatically transmitted to the base station so the wireless carrier's mobile switching office can check the call's validity. The ESN cannot be altered in the field. The ESN differs from the mobile identification number, which is the wireless carrier's identifier for a phone in the network. ESNs can be electronically checked to help prevent fraud.

Encryption/decryption. The translation of data into a secret code and back is called encryption and decryption, respectively.

Equifax. Credit-reporting agency.

Ethernet. The most widely used LAN technology. Uses a logical bus topology operating at 10, 100, and 1,000 Mbps.

Ethics. The rules or standards governing the conduct of the members of a profession.

eTRUST. Establish user trust and confidence in electronic transactions.

Experian. Credit-reporting agency.

Exploit. A prepared application that takes advantage of a known weakness or vulnerability.

Extensible authentication protocol (EAP). Implements a number of authentication mechanisms, including MD5 and S/Key. It is implemented in many wireless networks.

Extranet. Extranets are extensions of corporate intranets and usually allow access via the Internet; sensitive data can be kept private via the use of a firewall.

F

Face recognition. Biometric process to identify human faces.

False acceptance rate (FAR). In biometrics, the instance of a security system incorrectly verifying or identifying an unauthorized person.

False rejection rate (FRR). The instance whereby the system fails to recognize an authorized person and rejects that person as an impostor.

Fast Ethernet. An extension of the 10BaseT Ethernet standard that transports data at 100 Mbps.

Fault management. Ability to detect, isolate, and correct abnormal network conditions.

Federal Communications Commission (FCC). The government agency responsible for regulating telecommunications in the United States.

Federal Deposit Insurance Corporation (FDIC). An agency of the federal government that insures bank deposits up to a stated maximum.

Federal Trade Commission (FTC). Government agency responsible for protecting the public against unfair business practices, including false and misleading advertising. The FTC has very broad antitrust and consumer protection powers.

File-infecting virus. Virus that infects executable files with com, exe, and ovl extensions.

File transfer protocol (FTP). Used for file transfers between remote systems on TCP ports 20 and 21.

Filters. See access lists.

Firewall. Any software program or hardware device designed to prevent computers on a network from communicating directly with external computer systems by filtering the information coming through the Internet connection into the private network or computer system.

Forensic analysis. A process to preserve, identify, extract, document, and interpret computer data. It is often more of an art than a science, but as in any discipline, computer forensic specialists follow clear, well-defined methodologies and procedures.

Fraud. A deception deliberately practiced in order to secure unfair or unlawful gain.

G

Gap analysis. A methodology for testing the authenticity, integrity, and confidentiality of an organization's hardware and software systems; it can provide an assurance that security implementations are consistent with the real requirements.

Gateway. An entrance and exit into a communications network that performs code and protocol conversion processes.

Grey hat. In the hacking community, refers to a skilled hacker who sometimes acts legally, sometimes in goodwill, and sometimes not.

H

Hacker. The most common usage of this term in the popular press is to describe those who subvert computer security without authorization.

Hacktivist. A hacker who utilizes technology to announce a political message. It should be noted that Web vandalism is not necessarily hacktivism.

Hand geometry. Biometric process for identifying hand structure.

Hash function. Maps a variable-length data block or message into a fixed-length value called a hash code.

Health Insurance Portability and Accountability Act (HIPAA). Enacted by the U.S. Congress in 1996.

Hijacking. The network attacker takes control of a session between two entities and masquerades as one of them.

Hoax. An act intended to deceive or trick. These false messages might contain dire warnings about devastating new viruses, Trojans that eat the heart out of your system, and malicious software that can steal the computer right off your desk.

Hotspot. A public location such as an airport, shopping mall, or conference center that has readily accessible wireless networks, usually 802.11b or 802.11a.

Hypertext markup language (HTML). Web pages are usually constructed using this language.

Hypertext transfer protocol (HTTP). The language of the WWW, used to transmit on the Internet. Operates on TCP port 80.

I

Identification. Procedures and mechanisms that allow an entity external to a system resource to notify that system of its identity.

Identity theft. Someone wrongfully obtaining and using another person's personal data in some way that involves fraud or deception, typically for economic gain.

Identity Theft Resource Center® (ITRC). A nonprofit, nationally respected organization dedicated exclusively to the understanding and prevention of identity theft.

Incidence response. Processes and tactics for a successful response to some incident.

Incremental backup. Copies elements that have been created or changed since the last backup.

Inference. The ability of users to infer or deduce from information about data at sensitivity levels for which they do not have access privileges.

Information warfare. The offensive and defensive use of information and information systems to deny, exploit, corrupt, or destroy an adversary's information and systems while protecting one's own.

InfoSec. Meaning information security, which describes the protection of classified information stored on computers or transmitted by radio, telephone, teletype, or any other means.

Integrity. Defined as rigid adherence to a code or standard of values; the quality or condition of being unimpaired and sound.

Integrity threat. Any unauthorized change to data stored on a network resource or in transit between resources.

Intellectual property. Includes copyrights, trademarks, and trade secrets.

Interactive Voice Response (IVR). Guides the caller through keypad options.

Internet. (Capital I) A self-regulated network of computer networks.

Internet Protocol (IP) address. Network device addresses containing 32 bits arranged in groups of eight bits, called dotted-decimal notation (10.10.10.1).

Internet Service Provider (ISP). Provides the vital link between the user and the Internet.

Intranet. An internal network, usually within a department or business.

Intrusion detection (ID). The art of detecting and responding to situations involving computer, database, and network misuse. Can identify intruders and assist in the detective analysis of intrusion attempts. It can also create a sampling of traffic patterns.

Intrusion detection system (IDS). A conglomeration of capabilities to detect and respond to threats.

IP Security (IPSec). A standard created to add security to TCP/IP networking.

Iris imaging. Biometric process for identifying iris images.

ISO 17799. A detailed security standard.

K

Kensington security lock. A device consisting of aircraft-grade steel cable for securing laptop computers.

Key. Described as a number of characters within a data record used to identify the data. A key can be either public or private or a combination of both.

Keylogger. A type of surveillance software or hardware that has the capability to record every keystroke a user makes to a log file.

L

Local Area Network (LAN). Group of devices linked to each other within a limited geographical area.

Logic bomb. A Trojan horse with a timing device.

M

MAC filtering. A network checks a device's MAC address against a database to see if it is authorized to access the network.

Macro virus. Virus that includes executable programs that attach themselves to documents created in Microsoft Word and Excel.

Malware. Slang for malicious software. Software designed specifically to disrupt a computer system. A Trojan horse, worm, or a virus could be classified as malware.

Man-in-the-middle attack. Occurs when an attacker gets between two parties and intercepts messages before transferring them on to their intended destination.

Masquerade attack. Takes place when an entity pretends to be a different entity.

Media. Wire, fiber optics, and air used as a transmission medium.

Media access control address (MAC address). The unique physical address of each device's network interface card (NIC).

Monitoring. Contains the mechanisms, tools, and techniques that permit the identification of security events that could affect the operation of a computer facility.

Multi-part virus. This virus infects boot sectors as well as executable files.

N

National Institute of Standards and Technology (NIST). Established by Congress to assist industry in the development of technology needed to improve product quality, modernize manufacturing processes, ensure product reliability, and facilitate rapid commercialization of products based on new scientific discoveries.

Netcat. Backdoor tool.

Network address translation (NAT). Translates private, non-routable addresses on internal network devices to registered IP addresses when communicating across the Internet.

Network analyzer. A monitoring, testing, and troubleshooting device used by network administrators and technicians.

Network management. A general term describing the protocols and applications used to manage networks.

Network management system (NMS). Defined as the systems or actions that help maintain, characterize, or troubleshoot a network.

Nonrepudiation. A mechanism that prevents a user from denying a legitimate, billable financial transaction.

O

Obscenity. Forms of pornography that society considers most harmful to sexual morality.

One-time password. A system that requires a new password for each session.

Open Systems Interconnection (OSI). International framework of standards for electronic communications between different systems.

Orange Book. Called the Trusted Computer System Evaluation Criteria (TCSEC).

P

Packet sniffer. A software application that uses a hardware adapter card in promiscuous mode to capture all network packets sent across a LAN segment.

Palm imaging. Biometric process for identifying palm prints.

Passive system. Includes monitoring and eavesdropping on a transmission.

Password. A word or string of characters recognized by automatic means, permitting access to a location, database, or file storage.

Patent. A grant made by a government to an inventor, ensuring the sole right to make, use, and sell an invention for a certain period of time.

Performance management. Provides for computer network monitoring and controlling.

Personal identification number (PIN). A code used by a mobile telephone number in conjunction with a SIM card to complete a call.

Pharming. Similar in nature to e-mail phishing as it seeks to obtain personal or private financial-related information through domain spoofing.

Phishing. A type of fraud whereby a criminal attempts to trick their victim into accepting a false identity presented by the criminal.

Phishing scam. An identity theft scam that arrives via e-mail.

Phone phreaking. The art of exploiting bugs and glitches that exist in the telephone system.

Phreaking. The art of exploiting bugs and glitches that exist in the telephone system.

Physical security. Technique oriented toward keeping the asset, resource, and user safe.

PING. A popular utility that uses simple ICMP messages to test the connectivity and availability of network devices.

Point-to-point protocol (PPP). The most commonly used protocol for dial-up access to the Internet.

Point-point tunneling protocol (PPTP). Enables PPP to be tunneled through a public network. It used native PPP authentication and encryption services.

Polyinstantiation. Several views of a database that determines the user's access security level.

Polymorphic virus. This virus changes its appearance to avoid detection by anti-virus software.

Pop-up. A form of online advertising on the World Wide Web intended to increase Web traffic or capture e-mail addresses.

Pornography. Presentation of sexually explicit behavior.

Port. Possible network connections on a computer. Port 80 is for HTTP (RFC 1700).

Pretty Good Privacy (PGP). An encryption and digital signature utility for adding privacy to electronic mail and documents.

Privacy enhanced mail (PEM). Proposed standard for providing e-mail confidentiality and authentication.

Private branch exchange (PBX). A telephone system.

Private communication technology (PCT). A protocol that provides secure encrypted communications between two applications over a TCP/IP network.

Private key. Encryption that utilizes a shared secret key between one or more parties. The private key is used in a symmetric encryption system.

Protocol. A set of rules that govern communication between hardware and/or software components.

Protocol analyzer. A tool used for troubleshooting network problems and monitoring for excessive bandwidth usage.

Prototyping. Involves developing a scenario concerning a security violation and determining the effect on the organization.

Proxy. An application running on a gateway that relays network packets between a trusted client and an untrusted host.

Proxy server. Like a firewall, this server is designed to protect internal network resources that are connected to other networks, such as the Internet.

Public key. Used in an asymmetric encryption system. It is used in conjunction with a corresponding private key.

Public-key infrastructure (PKI). Enables users of a public network such as the Internet to securely and privately exchange data and funds through the use of cryptographic keys that are obtained and shared through a trusted authority.

Pyramid scheme. A non-sustainable business model that involves the exchange of money primarily for enrolling other people into the scheme, usually without any product or service being delivered; it is highly illegal.

R

Radio-frequency fingerprinting. A process that identifies a cellular phone by the unique "fingerprint" that characterizes its signal transmission. RF fingerprinting is one process used to prevent cloning fraud, because a cloned phone will not have the same fingerprint as the legal phone with the same electronic identification numbers.

Red Book. Called the Trusted Network Interpretation (TNI).

Redundant array of inexpensive disk (RAID). Storage device used to improve performance and automatically recover from a system failure. RAID allows for data to be written across multiple disk drives, improving performance and protecting data.

Remote Authentication Dial-In User Service (RADIUS). Provides authentication and accountability.

Replay. Involves the passive capture of a data unit and its subsequent retransmission to produce an unauthorized effect.

Retina scanning. Biometric process for identifying one's retina.

Risk analysis. The process of understanding how the loss of an asset will affect an organization.

Rootkit. A toolkit for hiding the fact that a computer's security has been compromised.

Router. Intelligent device, operating at Layer 3 of the OSI model, that connects like and unlike LANs, MANs, and WANs. Routers work with packets that include logical addressing information.

S

Scam. Generally described as a fraudulent business scheme or a swindle. Criminals are using the Web, e-mail, and unlawful techniques to defraud the general public.

Scam baiting. The practice of eliciting attention from the perpetrator of a scam by feigning interest in whatever bogus deal is offered.

Scammers. Refers to people who use a confidence trick, confidence game, or con for short (also known as a scam) in an attempt to intentionally mislead a person or persons (known as the mark) usually with the goal of financial or other gain.

Screened host. Uses a screening router that directs all Internet traffic to a bastion host, which is located between the local network and the Internet.

Script kiddie. A person with little or no skill.

Secure Electronic Transaction (SET). An open specification for handling credit card transactions over a network, with emphasis on the Web and Internet.

Secure HTTP (S-HTTP). Works in conjunction with HTTP to enable clients and servers to engage in private and secure transactions.

Secure MIME (S/MIME). A secure method of sending e-mail.

Secure Remote Procedure Call (S-RPC). Used to request services from another computer on the network. It provides public and private keys to clients and servers.

Secure Socket Layer (SSL). A Web protocol that sets up a secure session between Web client and server.

Security Act. The Government Information Security Reform Act.

SecurID. Security dynamics token.

Security audit. Tasks involved in maintaining a secure network.

Security management. Provides the ability to monitor and control access to network resources.

Security policy. A formal statement of rules by which users with access to an organization's technology and database assets must abide.

Sensor. The processor that monitors a network for intrusion attempts. Some sensors store all records locally, while others send reports to a console application or back-end database. Sensors usually run in promiscuous mode, often without an IP address.

Service access point (SAP). An identifying label for network endpoints used in OSI networking.

Session hijacking. Instead of attempting to initiate a session via spoofing, the attacker attempts to take over an existing connection between two network computers.

Signature scanning. Biometric process for scanning an individual's signature.

SIM card. A small memory card used in GSM phones to hold phone numbers and other information. Can be removed and inserted into other GSM phones, allowing the user to keep his or her numbers and to place and receive phone calls.

Simple mail transfer protocol (SMTP). Used to send and receive e-mail across the Internet. Operates on TCP port 25.

Simple network management protocol (SNMP). Part of the TCP/IP suite that is used for network management. Operates on TCP port 161.

Single sign-on (SSO). A specialized form of software authentication that enables a user to authenticate once and gain access to the resources of multiple software systems.

SiteKey™. A security feature that is an additional layer of identity verification for signing in to online banking.

Smart card. Contains a microprocessor chip that performs various security tasks.

Smurfing. Uses a directed broadcast to create a flood of network traffic for the victim computer.

Snarfing. See eavesdropping. Also called packet snarfing.

Sniffer. An application that captures password and other data while it is in transit either within the computer or over the network.

Social engineering. A deception technique and manipulation skill used by an attacker to gain access to a resource and obtain some form of information.

SOCKS. An authentication protocol used to communicate through a firewall or proxy server.

Spam. Defined as commercial advertising, often for dubious products, get-rich-quick schemes, or other services. Adds considerable overhead to network utilization and considerable costs to businesses.

Spammers. Individuals use spamming techniques to send unsolicited messages in bulk.

Spear phishing. An e-mail spoofing fraud attempt that targets a specific organization.

Spoofing. A type of attack in which one computer disguises itself as another in order to gain access to a system.

Spread spectrum. Jamming-resistant and initially devised for military use, this radio transmission technology "spreads" information over greater bandwidth than necessary for interference tolerance and is now a commercial technology.

Spybot. Privacy software designed to search and destroy spyware and Trojan horse programs.

Spyware. Any software that covertly gathers user information through the user's Internet connection without the user's knowledge, usually for advertising purposes. Also called adware and malware.

Stealth virus. This virus attempts to hide itself from the operating system and anti-virus software.

Steganography (stego). The art and science of hiding information by embedding messages within other, seemingly harmless messages.

Storage area network (SAN). A high-speed sub-network of shared storage devices.

Subscriber fraud. A deception deliberately practiced by an impostor to secure wireless service with intent to avoid payment. This is in contrast to bad debt, which occurs when a known person or company has a payment obligation overdue and the debt cannot be collected.

Symmetric encryption. A form of cryptosystem in which encryption and decryption are performed using the same key.

SYN flood. Techniques for launching a packet flood.

T

Telnet. Provides for remote access to system resources. Operates on TCP port 23.

Terrorism. The unlawful use of force or violence against persons or property to intimidate or coerce a government, the civilian population, or any segment thereof, in furtherance of political or social objectives.

Threat. A threat to the computer network is described as any potential adverse occurrence that can do harm, interrupt the systems using the network, or cause a monetary loss to the organization.

Trademark. A word, name, symbol, or device that is used in trade with goods to indicate the source of the goods and to distinguish them from the goods of others.

Trade secret. A trade secret may consist of any formula, pattern, physical device, idea, process or compilation of information that provides the owner of the information with a competitive advantage in the marketplace.

Transmission control program/Internet protocol (TCP/IP). The protocols, or conventions, that computers use to communicate over the Internet.

TransUnion. Credit-reporting agency.

Triple-A. This takes the form of identification, authentication, authorization, and accounting, collectively called AAA or triple-A.

Trivial file transfer protocol (TFTP). A very simple form of the file transfer protocol, implemented on top of UDP. TFTP provides no security features and operates without user authentication. Operates on TCP port 69.

Trojan horse. A type of computer program that performs an ostensibly useful function, but contains a hidden function that compromises the host system's security. Usually is called a Trojan.

Trust. The composite of availability, performance, and security, which includes the ability to execute processes with integrity, secrecy, and privacy.

Trusted network. Secure internal or corporate internetworks protected by security devices and policies.

Tunneling. A vehicle for encapsulating packets inside a protocol.

U

Uninterruptible power supply (UPS). Stores electrical energy to provide backup power during power outages.

Untrusted network. The Internet or insecure network, outside the organization's control, and there is no control over the administration or security policies.

V

Virtual local area network (VLAN). A grouping of network devices not restricted to a physical segment or switch.

Virtual private network (VPN). A private data network that makes use of the public telecommunications infrastructure, which maintains privacy through the use of tunneling and security procedures.

Virus. A small piece of software that piggybacks on real programs. Each time the host program runs, the virus runs, too, giving it the chance to reproduce or wreak havoc.

Voice over Internet protocol (VoIP). The technology used to transmit voice conversations over a data network using the Internet protocol.

VPN (Virtual Private Network). A private data network that makes use of the public telecommunications infrastructure.

Vulnerability. A characteristic of a computer system or a network that makes it possible for a threat to occur.

Vulnerability scanner. A tool used to quickly check computers on a network for known weaknesses.

W

Wannabe. Grey hats; potential black hats, criminals, or consultants.

War chalking. The practice of marking a series of symbols on sidewalks and walls to indicate nearby wireless access. That way, other computer users can pop open their laptops and connect to the Internet wirelessly.

War dialer. A program that tries a set of sequentially changing numbers to determine which ones respond positively.

War driving. Driving around with a laptop computer, with a wireless card installed, or a wireless LAN adaptor, in order to find unsecured wireless local area networks. Users can gain free Internet access or access the organization's data illegally.

White hat. Defined as a hacker who breaks security but who does so for altruistic or at least non-malicious reasons. Also known as a sneaker or grey hat.

Wide area network (WAN). A geographically dispersed network.

Wi-Fi (wireless fidelity). A wireless networking technology for PCs and PDAs that allows multiple devices to share a single high-speed Internet connection over a distance of about 300 feet. It can also be used to network a group of PCs without wires. It can transmit data at speeds of up to 11 megabits per second.

Wi-Fi 5. A new version of Wi-Fi that is even faster, with a maximum speed of 54 megabits per second.

Wi-Fi protected access (WPA). A system to secure Wi-Fi networks, intended to replace the current, less secure WEP (Wired Equivalent Privacy) system. Part of the IEEE 802.11i standard.

Wired equivalent privacy (WEP). An encryption system that encrypts data on wireless networks that can only be read by authorized users with the correct decryption key.

Wireless application protocol (WAP). A worldwide standard for providing Internet communications and advanced telephony services on digital mobile phones, pagers, personal digital assistants (PDAs), and other wireless devices.

Wireless local area network (WLAN). Using radio-frequency (RF) technology, wireless LANs or WLANs transmit and receive data over the air, minimizing the need for wired connections. Thus, wireless LANs combine data connectivity with user mobility.

Wireless Network Interface Controller (WNIC). A network card that connects to a radio-based computer network.

Wireless Transport Layer Security (WTLS). The security layer of the WAP providing privacy, data integrity, and authentication for WAP services.

Wiretapping. Unauthorized or court-authorized user listening for a transmission and not changing the contents.

World Wide Web (WWW). A way of accessing information over the medium of the Internet. It is an information-sharing process that is built on top of the Internet. Also known as the Web.

Worm. A worm is a program that can replicate itself and send copies from computer to computer across network connections.

Selected Bibliography

Anti-Phishing Working Group (APWG). *http://www.antiphishing.org/*. Accessed December 28, 2007.

Antivirus-Software-Reviews. *http://www.6starreviews.com/* and *www.antivirus-software-reviews.com/*. Accessed December 26, 2007.

California Financial Information Privacy Act. *http://library.findlaw.com/2003/Sep/30/133060.html*. Accessed December 26, 2007.

CAUCE. Coalition Against Unsolicited Commercial Email. *http://www.spamunit.com /anti-spam-organizations/cauce/*. Accessed December 14, 2007.

CCIPS. *www.cybercrime.gov*. Accessed January 6, 2008.

Check verification. *http://en.wikipedia.org/wiki/Check_verification_service*. Accessed January 4, 2008.

Ciampa, Mark. *Security Awareness: Applying Practical Security in Your World*. Boston: Thomson/Course Technology, 2004.

Consumer Alerts. "Consumer Alerts—Fair and Accurate Credit Transactions Act (FACT Act)." *http://www.ftc.gov/opa/2004/06/factaidt.shtm*. Accessed December 7, 2007.

Consumer Law Page. *http://consumerlawpage.com/brochure/tradmark.shtml*. Accessed December 7, 2007.

Cornell Law Center. U.S.Code. *http://www4.law.cornell.edu/uscode/search/index.html*. Accessed December 25, 2007.

Dhillon, Gurpreet. *Principles of Information Systems Security*. Hoboken, NJ: Wiley, 2007.

DNC Registry. Maintained by the Federal Trade Commission. *https://www.donotcall.gov/*. Accessed December 14, 2007.

Equifax. Equifax Credit Reporting Bureau. *http://www.equifax.com/*. Accessed December 7, 2007.

Experian. Experian Credit Reporting Bureau. *http://www.experian.com/*. Accessed December 7, 2007.

Finkelhor, David, Kimberly J. Mitchell, and Janis Wolak. "Online Victimization: A Report on the Nation's Youth." *http://www.experian.com/*. Accessed December 14, 2007.

Fraud. "Frauds and Scams." *www.fraud.org/internet/intinfo.htm*. Accessed January 6, 2008.

FTC. Federal Trade Commission. *https://rn.ftc.gov/pls/dod/*. Accessed January 8, 2008.

Gollmann, Dieter. *Computer Security,* 2nd ed. London: Wiley, 2006.

Gramm-Leach-Bliley. Gramm-Leach-Bliley Financial Services Modernization Act. *http://banking.senate.gov /conf/grmleach.htm*. Accessed December 30, 2007.

443

Greene, Sari Stern. *Security Policies and Procedures: Principles and Practices*. Upper Saddle River, NJ: Prentice Hall, 2006.

ICANN. Internet Corporation for Assigned Names and Numbers. *http://www.icann.org/*. Accessed December 26, 2007.

IDS. Intrusion Detection Tools. *http://insecure.org*. Accessed January 8, 2008.

Internet Crime Complaint Center. *www.ic3.gov*. Accessed January 4, 2008.

ITRC. Identity Theft Resource Center. *http://www.idtheftcenter.org/*. Accessed January 4, 2008.

Lipner, Steve, and Michael Howard. "The Trustworthy Computing Security Development Lifecycle." Security Business and Technology Unit. Microsoft Corporation. March 2005.

McRee, Russ. "Putting Snort to Work," *Information Security*. October 2007.

Merkow, Mark, and Jim Breithaupt. *Information Security: Principles and Practices*. Upper Saddle River, NJ: Prentice Hall, 2006.

Missingkids. National Center for Missing and Exploited Children and Cox Communication. *http://www.missingkids.com/missingkids/servlet/ProxySearchServlet?keys=walsh*. Accessed December 28, 2007.

Missingkids. "Online Victimization of Youth: Five Years Later." *http://www.missingkids.com/missingkids /servlet/ResourceServlet?LanguageCountry=en_US&PageId=2530*. Accessed December 14, 2007.

National Fraud Information Center. "National Fraud Information Center for 2006." World Wide Web. *http://www.fbi.gov/majcases/fraud/fraudschemes.htm*. Accessed December 7, 2007.

NetSmartz. *http://www.netsmartz.org/lawenf.htm*. Accessed December 14, 2007.

Networkworld. Networkworld Reviews. "IPS Reviews." *http://www.fraud.org/internet/intinfo.htm*. Accessed December 26, 2007.

Proctor, Paul E. *The Practical Intrusion Detection Handbook*. Upper Saddle River, NJ: Prentice Hall, 2001.

Request for Comments (RFC) 1700 (assigned numbers). *http://www.ietf.org/rfc/rfc1700.txt*. Accessed December 30, 2007.

Roiter, Neil. "Raise the Standard(s)—SIEM Vendors Champion Solutions to a Mishmash of Log Formats," *Information Security*. November 2007.

SANS. "Solutions." *http://www.SANS.org/resources/*. Accessed January 5, 2008.

Scambusters. "Credit Card Scams." *http://www.scambusters.org/*. Accessed January 8, 2008.

Schneier, Bruce. "Security Certifications." *http://www.schneier.com/blog/archives/2006/07/security_certif.html*. Accessed December 26, 2007.

Shopping Online. "Shopping Safely Online." *http://www.nclnet.org/shoppingonline*. Accessed December 30, 2007.

Software Engineering Institute. Carnegie Mellon University. *http://www.sei.cmu.edu/*. Accessed January 8, 2008.

Standards. "Wireless Standards." *http://standards.ieee.org/getieee802/download/802.11–1999.pdf*. Accessed December 30, 2007.

Strom, David. "Log Wild." *Information Security*. October 2007.

TransUnion. TUC Credit Reporting Bureau. *http://www.tuc.com/*. Accessed December 7, 2007.

USDOJ. U.S. Department of Justice. "Identity Theft." *http://www.usdoj.gov/criminal/fraud/idtheft.html.* Accessed December 27, 2007.

USPTO. U.S. Patent and Trademark Office. "Basic Facts about Trademarks." *http://www.uspto.gov/web /offices/tac/doc/basic/.* Accessed December 7, 2007.

Virus List. *http://www.viruslist.com.* Accessed December 21, 2007.

Whitman, Michael, and Herbert Mattord. *Principles of Incident Response and Disaster Recovery.* Boston: Thomson/Course Technology, 2007.

Index

D